RURAL DEVELOPMENT

About the Editor

Dr. M.R. Biju, Editor of *South Asian Journal of Socio-Political Studies* (SAJOSPS) has been actively engaged in his researches on the area of decentralized governance in the past 27 years. He has made significant contributions to the theory and practice of grass root governance in India. As a mark of its national recognition he has been conferred with the post-doctoral research award by the University Grants Commission, New Delhi in 2004.

As prolific writer, he has published 22 outstanding books and 104 research papers on various aspects of decentralization, development, democracy, human rights, development management, strategic management, women empowerment, etc. He is also heading three major research projects on Panchayati Raj funded by the Ministry of Panchayati Raj, Government of India and University Grants Commission, New Delhi. Dr. Biju is currently Associate Professor of the Post-Graduate and Research Department of Political Science, Sree Narayana College, Kollam, Kerala.

RURAL DEVELOPMENT

GOVERNANCE AND PARTICIPATION

Dr. M.R. BIJU

CONCEPT PUBLISHING COMPANY PVT. LTD.
NEW DELHI-110059

ISBN-13 : 978-93-5125-051-7

First Published 2014

Published and Printed by

Concept
Since 1974

Concept Publishing Company Pvt. Ltd.
A/15-16, Commercial Block, Mohan Garden
New Delhi-110059 (India)
T: 25351460, 25351794, *F*: 091-11-25357109
E: publishing@conceptpub.com, W: www.conceptpub.com
Editorial Office: H-13, Bali Nagar, New Delhi-110 015, India.

Cataloging in Publication Data—*Courtesy:* D.K. Agencies (P) Ltd. <docinfo@dkagencies.com>

Rural development : governance and participation / M.R. Biju.
p. cm.
Contributed articles.
Includes bibliographical references and index.
ISBN 9789351250517

1. Rural development—India. 2. Rural development—Government policy—India. 3. Rural development projects—India—Electronic information resources. 4. Decentralization in government—India. 5. Political participation—India. 6. Local government—India. 7. Community development—India. I. Biju, M. R., 1965-

DDC 307.14120954 23

Dedicated to
the ever-loving and ever-lasting
memory of my beloved wife

JAYA BIJU

(7th September 1969 – 31st August 2012)

Preface

People's participation and governance in rural development is an ongoing process of mobilisation and self-organisation that shapes and reshapes the community itself. Any research connected with the concepts of 'participation' and 'governance' can adopt a variety of different perspectives upon which to focus in examining these concepts. We could examine both these concepts as a societal process of the gradual incorporation of peripheral areas into the central society; we could examine it in terms of broad political processes and the increasing involvement of previously disenfranchised groups in the political life of a country like India; or we could approach it from an essentially bureaucratic perspective in terms of the involvement of local people in formal, administrative structures.

The process connected with participation and governance starts with the identification and description of problems, needs and opportunities, continues through grass-roots involvement in conception, planning and implementation and carries on through monitoring and evaluation. The present global trend in self-governance is democratic decentralization and strengthening of the local self-governments as strong grass-root level institutions with appropriate safeguards for weaker sections.

Acquiring a Constitutional status in 1993, the Panchayati Raj Institutions in India gave the vision of a democratic governance down even to village level (the Gram Sabha) by decentralizing State's developmental functions, finance and functionaries to PRIs, granting them autonomy so that they function as institutions of self-government, securing people's participation in local development and ensuring accountability and transparency of the government to the people. It is not only a system of participative self-governance but it ensures political empowerment to the poor, the marginalized and the oppressed. The Constitution (73rd Amendment) Act has made Panchayats instruments of local governance with potential space for women and marginalised groups in the federal set-up. It has perceptually widened the democratic base providing the potential for local-level planning and implementation of development programmes. These potentialities include the participation and self-governance by ensuring political empowerment to the poor, marginalized and oppressed — Scheduled Castes, Scheduled Tribes and women — at the grass root level.

The present volume attempts to address the issues pertaining to rural governance, people's participation, financial inclusion, environmental sustainability and watershed development initiatives. The volume contains twenty two research papers and articles contributed by senior academics, administrators and rural development activists with rich experience on the core areas of the study. In their sub-missions, the authors have tried to explore the existing problems faced by rural development in the aforesaid areas and present solid suggestions to revamp the system.

Acknowledgements

I would like to express my gratitude to those who have been kind enough to help me in the preparation of this volume. I wish to express a deep sense of gratitude to the esteemed contributors to this anthology of articles. The views and opinions expressed by the contributors are of immense value for researchers, policy-makers, planners for rejuvenating policies and strategies on Rural Development and Decentralized Governance in India. I am extremely thankful to Shri Ashok Kumar Mittal of Concept Publishing Company Pvt. Ltd., New Delhi, who brought out the volume in an elegant form. I also wish to express my sincere thanks to Prof. V.S. Lee, Principal, Sree Narayana College, Kollam for his support.

I also express my deep sense of affection, love and gratitude to my beloved wife—Jaya for her support, care and exceptional sincerity. I lost her on 31st August, 2012 at an early age of 42. Whatever little academic activity I had undertaken hitherto was due to her solid support. Jaya came to my life on 14th November 1993. From the day onwards she supported me like a friend and motivator. She inspired me a lot and she had given a new meaning and dimension to my life. All the twenty-two books I have published so far, I have concluded my Preface by showering petals for her and our kids. Now for this volume, she turned as a fragrant memory. At this moment of grief and deep sorrow, I pray to the Almighty to give her soul eternal peace and guide my kids—Aishwarya and Ananthapadmanabha and myself, with the courage and strength to face the days to come.

Finally, I am also thankful to Sri Ompraksh of Datasoft, Kollam for his page setting.

Kollam
19-02-2013

Dr. M.R. Biju
Associate Professor & Formerly Head
PG & Research Department of Political Science
Sree Narayana College, Kollam, Kerala, India.

Contents

List of Contributors

Abraham, Bijith George, Research Assistant at CSSEIP, Cochin University of Science and Technology, Kochi-22, India.

Biju, M.R., Associate Professor PG & Research Department of Political Science, Sree Narayana College, Kollam, Kerala.

Chandrashekar, E., Assistant Professor, Dept. of Sociology/Adult Continuing Education, Extension and Field Outreach, Kuvempu University, Shankaraghatta-577451, Shimoga Dist., Karnataka, India.

Chathukulam, Jose, Director, Centre for Rural Management (CRM), Kottayam, Kerala-686028.

Chaturvedi, Sonalika, Planning Commission, Government of India, Sansad Marg, New Delhi-110001.

Dam, Supriya, Assistant Professor in Commerce, Govt. Degree College, Dharmanagar, North Tripura.

Garg, Priti, Professor, Department of Public Administration, V.N. South Gujarat University, Surat.

Hazra, Ayan, Astt. Professor in Sociology, Hidayatullah National Law University, New Raipur, Chhattisgarh.

Kala, K., Full Time Ph.D. Management Studies Scholar in School of Management Studies, Anna University of Technology, Coimbatore.

Karna, Ashok Kumar, Research Scholar (PhD), Centre for the Study of Law & Governance, Jawaharlal Nehru University, New Delhi.

Kulsheshtra, Lekshmi Rani, Head, Deptt. of Economics, Faculty of Social Sciences, Dayalbagh Educational Institute, Agra.

Kumar, K. Anil, Guest Faculty, Department of Politics and Public Administration, Andhra University, Visakhapatnam.

Laskar, Nazmul Hussain, Ph.D. Scholar, Deptt. of Political Science, Assam University, Silchar-11.

Makar, A.K., Associate Professor and Head, Department of Rural Development and Planning, School of Agricultural Sciences and Rural Development, Nagaland University, Nagaland-797106.

Mallick, Ayub, Department of Political Science, University of Kalyani, Kalyani Nadia, West Bengal.

Mondal, Sagar, Associate Professor, Department of Agricultural Extension, Bidhan Chandra Krishi Viswavidyalaya, PO - Krishi Viswavidyalaya, Mohanpur, Nadia, West Bengal-741252

Munikrishna, Assistant Professor, Deptt. of Political Science, Government First Grade College, K.R. Puram, Bangalore.

Narayana, E.A., Head, Department of Politics and Public Administration, Andhra University, Visakhapatnam.

Negi, M.K., Assistant Professor in Production Engineering, Department of A.V.C.O.E., Sangamner (M.S.).

Odyuo, M.N., Research Scholar, Department of Agricultural Extension, School of Agricultural Sciences and Rural Development, Nagaland University, Nagaland-797106.

Panda, Snehaletha, Professor Emeritus, Department of Political Science, Berhampur University, Orissa.

Patra, N.K., Assistant Professor, Department of Agricultural Extension, School of Agricultural Sciences and Rural Development, Nagaland University, Nagaland-797106.

Rajasenan, D., Director, Centre for the Study of Social Exclusion and Inclusive Policy (CSSEIP) Cochin University of Science and Technology, Kochi-22, India.

Rao, S. Nagabhushana, Assistant Professor (CRI), National Institute of Rural Development, Rajendranagar, Hyderabad-500030.

Rekha, V., Associate Fellow, Centre for Rural Management (CRM), Kottayam, Kerala-686028.

Satsangi, Rupali, Astt. Professor in Economics DEI, Dayalbagh Educational Institute, Dayalbagh, Agra, Uttar Pradesh

Satsangi, Rupali, Department of Economics, Faculty of Social Sciences, Dayalbagh Educational Institute, Agra.

Sharma, Arjun, Principal, K.L.S. College, Nawada (M.U.).

Shrivastava, Rajeev R., Department of Geography, St. Xavier's College, Ranchi.

Sreedevi, V., Professor and Head, Department of Management Studies, Ponjesly College of Engineering, Nagercoil, Tamil Nadu.

Thawani, Madhu, Assistant Professor, Department of Public Administration, V.N. South Gujarat University, Surat.

Venkatesh, J., Assistant Professor, School of Management Studies, Anna University of Technology Coimbatore.

Introduction

Content of the Volume

In the inaugural paper **S. Nagabhushana Rao** observes that a change in the attitude of the people is visible throughout the nation. According to him, this change is anti-establishment factor. This is because most of the State governments and Government at Centre failed to live up to the expectation of people to meet the wave of liberalisation and globalisation. The Government at Centre and State governments are failed in addressing the needs of the people. So in present context good governance is "a government actually delivers". This means bringing more professionalism and efficiency in the government by bringing reforms in the 'hierarchy bound' civil service to deliver with speed and efficiency. The former Andhra Pradesh Chief Minister Shri N. Chandrababu Naidu rightly said "Andhra Pradesh had 47 levels of bureaucracy from the top to bottom. Such a complex structure could not deliver with speed and efficiency and needed to be replaced by a lean and nimble-footed public service".

Rao further states that, India is a nation of villages. The rural mass in the nation comprises the core of Indian society and also represents the real India. According to the Census data of 2012 about 72.2 per cent of the population lives in 6,38,000 villages. So development of these rural mass is one of the key areas of consideration in government policy formulation. At independence, the Indian State had given priority to development along with the task of reducing poverty. The bureaucracy was the chief instrument for the accomplishment of this task. The failure of bureaucracy has resulted in innovations and departure from traditional notions of government to governance. Particularly in 1990s, governance aspects were more emphasized, because Indian democracy confronted new challenges of economic, political and social aspects. These challenges are departures in economic policy in the wake of liberalization and globalization and political assertions of Backward Classes, Scheduled Castes and Scheduled Tribes.

According to Rao, rural development is concerned with the improvement in the living standard of the rural people by providing adequate and quality social services and minimum basic needs. The Government of India has started many programmes aimed at improving the standard of living in rural areas. The present strategy of rural development mainly focuses on poverty alleviation, better livelihood opportunities, provision of basic amenities and infrastructure facilities through innovative programmes of wage and self-employment, etc. But success of these RD Programmes is dependent upon Good Governance at village level.

E.A. Narayana and **K. Anilkumar** have presented a paper on Rural Development strategies and programmes in India. According to them, India has a very long history of government intervention in the rural sector, with a view to improve the socio-economic condition of rural people, especially the poor. However, there is no comprehensive integrated national policy for agricultural and rural development yet declared and adopted by the government (Katar Singh, 2008). Do these various approaches to rural development cover all these components? Certainly not. Mere extension of past concepts and practices which are away from reality would not serve the purpose and major re-thinking is required to develop the rural India and the whole handling calls for adaptation, modification and experimentation, depending upon the exigencies of the situation in our country (Hoshiar Singh, 1995).

Both of them further states that the rural development strategy plans so far have led to vertical mobility in the society and increase in social inequality. Keeping in mind the rise in rural poverty and the need to control fiscal deficits, the rural development plans here onwards should try to largely focus on the development of the women and other marginalized sections. Efforts have to be made to understand and incorporate the problems and sufferings of people while framing rural development strategies. To make popular participation and decentralization work for rural people, the rural people will have to be empowered enough economically and educationally so that they can think and act for themselves.

Snehalatha Panda has presented a paper on cyclical approach to Empowerment. According to her empowerment process may be cyclical for a woman that is determined by gender as well as generation. It attempts to focus on these factors by analyzing selected groups of age specific, educated and employed women in an urban area. Data for verification of gender and generational determinants in a cyclical process of empowerment and disempowerment was collected through interactions and observations. The study is organized in three sections. In the first section, important concepts and definitions of power have been discussed. In the second section empowerment is analysed highlighting probable disempowerment. Field data is analysed in the third section and the hypothesis that empowerment is not linear and selected independent variables have less impact in empowering women has been examined.

Sonalika Chathurvedi presents an analytical framework for conceptualizing the governance function within health systems. As we see governance is increasingly recognized by the World Health Organization and other global and national actors to be a fundamental health system function, and is a central part of their health sector and developmental strategies. Governance is a multidimensional concept, and there are normative, instrumental, and pragmatic models of stewardship. Governance failures, in health systems or in the wider society, have been perceived as obstructing progress towards national as well as international goals such as the Millennium Development Goals for health. These failures include the lack of a long-term vision and planning for essential interventions, the absence of a functional regulatory framework, failure to address corruption, and limited efforts to assess performance.

M.R. Biju has made a detailed study on the local body polls 2010 in Kerala. According to him, the civic polls assumed greater significance because local level democracy is the basic foundation on which the entire democratic edifice rests. The legitimacy of these elections as crucial instruments of a democratic political process at the local level is increasing day by day. Obviously all the social, economic and political factors affecting the States and parliament elections influence the local government elections too. The present study examines the diversified aspects of the recently held local body polls in Kerala. The State of Kerala went for local body polls on 23rd and 25th October 2010, for the eighth time since independence. The first poll was held in 1953 under the provisions of the then Travancore-Cochin Panchayat Act 1950. The second election was held in 1963 after the formation of the State in 1956 and after the passing of Kerala Panchayat/Municipality Acts of 1960. It was followed by elections in 1979, 1988, 1995, 2000 and 2005.

M.R. Biju further states that, the people's verdict in the 2010 polls clearly shows that, for the first time the UDF has stormed grass root citadels that were hitherto monopolised by the Left. UDF's muscular showing has decimated the myth that Grama Panchayats and Block Panchayats are the bastions of cadre-based political parties. The Congress, finally, has bridged the urban-rural divide. The Congress war cry, which was generally considered suited only for the Assembly and the Lok Sabha polls, percolated right down through the three tiers of the Panchayati Raj system. Taking even the Congress leadership by surprise, the party has put up an unprecedented performance in the local body polls almost sweeping the entire Central Travancore and even some of the Marxist bastions in the southern districts.

The author also feels that if the UDF outplayed the CPM-led LDF in Kochi and Thrissur Corporations, it shocked the Marxist Party in Thiruvananthapuram. The UDF has secured an absolute lead in the Grama Panchayats, Block Panchayats, municipalities and district Panchayats. Among the Block Panchayats, the UDF is leading in 79 while the LDF could secure lead only in 60. The Grama Panchayats, perhaps, threw up the biggest surprise. The UDF is leading in 510 Panchayats while the LDF has led only in 362. Among the municipalities, the UDF is leading in 39 and the LDF is leading only in 18. Among the district Panchayats, the UDF is leading in eight and the LDF only in five. This is the first time that the UDF has secured such a massive lead in all the sectors irrespective of the rural and urban areas of the State. Kollam, Alappuzha, Palakkad and Kannur are the only districts where the CPM-led LDF could put up a good show. In all the other districts, the UDF has given a tough fight for the CPM. In the districts of Thiruvananthapuram, Pathanamthitta, Idukki, Kottayam, Ernakulam, Thrissur, Malappuram, and Wayanad, the Congress-led UDF has dominated the show.

The author concludes his study by stating that:

- In the 2010 polls for the first time the UDF has stormed grass root citadels that were hitherto monopolised by the Left. UDF's muscular showing has decimated the myth that Grama Panchayats and Block Panchayats are the bastions of cadre-based political parties. The Congress, finally, has bridged the urban-rural divide. The Congress war cry, which was generally considered suited only for the Assembly and the Lok Sabha polls, percolated right down through the three tiers of the Panchayati Raj system. Taking even the Congress leadership by surprise, the party has put up an unprecedented performance in the local body polls almost sweeping the entire Central Travancore and even some of the Marxist bastions in the southern districts.

- The UDF captured absolute control over corporations in Kochi and Thrissur. Similarly, the UDF captured absolute control over Grama Panchayats, Block Panchayats and district Panchayats throughout the State. In Block Panchayats, the UDF got 89 and the LDF captured 49. The Grama Panchayats, perhaps, threw up the biggest surprise. The UDF got control in 525 while the LDF got 301. The BJP had established control over 2 and others in 75. Among the municipalities, the UDF got 34 and LDF got 12. In 11 municipalities none got absolute majority. Among the district Panchayats the UDF got 8 and LDF got 5. This is the First time that the UDF has secured such a massive lead in all the sectors irrespective of the rural and urban areas of the State. Kollam, Alappuzha, Palakkad and Kannur are the only districts where the CPM-led LDF could put up a good show. In all the other districts, the UDF has given a tough fight for the CPM. In the districts of Thiruvananthapuram, Pathanamthitta, Idukki, Kottayam, Ernakulam, Thrissur, Malappuram, and Wayanad, the Congress-led UDF has dominated the show.
- If a mandate is a slice of social psychology, then the Left in the State has failed to read the mind of its people. The miscalculation that development agenda would eclipse all political controversies have poorly failed. The deliberate attempt to show case development and steer public mind from politics and communal factors only brought them to the fore-front.
- Long before the UDF zeroed in on its candidates or even thought of the word campaign, the LDF was taking the development activities undertaken by local bodies to the far and wide of the State. Its grass root machinery had jumped into the election scene much before others had even given it a thought. Seminars,

exhibitions, Kudumbasree melas... every possible idea was utilised. Rice for Rs. 2, EMS Housing scheme, Asraya project and a lot more for the welfare of the poor was projected. But all went in vain.

- The ballot has shown that it is a misconception of the Left that half the voting population are beneficiaries of their various welfare schemes. If the beneficiaries form a mere 20-30 per cent, it is to be assumed that the rest of 60-70 per cent decided the fate of the Left this time. For the latter, it is not rice or house that matters. But improvement of living conditions, roads, undisrupted water supply and better facilities. Even the behaviour of politicians in public sphere matters for this group.
- The Left often forgets that it can be a centralised and closed party but it cannot impose its character on the people. The party needs to converse with the upper levels of society just the way they communicate with the grass root. Before concluding, the LDF particularly the CPI(M) needs to politically educate its grass root cadres and not feed them on development activities which have gained acceptance.

Arjun Sharma's paper titled e-panchayat initiatives aims to delve into electronic governance experiments in the State of Bihar. According to him e-governance is the effective use to IT (Information Technology) to improve the system of governance that is in place and thus provides better services to the citizens. IT is a multidisciplinary field emerging from computer technology and internet technology. IT and communication technology now popularly referred to as ICT (Information & Communication Technology) embody satellite broadcasting network, television, video, digital radio, internet, extranets, wireless communication, devices (mobile phones), DVD (Digital Video Disk) CD-Roms, video or voice mail, e-mail, e-commerce, e-conferencing and so on. We have moved into IT to ICT and now are advancing towards IS (Information Society). Truly speaking, e-governance is an attempt of government to harness ICT to improve the efficiency of the executive function to the government including the delivery of public services. The application of electronic means in the interaction between government and citizens, between government and business and between government and government It is to simplify and improve democratic government and business aspects of governance. It is all about how government business and citizens interact on an ongoing basis.

The study further reveals that the system of e-governance is supported by the C^5 Computer, Connectivity, Content, Consumer and Confidence. Computer refers to all the hardware and software requirements of government. Connectivity refers to all the information carriers system, bandwidth, etc. Content refers to the information that is exchange between 'Consumer' of the system. Consumer refers to the entire human and human substitutes system that access and uses the 'Content' in the e-governance system. Confidence building refers of such of these measures that help the citizens develop a confidence in the e-governance and encourage them to take to e-transformation. '*Sushasan*' has become an integral part of administration and democratic system in Bihar today, so e-governance has been accepted as a tool to accomplish good governance. It focuses in bringing improvements in the service delivery, dissemination of information, transparency, public and private partnership, efficiency and accountability. Government and its numerous agencies being the largest service providers in Bihar specially in rural areas feel the need to make extensive use of ICTs for its major services.

The author is of the firm opinion that, to achieve the targets of good governance in Bihar, the government has taken bold steps to implement e-governance at the grass root levels of Panchayati Raj Institutions. And this effective use to ICT in the affairs of local administration has been termed as e-Panchayat. So, e-Panchayat has become synonym of e-governance in rural Bihar. e-Panchayat is now concerned with the new form of e-governance. We know that our economy is based on agriculture and people in one way or the other depend on agriculture. A large chunk of our population is poor and socio-economically deprived. More than one-third population lives below poverty-line. So, the State has to take such steps that development of ICTs reaches the deprived section of society. e-Panchayat or e-Governance is a very bold step taken in this regard. In this context, poor need 'intelligent intermediaries' for using the ICTs who can be drawn from the NGOs working at the grass roots level. ICT has become vehicles of enrichment of democratic outlook among the people as the scientific ethos and democratic spirit have the similar nature *viz.* not prejudiced with caste, class and regional feelings.

The rural leadership, according to Arjun Sharma, forms an important fabric of rural-socio and political system. Their perception of the local institution goes a long way in improving and delivering the appropriate service to the village community. e-Panchayat refers to the application of ICTs by government agencies intending to transform relations with citizens. It deals with the attempts made in the remote areas to implement e-governance in various areas of administration including food, nutrition, health, environment, education, energy, water, electricity, revenue, civil supplies, agriculture, irrigation, civil services and others.

In short, Arjun Sharma through this chapter attempted to analyse the very conceptual intersections of terms involved for e-Panchayat such as governance, good-governance and e-governance. The role of ICTs today in the era of globalization has also worth mentioned. e-Panchayat Policy adopted by the Government of Bihar has been illustrated. Initiatives and measures have been reviewed in this regard. Constraints on the ways of ICT revolution have been focused with prospects to remove them and to meet the challenges of the tweenty first century. Solutions have been suggested to make Bihar ready for radical change and sustainable development.

Technology as an effective tool to reduce mass poverty is the central theme of discussion of the chapter by **A.K. Karna**. This chapter scrutinizes how technology can be applied effectively to encounter the growing number of problems caused by the poverty. This chapter has also wrapped the dangers and vulnerabilities of applying technology without due regard and restraint. The necessity for proper and effective acquisition and utilization of technology in developing countries is becoming more and more evident. This is because technology is not neutral and can be used for different aims and objectives. While technology can be used to promote and enhance social and economic development thereby reducing poverty, the same technology can and is often used as an instrument of exploitation, domination and underdevelopment by those who own and control the technology.

Nazmul Hussain Laskar discusses in depth on the people's participation at grass root level in the north-east of India. To him, studies carried out in number of State all over India have also found that by large, PRIs have not yet become the real institutions of self-governance largely due to lack of people's participation, especially women, the poor, and other marginalized groups because of ignorance, poverty and lack of distributive justice. Reluctance on the part of the higher tiers of the government to devolve financial and administrative powers to control the planning and implementation of developmental schemes to the PRIs is another factor contributing to it. A pathetic attitude of bureaucrats and politicians is another serious hurdle. Besides, insufficient capacity and resources of the PRIs in running their activities effectively, and lack of organic linkages among the different tiers of PRIs also adversely affect the emergence of these in situations as meaningful agencies of self-governance. If the Panchayats are to function as effective as well as meaningful institutions of self-governance at the grass root level, then they have to fulfil three basic conditions, namely (1) institutional existence in the sense that the decisions are taken by the people's representatives, (2) institutional capacity in the form of empowering institutions to make their rules independently, and (3) financial viability in terms of sufficiently empowering Panchayats in raising resources to meet their responsibilities. In other words, the Panchayats should enjoy administrative and financial autonomy. However, these things are easier said than actually realised, and we have to find the ways and means to actually realise these things.

According to Nazmul, the need for sensitising the members of the PRIs as well as the public to the multidimensional issue of rural development is another thing which requires proper attention. PRI personnel as well as the people in rural areas have to be made really aware of the different rural development programmes so that these may be meaningfully implemented. In many cases, gaps in implementation process and observance of basic guidelines have been due to the lack of awareness among the concerned people at various levels. Apart from their just sensitization to the urgent needs of the rural people, there is also need for a real sense of commitment and sincerity on the part of the PRI personnel while discharging their duty in the course of implementing various programmes. For the people in rural areas also, they are often ignorant of the opportunities offered to them by the various schemes that are there for their development. Once they are not aware of their entitlements, it becomes easy for persons with vested interests to misappropriate the benefits thereby depriving the target group of the various schemes.

Nazmul concludes his meaningful enquiry by stating that, Panchayati Raj and people's participation cannot be separated from one another. There is an organic relationship between the two in the sense that there can be no meaningful and healthy existence of one in the absence of the other. The PRIs are basically meant to promote self-governance and self-sufficiency on the part of the people. This obviously requires that people should come forward and participate in the management of their own affairs. Similarly, the people also require certain basic institutions through which they can participate in the management of their own affairs. The PRIs facilitate this requirement. However, the present state of PRIs and people's participation in North-East India is far from being fully satisfactory. Even after almost two decades of the 93rd Amendment, meaningful implementation of rural development programmes through PRIs and people's participation remains an unfinished agenda, a dream yet to be realised. Lack of political will on the part of the most of the State governments to really devolve power into the hands of the PRIs, lack of awareness on the part of the PRI personnel as well as the rural people at large, etc., obstruct effective participation of the people in the rural development programmes through these institutions. The conflict between the State government and the PRIs over the issue of devolution of power is another basic issue that needs to be properly addressed.

Ayub Malik in his chapter has made an enquiry on decentralised governance in rural West Bengal during the Left regime. According to him, the representation of SCs and STs to the Panchayati Raj institutions does not correspond to their proportion of the total population. The representation of the poor and disadvantaged has been increased in Panchayati Raj institutions, but this representation has not resulted in any significant increase in their control over these institutions. Due to the lack of this class organization, the poor and disadvantaged groups, *i.e.*, Scheduled Caste and Scheduled Tribe members seldom speak up in Gram Panchayat meetings. The real problem is the lack of organizational effort on class lines among the poor and disadvantaged groups. '... the CPI (M) and the Left Front mobilized the rural masses by appealing to their class identities, these parties have neither seriously advanced the class struggles in the countryside, nor, apparently, do they mean to do so in the next round'. In fact, the whole situation is judged by the Left Front 'not in terms of classes but in terms of party affiliations'. The party does not vigorously oppose the vested interests for pre-occupation to secure votes in spite of its desired objectives of 'grass roots democracy, mass initiative and involvement, and enhancement of right'. Often vested interests do 'manage to extract support from a substantial proportion of the poorer sections among the rural poor in their fight against reform measures'. 'The political leadership of the party is established only when people ... accept the political perspective of the party as their own.' The party has drifted from its tasks of making people conscious about the existing exploitative system and of developing the 'revolutionary spirit'. It is the party which 'imposes its prior decision which violate democratic right of the members of the elected bodies. The common people have not been involved in the functioning of Panchayat'. In fact 45 per cent of the CPI (M) members belong to the agricultural labourer and small peasant families. 25 per cent comes from the middle peasants and small businessman. Though the agricultural labourers and small peasants form the majority in the Panchayats, the middle peasants control the power pool, in spite of the professed goal of the Panchayats in bringing about an 'equilibrium of class force in favour of the people' (West Bengal State Committee, 1994; 1). 'Panchayats are heavily dependent on the Pradhans' who are party men. The issue of mass initiative has been neglected. People are not involved in the development process. People and Panchayat members are less interested in the decision-making process. The rationality of decisions is not explained before the people and the elected members of the Panchayats. 'There is an indifference to involve the people in the decision-making process of the Panchayat. It is quite impossible to activate for implementing the decision by those who do not take part in decision-making process. We noticed the indifference of the elected members and ordinary people in running the Panchayats.' This overpoliticization process is the 'unpolitical science' of the Panchayats.

According to the author, experiences over the years have shown that, the Panchayats are still dominated by small and marginal farmers. Panchayats are not effectively providing 'power to the people' and there is every danger of bureaucratic ills and political nepotism. A process of socialization through a movement of education based on autonomous model of literacy campaign is the new challenge before the West Bengal left. Registering the names of the share-croppers and giving few reliefs to them through the institution of Panchayats, the Left Front has subdued the intensity of politicization of a huge chunk of the deprived population in West Bengal. Panchayats have been used by the CPI (M) as institution in order to penetrate into the masses, to incorporate the masses in the democratic process through 'electioneering and various developmental programmes'. However, Panchayats have become successful in bringing about a change in the living conditions of the SCs and STs and down-troddens through various development programmes, political mobilization and decentralized planning and in giving power and privileges to the poorest sections of society. N. Bhattacharya, M. Chattopadhyay and A. Rudra in their study on the levels of living in terms of private consumption, housing conditions, social consumption, consumer durables, perceptions of the people etc. have found that mild improvements have occurred in the overall level of consumption of private goods in the period between 1972-73 and 1985-86. Consumption of clothing, footwear and consumer durables showed improvement and housing conditions also showed improvement, on an average. The rural poor consumed more food items than that of non-food items. The mild improvements in non-food consumption affected only the upper strata. There were substantial improvements in the distribution of expenditure between 1977 and the late eighties. The Gini co-efficient which was around 0.31 in 1972-73, as well as in 1977-78, fell to around 0.29 in 1983 and to 0.25 in 1989-90. The comparison with other States that experienced agricultural from around 1983 onwards is also enlightening. Between 1983 and 1989-90, the Gini co-efficient for consumer expenditure in rural areas registered a decline for West Bengal and Bihar. The decline (i.e., improvements in the distribution of expenditure) was most pronounced in West Bengal. With regard to the people's consciousness of their own rights there has occurred a revolutionary change with the activation of decentralized governance through Panchayati Raj institutions. Economic dimension has become more important than that of caste dimension, which has not taken deep inroads into the socio-economic fabric of the rural society. 'Caste has stopped being a factor in politics, and even in social intercourse, there is a free mixing of castes. No longer is there any inhibition on sharing food and tea from the same plate, a habit which only a decade ago was not practiced and a thing that was not so dominant in the past now become obvious, and that is, a bond between the men of the same economic class of neighbouring villages as well.

The author concludes his study by stating that in West Bengal the social relations are acted upon the notion of a community, a prior collective authority from which all rights and entitlements flow. Caste here does not become a fundamental organizing principle in terms of which the social division of labour is conceived. Castes have disappeared from the political consciousness of the people. A study of electoral mobilization in some Midnapore villages has shown that the upper and middle sections of the peasantry would be divided in their support to various parties and the poorest sections of the peasantry, the Scheduled Castes and Scheduled Tribes would be spontaneously mobilized through self-generation during election campaign. This support is the result of a particular choice of linkage with the structure of organized politics of a group identifying itself as an exploited peasant community rather than its absorption into the organized structure of politics as a group conscious of itself as constituting part of a class. Hence, there can be no *a priori* ruling out of the possibility of political mobilization on appeals to caste or tribal or religious loyalties. Huntington says, "No social group is more conservative than a landowning peasantry, and none is more revolutionary than a peasantry which owns too little land or pays too high a rental. But, class consciousness among the peasantry has not yet developed in rural West

Bengal. The growing rural unemployment and underemployment, inadequate surplus land distribution, and increasing population have had tended to increase the two related aspects: 'poverty of the labouring classes and relative surplus of labour', even after the relative disappearance of the landlords-traders-moneylenders nexus."

The study of **Chandrasekhar** relates to Panchayati Raj Institutions with particular reference to the Gram Panchayat (Local governance) and Empowerment of elected women representatives in rural Karnataka. Though in Karnataka the Panchayati Raj System is based on three-tier system, this study is focused on the basic tier, i.e., Gram Panchayat. This is done with a view to explain the basic units of Local Government in Karnataka. Here there is scope for people's participation and particularly for women's representation. It is very difficult to study in detail the whole system of Panchayati Raj, as the subject covers vast area. In this study, an attempt is made to analyse the empowerment of women representatives in Gram Panchayat – A case study of 10 Gram Panchayats in Shimoga district.

Chandrasekhar further states that in all the thirty two Panchayats, it has been found that women are fairly young in age, which indicates that the younger generation of women have realized the value of political participation. It has been observed that the participation of respondents with below secondary education tends to be more in a decentralised democracy. Regarding the caste profile, one-third of the representatives belonged to Scheduled Castes and Scheduled Tribes. The reservation of seats for these groups ensured their participation in Gram Panchayats. It is found that the Christians had a better representation than Muslim members in the Gram Panchayats. It reveals that majority of the respondents are married and are able to balance their roles in family life and political life. An overwhelming majority of the respondents come from joint family background. The occupational status of the respondents shows that, majority of them were housewives engaged in the household related activities. A majority of the respondents belonged to low income groups. Most of the women are from non-political background and entered politics due to the pressure of political parties, husband and family members. Social status of the family tends to bear a strong influence in determining women empowerment in Gram Panchayat than the economic status of the family. Majority of the respondents are only the members in Gram Panchayats. It is found that a majority of the Gram Panchayats are headed by male presidents. Majority of the respondents have represented their wards for the first time. It indicates the lack of experience, skill and ability of participation on the part of members. The members have secured self-satisfaction and self-respect and also acquired a new identity because of their participation in welfare services. Most of the respondents knew that reservation of seats had been made for women from the 73rd Constitutional Amendment Act and they were in favour of the Bill. This shows that the awareness level of women in Gram Panchayat is quite high. Majority of the respondents have awareness of their roles and responsibilities. They always visit the ward and interact with people to identify the problems of the wards.

According to the author, the nature of participation by the respondents in Panchayat proceedings and the ward sabha are quite encouraging. Involvement of women in the public activity is important for empowerment of women. Majority of the respondents have strong consciousness of their role in Panchayats and are capable of handling issues independently. The respondents in most of the Gram Panchayats discuss village problems in meetings, interact with people to identify the needs of the community and implement developmental programmes. Majority of respondents have made specific contributions in the form of taking initiative to provide basic infrastructure and water connection for ward.

Chandrasekhar further observes that, decision making role is important for empowerment. Majority of the respondents have involved themselves actively in decision-making process. They have also exhibited potentiality to emerge as decision-makers. Large proportions of respondents present the problems in the meetings and get the approval. They are aware of their responsibilities and discharge their functions in Panchayat independently. Dominance by male members still exists in the Panchayat. The respondents think that only illiterate and ignorant members are dominated by male members. A majority of respondents have shown interest in continuation in politics. A large proportion of the respondents' opinion is that women leaders have got extra responsibilities towards women. Most of the respondents are of the opinion that training should be imparted to newly elected representatives. The problems faced by majority of the women in politics are balancing family life and professional career, lack of previous political experience, lack of knowledge of the Panchayat Act, lack of awareness, inferiority complex and lack of self-confidence.

Munikrishna has presented a chapter on the framework of PRIs in Karnataka. To him, representative institutions in a democratic process have often been viewed, as forums for the expression of popular will. John Stuart Mill eloquently outlined the role of such representative institutions. In modern democracies, representative institutions were perceived to be 'pillars of democracy and rule by popular consent (that) mirror the aims, aspirations and sentiments of the people'. From the perspective of a conscientious citizen, the representative assembly is the 'conscience keeper of the nation and the repository of public confidence Representative assemblies provide a better and more visible access to positions of power and legislators have an opportunity to make an important intervention on issues that touch the live of common people'.

Jose Chathukulam and **Rekha, V.** have presented a chapter on random survey of habitations in Kerala. According to the authors, the main objectives of this survey are to verify the results of the Rural Habitation Survey 2003 and to ascertain the exact position of the status of the rural habitation with regard to availability and quality of drinking water in the State of Kerala. This survey will help in categorization of the habitations into Not Covered (NC)/Partially Covered (PC)/Fully Covered (FC) as per the position in 2003. Based on random sampling, it will be possible to identify the reasons and extent of slippages and emergence of new habitations.

Other major objectives of the random sample survey are the following:

1. Whether the categorization of habitations into Not Covered (NC)/Partially Covered (PC) are correct as per Habitation Survey 2003;
2. The position of NC/PC as on date;
3. The reasons for slippage from FC to PC, PC to NC or FC to NC;
4. Type of water quality problem, if any;
5. Whether new habitations have emerged since the last survey; and
6. The sources of drinking water supply, management and maintenance system that exists in the surveyed habitations.

The study covered the entire State of Kerala. The data has been collected from 5,600 households in 30 Blocks of 14 districts of the State and 30 Block level officers of the rural water supply departments (Kerala Water Authority). The present study seeks to verify the results of the Rural Habitation Survey 2003 and to ascertain the exact status of rural habitations with regard to quantity and quality of drinking water available.

Lekshmi Rani Kulsheshtra and **Rupali Satsangi** in their chapter on Micro-insurance in India states that, micro-insurance is a first step in providing social and economic security to the poor, particularly business and livelihood security. Micro-insurance refers to protection of assets and lives against insurable risks of target population such as micro-entrepreneurs, small farmers and the landless, women and low-income people through formal, semi-formal and informal institutions. These groups have to pay specific amounts as regular premiums, proportionate to the livelihood and the cost of risk against which they are insuring their life, those of their family members and property. Micro-insurance is normally offered to that group of people who are not encompassed by the mainstream of commercial and social insurance schemes because these people do not have access to the products offered in the general line. Insurance companies also ignore them because these groups do not have a regular and predictable source of income.

According to the authors, in principle, micro-insurance works like any typical insurance business. But there are several things that differentiate it from normal insurance. It is group insurance that can cover thousands of customers under one contract. (e.g., in India, Allianz covers 42,000 customers under one contract); it requires an intermediary between the customer and the insurance company, e.g., NGO or MFIs, etc., and it is a low value product (involving modest premium and benefit package) which requires different design and distribution strategies such as premium based on community risk rating (as opposed to individual risk rating) and active involvement of intermediary agency representing the target community and bundling with micro-saving and micro-credit. This way, micro-insurance combines positive features of formal insurance (pre-paid, scientifically organized scheme) as well as those of informal insurance (by using local information and resources that helps in designing appropriate schemes delivered in a cost-effective way). Micro insurance is a form of health, life or property insurance which offers limited protection at a low contribution (hence micro). It is aimed at poor sections of the population and designed to help them cover themselves collectively against risks (hence insurance).

Tracing the evolution of the subject, the authors further states that historically in India, a few micro-insurance schemes were initiated, either by non-governmental organizations (NGOs) due to the felt need in the communities in which these organizations were involved or by the government. The government on its own and through the nationalized industry brought in several schemes to alleviate the financial losses that the low-income groups in rural areas suffered. Two schemes introduced by the government were: The Personal Accident Social Security (PASS) schemes and the Hut Insurance. The PASS scheme covered persons with income below the poverty line for Rs.3,000 sum insured against accidental death; the Hut Insurance Schemes covered the destruction of huts by fire and natural calamities to enable rebuilding them up to Rs.5,000 each. The government had also simultaneously embarked on numerous schemes in the 1970s and 1980s to develop the earning power of the low-income groups in the rural areas and concentrated on loans being made available to them to purchase milch cattle, engaging in horticulture and other economic pursuits. The nationalized General Insurance Corporation (GIC) administered both the schemes for the Government of India on a reimbursable basis. The GIC itself as an instrument of social change, which was the primary purpose of nationalization, brought in a new personal accident scheme in 1975 known as Janata Personal Accident Insurance, making it available at a cost of Rs.12 for sum insured of Rs.10,000 against death and permanent disability. This scheme turned out to be very popular and was extensively availed of by a large number of low-income individuals and by Cooperative Banks as a cover for credit-life. Several community based organizations in India have focused on developing Community Based Health Insurance (CBHI) schemes during the last decade. Most of these CBHI schemes are also known as Micro Health Insurance Schemes

Both of them have concluded their study by stating that the micro-insurance schemes have now gathered momentum partly due to the development of micro-finance activity, and partly due to the regulation that makes it mandatory for all formal insurance companies to extend their activities to rural and well-identified social sector in the country (IRDA: 2000).The Insurance Regulatory and Development Authority (Micro-Insurance) Regulations 2005 provided that any micro-insurance product issued as per the regulations will qualify for rural and social sector obligations of the insurer. The social obligations are in terms of number of individuals to be covered by both life and non-life insurers in certain identified sections of the society. The rural obligations are in terms of certain minimum percentage of total policies written by life insurance companies and, for general insurance companies, these obligations are in terms of percentage of total gross premium collected. Some aspects of these obligations are particularly noteworthy. *First*, the social and rural obligations do not necessarily require subsidizing insurance. *Second*, these obligations are to be fulfilled right from the first year of commencement of operations by the new insurers. *Third*, there is no exit option available to insurers who are not keen on servicing the rural and low-income segment. *Finally*, non-fulfilment of these obligations can invite penalties from the regulator.

Financial Inclusion and its role in rural development is the major theme of discussion in the chapter by **V. Sreedevi**. To her, India, where three-fourth of the population resides in rural areas, is needless to say, predominantly a rural economy. Rural development, therefore, is the urgent need of the hour for planning in India to facilitate the overall development of the country. Rural development may be defined as a process of bringing about structural change in the socio-economic situation of the poor in rural areas and making the process of development self-sustaining.

Rural development became a planning concern because the programmes and strategies adopted in India remained largely ineffective in solving the unemployment problem, ensuring distributive justice and alleviating poverty. Indian economy has witnessed considerable growth acceleration during the post-liberalization period. The economy has been growing at an annual growth rate of 9 per cent for the last four years. Our economy now has the potential to become the fastest growing economy in the world in the coming decades. The major factors of the growth acceleration are: demographic dividend, increase in the total productivity, aspirants of entrepreneurship and India's acceptance of globalization. This growth acceleration has substantially reduced in the percentage of people below poverty line. This growth rate is not easily achieved as some inter-regional, intra-regional and intra-personal inequalities in wealth and income do exist. India is still home to the world's largest number of poor.

Sreedevi further states that the urban rural gaps are getting wider day by day and sizable sections of the population, particularly the vulnerable groups, continue to remain excluded from even the most basic opportunities and services provided by the various sectors, especially financial sectors. Finance plays a major role in economic development. Financial development has an impact on the well-being of the people. It alleviates poverty apart from contributing to overall economic development. To enhance their income and improve their living conditions, poor people require finance. In most of the countries, however, all financial services are provided to high income people and large enterprises. The people below poverty line who actually require access to the financial services are being excluded from the basic services.

The banking sector, according to Sreedevi despite the fact that it has 47,000 branches, does not lend any financial help to a large section of the people in India. Only 27 per cent of farmers get some of the institutional credit, 22 per cent get credit from moneylenders and remaining 51 per cent do not get any credit at all.

J. Venkatesh and **Kala, K.** in their chapter on SHG based micro-finance observes that, women's livelihood has been prominently empowered by Microfinance. Serving the women through microfinance means fighting poverty and promoting gender equality. The weapon of choice can be said as microfinance. There are two special ways to look at this: one is that microfinance is excellent for women; the other is that women are excellent for microfinance. The lessons have exposed that women are liable to repay their loans than men. For any microfinance institution interested in profit it is significant. The methodology used by many microfinance providers have made the women more inclined to work in the cooperative to reach large number of clients efficiently. Microfinance is specifically considered as one way to correct some of the broader gender inequalities which are existing around the world. SHGs are the groups where a greater part of groups are linked with the help of NGOs. And it provides support in financial services and specialized training which has a higher scope to create a positive blow on women empowerment.

M.K. Negi has presented a chapter on environmental sustainability in context of rural development. According to Negi, environmental sustainability involves making decisions and taking action that are in the interests of protecting the natural world, with particular emphasis on preserving the capability of the environment to support human life. It is an important topic at the present time, as people are realising the full impact that businesses and individuals can have on the environment. Environmental sustainability is about making responsible decisions that will reduce your business' negative impact on the environment. It is not simply about reducing the amount of waste you produce or using less energy, but is concerned with developing processes that will lead to businesses becoming completely sustainable in the future. Currently, environmental sustainability is a topical issue that receives plenty of attention from the media and from different governmental departments. This is a result of the amount of research going into assessing the impact that human activity can have on the environment. Although the long-term implications of this serious issue are not yet fully understood, it is generally agreed that the risk is high enough to merit an immediate response. Businesses are expected to lead in the area of environmental sustainability as they are considered to be the biggest contributors and are also in a position where they can make a significant difference.

According to Negi, the main reason behind the increase in pollution and global warming is the increase in number of industries. Number of industries have increased due to increase in demand of materials or devices. Demand is increased due to two reasons. Increase in population-Greediness—the desire to collect more and more. Life seems to have become the treasure of impatience and corruption due to loss of self-consciousness and discipline in life. There is the difference between the requirement and desire. A person unnecessarily collect the materials/devices often misutilises them. This.unnecessary extra collection increases the demand of the products in the market thus industries have to increase their production. Another reason for increase in population is the lack of will power to control sexual desire. Thus, immorality/impurity introduced in our minds is directly responsible for the increased population and global warming.

Negi further states that if we want to get rid of this external pollution we will have to make free our minds from internal/mental pollution and for this purpose self-discipline or adoption of moral values in our lives become an inevitable task. There is direct relationship between thoughts generated in mind and our attitude/actions. So, naturally if we want to change our actions we will have to change our thoughts. We have to cut short our desires, avoid the misuse. It is the responsibility of every citizen to be firm regarding controlling of thoughts and thus desires.

Most of the industrialists, according to Negi, are self-centred that so why they do not think about the possible harmful effects causes to the society arising due to pollution. Now this is the call of time to think globally, to have the well-wishes for all, keep aside selfishness. If we do not change our view today, tomorrow it will be too late and then everything will be out of our control. Organising the self-awareness programmes, planning exhibitions in different parts of the countries to be aware of global warming are some of the steps we can initiate. We must show the necessary courage to take these steps and to bring our positive selfless actions to a logical completion.

Negi further observes that there is a need for sustainable development. The development which focuses on combined needs of environment, economics and society. Present model of development is mainly based on economic development which has not delivered equity in the society and thus is responsible for impatience of society. It is also an indirect reason of growing intolerance for injustice, corruption and uncaring corporate behaviour.

Measure of level of any country's development is GDP (Gross Domestic Product), which does not indicate the level of sustainable living, i.e., the factors of environmental impact, societal impacts have not been taken into account. Environment should not be degraded in the process of economical growth (in contrast to what has been happening at present). Someone from amongst the demonstrating people gathered near White House in America threw a smoke bomb, which was the result of an irritation against the economical policies of America, due to which their country's economy was regularly declining. Degradation of atmosphere may be viewed in the light of corruption. Corruption does not mean just taking bribe for doing any job but it also includes intolerance for small matters. If work is delayed, call is not responded, some desire/wish is not fulfilled, people becomes short tempered, which not only pollutes the atmosphere but vitiates/develops crack in the relationship also. In this way environmental and social circles get negatively charged.

D. Rajasenan and **B.G. Abraham** in their chapter on livelihood security and socio-economic community based ecotourism states that Tourism Industry is a major source of income and employment which is expected to grow at a considerable pace, because of its buoyant growth. Within the tourism sector, the growth of ecotourism has been phenomenal during the last decade with the increase in tourist inflow and associated activities. In Kerala, most of the Ecotourist destinations are inhabited by the weaker sections of the society including tribes who still lag in the path of development set-up experienced in other parts of the State. 56 potential ecotourism destinations from 14 districts have been generally accepted by Kerala Tourism Department (Government of Kerala, 2006). Ecotourism projects in Kerala are based on the concept of sustainability in the tourism sector where there is a balance between the nature and the people living there. 15 wildlife sanctuaries and 5 national parks form a predominant role in the ecotourism initiative of the State. These projects are successfully undergoing because of popularity and tourist demand. The ecotourism development of Kerala and the simultaneous increase in the flow of tourists to these ecotourist destinations would help in providing livelihood opportunities to the local communities and the betterment of their lives.

According to the authors, community based ecotourism initiatives on the part of the government has benefited the community in a big way as 56.20 per cent of the community members in the sample solely depend on ecotourism as their only livelihood. Any setback, either seasonal or random, will have deleterious effect on their income and livelihood options inasmuch as they find it difficult to unearth alternative avocations in this alienated and difficult terrain. Moreover, the community is also striving hard to conserve the forest and ecosystem with a view to attracting more and more ecotourists, which in a way expands their livelihood base. This has been well specified by the respondents when asked about their main occupation, of which about 95 per cent of the community members answered that their primary occupation is only related to ecotourism. Most of the socio-economic indicators of the community in the ecotourist centres show a positive trend once these centres have been active with tourists. This has reflected in monthly income earnings, education attainment of the community, saving habits and related attainments. Chi Square analyses pertaining to various socio-economic analyses have also confirmed this.

The authors further state that zone-wise analysis shows that the community members have benefited totally from tourism development in the region as they have got both employments as well as secured livelihood options. This has helped to draw attention to reduce overall exploitation of forest land by these communities which in turn perpetuates sustainable development of ecotourist sites and ecotourism in Kerala. Inter-zone analysis to highlight the differences in the socio-economic aspects brings to the fact that difference between and among zones is marginal. This may be either due to the small geographical area of Kerala and as such the in-bound and out-bound ecotourism happening almost equally with all the ecotourist centres or may be due to different niche ecotourist sites are equally preferable to all the visitors coming over to Kerala for ecotourism activities.

Supriya Dam's chapter is on the issues of community based ecotourism in Sikkim. To her, ecotourism is a global phenomenon in recent years, especially during the early years of twenty first century. The early definition of ecotourism was presented by the International Ecotourism Society (IES:1991) which defines it as "responsible travel to natural areas that conserves the environment and sustains the well-being of local people". Ceballos-Lascurain (1996) has given a comprehensive definition on ecotourism which states "ecotourism is environmentally responsible travel to natural areas in order to enjoy and appreciate nature (and accompanying cultural features, both past and present) that promotes conservation have low visitor impact and provide for beneficially active socio-economic involvement of local people". In a similar vein, UN World Tourism Organisation (WTO) defines it as "travelling to relatively undisturbed natural areas with the specific object of satisfying, admiring and enjoying nature and its wild plants, animals as well as existing cultural aspects (both past and present) found in these areas". Thus, ecotourism is understood as purposeful travel to natural areas for understanding and appreciating cultural, natural and ecological environment for not altering the ecosystem; while making allowances for conservation of natural resources which are beneficial to local populace. According to the data released by the World Tourism Organisation (2006), eco-touristic journeys comprised up to 7 per cent (45 million of all journeys), while it is expected that the number will increase up to 80 to 85 million by the year 2013. Ceballos-Lascurain (1996) shows that the share of ecotourism journeys reaches 20 to 60 per cent of all journeys.

She further states that the diversity in geography in India provides a wealth of natural areas that could support ecotourism activities. The natural reserved areas for the tourists include national parks, biosphere reserves, wetlands, mountain areas and forests, coral reefs and mangrove under ecotourism. In this way, the natural reserved areas have been opened for the tourists that include 13 biosphere reserves (to limited extent in outer buffer zone), 89 natural parks and 490 wildlife sanctuaries (MoIB:2004).

The Government of India, according to Supriya Dam through policy initiatives, has acknowledged the significance of ecotourism with policy measures. Both the Ministry of Tourism and the Ministry of Environment and Forests have responded to the development in the field of ecotourism. The Department of Tourism issued Policy and Guidelines on ecotourism in July, 1998. The policy lays down the objectives for ecotourism which contains operational guidelines for major stakeholders. During 2000, Territorial Forest Divisions recognized ecotourism in protected areas as one of the fifteen thrust areas of the Ministry of Environment and Forests. The Indian chapter of the Pacific Asia Travel Association (PATA) has formulated an action plan for National Ecotourism Policy, which has been forwarded by the Ministry of Tourism for the State Governments for review (Boora:2005).

According to Supriya the foregoing discussion points to fact that the spread of ecotourism destinations in Sikkim are confined a few select tourism pockets resulting congestion and has a serious implication on its sustainability. Promotion of satellite areas could be one of the possible options. But, again development of such areas involves huge amount of costs and feasibility related issues. Moreover, in spite of having outstanding plans and policies, the stakeholders found wanting in its proper execution. Though, this is not an exception to the Sikkim alone.

Ecotourism in its purest form embraces positive environmental ethic, fostering preferred tourist behaviour. It does not denigrate the resource or erosion of resource integrity. The environment must experience a net benefit from the activity including social, economic, political or scientific benefits. It promotes firsthand experience with the natural environment and not a thrill seeking or physical achievement which are consistent with adventure tourism (Butler:1992). From this point of view, tourism practiced in Sikkim cannot be termed as ecotourism, rather a branch of nature based tourism having a concern for sustainability. However, each of the tourism destinations has its own specificities which make it imperative for them to employ the term suit their desirable ends. The promotion of Sikkim as the 'Ultimate Ecotourism Destination' is a part of building brand image to the world in general and India in particular without disregarding its sustainability concerns. Stakeholders including policy makers, who are directly associated with tourism, must understand these basic needs and take appropriate measures for the well-being of future generations.

It can be recalled that high tourism intensity destinations in the State is experiencing tourism congestion which invariably lead to environmental degradation. Silori's study (2004) observed that growth of tourism should not be entertained cost of environment; rather closure of tourism activity in those destinations can be an option which the policy makers can ponder over. However, in such cases, there should be an arrangement for alternative employment opportunities for local inhabitants.

According to Leong (2008), many countries have made unwise investment in tourism that is often imposed on local communities, especially rural and minority communities, at a level and speed that causes great social disruption. Darjeeling and Simla, two popular hill stations in the North-Eastern and North-Western India, since British colonial rule, have been victim of resource use conflict and depletion of natural resources due to expanding hotel and tourism industry (Luhomi:2006). Dodd's (2010) remarked that many destinations did not address the issue of sustainability until negative pressures were felt. In the face of such impending challenges, ecotourism industry in Sikkim is heading for a testing time in the future ahead.

N.K. Patra *et al.* have presented a paper on prioritization of extension activities for development work in Nagaland. According to Patra, the present-day context of liberalization of economy, privatization of public sector, globalization of trade and the revolution in information technology gave rise to the concept of 'Global Village'. Research sector has continuously been swelled enormously with the sack of technology and the applicability of the invention or re-invention in development and farming sector has also been proved, but most of them are not adopted and popularized. Accordingly vehement changes have also taken place in development sector and their extension approaches for transfer of technology. Extension is a science of developing capability of the people for sustainable improvement in their quality of life (Ray: 2008) and for that various activities and approaches are present. The approach of altruism, providing inputs with subsidized or free of cost and prescribing technology practices to the beneficiaries have been suppressed by the skill up-gradation, capacity building and empowerment of the beneficiaries with effective participation of beneficiaries in development work. Development is a continuous, pluralistic and widely participatory process and basically it means, advancement of an area, revealing, unfolding or opening up something which is latent and a change that is desirable. It is referred to as a continuous and rigorous process of progress, mobilizing the people towards self-reliance, assuring and/or ensuring equitable distribution or benefit of opportunity, resource and social justice among all sections of the society. It may be defined as, the process of creating and maintaining a situation in which all citizens of the country can lead a desirable and satisfying life. When, development is a continuous process then activities for development, that is extension work or activities are obviously simultaneous.

Government sector is unable to reach quantitatively to all the resource poor and backward people for upliftment of their existing condition. As a result they are also pressurized to change their development approach to reach the destination. Possible ways are only a few like privatizations of development activities, private-public partnership, and GO-NGO (Government-Non-Government Organization) collaboration and so on.

In development sector, according to Patra, Non-Governmental Organizations (the organizations which are outside the direct control of government agencies or autonomous bodies and are engaged in providing financial and non-financial services to the community are called Non-Governmental Organizations or NGOs) are playing major role since time immemorial. For the purpose of development of beneficiaries, NGOs adopted various extension activities.

Rupali Satsangi and **Ayan Hazara** have presented a chapter on gender equality through watershed development programme. According to the authors, the importance of increasing women's participation in watershed development has been recognised, and efforts are being made in this direction. However, there is still need to sensitise policy-makers and staff of project implementing agencies to the core issues in ensuring benefits to women from watershed development projects.

According to Rupali and Ayan, a major component of watershed development is to improve agriculture and increase land productivity. Agricultural development programmes have always targeted men rather than women, since women are rarely viewed as 'farmers'. Therefore, in watershed development too, it is male farmers who first come forward to participate in the programme. Women, however, often perform more task and spend more hours than men in agricultural production. This becomes all the more important since more than women are shifting to non-farm livelihoods, leaving agricultural tasks to women. However, in the absence of the men, women are not able to take any decisions related to the land, since the land titles do not belong to them. It is (male) landowner who is nominated to the decision-making body for watershed development projects, although the woman may be actually farming the land. Agarwal (1994) argues that allowing women to hold land titles would motivate them to increase output and adopt better farming practices, besides increasing their access to credit, inputs and technology. Access to arable land is mainly through inheritance, which varies by region and religion. Although laws today give more rights to women, significant inequalities remain, more so because of the disinheritance that takes place in practice. Some of the important reasons leading to disinheritance are male reluctance to endow daughters with land, women's forgoing of their shares in parental property in favour of their brothers, and obstruction by government officials in the implementation of laws in favour of women.

Women's needs and priorities are similarly overlooked in relation to common-pool resources. These resources provide women with livelihoods options that are not always visible. Restricting access to them increases drudgery in fuel and fodder collection, and reduces the livelihood options available to women. Assessing the interface between livelihoods and the resource base can help keep in focus issues related to the economic survival of women resource-users through the planning and implementation stages of the project.

Rupali and Ayan concludes their study by pinpointing that in many Indian cultural traditions, women have been given a lower economic and social status than that of men. Many of the attempts currently being made to break these moulds regard women potentially as passive beneficiaries of special concessions. In reality, women are strong contributors to the economic and social well-being of rural areas and should be regarded as such. This implies that they should be given equal representation with men on the various committees dealing with watershed development, and equal wages in construction and other work. But they should also be given the technical and social support (such as childcare) necessary to allow them to play a role in watershed development. In addition, if women's interests are to be adequately represented, it will be necessary for government and project officers to be sensitised to women's roles and needs, and to ways of meeting those needs. Ways will have to be found of increasing the proportion of women officers on watershed committees and elected bodies and, especially in the case of watershed development teams, of making it easier for them to undertake field duties. Monitoring systems must be established to assess how women's interests are being defended.

Capacity building of communities under watershed development programme is the core area of discussion in the chapter by **Madhu Thavani**. According to her, capacity is essential lubricant of development; more important even than finance. The UN Development Programme has defined "capacity" as "the ability of individuals, institutions and societies to perform functions, solve problems, and set and achieve objectives in a sustainable manner". According to Madhu, Capacity Building should include the following:

- Human resource development, the process of equipping individuals with the understanding, skills and access to information, knowledge and training that enables them to perform effectively and strengthens the capacity of people to achieve sustainable livelihood.
- Organizational development, the elaboration of management structures, processes and procedures, not only within organizations but also the management of relationships between the different organizations and sectors (public, private and community) and emphasis on technological change and innovation.
- Institutional and legal framework development, making legal and regulatory changes to enable organizations, institutions and agencies at all levels and in all sectors to enhance their capacities.

- "Economic Capacity Building" which increases the capacity of any developed or developing society to improve trade, employment, economic development and quality of life.

This chapter focuses on Community Capacity Building with special reference to community capacity building under the Watershed Development Programme in Songadh Taluka, Tapi District in State of Gujarat. A qualitative and quantitative approach was adopted for the study. For this available government records, knowledgeable people — government officials, members of NGOs, elected members. Certain beneficiaries were initially contacted to understand various dimensions of the study. In-depth interview of abovementioned categories of knowledgeable people were conducted to probe various aspects related to the topic. After identifying the various dimensions and attributes survey method was adopted for research.

The focus of the research study is Songadh taluka of Tapi District. Tapi district comprises of 5 talukas (Valod, Vyara, Songadh, Uchhal and Nizar talukas). Out of these 5 talukas Watershed Programme is implemented in 4 talukas. In Songadh taluka there are 177 villages out of which 29 villages are covered under Watershed Development Programme. For the purpose of the study, we selected all 29 villages of Songadh taluka where Watershed Development Programme has been implemented. For collecting primary data 10 functionaries, who were working at different levels were contacted and interviewed. At the Village Level 122 beneficiaries (Self-help groups and user groups) were contacted to study the Community Capacity Building task undertaken under Watershed Development Programme in Songadh taluka. Convenience sampling method was adopted for contacting self-help groups and user group members.

Both secondary and primary data sources were tapped to collect the data. A checklist was developed. Based on this checklist in-depth interview was conducted for the functionaries. An undisguised structured questionnaire was developed for the beneficiaries. Many of the questions were of multiple choices though there were certain open ended questions also to elicit their opinion. Contact method used was personal.

Madhu Thawani concludes her study by stating that under Watershed Development Programme various measures were adopted in different areas for Community Capacity Building like Institutional Building at Village Level, Financial Capacity Building and Community Skill Development. Under Institutional Building Watershed Committee,

Watershed Association, Self Help Groups and User Groups were created in which some of the beneficiaries of the programme were members. Participatory Rural Appraisal Exercise and Entry Point Activities were also undertaken. This has led to people's participation and they themselves identifying their needs and having control over the activities. Local level leadership was also developed as the chairman of WC and some of the members were from amongst the villagers. The beneficiaries were motivated to choose on their own the work that could be taken up for development of the project area depending upon their needs and also organize themselves into self-help groups and user groups. This also helped them to administer the Watershed Project Account and Watershed Development Fund. Besides this, it is the Gram Sabha which sanctions the Watershed Plan after identifying the needs and problems of the people. This has led to effective planning, implementation and evaluation of the programme on sustainable basis. Apart from this, under Watershed Development Programme skills of the people were upgraded through Training and Exposure Visits and organizing Cattle Camps. They were also taught about new technological developments in agriculture, and different methods for soil and water conservation. All this helped the respondents indulge in alternative economic activity. Thus, under Watershed Programme efforts are being made by Government for Community Capacity Building like Resource Development—Natural, Financial Development, Human Resource Development; Institutional Development, Technological Development and Economic Capacity Building.

However, there is still need to strengthen links with other institutions, and diversify training programmes. Forward and backward linkages also need to be provided along with skill development. Further for equity and social cohesion it is necessary that the whole village benefit under the programme and not part of the village only which is covered under Watershed Development Programme.

In the concluding chapter **Rajeev R. Shrivastava** has made a study on water resource management. According to the author, all lands on the earth are a part of one watershed or another. The comprehensive development of a basin to make productive use of all its natural resources with a focus on the social and environmental aspects is termed as watershed management. Rajeev further observes that hydrological watershed could be defined as an area from which the runoff is drained through a particular point in the drainage system. Watershed management as found in the international Glossary of Hydrology is "planned use of drainage basin in accordance with the predetermined objectives" or "optimization of the quantity and quality and timing of run-off through planned use of drainage basin". The concept of developing an area on the watershed basis started playing an important role since 1920s. Watershed Management (WSM) has emerged as a new paradigm for planning development and management of land, water and biomass resources with a focus on social and institutional aspects apart from biophysical aspects. Watershed programmes are being implemented under array of national schemes/programmes (IWDP, DPAP, RVP, and Flood prone River, NWDPRA, etc). Most of the millions of people living in our country depend on agriculture and natural resource management for their livelihoods. The development planners are eager to implement productive, environmentally sustainable land and water management.

Before concluding, I would like to express my gratitude to those who have been kind enough to help me in the preparation of this volume. I wish to express a deep sense of gratitude to the esteemed contributors to this anthology of articles. The views and opinions expressed by the contributors are of immense value for researchers, policy-makers, planners for rejuvenating policies and strategies on Rural Development and Decentralized Governance in India. I am extremely thankful to Shri Ashok Kumar Mittal of Concept Publishing Company Pvt. Ltd., New Delhi, who brought out the volume in an elegant form. I also wish to express my sincere thanks to Prof. V.S. Lee, Principal, Sree Narayana College, Kollam, for his support.

I also express my deep sense of affection, love and gratitude to my beloved wife—Jaya for her support, care and exceptional sincerity. I lost her on 31st August, 2012 at an early age of 42. Whatever little academic activity I had undertaken hitherto was due to her solid support. Jaya came to my life on 14th November, 1993. From the day onwards she supported me like a friend and motivator. She inspired me a lot and she had given a new meaning and dimension to my life. All the twenty-two books I have published so far, I have concluded my preface by showering petals, for her and our kids. Now for this volume, she turned as a fragrant memory. At this moment of grief and deep sorrow, I pray to the Almighty to give her soul eternal peace and guide my kids—Aishwarya and Ananthapadmanabha and myself, with the courage and strength to face the days to come.

Finally, I am also thankful to Sri Omprakash of Datasoft, Kollam, for his page setting.

References

Aiyar, Mani Shankar, Panchayati Raj: The Way Forward, *EPW*, 3rd August, 2003.

M.R. Biju, *Rural Development under Decentralized Governance*, Concept, New Delhi, 2012.

Pal Mahi, Panchayati Raj and Rural Governance, *EPW*, Vol. XXXIX, 2004.

Ratna Naik Murdia, Participatory Rural Governance in India, paper presented at the Network of Asia Pacific School and Institute of Public Administration and Governance, annual conference, December 2005, Beijing.

1

Good Governance: Transforming Rural India

A Case of Hivre Bazar

S. Nagabhushana Rao

Introduction

The development thinking in 1990s is increasingly focused on governance. Governance literally means 'action or manner of governing'.[1] Till later 1980s 'governance' was not heard frequently within development community. But today the United Nations, multilateral and bilateral agencies, academics and voluntary organizations heavily use the term 'governance'.[2]

The governance debate is wide-ranging and complex. The term governance is having variety of meanings and has a plethora of users. The traditional use of 'governance' and its dictionary entry defined it as a synonym for government. The theoretical work on governance reflects the interest of the social science community in a shifting pattern in styles of governing. In current development, governance is being used in different ideological persuasions.[3]

Works on governance suggest that there is a redirection in its use. Governance signifies a change in the meaning of government, referring to a new process of governing or a changed condition of ordered rule or the new method by which society is governed. 'Governance is ultimately concerned with creating the conditions for ordered rule and collective action. The outputs of governance are not different from those of government. It is a matter of a difference in processes'.[4]

Gerry Stoker defines governance as a "positive attempt to tackle social and economic challenges in innovative ways but not as a panacea".[5]

From Government to Governance

The concept of governance assumed global context by entering into the arena of developing countries. The international financial institutions used the term governance in the context of volume of funding to Third World countries. By talking about governance rather than state reform or social and political change, multilateral banks and agencies within development establishment have been able to address sensitive questions.[6] The efforts of international financial and donor communities to promote good governance in 1990s are presented as elements in the programme of institutional reform.[7]

The term governance is first applied to the governments of Third World countries by the World Bank. The World Bank applied it to a commitment to efficient and accountable government. The broad use of governance is that, the interdependence of public, private and voluntary sectors in developing countries. Niraj Gopal rightly says, "The term 'governance' first landed on Southern shores as the medicine prescribed by the good doctors of the Bretton Woods Institutions, to remedy laggard and inefficient development performance of these states".[8]

Governance was first problematized in a World Bank document of 1989 on sub-Saharan Africa, which suggested that the Bank's programmes of adjustment and investment in that region were being rendered ineffective by a 'crisis of governance'.[9] Good governance soon came to be equated with 'sound development management', and was defined as 'the manner in which power is exercised in the management of a country's economic and social resources for development'.[10] Accordingly, four aspects of governance were specified. They are (i) public sector management (capacity and efficiency); (ii) accountability; (iii) the legal framework for development; and (iv) information and transparency.[11]

The Third World countries like Bosnia, Liberia and Rwanda, the United Nations and bilateral donors and non-governmental development organizations confronted conflicts in civil society in their extreme form and led to social disintegration.[12] Describing the civil society in these countries Hewitt says, (i) neighbours have killed neighbours; (ii) families have been torn apart; (iii) political and administrative capacity of the state has largely been destroyed.[13] The important aspect in these countries is strengthening of civil society and restoration of legitimacy of authority.

The financial crisis in East Asian countries exploded the myth of market economy and expressed that it is not the complete panacea for the countries of the South. Accordingly, the definition of governance has transcended and alternative concepts of governance have emerged. These concepts are not driven by donor interests or tied to aid conditions. Martin Minogue describing new concept of governance says, "Governance or good governance is a broad reform strategy and a set of initiatives to strengthen the institutions of civil society with the objective of making government more accountable, more open, transparent, and more democratic".[14] Now in the context of governance, there is a greater emphasis on (i) participation, (ii) decentralization, (iii) accountability, (iv) governmental responsiveness, (v) social equality, and (vi) justice. Most recently, governance is also linked with the agenda of human rights.[15]

Good Governance

Good governance implies involvement of people in the political process, transparent administration and ***reducing the gap between people and the system***. For this, the rules should be simplified and the complexities of rules should be eliminated. The rules, norms and regulations relating to governance should be made transparent.

Good Governance and Indian Democracy

In India, governance has a wide ambit and encompassed a variety of spheres. These are: (i) political, (ii) economic, and (iii) social. The political implies equal application of the rule of law, accountability and transparency, right to information and corruption in public life. The economic refers to corporate governance; regulation of the private sector and financial markets and social implies expression of civil society in its various manifestations like assertion of *dalits* and weaker sections.[16]

Good Governance in India's Context

In India, a change in the attitude of people was noticed. This change is anti-establishment factor. This is because most of the State governments and government at Centre failed to live up to the expectation of people to meet the wave of liberalisation and globalisation. The government at Centre and State governments have failed in addressing the needs of the people. So in present context good governance is "a government actually delivers".[17] This means bringing more professionalism and efficiency in the government by bringing reforms in the 'hierarchy-bound' civil service to deliver with speed and efficiency.[18] The then Andhra Pradesh Chief Minister Shri N. Chandrababu Naidu said that "Andhra Pradesh had 47 levels of bureaucracy from the top to bottom. Such a complex structure could not deliver with speed and efficiency and needed to be replaced by a lean and nimble-footed public service".[19]

Good Governance and Rural Transformation

India is a nation of villages. The rural mass in the nation comprises the core of Indian society and also represents the real India. According to the Census data of 2012 about 72.2 per cent of the population lives in 6,38,000 villages. So development of these rural mass is one of the key areas of consideration in government policy formulation.

At independence, the Indian State had given priority to development along with the task of reducing poverty. The bureaucracy was the chief instrument for the accomplishment of this task. The failure of bureaucracy has resulted in innovations and departure from traditional notions of government to governance. Particularly, in 1990s, governance aspects were more emphasized, because Indian democracy confronted new challenges of economic, political and social. These challenges are departures in economic policy in the wake of liberalization and globalization and political assertions of Backward Classes, Scheduled Castes and Scheduled Tribes.

Rural Development is concerned with the improvement in the living standard of the rural people by providing adequate and quality social services and minimum basic needs. The Government of India has started many programmes aimed at improving the standard of living in rural areas. The present strategy of rural development mainly focuses on poverty alleviation, better livelihood opportunities, provision of basic amenities and infrastructure facilities through innovative programmes of wage and self-employment etc. But success of these RD Programmes is dependent upon Good Governance at village level.

Panchayati Raj—An Institute of Rural Transformation

To develop rural areas, the rural institution, *i.e.*, system of Panchayati Raj (A system of rural governance) was selected. Panchayats have historically been an integral part of rural life in India, and the Constitution has institutionalized through 73rd Amendment at village, intermediate and the district levels, as the third tier of governance.

Governance in PR is a reform strategy and an initiative to strengthen institutions with the objective of making government more accountable, more open, transparent and more democratic. Ramesh Kumar identifies five parameters of good governance. They are: (i) participation, (ii) legitimacy, (iii) accountability, (iv) openness and transparency, and (iv) competence.[20]

Participation refers to direct involvement of the entire society in areas hitherto kept exclusively for public domain. Legitimacy emphasizes the need for the assent of the governed and provides means to give or withhold their assent. Accountability is the mechanism to ensure politicians and officials are answerable for their actions, use of public resources and performance. Openness and Transparency implies public access to information and making transparent all transactions in which public interest is involved. Competence refers to create effective policy and decision making process to achieve efficient delivery of public services.[21]

S.K. Dey, Minister for Community Development in Nehru's cabinet and the architect of Panchayati Raj after Independence, elevating the idea of PR to a philosophical level viewed PR as "an instrument which linked the individual with the universe."[22] Within the sphere of national democracy, he has visualised an organic and intimate relationship between Gram Sabha and the Lok Sabha.[23]

Panchayati Raj and Seventy-Third Constitutional Amendment Act 1993

The 73rd Constitutional Amendment provides certain aspects with basic structural framework for Panchayati Raj Institutions to withstand external interference and establish themselves as effective and strong people's institutions to perpetuate good governance.[24] Kumar points out that, "parameters of good governance or governance are included in the 73rd Constitutional Amendment. However, some aspects are left to the discretion of State legislatures to make suitable provision in their State Acts like providing reservation to Backward Castes".[25]

The parameters of good governance in this act Are: (i) Legitimacy, (ii) Democratization, (iii) Participation, (iv) Decentralization, (v) Devolution, and (vi) Accountability.

Good Governance in Rural Transformation: A Case of Hivre Bazar

Hivre Bazar in Ahmednagar district of Maharashtra State was transformed into a model village in development with aspects/principles of good governance at village level. The present case study talks about the transformation of village in good governance perspective.

The village Hivre Bazar is located at 17 km towards western side of the Ahmednagar District of Maharashtra State. The village is a drought prone, receives little rainfall, approximately 250 mm to 450 mm per annum. It has a low watertable that resulted in perennial water problem for irrigation and drinking problem in summer season. The village has porous soils and 90 per cent is hard rock and hardly retains any moisture. This resulted in low agriculture productivity which helped only few farmers in the village. But slowly the past situation has changed as the village has adopted the principles of good governance.

History of Hivre Bazar

Till 1972 the village was full of natural resources like water, forest, vegetation and seasonal fruits were plenty. But in 1972 severe drought took place in India. From 1972 to 1989 is a dark period in the history of Hivre Bazar. During the years of 1972-1989, the village suffered frequent droughts; there was a major migration of the villagers towards the industrial areas. The village was also lacking the basic facilities of primary education and health. This forced many families to city for further education. The well-to-do families has shifted their children to the cities for education but those left behind in the village later on turned towards illegal income generation for their sustenance. The people have selected 'two' livelihood activities, i.e., local liquor preparation and selling and cutting the trees in Sahyadri forest, which is near to the village and selling the wood in urban areas. This gave birth to other evil activities like alcoholism, gambling, in-fighting and factionalism. Due to liquor preparation and selling, the villagers are recognized as criminal villagers in government records.

The failure of agriculture and continuance of drought has made the economic life of the people very hard. Besides this, bad habits have increased. The water crisis has started and internal strife has also started. **Milk replaced Liquor**. The school has become 'liquor taking institution'. Violence has become everyday affair. Duo to liquor youth started quarrelling among them. Wife beating has become a common feature. The village got bad reputation.

The police started believing that the village was vulnerable to violence, because, in this village 90 per cent people are drunkards. The Government officers used to believe that posting or transfer to this village was a punishment. Habib a villager says that "In this village the officer should take liquor or should provide liquor to others". Marriage has become a difficult task to the boys of village, because no one is ready to dare to send girls to this village. In this small village, 20 liquor shops existed.

Hivre Bazar in Cameo

Sl. No.	*Item*	*No.*
1.	Name of the village	Hivre Bazar
2.	Tahsil	Nagar
3.	District	Ahmednagar
4.	Area of the village	976.84 ha.
5.	Rainfall	250-450 mm
6.	Population	1215
7.	No. of males	619
8.	No. of females	596
9.	No. of farm families	205
10.	No. of landless families	02
11.	Cattle	1140
12.	No. of Milk animals	488
13.	No. of farm use animals.	216
14.	Total Geographical Area	976.84 ha.
15.	Cultivable land	795.23 ha.
16.	Forest land	70.03 ha.
17.	Pasture Land	6.75 ha.
18.	Irrigated Land	580.40 ha.
19.	No. of functioning wells	252
20.	Slope of the watershed	3 to 25%

Source: Gram Panchayat records.

The principle of good governance has turned the Hivre Bazar towards development path. These principles are:

1. Good Leadership;
2. People's Participation;
3. Watershed Approach;
4. Panchasutri's or Project Conditions;
5. Decision Making in Gram Sabha;
6. Water Budgeting; and
7. Equity and Social Integration.

1. Good Leadership

For any achievement, particularly in developmental aspects good leadership is necessary. However, defining leadership has been challenging and definitions can vary depending on the situation. Chemers says that, "Leadership is a process of social influence in which one person can enlist the aid and support of others in the accomplishment of a common task".[26] Alan Keith of Genentech states that, "Leadership is ultimately about creating a way for people to contribute to making something extraordinary happen".[27]

But the comprehensive definition is given by Ann Marie E. McSwain, Assistant Professor at Lincoln University. According to Ann "leadership is about capacity: the capacity of leaders to listen and observe, to use their expertise as a starting point to encourage dialogue between all levels of decision-making, to establish processes and transparency in decision-making, to articulate their own values and visions clearly but not to impose them. Leadership is about setting and not just reacting to agendas, identifying problems, and initiating change that makes for substantial improvement rather than managing change".[28]

The leadership has certain characteristics. There are number of studies which propose a number of characteristics that distinguish leaders from non-leaders. To name few characteristics (i) Intelligence, (ii) Dominance, (iii) adaptability, (iv) persistence, (v) integrity, (vi) socio-economic status and self-confidence. Hivre Bazar has succeeded because of good and committed leadership that made the people to unite and think towards development.

From 1989 onwards the things have started changing in Hivre Bazar. In 1989, the Gram Panchayat election were declared by the Government of Maharashtra. The subject of election was a fearful factor in the minds of the villagers because of violence, in-fighting and factionalism. But the young people have realized that "the young and educated blood is needed for development of their village". In these circumstances, the youth found Mr. Popat Rao Pawar, a young and only post-graduate (in commerce from Pune University) person from this village. He was looking for the job where he can serve the community.

The village youth invited him for Panchayat chairman for one year. Popat Rao Powar accepted the invitation and he was unanimously elected. In fact, entire Panchayat members were elected unanimously. His leadership was accepted because he was from the same village, educated and exposed to the outside world and the villagers believed that he may bring changes in the village. Priya Sangameswaran asserts the same. She says that "Initially the people have suspected him about ulterior motives. But Popat Rao Powar neutralised himself and did not identify with any group. Finally, he was accepted as a leader by the villagers. The fact that he was originally from the village facilitated his acceptance and his education and exposure to the outside world made to believe the villagers that he can bring changes in the village".[29] As people expected Mr. Popat Rao Powar also lived up to their expectations.

Popat Rao Powar has observed the following problems in the village. These are:

1. No Water,
2. No Education,
3. Unemployment,
4. No rainfall,
5. Disappearance of vegetation, and
6. All the natural resources were degenerated.

The 'journey of development of village' has started with humble beginning. First priority was given to education. The problem in the village was students are more and the rooms are less in the school. The government has sanctioned budget for construction of one room for the school. But the school was in need of 'two' rooms. He has requested the people for *shramadan* (voluntary labour) and donation of land to the school. Few farmers came forward and donated the land to the school. All people in the village have contributed *shramadan* and constructed two rooms for the school. Within the budget of one room the people with *shramadan* were able to construct two rooms for the school. With this 'community work' Popat Rao Powar has won the people's faith and his term of Gram Panchayat President was extended up to 1994.

In 1993, the school was upgraded to upper primary (5th to 7th standard) school. The problem was that the school was granted but the teachers were not provided to the school by the government. At that time Popat Rao Powar has requested the educated youth of village to teach students of 5th to 7th standard. This has strengthened his leadership.

After consolidating his leadership, he has recognized the needs of the village. These are:

1. Food Security,
2. Education,

3. Health,
4. Roads, and
5. Power.

In the process he has also recognized '**enemies**' of the village. These are:

1. Drought,
2. Poverty,
3. Unemployment, and
4. Ill-health.

He started his war against these enemies. His development agenda was:

1. Jan (People),
2. Jal (Water),
3. Jungle (Forest), and
4. Janwar (Animal Resources).

Shri Popat Rao Powar was honest and true leader and every penny was utilized towards development of the village. The good leadership with vision of development can transform village as a model village. Since 1989 till now he was unanimously elected as a Sarpanch. He has refused to become M.L.A. and M.P., as he is interested in making Hivre Bazar as a model village in the country. At present he was given as a Minister status by the Government of Maharashtra.

2. People's Participation

People's participation is central to development in democratic systems. "Participation refers to taking part or sharing".[30] Participation means involvement of people in the economic, social, cultural and political processes that affect their lives. People may, in some cases, have complete and direct control over these processes. In other cases, the control may be partial or indirect. One important aspect of participation is that the people should have constant access to decision-making and power. Participation in this sense is an essential element of human development.[31]

The concept of participation is understood differently in different contexts. Stan Burkey (1993) defines participation "as an essential part of human initiative, creativity, responsibility, pride and cooperation.[32] Burkey understands that "participation as a process by which people learn to take charge of their own lives and find solutions to their own problems". The operation of democracy results in innovations and provides opportunity for citizens to participate in the activities of democratic functioning and developing themselves.

People's participation is hallmark in development of Hivre Bazar. From the beginning the participation is high in the village. The participation has started with *shramadan* in the village. The *shramadan* concept was drawn from its predecessor, another model village 'Ralegaon Siddhi' in same district. **Shramadan is a contribution of voluntary labour by the villagers for creation of community assets.** All families in the village provide voluntary labour to the developmental works.

Shramadan has started in 1989, when the people have constructed two rooms for the school. The two rooms were constructed within the budget of one room. This has created a feeling of **unity and pride in their work**. The people felt that *shramadan* brings development to the village. From that day onwards participation in *shramadan* has become a tool for unity and development of village. The *shramadan* is having many advantages besides creating assets. It is an expression of unity and cooperation by the village community. The people contribute their labour forgetting all barriers like caste, class, religion and gender.

The benefits of people's participation in *shramadan*:

1. It has brought unity among the villagers and a sense of togetherness was developed.
2. It resolved all conflicts, in-fighting among the community.
3. *Shramadan* created many assets for welfare of the community.
4. All water and soil conservation works were done with the help of *shramadan*. It has brought immense benefits to the village.
5. A 'sense of ownership' was developed among themselves. This made them responsible for maintaining the structures created by them.
6. *Shramadan* helped to save the money from developmental scheme. In turn this surplus money was utilized for another community works.
7. This has helped backward communities economically.
8. Most important thing is that it helped to get further government funds from government for development of their village.

The people express different opinions of participation in *shramadan*. These are (i) expression of unity; (ii) it is a responsibility because it creates assets to develop the village; (iii) it is a pride and prestige in participation of *shramadan*. An economically backward people feel that they are always in good books of Sarpanch of the village and some get favours from Sarpanch. Priya Sangameswaran sums up the different motives and explanation of the people on *shramadan*. She says that the high contribution of *shramadan* has had a variety of other motivations and explanations. These are:

1. Some felt that *shramadan* was an important means of making themselves visible.
2. This will help the people to get favours from Sarpanch.
3. It is an ideological commitment.
4. This is a bid to maintain one's prestige and position in society.
5. *Shramadan* is a precondition for ensuring the village got its share of funds from the government. So not contributing to *shramadan* means the 'required' percentage of *shramadan* would not be met, adversely affecting the granting of funds and this in turn could invite the ire of other villagers.[33]

Whatever the motives behind the participation in *shramadan*, it has brought the unity and development to the village. The present norm of *shramadan* is 'one person from each family should contribute two days of labour per month'.

3. Watershed Approach

The motivation of watershed approach was drawn from another model village, i.e., Ralegaon Siddhi, which was developed through watershed approach. Hivre Bazar village is in semi-arid area. The village is a drought prone and receives little rainfall. Thousands of rupees of investment on water (bore wells) will not fetch a single drop of water. Farmers are difficult to survive. It was very difficult to grow crops. It is difficult to trust rain water (only 400 mm).

The main problem of the village was 'WATER'. Due to continuous droughts and low rainfall the village has suffered water scarcity for irrigation and drinking water in summer season. Low agriculture productivity was concern of all the villagers. All villagers went and requested the Sarpanch Mr. Popat Rao Powar to solve the water problem.

From that day onwards all developmental schemes were centred on water and soil conservation works to conserve the water.

In this situation the people of Hivre Bazar has declared the war against "WATER DROUGHT". As an initial step the people of Hivre Bazar have stated protecting "water resources". The people have started 'two' pronged strategy. These are (i) soil and water conservation works from ridge to valley, and (ii) the plantation for vegetation. They have started regeneration of forests. For protection of plantation fencing was done. Slowly in 70 hectares the greenery has started.

In 20 years, 50 lakhs plantation was done. "Water conservation and protection was the main mission (aim). Accordingly, the people have prepared five-year perspective plan. All the government funds were utilized towards soil and water conservation. Every rupee was sincerely utilized. 600 sunken ponds (pits) were done in hill areas. Many check dams and percolation tanks were constructed. Besides this, 2,00,000 trees were planted in the village. At present in 330 hectares 11,00,000 plantation was done, which includes private lands. 3,000 loose boulders structures were constructed.

Due to sincere implementation of watershed works, the watertable has increased. The water started percolating and the groundwater has recharged. The people have started getting benefits. The multiple crops were grown. The cropping pattern has shifted from subsistence crops to commercial crops. The quality of life of villagers has increased. Due to control of grazing, the grass has come up. The grass availability has increased the dairy production. The people have got immense benefits. Some of them have become millionaires in the village, due to water availability for irrigation.

4. *Panchasutri* (or) Project Conditionality

Another principle which helped the Hivre Bazar is project conditions called as *Panchasutri*. In 1995, Government of Maharashtra was celebrating 'Golden Jubilee of State formation'. On this auspicious occasion, the State Government announced the "Adarsh Gaon Yojana" for providing (i) drinking water, (ii) employment, (iii) Green fodder, (iv) education, and (v) health. This is to create self-sustainable village through watershed approach and arresting the migration of villagers towards cities. The programme implementation was based on *Panchasutri* (Five Principles). These are:

1. Ban on cutting of trees,
2. Restriction on free grazing,
3. Ban on alcohol dens (Ban on liquor),
4. Family Planning, and
5. Voluntary *shramadan.* (voluntary labour)

Ban on Cutting of Trees

Ban on cutting of trees was the first condition imposed by the Forest Department when they have implanted JFM in forest areas of Sahayadri Hills. The forest department has put this condition because, in drought period, the people have cut the trees for their livelihood. Slowly the entire forest was destroyed. With this rains have decreased. The water drought has started. The people began to suffer with low agriculture productivity. The people of Hivre Bazar has requested the Forest Department to implement the JFM and other water and soil conservation works. The Forest Department has agreed to implement the programme with conditions. The people should not cut the trees and restriction on grazing. The villagers had agreed for these conditions. The people stopped cutting trees. In addition the people have planted trees for regenerating forest.

Restriction on Free Grazing

Open grazing was completely banned to protect soil degradation and to conserve water. After the ban on grazing, the grass has grown in the village. The Gram Sabha allowed the cutting of the grass with certain conditions. At present ₹ . 100 is charged per person per head load per day for one year. Slowly, neighbouring villages also started depending upon Hivre Bazar for grass. The grass has helped the Animal Husbandry activities. As a result, the dairy activities were also increased. Number of milk animals have increased from 19 to 476. Accordingly, the milk production has increased from 140 litres to 3000 litres per day. This achievement is within a decade.

Ban on Alcohol Dens (Ban on Liquor)

During drought period, liquor preparation and selling was one of the means of livelihood. This gave birth to all other evil activities like gambling, in-fighting and factionalism. Due to liquor preparation and selling, the villagers were recognized as criminal villagers in the

Government records. As liquor has become a menace, the AGY (Model village) guidelines have become boon to the village. With this the Gram Sabha banned the liquor preparation and selling in the village.

Family Planning

The village has adapted a family planning. One child and one family was the norm adopted by the village. But, in the village two to four children's families do exist. To maintain the 'Adarsh Gram Yojana' status the village has continued on the condition of family planning, i.e., 'one child norm'.

Shramadan (Voluntary Labour)

Shramadan is a voluntary contribution of labour by the villagers for creation of community assets in the village. The Hivre Bazar has started '*shramadan*' in 1989 even before declaring of model village. *Shramadan* has become the part of their lives for creation of community assets.

All these conditions not only fulfilled the 'Adarsh Gaon Yojana' guidelines, but helped the village to develop beyond their expectations. Due to implementation of all *panchasutri* or project conditions Hivre Bazar was selected as a model village by the Government of Maharashtra. For model village ₹ 2,50,000 was given to Hivre Bazar Gram Panchayat. But ₹ 74,000 was returned to the government after utilizing the fund for developmental purpose. Due to *shramadan* money was saved by the villagers. The saved money was utilized for other developmental works.

5. Decision Making in Gram Sabha

The Gram Sabha is an important institution in village governance. It expresses the unity, cooperation and coordination of the village in decision making. In fact, "Gram Sabha is a voice of all people in the village". At present 'Gram Sabha' is considered as 'development agency' of village. All important decisions pertaining to development taken in Gram Sabha.

First important meeting of Gram Sabha was held on 26th January, 1990 under the leadership of Mr. Popat Rao Powar. In this Gram Sabha, the basic needs of the village were discussed. The basic needs identified are:

1. Drinking water,
2. Fodder to cattle,

3. Irrigation to Agriculture,
4. Educational Facilities,
5. Health Facilities,
6. Village Roads,
7. Electricity, and
8. Employment.

Gram Sabha also prepared 'five years' perspective plan for the period 1990-95. The needs and requirements of the village were prioritized. First priority was given to the education facilities in the village. The idea for selecting the education is explained in below mentioned phrase.

"One educated man can change - A Home,
One Educated Home can change - A village, and
One educated village can change - Everything".

Again the Gram Sabha came to an understanding that "WATER" is very important and can solve the village problems. Water is a basic requirement for an agrarian society. As village is rainfed, most of the farmers depend on rainwater or groundwater, which is fast depleting and can be sustained only by harvesting rainwater.

Gram Sabha took some important decisions regarding water conservation. These are:

For Water and Soil Conservation

1. Constructing small bunds using several government schemes.
2. Passing a resolution not to cultivate water intensive crops.
3. Planting more trees on the hills to let water soak into the ground.
4. One head load of fodder for their animals everyday (after paying a nominal fee – to remove the notion that anything comes for free).
5. Everyone was made to contribution of voluntary labour (*shramadan*) for bund and pond construction.
6. Savings were utilised to build temple and mosque in the village (even when there were only 2 Muslim families in the village, they decided to build a mosque) passing the message that efforts of people went for a noble cause.
7. No one was allowed to sell the land to anyone from outside the village.

8. Even when someone gets richer and decides to build a house, it was decided that all houses (small, big, *kutcha* or *pukka*) will have same facade design and colour to show equality.
9. New roads were constructed but a small part of the entrance of the village where people used to break the coconut on auspicious occasions was preserved as cultural entity.
10. The village land should be sold to villagers only. Other villagers cannot purchase the land of Hivre Bazar. First option is given to the landless people to buy the land. If they were not able to buy, marginal and small farmers were given the option to purchase land. Finally, the rich were given option of buying the land.

HIV Certificate

In 2001, the Gram Sabha took important decision to protect the village from HIV-AIDS. Before marriage HIV test was made mandatory. The test should be done and the certificate should be deposited in Gram Panchayat. After depositing the certificate, the couple is allowed to marry.

Gram Sabha has taken few positive steps for social integration. These are:

Women's Thrift Groups

1. Women's Milk Dairy Society,
2. Bhajani Mandal,
3. Youth Clubs,
4. Co-operative Society,
5. Common Crematorium,
6. Common Drinking Water source, and
7. Adoption of one family and one child concept.

All above decisions of Gram Sabha have contributed to the social integration of Hivre Bazar.

Future Agenda of Gram Sabha

The Gram Sabha has adopted agenda for future. The agenda is mentioned below:

1. To make best village in India.

2. Purchasing land from landed people to provide it to landless people.
3. Food Security.
4. Water.
5. Electricity.
6. No Disputes
   - Political,
   - Social, and
   - Economical.
7. Social Integration.

Goals by the Gram Sabha

The Gram Sabha has adopted few goals for future:

1. No person should be landless,
2. No person should be BPL,
3. 100 per cent Sanitation and one house – one latrine,
4. Complete literacy, and
5. Condition for selection of GP Members is that "the Members have to work for two hours in a day for developmental purpose".

Women Gram Sabha

The Women Gram Sabha would be held to solve the women problems. Some of the important decisions taken in Women Gram Sabha are:

1. Blood Group Testing,
2. Discussing Family problems,
3. Solving family problems,
4. Greater Participation of women mainly participation of women from landless, marginal and small households,
5. Better access to health and education facilities, and
6. Access to improved drinking water facilities.

The Women Gram Sabha focuses on following aspects:

1. Security,
2. Education,
3. Food Security, and

4. Employment Generation.

Thus, the Gram Sabha is an important institution that made the people to participate in decision making in development of the village.

6. Water Budgeting

"To day you save the water
Tomorrow it will be useful
As long as water is there the story of life continues".

This reflects the water policy of Hivre Bazar. The people, who have suffered with scarcity of water, started managing the water judiciously. The village has put up conditions for judicious management of water. These conditions are:

Total Ban On

1. No tubewells for irrigation. The bore wells are for drinking water purpose only.
2. Only dug wells are used for irrigation.
3. Sugarcane and banana is completely banned due to the water consumption. Only half acre of sugarcane is allowed. This is for fodder availability for animals only.
4. Only Drip Irrigation.
5. Biogas in every house.

To protect and save water resources, the people have started water budgeting. Every year the rainfall is recorded. Every month the water in the open wells were measured. In Gram Sabha the crops were decided for cultivation depending upon the rainfall and water availability. Accordingly, the crops grown will be decided for that particular year. **For Instance:** –300 mm rain is received in one particular year. The crops which can be grown in 300 mm will be selected. Depending upon the water availability, the 'Gram Sabha' decides following things:

1. The priority is given to the Drinking Water and for Animal Resources.
2. 30 per cent of water is for groundwater recharge.

3. 70 per cent for agriculture, and every year the rainfall is recorded. The rainfall from 2007 to 2009 is depicted in tabular form.

Rainfall in Hivre Bazar

Sl. No.	*Year*	*Rainfall (in. mm)*
1.	2007	345 mm
2.	2008	277 mm
3.	2009	427 mm

Source: Hivre Gram Panchayat.

Every month rainfall will be recorded. Month-wise rainfall in the year 2009 is depicted in tabular form.

Rainfall in the Year 2009

Sl. No.	*Month*	*Rainfall (in. mm)*
1.	June	79 mm
2.	July	15 mm
3.	August	77 mm
4.	September	135 mm
5.	October	55 mm
6.	November	66 mm
	Total	427 mm

Source: Hivre Bazar Gram Panchayat.

Measuring the Depth of Wells

'Three' open wells will be taken to measure the depth of wells in different areas. **For Example**: Watertable in one open well was measured in 2009.

Measurement of Water in Open Well

Sl. No.	*Month*	*Water (in metres)*
1.	May	12.5
2.	June	12.5
3.	July	11.5
4.	August	6
5.	September	5
6.	October	5
7.	November	5
8.	December	5.5

Source: Hivre Bazar Gram Panchayat.

The water measurement in open wells, water budgeting, dividing the water for drinking and for irrigation explains the judicious and efficient management of water. 30 per cent of water is saved for future purpose and the crops cultivation with availability of water makes Hivre Bazar as one of the best village and also model village in India.

The availability of water made the people to shift to commercial crops. In 2009, the farmers of Hivre Bazar have sold 2 crores of onions. Table below presents the change of cropping pattern from 1992 to 2010.

Changing Cropping Pattern in Hivre Bazar

Sl. No.	*1992*	*2010*
1.	Jowar	Onions
2.	Bazra	Vegetables
3.	Chenna	Potato
4.	Wheat	Floriculture

Due to availability of water and irrigation facilities in the village the land rates have increased from ₹ 5,000 to 50,000 per acre. The present rate is ₹ 1,00,000 to 6,00,000, depending upon the quality of land. The availability of grass has helped the animal husbandry. The livestock has increased and the milk production has also increased.

Milk Production in Hivre Bazar

Sl. No.	*Year*	*Production of Milk (in litres)*
1.	1992	120 litres per day
2.	2010	3,000 litres per day

As people succeeded in commercial crops and animal husbandry activities, the quality of life of villagers has improved. Some of them have become millionaires in the village. The per capita income is also increased. Hivre Bazar has proved that judicious use of water makes village prosper.

7. Equity and Social Integration

Equity is one of the important aspects of good governance. Many factors have contributed to the equity and social integration. For equity and social integration, separate plans were prepared for different social groups.

For Instance: There are only 'two' Muslim families in the village. The people with *shramadan* have built a '*masjid*' for them. This is a high expression of social integration in the village. Further, there is a separate plan for OBCs, SCs and STs and for landless in the village. For OBCs community hall was constructed with *shramadan.* Open wells were provided to the SCs and STs who own a land and pipeline (drip irrigation) in the fields and electricity to the houses and in the field also provided. For landless people animals were provided through Gram Sabha, bank loan for houses and access to the grass in the forest was given to them. All these economic measures to different social groups brought social integration in the village. Although some minor differences arise the Sarpanch used to solve them.

To maintain the equity developmental schemes were given to the needy and socially economically backward people.

For Instance

1. 80 per cent of housing schemes went to the landless.
2. 67 per cent animals were provided to the landless.
3. Schemes for wells went to small and marginal farmers (Most of them are OBCs, SCs and STs).
4. 22 per cent of other schemes such as sanitation etc. benefited poor and women.

The Sarpanch played a vital role in equity and social integration. Mainly, he has distributed the benefits to the real needy persons in the village and stopped the marginalization of poor people by the rich and cornering the benefits of developmental schemes.

For Instance: A reasonably well-to-do farmer tried to get a housing scheme meant for the landless on his daughter-in-law's name (who did not have any land on her name). The Sarpanch intervened and convinced him against applying for the scheme. He pointing out that one should not benefit of their economic status to try and take advantage of bureaucratic loopholes to get a scheme which they really did not need. The scheme was given to the really needy persons in the village. This and similar interventions by the Sarpanch have served the purpose of legitimizing his role as a leader and also integrating the society together in the village.[34]

The leader also resolved the differences with other members by personally talking and persuading them. Priya Sangameswaran says that "The Sarpanch was facilitator for everything, be it getting a new government scheme, an electricity connection, a bank loan, or entry into the military".[35] This type of measures by the *Sarpanch* i.e., giving all government schemes to needy people had prevented conflicts between various classes that could arise because of differential distribution of costs and benefits of the watershed programme.

To control in in-fighting among youth and to inculcate good habits, few bad things were banned in the village. These are:

1. No Hotel;
2. No *Pan*;
3. No Tobacco (1992);
4. No Gutkha; and
5. No to liquor.

Another factor is that most of the families live in their fields (farm houses) which are far away from main village and most of their time is spent in their fields. This has contributed to increase production and avoidance of social conflicts in the village. Hivre Bazar is a complete hygiene village. The Sarpanch, Popat Rao Powar, says that "If any one show a single mosquito, I will pay Rs 100 to them". Sarpanch believes that 'equity and social integration' is necessary to develop the village.

CONCLUSION

Good governance is a process. Every village can adopt their own aspects/principles of good governance to develop the village. But the core aspects/principles of good governance should be followed. These are:

1. Good Leadership;
2. Participation;
3. Transparency;
4. Collective Decision Making; and
5. Equity.

The good governance has developed the Hivre Bazar village and has brought immense benefits to the people. At present Hivre Bazar is having many infrastructure facilities that can be equal to urban environment.

At present HIVRE BAZAR is having:

- Gym;
- Library;

- PHC;
- Veterinary Hospital;
- Auditorium;
- High School (Up to Tenth Standard).

All these are built by the people with their voluntary labour. At present Hivre Bazar can boast of 99 per cent literacy in the village. The village can also boast of producing many educated people and employed:

70 – Army;
82 – Primary Teachers;
4 – Engineers; and
25 – D. Pharmacy Engineers.

Vehicles in Hivre Bazar

Year	*Bikes*	*4-Wheeler*	*Tractors*
1992	1	—	2
2010	216	10	22

Hivre Bazar has got many awards in different fields. Some of them are mentioned below:

Sl. No.	*Year*	*Award*
1.	1995	Ideal village (Govt. of Maharashtra)
2.	1997-98	Best Model Village
3.	1998	National Productivity Award (For Dry Land Farming) (First village in Maharashtra)
4.	1998	Vansri Award
5.	2000	Yeswanth Gram Award (Govt. of Maharashtra)
6.	2002	Ideal Sarpanch in Maharashtra
7.	2005	Mahatma Jal Bhumi Award
8.	2005	Tukaram Van Gram Award
9.	2007	Van Gram Award (Govt. of Maharashtra)
10.	2007	National Water Award
11.	2007	Nirmal Gram Award (Total Sanitation Award)

Hivre Bazar has followed the principles of Good Governance and has become the model village. So the good governance is a process and always has relevance in transformation of rural areas.

Notes

1. Oxford English Dictionary (2001), Oxford University Press, New York, p. 257.
2. Cynthia, Alcantara Hewitt de. (1998), "Uses and Abuses of the Concept of Governance", *International Social Science Journal*, Vol. L, No. 1, Blackwell Publishers Ltd. for UNESCO, March, p. 105.
3. *Ibid.*, p. 106.
4. Stoker, Gerry. (1998), "Governance as Theory: Five Propositions," *International Social Science Journal,* Vol. I, No. 1, Blackwell Publishers Ltd. for UNESCO, March, p. 18.
5. *Ibid.*, p. 17.
6. Cynthia, Alcantara Hewitt de. (1998), *op. cit.*, p. 107.
7. *Ibid.*
8. Gopal, Jayal Niraja. (2001), "Reinventing the State: The Emergence of Alternative Models of Governance in India in the 1990s", in Niraj Gopal Jayal & Sudha Pillai (ed.). *Democratic Governance in India: Challenges of Poverty, Development and Identity*, Sage Publications, New Delhi, p. 132.
9. *Ibid.*
10. World Bank. (1992*),* "Governance and Development", World Bank, Washington, D.C., p. 3.
11. *Ibid.*
12. Cynthia, Alcantara Hewitt de. (1998), *op. cit.*, p. 107.
13. *Ibid.*
14. Syedur, Rahman. (2001), "*Governance and Local Government System*" in Hasnat Abdul Hye (ed.). *Governance: South Asian Perspectives*", The University Press Limited, New Delhi, p. 233.
15. Gopal, Jayal Niraja. (2001), *op. cit.*, pp. 132-150.
16. *Ibid.*
17. Advani may. "Head Panel on Good Governance", *The Hindu*, 29.08.2003, p. 1.
18. "Naidu calls for Civil Service Reforms", *The Hindu*, 28.08.2003, p. 1.
19. *Ibid.*
20. Kumar, Ramesh G. M. (2001), "Local Government for Good Governance: Experience in Andhra Pradesh", in Hasnat Abdul Hye (ed.). *Governance: South Asian Perspectives*, The University Press Limited, New Delhi, p. 247.
21. *Ibid.*, p. 248.
22. Mathew, George. (1995), "Status of Panchayati Raj in the States of India", *Institute of Social Sciences*, Concept Publishing Company, New Delhi, p. 5.

23. *Ibid.*
24. Kumar, Ramesh G. M. (2001), *op. cit.*, p. 249.
25. *Ibid.*, p. 251.
26. Chemers, M. M. (1997). "An integrative theory of Leadership", Lawrence Erlbaum Associates, Mahwah, NJ07430 (USA), p. 1.
27. Keith, A., "Personal communication", quoted in Kouzes & Posner, 2007, p. 3.
28. Dr.Ann Marie E. McSwain (from http://www.Medpedia.com; Professional summary)
29. Priya Sangameswaran, "Journal of Development Studies", (March 2008), Vol. 44, No. 3, p. 399)
30. Buch, Nirmala (2003), "Panchayats in India—Forum for Citizens Participation in Local Governance: Representation and participation of Rural Women, Experience and Challenges", http://www.ciff.on.ca/Reference/documents. MS-936-1, files/Papers/Buch,html, 1/9/03, p.1.
31. United Nations Development Programme (1993), *Human Development Report,* New York, p. 1.
32. Burkey Stan (1993), "People First: A Guide to Self-Reliant Participatory Rural Development", Zed Books, London and New York.
33. Priya Sangameswaran, *op. cit.*, p. 399.
34. *Ibid.*, p. 399.
35. *Ibid.*, p. 399.

2

Rural Development Strategies and Programmes in India

An Overview

E.A. Narayana and *K. Anil Kumar*

Mahatma Gandhi famously noted that *India lives in its villages*. If the village perishes, India will perish too. This truth about the social, economic and political development of rural areas is valid even today. There are cascading affects of poverty, unemployment, poor and inadequate infrastructure in rural areas and consequential social and economic tensions being manifested in economic deprivation and poverty. The imbalances in the society, hampers development. Hence, rural development, which is concerned with economic growth and social justice, improvement in the living standard of the rural people by providing adequate and quality social services and minimum basic needs, becomes essential. Along with the traditional needs seen in rural areas, a host of new challenges have emerged in response to our globally connected society. So, rural development occupies a prominent position in the hierarchy of tasks before Indian planners.

The interest and public concern about rural development have been given a fair trial ever since the commencement of the Five Year Plans (C.M. Jain and T. Cangan, 1993). During this period several changes have taken place in the policy framework of rural development. Many rural development programmes have been launched both by the Central and State governments. The rural development programmes are aimed at improving the condition of the poor people. Many approaches have been given trial in the field of rural development during last sixty years. During this time, the focus of rural development programmes has shifted from multi-purpose approach to target sector development approach, and from target group development approach to area development approach and integrated rural development approach. An examination of these approaches concerning the rural development has been presented in this chapter. The programmes initiated under the different approaches and strategies have also been examined in this chapter.

1. Multi-purpose Approach

The rural development in India based itself, to begin with, on the Gandhian philosophy. It aimed at integrating the efforts of the people and the government to improve the economic, social and cultural conditions of society through self-help and self-reliance techniques. The basic idea which influenced the thinking of planners at this stage was the so-called "multi-purpose approach", based on the principle of all-sided development. Under this approach, the Community Development Programme (CDP) and National Extension Service (NES) were conceived for all-sided development of rural people.

The community development programme which was formally inaugurated on 2nd October, 1952, is a conscious effort to bring about an all-round improvement in living standards of rural population. In other words, it is a plan of prosperity for the millions. The government provides the necessary incentive by way of financial and technical assistance to the rural population, but the major part of execution is to be accomplished by the rural folk themselves. It is basically and substantially a project of the people, for the people and by the people. It is really a concept of all-sided development distinguished from the development of a particular aspect of rural life like agriculture, education, health, animal husbandry, sanitation and cottage industries. In other words, this approach is based on the realization of the problem to be tackled is essentially a human problem and the target aimed at is giving the villager a fuller and richer life. The community development programme aims at solving all the major problems of the villages. The object of the programme has been to bring about improvement in the quality of life itself. The economic recovery through improvement of agriculture and expansion of cottage industries is to be pursued side by side with educational campaign among people of all ages, provision of speedy means of communications and transport, measures for better health, sanitation and medical aid, construction of reasonably comfortable dwellings and better opportunities for refreshing the mind and the body in recreation. Thus, the Community Development Programme is multi-purpose (J.L. Nehru's Speeches, July 1955).

The National Extension Service (NES) was evolved and launched in 1953. The NES scheme was designated to provide the essential basic staff and a small amount of funds, with which the people could start the development work, essentially on the basis of self-help. The NES Blocks were subsequently converted into CDP Blocks. The pattern of the CDP was further revised with effect from 1st April, 1958. According to this pattern, the CDP Blocks had a life of 10 years, consisting of stages I and II of equal duration, the budget provision in stage I being higher. Besides, a one-year pre-extension phase preceding stage I, with attention exclusively devoted to agricultural development was introduced from 1st April, 1959. From 1st April, 1969, the CDP was transferred to the State sector.

2. Specific Purpose Approach

The multi-purpose approach with multi-sectoral components directed at a wide spectrum of the rural population could not make much headway. Thus, multi-purpose approach yielded place to limited or specific purpose approach. The programmes covered under Specific Purpose Approach are:

1. Intensive Agriculture District Programme (IADP);
2. High Yielding Varieties Programmes (HYVP); and
3. Pradhan Mantri Gram Sadak Yojana (PMGSY).

The Intensive Agricultural District Progamme (IADP) popularly known as the package programme represents a significant departure in approach from the Community Development Programme. The IADP started in 1960-61 to boost agricultural production concentrated in areas (16 selected districts) with better prospects of higher yields. The success achieved in increasing agricultural production under this programme led the government to extend it to another 117 districts in the country in March, 1964. By 1966, the basic concept of concentration, effective use and better management of resources had gained national importance, and had emerged as the foundation of India's present strategy of agricultural development. The IADP clearly demonstrated that India can, in future, produce the food required for its needs (Katar Singh, 2008).

The adoption of High Yielding Varieties (HYVS) of seeds backed by use of fertilizers, pesticides, adequate water supply, agricultural machinery and other equipments in August 1965 marked a turning point in the modernization of traditional agricultural system. This programme became the instrument of agricultural growth. The draft outline of the Fourth Five- Year Plan, stated: "It is necessary to make for greater use of modern methods of production and to bridge the gap between demand and production by the application of the latest advance in the science of agriculture". (Fourth Five Year Plan)

Rural road connectivity is not only a key component of rural development in India; it was also recognized as an effective poverty reduction programme. Government of India has resolved to provide rural road connectivity to all habitants. On the 15th August, 2000, the Prime Minister announced a centrally sponsored scheme called the Pradhan Mantri Gram Sadak Yojana. Every village that has population of more than 1,000 should be connected through good all-weather roads and every village of more than 500 persons similarly connected by the year 2007. The primary focus of the programme will be construction of new roads. However, upgradation of existing roads will be permitted to be taken up under the programme so as to achieve connectivity through good all-weather roads. The programme shall cover only Other District Roads (ODRs) and Village Roads (VRs). A sum of ₹ 25,000 million was made in the budget for the year 2000-2001 for this programme.

3. Target Group Approach

The All India Rural Credit Survey Committee suggested that special agencies be established for the development of small and marginal farmers. This suggestion was based on the target-group approach. In this approach a particular group is taken up for in-depth studies and plan priorities are accordingly modified. This approach produces a client-oriented design and the ultimate goal is to transfer all the responsibilities of planning and development to the clientele themselves (Hoshiar Singh, 1995). Various target group programmes were taken up by the Centre in rural areas. These programmes were basically based on the assumption that the main problem of the agricultural sector is the non-availability of credit to the weaker sections specially Scheduled Castes and Scheduled Tribes. The existing occupations of these sections could be made available with the support of credit and subsidy. The SFDAs and MFALAs were recommended for the development of small and marginal farmers and agricultural labours. The recommendation was accepted by the government and 46 pilot projects for small farmers and 41 projects for marginal farmers and agricultural labourers (MFAL) were started in selected districts in 1970-71.

The Minimum Needs Programme (MNP) is another programme started under the target group strategy. The MNP was first introduced in 1974-75 with the objective of establishing a network of basic services and facilities of social consumption designed to assist in raising consumption levels of those living below the poverty line and thereby improve the productive efficiency of the people. The basic needs of the people identified for this programme include elementary and adult education, rural health, rural roads, rural water supply, rural housing, rural electrification and nutrition. The implementation of the MNP for a decade between 1974-75 and 1984-85 provided certain lessons on the basis of which the major thrust of the programme during the Seventh Plan was oriented towards integration of the MNP with other rural development and anti-poverty programmes (M.K. Ghadoliya, 1993).

4. Area Development Approach

Since there are vast regional disparities in unemployment and poverty, it has been realized that the overall sectoral and regional allocation of resources and the elaboration of sector-wise development programmes and projects alone will not be adequate for the attainment of basic objectives of eradication of unemployment and reduction of poverty and inequality. A deliberate thrust on creating employment opportunities and thereby enabling the poor to cross the threshold of poverty line has been considered an area by area assessment of the potential and problems and a matching of the manpower resources with the development of the natural resources is necessary. The planning in India was designed towards such an 'area approach' with the major thrust on elimination of unemployment and eradication of poverty. Under this approach emphasis is laid on the development of the underdevelopment regions. The area development approach presumes that the growth centres have an even geographical spread effect and that the benefits of development percolate to the lower levels over a period of time. Drought-Prone Area Programme (DPAP), Command Area Development Programme (CADP), Tribal Area Development (TAD) and Desert Area Development Propgramme (DADP) were conceived under the Area Development Strategy.

The Rural Works Programme launched in 1970-71 was redesigned in 1973-74 as the Drought Prone Area Programme (DPAP) and integrated as an integrated area development programme with the objective of developing the productivity of land, water, livestock and human resources of the drought-prone areas. The principal objective of DPAP is to organize permanent works, to obviate scarcity relief and to generate adequate employment through labour intensive schemes such as major, medium and minor irrigation works, soil conservation, afforestation and vulture production. Under the DPAP, the village community including self-help/user groups, undertakes area development by planning and implementation of projects on watershed basis through watershed associations and watershed committees constituted from among themselves. The Government was to supplement their work by creating social awareness, imparting training and providing technical support through project implementation agencies.

The Desert Development Programme (DDD), a sister programme of DPAP was started in 1977-78 by the recommendations of the Agricultural Interim Report (1974). The objective of DDP was to mitigate the adverse effects of drought on production of crops and livestock and productivity of natural resources; control desertification, encourage restoration of ecological balance and provide self-employment to the assetless persons. Rajasthan, Gujarat and Haryana States of India have been considered as hot desert whereas the States of Himachal Pradesh and Jammu and Kashmir have been considered as cold desert States. The strategy adopted to achieve the objectives of programme, involved development of the area on watershed basis. In hot sandy desert areas and sand dune stabilization and shelter-belt plantations were given weightage. On the other hand in cold desert areas crop cultivation and afforestation could be taken up only through assured irrigation. The main activity in areas included water resources development, by construction of channels for diversion of water flow to the fields from the glaciers and springs and lift irrigation works in the valleys. The Desert Development Programme (DDP) is under implementation in 235 Blocks of 40 districts in 7 States. From 1995-96 to 2007-08, 15,746 projects covering an area of 78.73 lakh ha have been sanctioned and an amount of ₹ 2,060.17 crore has been released.

Command Area Development Programme (CADP) was launched in December 1974, for the improvement of water conservation and drainage system. The specific objective was of ensuring a faster and better utilization of irrigation potential in selected major and medium irrigation projects in the country thereby increasing productivity per unit of land

and water, which was to be achieved through an integrated system of effective water distribution and efficient socio-crop water management practices. The programme broadly covered, *inter alia*, farm development works which include construction of field channels and field drains, land sowing wherever necessary, farm roads, consolidation of holdings and realignment of boundaries, introduction of *warabandi* or the rational supply of water and setting up of WHF wireless network for better communication in order to ensure equitable assured supply of irrigation water to each and every farm holding, arrangements for supply of input and credit, agricultural extension, construction of market and godowns and the development of groundwater for conjunctive use (Divya Nigam, 2006).

The Tribal Area Development Programme has been conceived as an integrated programme for areas having 50 per cent or more of tribal population during the Fifth-Five Year Plan period. It was in the Second Five-Year Plan period that four multipurpose Tribal Development Blocks were established and on the recommendation of Elwin Committee during the Third Plan, the tribal development programme was extended to 20 more tribal development Blocks and converted the earlier four multipurpose Blocks into tribal development Blocks. During the Fifth Plan, the approach changed with the introduction of the new strategy called Integrated Area Development for identified areas of tribal concentration (T.D.S. Kumar, 1993).

5. Target Sector Approach

It is a limited purpose approach which takes a particular segment at a time and tackles it in-depth. Agriculture development became the main end, which later gave rise to the minimum package approach of inputs of a selected area basis. The practice of defining targets in terms of related physical quantities and a similar presentation of the total plan became firmly established. This approach was adopted with the hope that the fruits of development that would initially be concentrated in certain class-caste strata of rural society will gradually percolate down. Several supportive measures like progressive taxation, subsidies, rationalization, etc., were also adopted (S.C. Jain, 1976). The programmes covered under the target sector approach are (S.K. Sharma and S.L. Malhotra, 1977):

1. National Food for Work Programme.
2. National Rural Employment Programme (NREP).

3. Rural Landless Employment Guarntee Programme (RLEGP).
4. Training of Rural Youth for Self-Employment (TRYSEM).
5. Development of Women and Children in Rural Areas (DWCRA).
6. Jawahar Rozgar Yojana (JRY).
7. Jawahar Gram Samridhi Yojana (JGSY).
8. Prime Minister's Rozgar Yojana (PMRY).
9. Employment Assurance Scheme (EAS).
10. Mahatma Gandhi National Rural Employment Guarantee Act (MGNREGA).

Concluding Observations

India has a very long history of government intervention in the rural sector, with a view to improve the socio-economic condition of rural people, especially the poor. However, there is no comprehensive integrated national policy for agricultural and rural development yet declared and adopted by the government (Katar Singh, 2008). Do these various approaches to rural development cover all these components? Certainly not. Mere extension of past concepts and practices which are away from reality would not serve the purpose and major rethinking is required to develop the rural India and the whole handling calls for adaptation, modification and experimentation, depending upon the exigencies of the situation in our country (Hoshiar Singh, 1995).

The rural development strategy plans so far have led to vertical mobility in the society and increase in social inequality. Keeping in mind the rise in rural poverty and the need to control fiscal deficits, the rural development plans here onwards should try to largely focus on the development of the women and other marginalized sections. Efforts have to be made to understand and incorporate the problems and sufferings of people while framing rural development strategies. To make popular participation and decentralization work for rural people, the rural people will have to be empowered enough economically and educationally so that they can think and act for themselves.

References

C.M. Jain and T. Cangan, *Forty Years of Rural Development in India*, Printwell, Jaipur, 1993.

Divya Nigam, *Poverty and Poverty Alleviation*, The Associated Publishers, Ambala Cantt., 2006.

Government of India, Fourth Five Year Plan, *Planning Commission*, New Delhi, 1969.

Hoshiar Singh, *Administration of Rural Development in India*, Sterling Publishers Private Limited, New Delhi, 1995.

J.L. Nehru's Speeches, March 10, 1951, New Delhi, p. 57; also see C.L. Sulzberges, *Competitive Co-existence in India's Villages*, *New York Times* reproduced in S.K. Dey, "Towards a New Destiny", *Kurukshetra,* July 1955.

Katar Singh, *Rural Development: Principles, Policies and Management*, Sage Publications, New Delhi, 2008.

M.K. Ghadoliya, "Approaches to Rural Development and Agrarian Structure", in C.M. Jain and T. Cangan (eds.) *Forty Years of Rural Development in India*, Printwell, Jaipur, 1993.

S.C. Jain, *Community Development and Panchayati Raj in India*, Printwell, New Delhi, 1976.

S.K. Sharma and S.L. Malhotra, Integrated Rural Development—Approach, Strategy Perspectives, Abhinav Publications, New Delhi, 1977.

T.D.S. Kumar and T.D.J. Nagabhushanam, "Rural Development in Andhra Pradesh", in C.M. Jain, T. Cangan (eds.) *Forty Years of Rural Development in India*, Printwell, Jaipur, 1993.

3

Cyclical Approach to Empowerment

Case Study of Urban Women

Snehaletha Panda

Discourses on empowerment of women are by and large predisposed to gender. Therefore, the temporal, situational, generational as well as cultural factors which disempower empowered women have been ignored. The present study postulates that empowerment process may be cyclical for a woman that is determined by gender as well as generation. It attempts to focus on these factors by analyzing selected groups of age specific, educated and employed women in an urban area. Data for verification of gender and generational determinants in a cyclical process of empowerment and disempowerment was collected through interactions and observation. The study is organized in three sections. In the first section, important concepts and definitions of power have been discussed. In the second section, empowerment is analysed highlighting probable disempowerment. Field data is analysed in the third section and the hypothesis that empowerment is not linear and selected independent variables have less impact in empowering women has been examined.

In general, literature on empowerment of women has put it in sync with power. The prefix "em" means "put into". Therefore, empowerment is "cultivating a feeling of power in people who are considered to have little power". Thus power needs to be defined for applying it to specific groups of people including women. Defining power is difficult as disagreements are many though most of the views are variations of the same theme. Two significant dimensions on which the debate centres round are "power over" and "power to" though over the years empowerment has focused on "power with" and "power within". These are inherent in some of the classical as well as modern definitions of power. Empowerment of women has a different approach to power that is appropriate to explain the individual, collective and transformational aspects. However, the concept needs to be understood for its use in the context of the present study.

Understanding Power

Power has been defined by philosophers and social scientists in several ways. Aristotle distinguished between two aspects of power—active and inactive. Active power exists actually and inactive power exists potentially. A dormant power is essentially dependent upon a situation or person for being directed towards activity or actuality which proves that it exists.[1] According to him "*dunamis*" is the origin of change in another thing or in the thing itself."[2] His causal power has an agent and a passive component where the circumstance is important. The passive object or subject must be receptive to change. Rationality of the agent is essential to activate change. He distinguished between two meanings of the word *dunamis*. According to his understanding of nature, there was both a weak sense of potential, meaning simply that something "might chance to happen or not to happen", and a stronger sense, to indicate how something could be done *well*. A *dunamis* in this sense means a "power to change another thing". He explained both human agency and physical causal interactions by means of the notions of agent and passive powers which together achieve a single outcome. Each agent requires a corresponding receptivity to change in the object. He distinguished power that is inherent in things with souls and power that is inherent without a soul.[3] Every substance having power may express or use it at certain times. Human beings have a range of abilities which are innate as well as acquired.[4] His concept of causal power is almost undisputed and valuable for understanding empowerment of women.

Hobbes defined power as the "present means to obtain some future good". This is explicit from the statement that "The commonwealth-creating covenant is not in essence a relationship between subjects and their sovereign at all. Rather, what counts is the relationship among subjects, all of whom agree to divest themselves of their native powers in order to secure the benefits of orderly government by obeying the dictates of the sovereign authority".[5] Locke distinguished power located in various positions held by individuals in private life and public institutions which exist in different relationships.[6] Power according to Nietzsche is domination of others and also control over one's environment. It is relational so far as it refers to domination over others. Inherent in it is empowerment because power endows a person with the ability to control the environment. It is the main driving force in men for achievement, ambition, the striving to reach the highest possible position in life which is manifestations of the "will to power". It is universal which steers action imbued with a sense of duty led by conscience with a gender perspective. "The will to power" is a psychological presupposition as every human action is guided by the motive to inflict one's will on the other by a soft or a hard approach. This is universal which manifests in everything and everyone. The gender dimension is explicit though it includes a sense of duty.[7] Adler incorporated the "will to power" in his individual psychology. He was a supporter of feminism and believed that "feelings of superiority and inferiority are often gendered and expressed symptomatically in characteristic masculine and feminine styles".[8]

Power is an analytical tool in decision making according to Polsby which investigates "who participates, who gains and who loses from alternative outcomes and also who prevails in decision making where different persons have different preferences and what is actually said and done in decision making or negotiation procedure".[9] But Bachrach and Baratz go beyond decision making, as power might have been exercised before the decision was made by control over the agenda.[10] A set of predominant values (mobilization of bias), beliefs, rituals and institutional procedures operates to the benefit of certain persons, groups and perspectives at the expense of others. Through control of the agenda, certain issues and perspectives never enter the overt political agenda. This might take several forms like use of force, by norms, rules or procedures, existence of certain values, myths etc.

Dahl has a pluralist approach to power. He affirmed that "A has power over B to the extent that he can get B to do something that B wouldn't otherwise do."[11] However, Lukes states that "...A may exercise power over B by getting him to do what he does not want to do, but he also exercises power over him by influencing, shaping or determining his very wants, secure compliance by controlling the thoughts and desires. The thoughts and desires can be controlled by media, education, socialisation process etc."[12] Power relations are "deep rooted in social nexus", argues Foucault and "at every moment the relationship of power may become confrontational between adversaries and this confrontation will be operational mechanism of power which will make visible the phenomenon of domination".[13] It is immanent in social processes but it is a productive force as it produces our conceptions of reality and "the way things are".[14] Huagaard suggests that power has no single definition. Therefore, it should be understood as family resemblance concept. In such a concept power has two "members"—one episodic and the other dispositional. Episodic power refers to active non-decision making agent and dispositional power refers to the inherent capacities of an agent irrespective of the power being exercised or not. Episodic power is one dimensional that is where A prevails over B in decision making. Power is both episodic and dispositional as temperamentally powerful actors do not necessarily have to act. It is also systemic as organizations and systems inherently put in order some issues into politics while keeping aside other issues. The idea that power is family resemblance concept entails that there cannot be a single best definition of power. Such a concept gives theorists the freedom to create own suitable tools appropriate to deal with the problem based on pragmatic criteria concerning its usefulness.[15]

Gramsci identified "dual perspectives of consent and force in terms of the dialectical unity of the moments of force and consent in political action.".[16] People internalize that power of man is imbued with consent and in the culture of violence in marital relationship. It is consensual power convincing women that men are conventionally endowed with the privilege to exert power to direct women to act according to family dictate, convention, social convention etc. The virtue of family life is extolled in women. They are repository of all values of good family life. It is the usual characteristic of women to keep the family peace, raise the children within the culture and thereby preserve the social culture. Family reputation is also inherent in this concept.

Tarnow shows that the power of an individual can be enhanced if the group conforms to his or her command. This is just obedience to dicta. Power is enhanced if there is more number of conformists.[17] But for Lukes all social interactions involve power because ideas operate behind all language and action. "It cannot be measured but inferred from its existence, ideas which is fulcrum of social activity, they are routine, we do not consciously think about them."[18] Clegg proposes a circuit of power analogous to that of electric circuit which operate at micro and macro levels. All three independent circuits interact at "obligatory passage points" which are channels for empowerment and disempowerment.[19] Power is a continuous process shifting from one group to another which can be used positively as well as negatively.[20] Understood in this sense power has temporal dimension which can disempower the empowered.

French and Raven distinguished between power and influence. Power is the state of affairs which holds in a given relationship; for example the relation between A and B. It influences B in such a manner that B makes into the change desired by A. Power, therefore, exists in relationships where the influenced recognizes the quality of the influencer which motivates him to change his/her behaviour. The influencer must draw on the base or combination of bases appropriate for that relationship to get the desired outcome. Choice of wrong bases of power might have negative effect on the influencer's power. They have argued five significant qualities for the influencer. Handy has identified positional power which is legitimized by one's formal authority attached to the position and charismatic power which refers to the attributes of a person which attracts followers. An individual's skill and knowledge also imbue him/her with power (expert power). It can be reward power which means the capacity of the person to give benefits, desired gifts, etc. It is coercive if it withholds reward to ensure obedience of the subordinates for those under influence and informational denoting potential use of informational sources, presentation of factual data in conversations or falsifying any existing information with more authentic ones.[21]

Blent defined power "as the ability or the capacity to perform or act effectively including the situation not to act...In pluralist democracies power is not limited to the formal realm of politics but goes beyond; it is everywhere, relations of power are omnipresent, multiple and dynamic".[22] Basing on Weber and Dhal he postulates that power is positive as well as negative, it is omnipresent and it can be appropriated as well as reappropriated within the relationships. Knowledge and power are inseparable so also rationality and power. The central question is how power is exercised, not who and why. Exercise of power over another has been more disputed as it ignores the definition that "it is the ability or the capacity to act". Weber defines it "as carrying out the will despite resistance. Dhal too, agrees with this view though he calls it as intuitive power. Bachrach and Baratz's two dimensional concept is not far removed from the one dimensional view of Dhal. Foucalt also refers to "power over". Power for Hobbes is the present means of people to earn future good. Lukes views power as potentiality, not actuality. For Morris it is a dispositional concept.[23] Arendt has distinguished power from authority, strength, force and violence though she is not clear about the dispositional characteristic of power.[24] Many classical social scientists like Aristotle refer to its transformational attribute. Plato describes its egalitarian nature. Nitzche focuses on rationality though he excludes women from his framework of power. Toffler acknowledged knowledge as power which has the capacity to ensure change. Gramsci states that power is based on consensus in a society with a human and animal duality. Some have equated "power over" with "power to" and others have disagreed.[25] Huagaard and Clegg conceptualise power as the ways in a given social system.[26] The historical, economic, political, cultural attributes of social system enable some people to exercise power over others or inculcate certain abilities. But Saar states that power is individualistic at the operational level.[27] Thus, it is defined in a broader perspective encompassing the whole social system stretching to each age devolving from one group to another and also in a narrow perspective limiting it to influence and decision making. Its rational use is emphasized to clear out its negative impact while elasticity reckons with its expanse depending on conformists. The receptivity of the influenced is essential for being influenced which qualifies it for acceptability but its omnipresence in the system might impede discretion which is important for understanding its gendered perspective.

Feminist Approach

Assortment of definitions and concepts of power bring home the different dimensions from which scholars have examined the subject in different contexts. The broader view includes a gendered perspective but among the feminists there are different approaches. Liberal feminists conceptualise power as a positive instrument for social good but distributed unequally between men and women.[28] Therefore, it has to be redistributed to end the inequalities or empowerment of women. Disagreeing with the concept of redistribution of power, Young asserts that power exists in an ongoing process of action and interaction. In contemporary societies, it is widely dispersed and diffused but she agrees that there are innumerable ways to dominate in social relationships.[29]

Thus, power is not a resource for some social good. It exists in an unjust relation, which can be oppressive. In the context of women, it is power over domination by men in a situation of unequal relationship. Beauvoir analyses the historical, social, cultural and economic conditions which define women's existence. She states that the situation of women can be distinguished between "self conscious" subjectivity and "un-self conscious" incapability. Where men have transcended in having freedom women have been relegated to a state of "immanent other". Women willingly become the "Other" in certain cultures or they are compelled to assume the status of the Other.[30] While Beauvoir writes that women's physiology compels her to immanence, Young states that women exist as objects in patriarchal societies but undergo profound stress when they cannot think themselves only as objects.

Radical feminists conceptualise power relationship as dominance and subordination. MacKinnon stated "women/men distinction centres round difference of power and powerlessness".[31] Gender differences are socially constructed. In a gendered social system women's subordination is universal. But her view has been criticized by quite a few feminists for presenting women as helpless victims of male supremacy.[32] Frye has stressed accessibility as an important factor for power analysis. Oppression according to her is "a system of interrelated barriers and forces which reduce, immobilize and mould people who belong to a certain group, and effect their subordination to another group".[33] Carole writes that gender differences centre around domination[34] though Fraser suggests women's subordination in western societies need to be analysed basing on social practices, its structures and cultural norms.[35] According to Foucault "power is everywhere, not because it embraces everything but because it comes from everywhere".[36] It is not repressive rather it "produces reality", objects as well as subjects. His concept is not free from criticism but feminist analysis of power draws heavily from his arguments.

Socialist feminist approach to power acknowledges domination resulting from exploitation, oppression of women by men in a patriarchy which is omnipresent in any society. In capitalist societies oppression also includes class domination, alienation and specific tools for oppression. Young has identified the types of exploitation as economic exploitation, socio-economic marginalization, lack of power or autonomy over one's work, cultural imperialism, and systematic violence.[37] In some societies, the economic modes of exploitation are rampant while in others violence and cultural imperialism inhibit women to realize their potential.[38] Kimberle argues that power and domination are consistently associated with masculinity because power has been understood from the position of the socially dominant class and men. Therefore, power need to be understood from women's life experience, "beyond power over others. "Socialist feminists have broadened the theoretical frame to include class exploitation and women's subordination. Intersectional approaches however, have broadened it further by including race based subordination particularly the black women in western societies.[39] Post-structural feminist approaches to power exclude from power the exclusive characteristic of repression. According to Foucault, "modern power subjects individuals, in both senses of the term; it simultaneously creates them as subjects by subjecting them to power".[40]

Rational Choice Theory has been the base to analyse power as oppression from a feminist perspective.[41] It underscores that human beings (actors) can choose from a choice set of possible actions in order to try to achieve the desired outcomes. The incentive structure of an individual comprises (its belief about) different costs associated with different actions in the choice set and the likelihood that different actions will lead to different outcomes. Its major elements are, a set of choices, selection from the set, desired upshot, ability of the actor to ensure the desired change and ability to change the incentive structure of other actors in order to get the desired outcomes. This framework is useful in quite a few social transactions where one actor has the capability to exert power over the other. In male-female relationship, a powerful man can take the option away from a woman's choice set, change the relative cost of actions and also the likelihood that a given action will lead to a given outcome or change the beliefs about the incentive structure. This model is neutral regarding the use of coercion. According to Cudd individuals are harmed due to their membership of a group (including ascribed membership). Coercion is unjustified but such coercive condition exists when the "privileged group derive benefits from the unjust harm".[42] Thus, human action is directed by some benefit for the agent for which a choice is made according to the actual and perceived outcomes. Miller views that women's definition of power differed significantly from their perception of society's definition of power, as well as from the way power has traditionally been conceptualized.[43] Women would like to be powerful which concurrently enhances the power of others.[44]

Feminist scholars have focused on the oppressive and unjust power relationships. Many of them refer to power-over that is domination or control in male-female relationship. Some others have conceptualized it as power to or ability to change individually and collectively spawning a new understanding of power and empowerment of women. Power defined as dominance and submission to others will have led to control in hierarchical gender relationship. Power defined as transformation connotes empowering the self and others in an equitable relationship.[45] Hoagland defines power as "power from within "which is creative ability, a transformative but not controlling power."[46] Starhawk assumes that power is inherent in human beings which stimulates growth.[47] Luce contends that viewing power as transformative without remoulding its perceived essence as domination and coercion will keep its masculine nature intact. Therefore, it has to be redefined.[48] Harstock argues that power should be understood as "energy and competence".[49] Follet differentiates between power-over and power-with, the latter being collective ability which operates within group relationships of reciprocity.[50]

Power may be utilized in a planned manner by resorting to soft or hard approaches. The former refers to indirect methods like interpersonal interactions, socialization, etc., while the latter refers to force, coercion, cajoling, etc. Threats from deviation from norms set in a particular culture and ostracisation can also be methods of hard power. Rational approaches like judgement by arguments reasoning and logic, etc., may be used to exert influence and irrational approaches like appealing to emotion, information intended to deceive may also be used to wield influence. It may be unilateral where the target does not participate in any negotiation for influence. It is bilateral when the target and powerful exchange, negotiate and reciprocate. Use of power tactics varies from person to person. But Falbo and Peplau, argue that men tend to use bilateral and direct tactics whereas women tend to use unilateral and indirect strategy.[51] A 2008 survey of college students has brought into focus that power does not corrupt but enables a person to change one's life and surrounding, generate new ideas uninfluenced by others and counter opposing views.[52]

Plato was concerned about the non-utilisation of women's power for the benefit of the community. He saw no fundamental difference between men and women which made women unsuitable for useful labour. According to him, some women were just as good, indeed better than men.[53] Woman's suitability for a work should be judged by the merits of the case and not on any assumption about women-kind as a whole. Women should exercise the same as men, be educated the same as men go to war the same as men and generally be treated exactly the same as except that not so much be expected of them.[54]

The above discussion reveals that definitions of power are varied. Its positive contribution for change, rational choice as a variable for decision making, dispositional characteristics and individual and group receptivity help in understanding empowerment. The gender perspective in empowerment of women brings to fore the negative as well as positive aspects, individual, collective and transformational dimensions and disposition irrespective of sex. But power is changeable depending on several factors which might disempower an empowered women. It may be linear or sequential and simultaneous, experienced in the same or different situation by an empowered women basing on several factors. To understand disempowerment, exploring the concept of empowerment is essential.

Empowerment and Disempowerment

The concept of empowerment is as varied as power. But quite a few researchers have agreed that it refers to greater control over one's life. It may be dispositional or acquired through an agent, the degree of which may fluctuate depending on the receptivity of the person. It includes almost all definitions discussed above but the gender perspective has enriched the concept by delving deep into dominance and control. Empowerment of women has focused on gender and patriarchy. It is the extent to which women have the freedom to participate in domains that are either private or public, make decisions that influence their life and that of their family and the degree to which they can have control over resources. However, in most of the studies, it is conceptualized as linear without analyzing the possible changes in the capacity of the empowered women depending on the locale, situation, evolution processes and practical necessities. There are stages and situations in a woman's life when an empowered woman feels disempowered. This situation does not deny her to have a choice as the woman desires to choose decision which empowers other members in the family both men and women. Her choice enables them to take decisions in which she may not be an active participant but recipient of benefits at the cost of her autonomy. This is possible in case of women in a joint family, women holding a job, women with a job having young children, etc. It is age related. A young disempowered woman feels empowered if she is older and entrusted with the responsibility which a young mother cannot discharge due to several reasons and thereby influences household decision making. For example, mothers of young children prefer to leave infants in the care of their mother-in-law rather than outsiders. Of course such a decision may be influenced by the husband and non-availability of services from the young women's parents. In such cases, the generational factor affects empowerment. In the absence of young children, the generational factor may disempower women if the generational dimension of authority in the household minimizes interaction between the conjugal pair. Living with the mother-in-law might limit the autonomy of the daughter-in-law. But if the latter chooses to stay with the former for taking care of children, if she is employed and has young children then the loss of autonomy is not due to patriarchal control but due to her own autonomy in taking the decision which in due course might disempower her. In joint families senior men and women in the household have important voices in decision making. In some households the mother-in-law or the elder sister-in-law play a key role in decision making. So a person's lack of power is a function of gender as well as generation.

Most of the studies on empowerment have not investigated on the power of family members in a household apart from the husband in patrilocal and patriarchal families. Emphasis is given to equal distribution of power but maintaining balance of power is rather difficult in extended families. Empowerment and disempowerment depend on who are the decision makers in the family both men and women. A measure of empowerment is participation of women in household decision making. But household decision making differs according to the type of family. Mostly there is a gender component in decision making. However, in the Indian context where extended family system continues, elderly women in the household play an important role in decision making. In some households, the mother-in-law or the elder sister-in-law play a key role in decision making. Thus relatively young female member(s) might be disempowered by the husband as well as other senior family members by being marginalized in decision making even with educational attainment and economic self-dependence. Gender inequalities as well as generational factors might influence the empowerment of women. It is age, culture, situation and status specific. Gender inequalities focus on the husband as the primary decision maker and in joint families his father plays a key role in decision making. But senior women like the mother-in-law and sister-in-law also play specific roles in quite a few decisions. By ignoring the full dynamics of power distributions within a family, the fallacy to combine inequalities of gender with those of generation is inevitable which ignores the cyclical mode of empowerment. The following analysis brings into fore the gender and generational factors which affect empowerment.

Analysis

To examine the postulation, a sample group is selected from households where educated women with young children stay in joint families in Jeypore, a southern town of Koraput district of Odisha. For the most part, culture of this urban area is traditional but women's education and employment has been accepted by quite a few families. Employed young women with small children prefer extended family for care of their children. Such families were selected to understand the cyclical process of empowerment. Extended family included two types of family: one, where husband, wife, young children and mother-in-law stay and two, where two or more brothers with their wives and children stay along with the father-in-law and mother-in-law. Women belonged to two age groups, one, educated, employed women in the age group of 25-35 having young children; and two, senior women aged 50-65 years. The total number of women was 75. (The number of women in the first group was 45 and in the second group 30). Age was entered as reported by the sample group, duration of marriage was calculated by deducting the years of marriage from total age, number of children included as reported by the women, employment referred to full time employment, education was entered as stated by the sample and graded into general and technical education, and marriage arranged by the parents. Decisions referred as major or minor as viewed by the sample group because it depended on the nature of importance. But on the whole cooking, care of the sick were accepted as minor decisions whereas buying property, costly household gadget, marriage of the grown up children, etc., were some of the major decisions.

As revealed by the respondents all women in the lower age group were educated; thirty two had technical education and the rest thirteen had nontechnical education. All of them were employed having small children, their parental houses were far away from their in-law's house. Husband of two women were absent at the time of interview due to their posting in far-off places. All the respondents admitted that except cooking and caring for the sick and their children after coming from office they do not have any say in household decision making. Senior women and men have a major share in decision making including the menu for the day.

Interaction revealed that majority of the young women in the sample group married after employment except two who improved their qualification for making them employable. The latter had small children when they entered job. Being encumbered by the responsibilities attached to parenthood and the job they preferred joint family and the mother-in-law to look after the child. They have come from a background where marriage and having children are obsession. Thirty two of the mothers said that they were quite anxious about upbringing of the child. Being weighted down by the responsibilities attached to parenthood and the job, they preferred joint family and the mother-in-law to look after the child. Staying in a joint family has more advantages than disadvantages though many of the mothers were not well connected to the child or the senior women in the family. Mothers of school going children revealed that their children do not like their long absence at home which inflicts emotional pain. In all cases, the parents are mature, have delayed child birth but the cultural factor prevailed where the empowered women were marginalized in the house for the sake of the child.

Interactions between the sample group and male members of the household revealed that staying in extended family was a better option for an employed young woman. As household decision making is a good determinant to assess empowerment of women. Questions pertained to participation of elderly as well as young women, the husband of young and elderly women in minor and major household decisions. Senior women were compared with junior women in family decision making. Interactions were also held with separated, divorced, widowed and those women whose husbands were absent due to employment elsewhere in the older age group. Questions on household decisions covered cooking, care of the sick, purchases, job related matters, autonomy in spending. In addition to these, simple questions of empowerment were put on marriage practices, family structure, income, employment, relationship between the husband and wife. Responses as well as observation revealed that senior women decided the menu, movement of the younger women outside except office and questioned occasional delays in arriving home after the office hour. All of the employed young women had to sacrifice promotion in their respective jobs for the sake of the young children even with the presence of the mother-in-law. The reason being long absence of the young mother often resulted in psychological uneasiness due to the attitude of the senior women which compelled them to miss out on promotion for which skill enhancement was compulsory.

Regarding cooking the senior female members have more say than the male members, choice of items is according to the male members generally as they buy food materials daily. Young women have greater say on matters related to number of children to which the senior members also agree as most families in the sample group supported small family even though the mothers-in-law had more number of children. It may be because the young mother had to remain absent at home and in her absence the mother-in-law had to look after the infant, in most cases against her will. It was again for the same reason the daughter-in-law wanted not to compromise her autonomy by having more children and leaving them in the care of the mother-in-law. In extended families major decisions were taken by senior men as a cultural norm or relationship between the husband and wife or regard for assets at their disposal. In such cases, gender was an important determinant. Decisions like cooking was taken by the senior women in extended families while purchase or sale of assets were taken by senior men. In such families husbands of younger women have least say in major family decisions. Where the husbands' role is limited, the young wife was disempowered even if educated and employed. Therefore, generational inequalities disempowered women in major household decision making. Empowerment of the young educated and earning women is not a question of gender as the husband is not the independent variable to empower or disempower the wife. Separated women with assets were revered but dependence on children has restricted their freedom of choice. The absence of the husband reduces her importance. Widowed women prefer to devote to rituals, *ekadasi* (eleventh day in a fortnight of lunar month) being held twice in a month along with other rituals which fall almost every week. But a widow having resources is looked after better than those who depend on the income of their children or other family members but has no role in decision making. Those senior women whose husbands do not stay in the house but contribute financially are powerful. In such cases, empowerment of senior women is self generated from the financial position of the husband while the young women with her education and earning capability is marginalized. The economic position of the senior male persons in a family *vis-à-vis* the juniors determines their power in the family. This is so in cases where they have business, agricultural income and non-dependence on the income of the younger family members. This is gendered but the senior women derive power from the status of their husband. Thus it is both gendered and generational as it raises the authority of senior men *vis-à-vis* the women and senior women *vis-à-vis* the respondent. Assets and traditional family structure leverage the senior family members over the juniors. Senior women gain importance in family decision making with age even without formal education and income while younger women with education and earning capabilities are marginalized /excluded from decision making. Age, financial potential of the husband of senior women in the household, his attitude towards wife are important than the education and income of the senior woman. A younger, educated, employed woman's empowerment/disempowerment may follow from that of the senior woman's decision making power. Younger woman have a larger role in cooking, looking after the sick than participating in other important household decisions. Equal gender relationship with husband also impact on participation in other important household decisions as the husband's role has less leverage compared to the senior men in the household.

The following Figures 3.1 and 3.2 indicate the cyclical nature of empowerment and disempowerment.

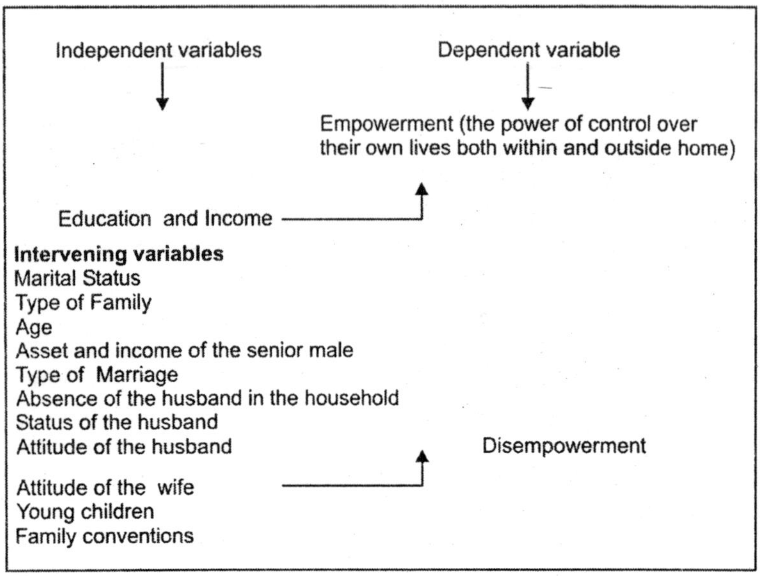

Fig. 3.1:

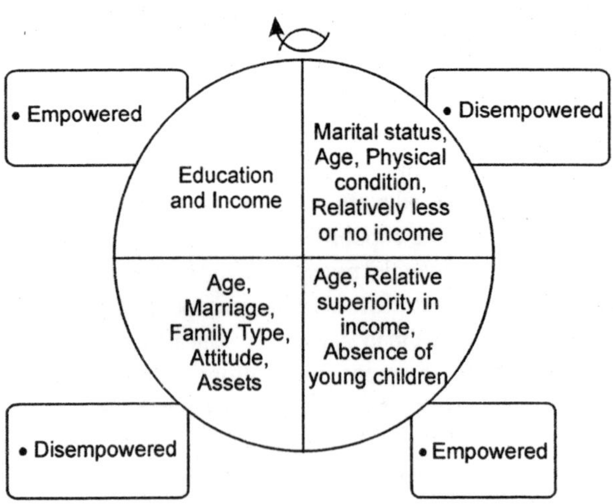

Fig. 3.2: Cyclical Representation of Empowerment

This chapter argues that to the extent that power of decision making is exercised by other family members, the young woman in a joint family (25-35 years) is disempowered. Family structure and culture disempowering women *vis-à-vis* the husband may be different from the factors that disempower women *vis-à-vis* other members both men and women. Therefore, it is relational within the family structure and culture. The age of women is an important determinant so also other centres of power in a family. Most of the studies have found that living with a mother-in-law lessens autonomy of the daughter-in-law.[55] The present study reveals that education and earning capability has disempowered young women having young children who live with their mother-in-law.

Where the senior women have more power in household decision making, the power of the husband in decision making and involvement of the young wife in the process depends on his attitude towards his wife and other senior female relatives. Generally, the young wife enjoys less trust compared to the parents with whom the husband has more intimacy since childhood. Also in joint families if the elder brother is more obedient to the parents, the female spouses of the younger brothers do not contravene the convention. If the husband leaves the wife with the parents due to job constraint (employed in defence, shipping corporation or outside the country, etc.) the young bride has no autonomy. The senior members of the household can influence decision of the younger women. This is also influenced by the husband's attitude. It may be difficult to divide which part of decision affecting the women is gendered and which is generational disempowering her but the study shows that it is gender which influences the generational factor. Kinship systems[56] and exogamy also affect empowerment of women. For example a woman married to a person of distant place deprives the woman emotional support which plummets her psychological ability to assert against discrimination. In such cases also, the passivity of the husband plays an important role. Inequalities based on gender have deep roots than generation but kinship structures in different cultures and rules of marriage structure both gender and generational qualities.

Most of the literature on empowerment stress financial autonomy of the women as an important tool for empowerment. But the responsibilities attached to income of the woman, the autonomy to spend, she being treated as an income generating tool, disempowers her even with her education and earning capabilities. This might be true of single woman who has to support young siblings and parents. But it does not empower the woman *vis-à-vis* the husband and in-laws or both. Education is a major determinant for empowerment of women as it exposes women to knowledge, generates self-confidence, inculcates decision making power, endows with freedom to choice, but generational factors as well as gendered attitude do not significantly correlate education and empowerment. In many families, education is perceived as a source for earning and the earning member as an asset. Therefore, employed women are preferred for marriage and in some cases after marriage many women are compelled to enhance qualification for getting a job. The usual argument is two earning members will ease the financial burden of a single earning member. But in fact the husband is reluctant to spend for the wife, provide her with adequate food and clothing for which the wife is compelled to pursue skill training for absorption in job. Women in the sample group have been compelled by the in-laws as well as the husband to improve qualification with this motive. If empowerment is perceived as choice to determine one's own course of action, lead a life of her own choice, if the women is forced to educate and employment contrary to her choice it questions such an understanding of empowerment. It may be argued after having independent income, the women is empowered through education. But where the cultural inhibitions do not allow women to have autonomy in spending, look for her income to meet family expenses the women might choose to have a life of her own at the cost of breach of her marriage. As women age in extended families, they gain respect so long they are not widowed. Young brides in nuclear families are empowered if the husband does not interfere in her personal life but those with small children have to compromise with autonomy for the sake of upkeep of the young child by living with the mother-in-law or a senior women from the husband's house. As the child grows up, and the woman has less burden of child care and grows in age, the degree of autonomy may increase. The number of children also affects empowerment. As long as the employed woman depend for their upbringing on the in-laws, they have less autonomy. However, the duration of marriage enhances security and confidence which adds to autonomy. Generally divorce is preferred less in traditional families even though employment and education are preferred for girls. But in such cases also, empowerment is dependent on relationship with other family members and attitude of the husband.

Notes

1. Barnes, Jonathan, (ed). *The Complete Works of Aristotle: The Revised*

Oxford Translation. Princeton: Princeton University Press, 1984, http://www.iep.utm.edu/aris-pol

2. *Dunamis* in Greek means capability, in Latin it corresponds to "potentia" and the English word "power" used by Hobbes and Locke is translated from Latin potential. It is the root of the English words dynamic, dynamite and dynamo. Depending on context it could be translated as potential, capability, strength, power, force, etc. It is strength, power ability which can be inherent power, power residing in a thing by virtue of its nature or which a person or thing exerts and puts forth, power for performing miracles, moral power and excellence of soul, the power and influence which belong to riches and wealth, power and resources arising from numbers, power consisting in or resting upon armies, forces, hosts, Hobbes and Locke used the English word power as translated from the Latin "potentia" which is similar to *dunamis*. But Blent Flyvbjerg writes that "power is derived from the French word "poeir" which means" to be able to act". Interestingly there are as many differences about origin of the word so are its meaning and definition.
3. In order to act, "an agent power like heat must meet up with something with the passive power to be heated, in the appropriate circumstances. And the agent power of heat can be defined by means of a specification of these activation conditions 'the wholesome produces only health, the calorific only heat and the frigorific only cold.' (1046b19-20) Indeed, Aristotle proposes to define a power in terms of its realization or activation conditions: "that which is capable of something and at some time and in some way (with all the other qualifications which must be present in the definition)." Some substances with soul have rational (metalogon) as well as non-rational (alogon) power. (1047b35-1048a2).
4. Charlotte Witt, in Ruth Groff ed. *Revitalizing Causality: Realism about Causality in Philosophy and Social Sciences*, Routledge, 2008. Barnes, Jonathan, ed. *The Complete Works of Aristotle: The Revised Oxford Translation*. Princeton: Princeton University Press, 1984. http://www.iep.utm.edu/aris-pol.
5. 1660 Leviathan, Ch. 6 and Leviathan II 18.
6. "The power of a magistrate over a subject may be distinguished from that of a father over his children, a master over his servant, a husband over his wife, and a lord over his slave. All distinct powers happening sometimes together in the same man, if he be considered under these different relations, it may help us to distinguish these powers one from another, and show the difference betwixt a ruler of a commonwealth, a father of a family, and a captain of a galley. John

Locke, Second Treatise on Government 1960 ch I http://libertyonline.hypermall.com/Locke/second/second-frame.html.

7. "Growth, self preservation, domination upward mobility all are characterized by the will to power". Women exert the will to power by throwing at men, love is their preserve, men dominate over women. The will to power also includes a sense of duty and conscience in which one feels a type of superiority over those who are really in power. It creates a sense of value to which they hold even those who are in power accountable. Travis J. Dennes on Nietzsche's "The Will to Power", http://www.infidels.org/
8. alfred-adler-individual psychology.htm
9. Nelson W. Polsby in John Scott (ed.) *Power : Critical Concepts*, Nelson W. Polsby, Routledge, London, 1994, *Community Power and Political Theory*, Yale University Press, 1963.
10. Bachrach, P. and M.S. Baratz, "The Two Faces of Power", *American Political Science Review* 56: 1962, pp. 947-52.
11. Robert A. Dahl, "The Concept of Power", *Behavioural Science*, Vol. 2, 1957, pp. 201-215.
12. Steven Lukes, *Power: A Radical View*, Macmillan, 1974, p. 23.
13. Alain Beaulien and David Gobbard (ed), *Michel Foucault and Power Today*, Lexington Books, 2000. To cite him "I would like to suggest another way to go further toward a new economy of power relations, a way which is more empirical, more directly related to our present situation, and which implies more relations between theory and practice. It consists of taking the forms of resistance against different forms of power as a starting point. To use another metaphor, it consists of using this resistance as a chemical catalyst so as to bring to light power relations, locate their position, and find out their point of application and the methods used. Rather than analyzing power from the point of view of its internal rationality, it consists of analyzing power relations through the antagonism of strategies. "Power over is evident from" if we speak of the structures or the mechanisms of power, it is only in so far as we suppose that certain persons exercise power over others. Michel Foucault and Hubert Dreyfus, *The Subject and Power is Beyond Structuralism and Herneneutics*, University of Chicago, 1983, p. 208 and p. 217.
14. Maarten Hajer, *The Politics of Environmental Discourse* (Oxford, 1995) ; Jacobson, K.C., and Crockett, L.J. (2000). "Parental monitoring and adolescent adjustment: An ecological approach." *Journal of Research on Adolescence*, 10, 65-97. Vivien Burr, *An Introduction to Social Constructionism.* London and New York: Routledge, 1995, p. 198.

15. Mark, Huagaard, "Power: A Family Resemblance Concept", *European Journal of Cultural Studies*, 13, 2010, pp. 418-438.
16. Analogous to Machiavellian centaur, a creature in ancient Greek stories, which has a human's upper body and the lower body and legs of a horse. "They are the levels of force and consent, authority and hegemony, violence and civilisation etc." Carl Cuneo's Notes on the Concept of Hegemony in Gramsci http://socserv2.mcmaster.ca/soc/courses/soc2r3/gramsci/gramheg.htm#new)
17. Tarnow, Dr. Eugen, *A Quantitative Model of the Amplification of Power Through Order and The Concept of Group Defense*, 2000 http://cogprints.org/4275/.
18. Steven Lukes, *Power: A Radical View*, Macmillan, 2nd Edition, 2005.
19. The micro level of power is episodic consisting of feelings, communication, conflict and resistance in day to day relationships. One of the two macro levels is a dispositional circuit consisting of socially construed rules and practices and the other is a facilitative circuit consisting of job, technology, environmental contingencies which might empower or disempower, punish or reward. Clegg, S.R., *Frameworks of Power*, Sage, London, 1989.
20. Alvin Toffler proposes three types of power which are violence (used negatively), wealth (used both positively and negatively) and knowledge (can be used positively as well as negatively and for transformation). Knowledge can be used for changing available technology, practices and strategically used for superiority. He argues that power has been shifting from one group to another and it is a continuous process. (During industrial revolution from the nobility to industrialists and now knowledge is power. Alvin Toffler, *Knowledge, Wealth and Violence at the edge of 21st Century*, Bantam Books, 1990.
21. French, J.R.P., Raven, B. "The Bases of Social Power." In D. Cartwright and A. Zander. *Group Dynamics*. New York: Harper and Row, 1959. see also Morgan Greth, *Images of Organisation*, Sage Publications Inc, 1986, Handy, Charles. 'Understanding Organizations'. Penguin Books, 1976.
22. Blent, Flyvbjerg, In pluralist democracies power is not limited to the formal realm of politics but goes beyond; it is everywhere, relations of power are omnipresent, multiple and dynamic What is Rationality? What is Power,www.sbs.oxford.edu/blentflyvbjerg.
23. Peter Moris, *Power: A Philosophical Analysis*, 2nd edition. Manchester: Manchester University Press, 2002.
24. Arendt, Hannah, *The Human Condition*, Chicago: University of Chicago Press. 1958.
25. Pitkin, Hanna Fenichel, *Wittgenstein and Justice: On the Significance*

of Ludwig Wittgenstein for Social and Political Thought, Berkeley, CA: University of California Press. 1972, press.uchicago.edu/ucp/books/series/CJ.html

26. Huagaard and Clegg (2010,1989) plato.stanford.edu/entries/feminist-power.
27. Saar, Martin, "Power and Critique," *Journal of Power,* 3 (1) pp. 7-20, 2010.
28. Mill, John Stuart, "The Subjection of Women" in *Essays on Sex Equality*, Alice Rossi (ed.), Chicago: University of Chicago Press. 1970. Okin, Susan Moller, *Justice, Gender and the Family*, New York: Basic Books. 1989.
29. Young, Iris Marion, *Justice and the Politics of Difference*, Princeton, NJ: Princeton University Press, 1990.
30. Simon de Beauvoir, *The Second Sex*, translated by H.M. Parshley, Penguin, 1972.
31. Mac Kinnon, Catharine, *Feminism Unmodified: Discourses on Life and Law,* Cambridge, MA: Harvard University Press, 1987.
32. See Butler, Judith, *Gender Trouble: Feminism and the Subversion of Identity*, New York: Routledge, 1990.
33. Frye, Marilyn, *The Politics of Reality: Essays in Feminist Theory,* Freedom, California; The Crossing Press, 1983.
34. Pateman, Carole, *The Sexual Contract*, Stanford: Stanford University Press, 1988.
35. Fraser, Nancy, *Unruly Practices: Power, Discourse and Gender in Contemporary Social Theory,* Minneapolis, MN: University of Minnesota Press, 1989.
36. *Op. cit*, 1978, 93.
37. Young, Iris Marion, "Five Faces of Oppression" in Thomas Wartenberg (ed.), *Rethinking Power*, Albany, NY: SUNY Press, 1992, pp. 183-193.
38. Hartsock, Nancy, *Money, Sex, and Power: Toward a Feminist Historical Materialism,* Boston: Northeastern University Press. 1983.
39. Crenshaw, Kimberle, "Demarginalizing the Intersection of Race and Sex: A Black Feminist Critique of Antidiscrimination Doctrine, Feminist Theory, and Antiracist Politics", in Katharine T. Barlett and Rosanne Kennedy (eds.), *Feminist Legal Theory: Readings in Law and Gender*, Boulder, CO: Westview Press, 1991.
40. *Op. cit.,* 1980.
41. Dowding, Keith, "Rational Choice Approaches to Analyzing Power", in Nash and Scott (eds.), *The Blackwell Companion to Political Sociology*, Oxford: Blackwell, 2001 and "Rational Choice Approaches", in Clegg and Haugaard (eds.), *The SAGE Handbook of Power,* London: Sage. 2009.

42. Cudd, Ann, *Analyzing Oppression*, Oxford: Oxford University Press 2006.
43. Cynthia L. Miller, "An Examination of Women's Perspectives on Power", *Psychology of Women Quarterly*, Vol. 16:4, Dec. 1992, pp. 415-428.
44. Jean Baker Miller, in Thomas E. Wartenberg (ed.), *Rethinking Power*, Suny Press, New York, 1992.
45. Held, Virginia, Feminist Morality: *Transforming Culture, Society, and Politics,* Chicago: University of Chicago Press, 1993.
46. Hoagland, Sarah Lucia, *Lesbian Ethics*: *Toward A New Value* undercoverpunk.wordpress.com
47. Starhawk, *Truth or Dare: Encounters with Power, Authority, and Mystery*, San Francisco: Harper, 1987.
48. Irigaray Luce, *This Sex Which Is Not One*, Ithaca, NY: Cornell University Press, 1985.
49. Hartsock, Nancy, *Money, Sex, and Power: Toward A Feminist Historical Materialism*, Boston: Northeastern University Press, 1983.
50. Follett, Mary Parker, "Power," in *Dynamic Administration*: *The Collected Papers of Mary Parker Follett,* Henry C. Metcalf and L. Urwick (eds.), New York: Harper. 1942.
51. Fablo, T., and Peplau, T. A., "Power Strategies in Intimate Relationship", *Journal of Personality and Social Psychology*, 38, 1980, pp. 618-628.
52. Jeanna Bryner, *US News and World Report*. (2008). *Power Doesn't Corrupt*, http://www.livescience.com, see also *The Journal of Personality and Social Psychology*, Dec. 2008.
53. http://www.idph.net
54. Republic 457a10, "the only need of sex is for procreation", (Republic454de) which was later reiterated by Gandhi.
55. Bloom, Shelah S., David Wypij and Monica Das Gupta, "Dimensions of Women's Autonomy and the Influence on Maternal Health Care Utilization in a North Indian City", *Demography* 38(1) : 2001, pp. 67-78. Jejeebhoy, Shireen and Zeba Sather, 2001, "Women's Autonomy in India and Pakistan: The Influence of Religion and Region," *Population and Development Review* 27(4) : 2001, pp. 687-712.
56. Dyson, Tim and Mick Moore. "On Kinship Structure, Female Autonomy, and Demographic Behaviour in India," *Population and Development Review* 9(1) : 1983, pp. 35-60.

4

Health Sector in Indian States

An Analysis of Governance through Health Sector Indicators

Sonalika Chaturvedi

PART I

Introduction

Over the years development planning in India has focused on reducing the burden of illness and mortality among women and children. A large number of development and public health programmes such as the Integrated Child Development Services (ICDS) have been geared towards this, since a long time. India is committed to achieve the Millennium Development Goals[1], particularly with respect to maternal and child health. In general, India's health indicators have continued to improve: Maternal Mortality Rate: from 301 per 10,000 live births in 2001-03 to 254 in 2004-06; Infant Mortality Rate: from 58 per 1000 live births in 2005 to 53 in 2008; and Total Fertility Rate: from 2.9 births per woman in 2005 to 2.7 in 2007. Institutional births, a main focus of the National Rural Health Mission, have increased from 41 per cent in 2004 to 47 per cent in 2008 (SRS Bulletin, 2011). Nevertheless, meeting the Millennium Development Goal (MDG) for infant mortality of 27 per 1000 live births by 2015 (Millennium Development Goals, 2009) represents a difficult challenge.

While there is no single metric to measure the performance of the health system, India compares poorly with countries at similar levels of development in most of the parameters. Progress in this area has not matched the country's economic growth as indicated by Table 4.1. As can be seen in the Table, the MMR is at 926 maternal deaths per thousand, which reflects poorly on the health sector inputs such as how many births were delivered in a health facility.

Table 4.1[2]**:** Health Indicators based on SRS Estimates, MoH&FW

Maternal mortality rate (2007-09)								
Sample Female Population	*Live Births*	*Maternal Deaths*	*MMR*	*95% CI*	*Maternal Mortality Rate*			
5,678,691	436,411	926	212	(198-226)	16.3			
Infant mortality rate (IMR) by sex and residence, 2009								
Total			*Rural*			*Urban*		
Total	*Male*	*Female*	*Total*	*Male*	*Female*	*Total*	*Male*	*Female*
50	49	52	55	54	56	34	32	35
Death rate by sex and residence, 2009								
7.3	7.8	6.7	7.8	8.4	7.3	5.8	6.4	5.3

Fertility rates outstrip those in most Asian countries, and maternal and infant mortality is one of the highest in Asia.[3] Of particular concern is the health of India's children, whose well-being will determine the extent of India's much-awaited demographic dividend. In fact, globally India's position with respect to various health indicators is quite poor as can be seen in Table 4.2. While in China the percentage of births attended by skilled personnel is about 96 per cent, in India it is less than 50 per cent with respect to the developed nations such as Australia, Canada, Japan, United Kingdom and United States of America.

The Central Government has focused new energy and attention on the health sector recently. National health budgets have increased significantly in the past years and additional resources have been promised. The Government proposes to increase health spending from the current level of a little more than 1 per cent of GDP to 2-3 per cent. (National Rural Health Mission, 2005-2012) Several new schemes have been launched in the last four years in pursuance of above initiatives. These include:

Table 4.2[4]: India's Comparison with Major Countries on Maternal Mortality Ratio and Percentage of Births delivered by Skilled Health Personnel

Location	*Time Period*	*Maternal mortality ratio (per 100,000 live births) – Inter-agency estimates*	*Births attended by skilled health personnel (%)*
Australia	2008	8 [6-10]	99.1
Bangladesh	2008	340 [170-660]	—
	2007	—	18
Brazil	2008	58 [38-87]	—
	2006	—	98.4
Canada	2008	12 [7-20]	—
	2007	—	100
China	2009	—	96.3
	2008	38 [23-60]	—
India	2008	230 [150-350]	46.9
Japan	2008	6 [5-8]	—
	2006	—	100
Nepal	2008	380 [210-650]	—
	2006	—	19
Pakistan	2008	260 [140-490]	—
	2007	—	39
United	2008	12 [11-14]	—
Kingdom	1998	—	99
United States	2008	24 [20-27]	—
of America	2006	—	99.4

(1) **National Rural Health Mission (NRHM):** Launched in 2005, this has helped reorganize departments at the State and national level government with particular focus on the poor performing States with respect to internal systemic problems. A lot of emphasis has also been laid on developing human capabilities and functions across the States through strengthening government delivery systems.

(2) **Rashtriya Swasthya Bima Yojana (RSBY):** This was launched in 2008 and caters to financial provision to families below poverty line with respect to their expenses on health problems and hospitalization. The federal and State governments are partners in funding along with insurance companies towards a PPP (Public Private Partnership) model of cashless health and hospitalization benefits. By March 2010, over 13 million BPL households have been enrolled in RSBY. The goal is to cover 60 million such BPL.

(3) **Janani Suraksha Yojana (JSY):** Under the NHRM, this programme was introduced by the Government of India which

brought about a modification to the existing National Maternity Benefit Scheme. This scheme looks at reducing both the Maternal Mortality Ratio as well as the Infant Mortality Rate through increase in institutional deliveries.

(4) **Integrated Child Development Services (ICDS):** The malnutrition of children up to six years of age is the most crucial period to keep in check the Infant Mortality Rate and the proper nutritional growth of the child. The ICDS is one such programme to tackle malnutrition and health of children at their most vulnerable age. The government brought about this programme through some Anganwadi Centres, slowly spreading to cover up most of the Blocks across the country.

Along with the Central Government's focus on health spending, a major challenge is to carry the momentum to the States. Increased funding will need to translate into greater access to health care and more effective delivery of health services. Low Effectiveness of Public Health Spending (Eleventh Five Year Plan, 2008) is mainly due to: (i) general absence of accountability arrangements and incentives for performance; (ii) ineffective targeting and inadequate emphasis on core public health functions; (iii) very weak information environment, including deficient monitoring and near absence of impact evaluations; (iv) insufficient engagement with non-government sector and absence of a "whole system" perspective; (v) inadequate human resources in both numbers and quality; (vi) insufficient capacity in the States, (vii) little attention to or assessment of quality of care; and (vi) variable political priority for health across States and poses a central systematic constraints in achieving stated goals in the health sector.

The Planning Commission in the Tenth Five-Year Plan (Tenth Five Year Plan, 2002-2007) has defined governance as "Governance relates to the management of all such processes that, in any society, define the environment which permits and enables individuals to raise their capability levels, on the one hand, and provide opportunities to realise their potential and enlarge the set of available choices, on the other".

Governance problems that confront health systems are often vaguely defined and poorly understood. Governance issues are interconnected and complex. Weak engagement of citizens in health policy dialogue can result from lack of capacity of civil society and limited incentives or capacity of Ministries of Health (MoHs) to share information and engage stakeholders.

This chapter presents an analytical framework for conceptualizing the governance function within health systems. As we see governance is increasingly recognized by the World Health Organization and other global and national actors to be a fundamental health system function, and is a central part of their health sector and developmental strategies. Governance is a multidimensional concept, and there are normative, instrumental, and pragmatic models of stewardship. Governance failures, in health systems or in the wider society, have been perceived as obstructing progress toward national as well as international goals such as the Millennium Development Goals for health. These failures include the lack of a long-term vision and planning for essential interventions, the absence of a functional regulatory framework, failure to address corruption, and limited efforts to assess performance.

For measuring the governance of health sector we require the most appropriate determinants of health to counter the high mortality rates, reduce the spread of communicable diseases such as malaria, TB, HIV/AIDS and others. The public health programme requires robust determinants of governance which, according to the Eleventh Five Year Plan (Eleventh Five Year Plan, 2008), focused on the following time bound goals:

- Reduction of Infant Mortality Rate (IMR) to 28 per 100 live births,
- Reducing MMR to 1 per 100 live births,
- Providing Clean drinking water for all by 2009 and ensuring no slip backs,
- Reducing TFR to 2.1,
- Raising the sex ratio for age group 0-6 to 935 by 2011-12 and 950 by 2016-17,
- Reducing anaemia among women and girls by 50 per cent,
- Reducing malnutrition among children of age 0-3 to half its present level.

Data Used in the Study

This chapter looks at a wide range of indicators which affect the output indicators of IMR and MMR to give us the governance deficit. The significant indicators that make the governance deficit are then tested using the Principal Component Analysis method to determine the governance index as a linear function of all these input variables. The important indicators that could affect the governance of health in the States are given below:

- Percentage who received all recommended types of antenatal care,
- Percentage of births delivered in a health facility,
- Percentage of Deliveries Assisted by Health Personnel,
- Doctors by ANC provider,
- Percentage of homes with toilet facility,
- Percentage using solid fuel for cooking,
- Percentage of children aged 12-23 months given all basic vaccinations,
- Percentage of children under five whose stools are disposed safely,
- Percentage of births assisted by trained personnel,
- Percentage of homes having tap water as principal source of water,
- Registered government doctors per million population, and
- Per capita expenditure on health and family welfare.

The width of indicators chosen are to provide robustness to the governance index which would specify clearly which indicators affect the State health and general public health of the country more and should be focused on in the future plans.

Annual Reports of Ministry of Health and Family Welfare, Government of India, provide with a very robust State-wise data on various health indices, IMR, ratio of male IMR, number of doctors per capita, percentage of births attended by trained personnel, sex ratio, per capita expenditure on health, etc., which have been used in this study. We also use SRS estimates and Census data. This data is freely available in the public domain.

We assume governance in the health sector as a linear function of IMR, MMR, percentage of births assisted by trained personnel, percentage of homes having access to tap water, registered government doctors per million population, sex ratio and per capita expenditure on health and family welfare. We used Principal Components Analysis (PCA) in this study. Using it, we estimate the relative weightage of various components of governance function, then by multiplying these weightage to respective columns we get cumulative index, and finally we rank different States in the descending order of index. Higher index reflects better governance, and *vice a versa.*

PART II (A)

The governance deficit has been measured taking two output indicators namely, Infant Mortality Rate (or IMR which is the probability of dying between birth and exactly one year of age expressed per 1,000 live births) and Maternal Mortality Rate (or MMR which is the number of maternal deaths per 100,000 live births in same time period). Using the statistical techniques of regression, the governance deficit is measured using the input indicators such as Percentage who received all recommended types of antenatal care, Percentage of births delivered in a health facility, Percentage of Deliveries Assisted by Health Personnel, Doctors by ANC provider, Percentage of homes with toilet facility and others. This can be seen in Tables 4.3a and 4.3b.

The initial R-square values for MMR and IMR were 0.808 and 0.799. To further fine tune the results the input variables were further regressed in different combinations to give the best fit and for both MMR and IMR, not using solid fuel for cooking, receiving all recommended types of antenatal care and doctors available through the ANC provider were the most important, common input factors affecting the output indicators, with R-square values of 0.652 for MMR. For IMR other very crucial input indicators were the safe disposal of stools for children under five, births delivered by health personnel and provision of health facility. The R-square for the important IMR indicators was 0.740.

It is clear from these tables that MMR is significantly affected by:

(i) Percentage of Deliveries Assisted by Health Personnel,
(ii) Percentage of births delivered in a health facility,
(iii) Doctors by ANC provider,
(iv) Percentage who received all recommended types of antenatal care,
(v) Per capita expenditure on health and family welfare, and
(vi) Percentage not using solid fuel for cooking.

This gives us the important input indicators for MMR that would affect the governance for it across the States in India. It is clearly evident that the health infrastructure of States has to be tightened by creating centres, making health personnel available and maintaining a regularity

Table 4.3a[5]: Effects of Input Indicators on Output Indicators MMR and IMR

Output Indicators/ Input Indicators	*Percentage using solid fuel for cooking*	*Percentage of children aged 12-23 months given all basic vaccinations*	*Percentage of children under five whose stools are disposed of safely*	*Percentage of homes having tap water as principal source of water (Census 2001)*	*Registered government doctors per million population**	*Per capita expenditure on health and family welfare**
Maternal Mortality	— 0.652970018	N/A	N/A	— 0.569232185	— 0.197563659	— 0.654893337
Infant Mortality Ratio (IMR)*	— 0.533255757	— 0.475044471	— 0.643578336	— 0.370575374	— 0.562807503	— 0.499439608

Table 3b[6]: Effects of Input Indicators on Output Indicators MMR and IMR

Output Indicators/ Input Indicators	*Percentage who received all recommended types of antenatal care*	*Percentage of births delivered in a health facility*	*Percentage of Deliveries Assisted by Health Personnel*	*Doctors by ANC provider*	*Percentage of homes with toilet facilty*
Maternal Mortality	— 0.692151498	— 0.811391922	— 0.832221692	— 0.739620255	— 0.368885097
Infant Mortality Ratio (IMR)*	— 0.539051898	— 0.612305179	— 0.591047056	— 0.69018582	— N/A

of supply. Even the State expenditure plays a crucial role in maternal and family care.

From Tables 4.3a and 4.3b, with respect to IMR, it is clear that the following input indicators affect the IMR of the Indian States:

(i) Doctors by ANC provider,
(ii) Percentage of children under five whose stools are disposed of safely,
(iii) Percentage of births delivered in a health facility,
(iv) Percentage of Deliveries Assisted by Health Personnel,
(v) Registered government doctors per million population, and
(vi) Percentage not using solid fuel for cooking.

The IMR of the Indian States are again emphatically affected by the health infrastructure which needs to be strengthened in the States with respect to the number of doctors provided by Anganwadi Centres (ANC), health facilities and health personnel. For reducing IMR, the hygienic conditions are necessary and, therefore, safe disposal of child's stools is emphasized.

The common indicators that affect the maternal and infant care are percentage of deliveries assisted by health personnel, percentage of births delivered in a health facility, doctors by ANC provider and percentage not using solid fuel for cooking. It is clear from this that for both the pregnant mother and the child health infrastructure should be provided, especially so in the rural areas, including the health personnel such doctors, nurses, etc., health facilities such as dispensaries, hospitals and others, in rural areas there must be doctors through the anganwadi centres and provision for using solid fuels for cooking would definitely help the cause of reduction in mortality and deaths.

PART II (B)

This section aims to analyse the input indicators State-wise and using the Principal Component Analysis, we put together the governance index for health based on the principal components. This would help us in deciphering the better and poor performing States and the governance deficit in the latter on the basis of these input indicators.

With the relevant input variables in now we have measured their performance using the Principal Component Analysis, giving weights to the relevant input variables that bring about the governance deficit.

This is a mathematical model which converts given values which may be correlated, through orthogonal transformation into uncorrelated set called principal components. The resulting principal components is usually less the original set of observations taken and this transformation entails high variance for the first principal components, which takes into consideration the variability in data. Successive components have highest variances possible with the restriction of it being orthogonal to the previous components (which are uncorrelated). Of course the data set has to be jointly normally distributed to be independent and the analysis is sensitive to the relative scaling of the original set of observations. To reduce dimensionality of the converted data, usually the first set of principal components is only used.

Table 4.4: Principal Components of Various Health Indices used in Governance Function

Indices	*Principal Component (weightage)*
IMR	0.12682053
Ratio of male IMR to female IMR	0.067093319
Percentage of births assisted by trained personnel	0.21921987
Percentage of homes having tap water as the principal source of water	0.19900848
Registered government doctors per million population	0.18333014
Sex ratio	0.10795487
Per capita expenditure on health and family welfare	0.18969448

As can be seen from Table 4.4, the health indices which have significant weightages on transformation as uncorrelated set, which could affect the governance function of the States in India are:

(i) Percentage of births assisted by trained personnel,
(ii) Percentage of homes having tap water as the principal source of water,
(iii) Per capita expenditure on health and family welfare, and
(iv) Registered government doctors per million population.

Based on these values of principal weightages are multiplied to reveal values for each States respective to each indicator and the overall values on summing the indicator values are then revealed which we call the governance index for that State.

Table 4.5[7]: Performance of various States in India according to their performance in the Health Sector

Big States	*Infant mortality ratio (IMR)**	*Ratio of male IMR to female IMR**	*Percentage of births assisted by trained personnel**	*Percentage of homes having tap water as principal source of water (Census 2001)*	*Registered government doctors per million population**	*Sex ratio (calculated for the year 2008 on the basis of population projections given in Health Ministry's Annual Report)*	*Per capita expenditure on health and family welfare**
Andhra Pradesh	52	0.944444444	74.9	48.1	55.5926173	987	191
Assam	64	0.953846154	31	9.2	76.53451707	945	162
Bihar	56	0.913793103	29.3	3.7	43.15180806	927	93
Chhattisgarh	57	0.982758621	41.6	15.5	51.0594843	992	146
Gujarat	50	0.960784314	63	62.3	39.73299428	907	198
Haryana	54	0.894736842	48.9	48.1	75.95898215	852	203
Himachal Pradesh	44	0.955555556	47.8	84.1	248	959	630
Jammu & Kashmir	49	0.941176471	56.5	52.5	194.0993789	959	512

(Contd.)

(Contd.)

Big States	Infant mortality ratio (IMR)*	Ratio of male IMR to female IMR*	Percentage of births assisted by trained personnel*	Percentage of homes having tap water as principal source of water (Census 2001)	Registered government doctors per million population*	Sex ratio (calculated for the year 2008 on the basis of population projections given in Health Ministry's Annual Report)	Per capita expenditure on health and family welfare*
Jharkhand	46	0.9375	27.8	12.6	57.1886 0803	942	155
Karnataka	45	0.95652 1739	69.7	58.9	87.3667 6568	971	233
Kerala	12	0.76923 0769	99.4	20.4	111.731 8436	1052	287
Madhya Pradesh	70	0.94444 4444	32.7	25.3	54.1976 0447	917	145
Maharashtra	33	1	68.7	64	41.2592 3175	916	204
Orissa	69	0.97142 8571	44	8.7	128.073 7705	977	183
Punjab	41	0.90697 6744	68.2	33.6	137.816 9791	862	247
Rajasthan	63	0.92307 6923	41	35.3	97.3899 4936	917	186

(Contd.)

(*Contd.*)

Big States	*Infant mortality ratio (IMR)**	*Ratio of male IMR to female IMR**	*Percentage of births assisted by trained personnel**	*Percentage of homes having tap water as principal source of water (Census 2001)*	*Registered government doctors per million population**	*Sex ratio (calculated for the year 2008 on the basis of population projections given in Health Ministry's Annual Report)*	*Per capita expenditure on health and family welfare**
Tamil Nadu	31	0.909090909	90.6	62.5	108.2954299	991	223
Uttar Pradesh	67	0.914285714	27.2	25	41.69098641	898	128
Uttarakhand	44	0.977777778	38.5	65.9	117.5502527	961	280
West Bengal	35	0.918918919	47.6	21.4	100.4722194	942	173

Source:

*Annual Report, Mo H&FW, 2009-10.

**Data for births assisted by trained personnel not available in the Annual Report, and taken from NRHM 2009 Report; Census 2001; SRS estimates.

Table 4.6 shows the ranking of States on the basis of this governance index (which is a function of uncorrelated values of infant mortality ratio, ratio of male IMR to female IMR, percentage of births assisted by trained personnel, percentage of homes having tap water as principal source of water, registered government doctors per million population, sex ratio and per capita expenditure on health and family welfare.

It is clear that Himachal Pradesh, Kerala, J&K[7], Tamil Nadu and Uttarakhand have performed well with high governance index (with respect to the input indicators). The health infrastructure of these States has been sufficiently provided and is relatively working efficiently. The southern States together have done very well and that shows that the overall governance in health sector in the southern region is efficient with respect to health, thereby reducing the mortality rates and illnesses here.

The central and Bimaru States have performed badly according to the governance index which is also evident from the high IMR and MMR in these States. The provisions for doctors per capita in these States have to rise along with health facilities, health personnel for births and expenditure on health and family welfare by the States.

Table 4.6: Ranking of the States on the basis of their performance in Table 4.5 (Ranking based on Performance of States)

Himachal Pradesh	West Bengal
Kerala	Haryana
Jammu & Kashmir	Rajasthan
Tamil Nadu	Orissa
Karnataka	Chhattisgarh
Uttarakhand	Madhya Pradesh
Andhra Pradesh	Assam
Punjab	Jharkhand
Maharashtra	Uttar Pradesh
Gujarat	Bihar

Results and Conclusion

As we can see from the Principal Component Analysis, the States which have performed well in the health sector namely, Himachal Pradesh, Kerala and Jammu & Kashmir which figure in the top three are not necessarily the States which do well in terms of the overall economic growth. An important point of consideration in this is that these States have consistent rates of expenditure on medical and public health and family welfare, around 5 per cent whereas States which have progressed economically and have higher standards of living such as Gujarat and Maharashtra allocate only about 3 per cent to 4 per cent towards this.

Normal perception of the northern States is of better governance, while the PCA suggests otherwise. States such as Gujarat and Maharashtra, which are financially sound, are in the middle of the rankings. This shows that there has been a neglect towards the health sector in these States, even though the overall economic scenario is stable. Therefore, these States and others in the middle ranking category such as Punjab, Haryana and others must focus of specific measures towards this end, to even out the process of development.

Though Bihar, Rajasthan, Uttar Pradesh and others may have done slightly well as per recent data, the mid-Eleventh Plan period shows that there is a lot left desirable in terms of governance in health sector and setting up the right infrastructure for speedy reduction in high mortality rates.

Serious policy interventions are required in Twelfth Plan to improve overall governance in the health sector and it is vital to use available resources most efficiently. The results above show the overall picture of the Health Sector in India through the governance lens. The central, northern, eastern and western States would benefit through enhanced governance systems greatly by adopting the methods and frameworks which the southern areas are using, which have proved to be better governed. The schemes as mentioned in the introduction of this chapter have initiated this process of covering the deficit in governance, but there is scope for much more.

Notes

2. SRS Bulletin, Volume 45. No.1 January, 2011 and Annual Report MoH&FW, 2009-10.
3. State of World Population Report, United Nations Population Fund, 2006.
4. WHO data on World Health Statistics.
5. The data for all the input and output indicators has been obtained from National Family Health Survey – 3 and SRS Estimates.
6. *Ibid.*
7. J&K data may have unreliable values, which may explain the anomalous result of its faring in the top three States. Further investigation for this State is required.

References

2002 : *Tenth Five Year Plan.* Planning Commission, Government of India.

2005 : *Mission Document. National Rural Health Mission.* Government of India.

2005 : *National Family Health Survey-3.* (2005). Ministry of Health and Family Welfare, Government of India.

2006 : *State of World Population Report.* United Nations Population Fund.

2008 : *Eleventh Five Year Plan, Social Sector,* Volume II. Planning Commission, Government of India.

2009 : *Annual Report, National Rural Health Mission.* Government of India.

2009 : *Millennium Development Goals.* United Nations.

2009-2010 : *Annual Report.* Ministry of Health and Family Welfare, Government of India.

2011 : *SRS Bulletin,* Volume 45. No. 1. (January). Government of India.

5

Local Body Polls 2010 in Kerala

UDF Smashes LDF Fortresses

*Dr. M.R. Biju**

Article 243-E and 243-U of the Constitution of India deals with the question of duration of Panchayats and Municipalities and periodicity of elections to the rural and urban local bodies. It says, "Every Panchayat/ Municipality unless sooner dissolved under any law for the time being in force shall continue for five years from the date appointed its first meeting and no longer". This constitutional provision also prohibits any dissolution of a Panchayat/Municipality during its life by amendment of law. It also provided that an election to constitute a Panchayat/Municipality shall be completed before the expiry of its duration of five years and in case it is dissolved, the election shall be completed before the expiration of six months from such dissolution. If, however, a dissolved Panchayat/municipality had a tenure of less than six months left, there is no need for election for such a short period. Thus, conduct of election to the rural and urban local bodies at a five year interval is mandatory.

Elections to the Local Body elections in Kerala assumed greater significance because local level democracy is the basic foundation on

* Dr. M.R. Biju is a prolific writer on Socio-Political and Developmental issues. Authored 22 books and 92 research papers. Heading two major research projects on Panchayati Raj funded by Ministry of Panchayati Raj, Government of India and UGC. Recipient of UGC Post Doctoral Research Award in 2004-07. Editor of *South Asian Journal of Socio-Political Studies* (SAJOSPS). E-MAIL : mrbijueditor@yahoo.com, web: www.sajospsindia.com

which the entire democratic edifice rests. The legitimacy of these elections as crucial instruments of a democratic political process at the local level is increasing day by day. Obviously all the social, economic and political factors affecting the States and parliament elections influence the local government elections too.

Against this backdrop the present study examines the diversified aspects of the recently held local body polls in Kerala. The State of Kerala went for local body polls on 23rd and 25th October, 2010, for the eighth time since independence. The first poll was held in 1953 under the provisions of the then Travancore-Cochin Panchayat Act 1950. The second election was held in 1963 after the formation of the State in 1956 and after the passing of Kerala Panchayat/Municipality Acts of 1960. It was followed by elections in 1979, 1988, 1995, 2000 and 2005.

I

Pre-Poll Scene

The local body elections 2005 had attracted more attention from political parties, media persons, and general public alike due to a number of reasons. Notable among them include:

(1) the local bodies both urban and rural are enjoyed with increased powers and resources, for example, a Grama Panchayat used to get barely ₹ one lakh a year for all its activities before decentralisation, the annual allocation is around ₹ 70 lakhs now;
(2) the most important factor deciding the fortunes of both UDF and LDF is likely to be the strategic alliances at the local level between parties belonging to even opposing political views and visions, a constant feature of local body polls in Kerala.
(3) For the LDF the civic polls 2010 was a means to examine whether the welfare, popular measures of V.S. Government namely, *viz.*, Rice for ₹ 2, EMS Housing Scheme, Asraya Project and a lot more for the welfare of the downtrodden, will produce positive outcome or not.
(4) The LDF also had tried to examine whether their well-oiled political and organisational machinery throughout the State will give gains to the front.
(5) The LDF had an edge over the selection of better women candidates through their organisational network and developmental initiatives

like Kudumbashree. Through the poll the party made an enquiry on the future prospects of this mechanism.

(6) The poll was also considered as a referendum on the issues like interference of the church in politics, alleged attempt of LDF for the consolidation of Hindu majority votes.

(7) The UDF on the other hand considered the poll to expose their political strength and mass base with new constituents like Socialist Janatha (Democratic) and Kerala Congress (Joseph).

(8) The UDF also tried to explore anti-incumbency factors by exposing the internal troubles within the leading partner of the LDF, personal rivalries between the Chief Minister and party secretary, charges of corruption, nexus with lottery and land mafia, etc.

(9) Compared to earlier polls, the internal troubles and deferences within the UDF camp was resolved well in advance particularly with JSS, CMP and Kerala Congress.

(10) The poll was also treated as a means to validate the strength of SJD in Malabar and Kerala Congress (M) in the Central Travancore. The Kerala Congress (M) was seeking a twin result — a vote against the LDF and reassertion of its claim of being a larger player in the region. Either way, political leaders believe that the results will have a long-standing impact on the State's politics as it moves towards the Assembly elections in 2011.

II

Polls in Two Stages

Elections to the Local Body polls in the State were held in two stages. First stage was on 23 October and the second stage was on 25th. Over 75.72 per cent of the voters exercised their franchise during the first stage held in seven districts, *viz.*, Thiruvananthapuram, Kollam, Pathanamthitta, Kozhikode, Wayanad, Kannur and Kasargod. Barring stray incidents of violence and booth capturing in Kannur district the polling passed off peacefully. According to electoral statistics, Wayanad recorded the highest polling 79.78 per cent and Thiruvananthapuram the lowest 69.27 per cent. The voter turnout in Kollam was 73.58 per cent, Pathanamthitta 70.54 per cent, Alappuzha 77.75 per cent, Kozhikode 76.99 per cent and Kannur 79.48 per cent.

The voter turnout in the second phase held on 25th October was pegged at 75 per cent. According to the official figures of the State

Election Commission (SEC) Alappuzha registered the highest polling 77.75 per cent, followed by Malappuram 75.6 per cent, Kottayam 75.64 per cent, Ernakulam and Palakkad 75 per cent and Thrissur and Idukki 73 per cent.

During the first phase of the poll barring few incidents of violence and booth capturing in Kannur, the polling passed off peacefully as referred earlier. Based on the Collector's report the SEC has ordered for repolling in five places. A marked indifference on the part of the voters in urban centres seemed to have upset the candidates and their campaign managers initially. The polling in the Thiruvananthapuram city limits remained below 10 per cent till 9 am. It gradually picked up to reach 36 per cent by 2 pm, and 52.5 per cent by 4.30 pm. Meanwhile the State average increased from 45 per cent at 2 pm to 64 per cent by 4 pm. The polling rate was by and large consistent in Kozhikode, Kannur and Wayanad. Kollam also recorded an impressive turnout of 46 per cent by 2 pm and 65 per cent by 4.30 pm.

During the second phase of the poll, violent incidents were reported from Alappuzha and Kannur where repolling was held at seven booths in five places, marred the election. A sub-inspector from special branch was hacked when he tried to tackle a person, reportedly a CPI (M) activist, who entered a booth at Ambalappuzha in Alappuzha district with a sword. The police officer sustained serious injuries. Three CPM and two BJP activists were reported to have suffered injuries in a clash that followed. Skirmishes were reported from polling booths at Kainakari in Alappuzha district. Ballot papers in a booth at Bharanikavu in the same district had to be replaced on detecting a mix up in the names of candidates.

The repolling in Kannur district was marred by complaints of intimidation of voters and clashes near the booths in Pattuvam and Thillankeri Grama Panchayats. This was despite a heavy deployment of the Kerala and Karnataka police. The booths recorded impressive turn-outs, Mattool 74.5 per cent, Pattuvam 73, Irikkur 79, Thillankeri 63 and Payyannur 80.47 per cent. The United Democratic Front (UDF) boycotted the repolling in two booths in the district alleging that the poll authorities failed to ensure free and fair polling. The UDF accused the CPI(M) of intimidating voters. A *hartal* called by the BJP in the district in protest against the attack on the vehicle of a Rashtriya Swayamsevak Sangh functionary at Kelanpeedika, near Iritty, on Sunday was neartotal. Three police personnel, including a Deputy Superintendent of Police, were injured in a bomb attack reportedly by BJP-RSS workers at Iritty following a protest march. The police opened fire in the air.

When polling drew to a close in the evening, queues were seen in Malappuram district, which witnessed heavy polling. As many as 254 booths in the district were identified as sensitive and 50 vulnerable, but no untoward incident was reported. Ernakulam district registered an impressive turnout. The rival fronts claimed that the higher turnout will work to their advantage. The State Election Commission has ordered repolling at Booth No. 4 in Ward 20 of Kochi Corporation on Tuesday. This was following a snag in the electronic voting machine.

Incidents of minor violence were reported from Palakkad, which witnessed a 10 per cent increase in the polling compared to the 2005 elections. Owing to a dispute over ballot papers, polling was held up for nearly 30 minutes at Ward 5 in Thrikkaderi Grama Panchayat. Following a minor scuffle, the police scared away CPI (M) and Janakeeya Vikasana Munnani workers at the Akkipadam booth in Kumaramputhur Grama Panchayat. Minor incidents were reported from the Thiruvzhamkun-nu and Attappady tribal belts.

Table 5.1: Voting Percentage in the Local Body Polls

District	*2010*	*2005*
Thiruvananthapuram	69.27	52.87
Kollam	73.58	59.50
Pathanamthitta	70.54	62.00
Alappuzha	77.75	62.80
Kottayam	75.64	64.34
Idukki	73.00	64.64
Ernakulam	75.00	56.90
Thrissur	73.00	58.76
Palakkad	75.00	61.00
Malappuram	75.60	63.73
Kozhikode	76.99	62.25
Wayanad	79.78	61.00
Kannur	79.48	63.00
Kasargod	77.68	60.00

III

Post-Poll Speculations

The polling percentage in the local body elections held in 2005 was 62.71 and it has gone up to 79.78 per cent in 2010. The total electorate in 2005 was 2.93 crore and it came down to 2.27 crore in 2010. This would mean that though the total number of electorate had come down in 2010, the polling percentage had gone up. It was the massive deletion of names from the voters' list which resulted in the decline of total number of voters. However, it is interesting to note that in the 2009 Lok Sabha elections, the total number of electorate in the State was 2.18 crore and the polling percentage was 73.33.

So, when the polling percentage was 62.71 in 2005, the LDF swept the local body polls. When the polling percentage was 73.33 per cent in 2009, the UDF swept the Lok Sabha polls in the State. Who will have an edge when the polling percentage reached at 79.78 becomes the million dollar question. It is evident that there has been an increase of 12.8 per cent in the polling percentage this time. But this cannot be claimed to be advantageous to any particular party. This proves the fact that neutral votes have been polled more this time and it would be a vital factor in determining the winners. A marginal swing of neutral votes would determine who will have the edge this time.

The high percentage of voting in the current local body elections signals the success of political parties in mobilising voters to polling booths. Given the average of 75 per cent voting in the two stages of elections, it is safe to assume that the issues that came up during the campaign, local as well as State-wide, have polarised the voters to come out in large numbers to vote.

The United Democratic Front (UDF) and the Left Democratic Front (LDF) leaderships, in their post-election analyses, have made tall claims about the outcome being in their favour on the basis of the higher percentage of polling. The focus of political parties is on the results of the district Panchayats, municipalities and corporations, which will provide a ready-made yardstick to gauge their performance. The fact that the percentage of votes polled will be later reckoned for recognition by the election authorities gives a competitive edge to the outcome.

While the secret was firmly locked in the ballot boxes and EVMs till counting day, it was becoming clear that the results would throw up answers to two issues: popularity or unpopularity of the LDF government, and the validation of redrawing of communal equations since the 2009 Lok Sabha elections.

Senior leaders observed that the voting would reflect the changed equations—the erosion in the LDF with the departure of the Socialist Janata (Democratic) and the merger of the Kerala Congress (J) with the Kerala Congress (M). A major poll issue was the "interference" of the Church in politics, with the LDF accusing the UDF of appeasing the Catholic Church, and the UDF leaders retorted that the LDF was trying to consolidate the Hindu majority votes. Sources said that the result would validate this process triggered off in the Lok Sabha elections. There is also a sub-script to the results for the UDF. The results would validate the strength of the SJD in Malabar and the Kerala Congress (M) in Central Travancore. The Kerala Congress (M) will be seeking a twin result — a vote against the LDF and the reassertion of its claim of being a larger player in the region. Either way, political leaders believe that the results will have a long-standing impact on the State's politics as it moves towards the Assembly elections early next year.

IV

People's Verdict 2010

The people's verdict in the 2010 polls clearly shows that, for the first time the UDF has stormed grass root citadels that were hitherto monopolised by the Left. UDF's muscular showing has decimated the myth that Grama Panchayats and Block Panchayats are the bastions of cadre-based political parties. The Congress, finally, has bridged the urban-rural divide. The Congress war cry, which was generally considered suited only for the Assembly and the Lok Sabha polls, percolated right down through the three tiers of the Panchayati Raj system. Taking even the Congress leadership by surprise, the party has put up an unprecedented performance in the local body polls almost sweeping the entire Central Travancore and even some of the Marxist bastions in the southern districts.

If the UDF outplayed the CPM-led LDF in Kochi and Thrissur Corporations, it shocked the Marxist Party in Thiruvananthapuram. The UDF has secured an absolute lead in the Grama Panchayats, Block Panchayats, municipalities and district Panchayats. Among the Block Panchayats, the UDF is leading in 79 while the LDF could secure lead only in 60. The grama panchayats, perhaps, threw up the biggest surprise. The UDF is leading in 510 Panchayats while the LDF has lead only in 362. Among the municipalities, the UDF is leading in 39 and the LDF is leading only in 18. Among the district Panchayats, the UDF is leading in eight and the LDF only in five. This is the first time that the UDF has secured such a massive lead in all the sectors irrespective of the rural and urban areas of the State. Kollam, Alappuzha, Palakkad and Kannur are the only districts where the CPM-led LDF could put up a good show. In all the other districts, the UDF has given a tough fight for the CPM. In the districts of Thiruvananthapuram, Pathanamthitta, Idukki, Kottayam, Ernakulam, Thrissur, Malappuram, and Wayanad, the Congress led UDF has dominated the show.

Factors worked for UDF in Central Travancore

In addition to the widespread resentment among the voters against the LDF dispensation, the massive mandate in favour of the UDF in the local bodies polls in Central Travancore underscores the sway of a host of other factors, especially the role of the Church in determining the final outcome in a decisive way. It is also notable that the Christian consolidation in favour of the UDF candidates had not led to a corresponding wave among the majority communities and favouring the opposite political camp. One of the salient features in the run-up to the current polls in the Christian dominated areas in the region was that the interference of the Church leadership was on a low key pattern in the eyes of common society, but piercing for the faithful.

The strategy has apparently worked out very well without creating bad blood among the majority communities and eventually helping the UDF in a big way. The Church was systematic in roping in every vote upon which it can have a say, going by the fact that all those associated with it and residing in far flung areas outside the district were directed to reach their native places and cast their votes. The phenomenon was visible everywhere on the polling day.

Despite the reservations expressed by some quarters within the UDF, the poll results reveal that the unification of the Kerala Congress factions led by K.M. Mani and P.J. Joseph has created an added political muscle for the regional party in its strongholds. Conversely, the UDF bandwagon in Central Travancore will never be the same again since the notable aspect will have to be addressed collectively by the front in any poll in the region in future. It could even give the much needed breather for a beleaguered Joseph politically, probably before the Assembly polls slated for early next year. The landslide victory of the UDF in Kottayam district has also brought out the role of a few prominent local CPM leaders into question.

It was well-known that over and above the cadre-based character and collectivity of the CPM, the final stamping on the candidature of many in the LDF banner was according to the wishes of such leaders, against whose style of functioning the people nurtured a deep grudge. The worst in the people's mandate against the Left was in Vaikom belt, considered to be one of a few strongholds and which was rated to give some relief for them amid the UDF sweep. The ruling LDF could manage just one-third of the total 26 seats in Vaikom municipality, indicating that the CPI, which had outstanding political issues with the major coalition partner, had pulled the rug from under the feet of the CPM, eventually immersing the front together. That even a highly politically conscious voter could take decisions on the basis of grass roots realities and will not get carried away with mere political considerations is also borne from the verdict.

The Church had played a crucial role in a few pockets in Vaikom also to hand out impressive gains for the UDF. The role of women voters against the backdrop of a large number of women candidates in the fray with scope of lot of them poised to take the reins of many local bodies, which was one of the factors which led to a huge poll percentage, is also believed to have aided the big sweep for the UDF across the district and adjoining ones. The trend among the voters in favour of the UDF was also noted with both urban centres and rural pockets working in unison to turn the tide.

UDF Conquered Territory that has hitherto Eluded

The United Democratic Front (UDF) has every reason to feel proud about its electoral performance given its record in the previous elections to the Panchayats and the civic bodies. The victory has been even across the three tiers of Panchayats, which many perceive as a vote against the Left Democratic Front's rule at the State and the local levels.

The victory, by and large, maintains a pro-UDF trend witnessed during the Lok Sabha elections in 2009 and the subsequent Assembly by-elections. Kollam district is, perhaps, the only exception with the opposition front way behind. The UDF went into the elections with reservations about delimitation of wards and the voters' list and apprehensions about bogus voting. But the results show that all these have been misplaced. Similarly, its misgivings about its chances with 50 per cent of the seats reserved for women appear to have been baseless, more so when the coalition appears to be the major beneficiary of this reform. Though the counting of votes in Kozhikode district will be held only on Sunday, the UDF has gained by the political shifts that took place in a year with the entry of the Socialist Janata (Democratic) into its fold and the merger of the Kerala Congress (J) with the Kerala Congress (M).

In Wayanad, the Socialist Janata (Democratic) has contributed much to its victory, but a clear picture will emerge only when votes are counted in Kozhikode. The election results in Kottayam, Idukki, Ernakulam and Thrissur indicate that the UDF has benefited from the consolidation of the Catholic community behind it. In Malappuram, parts of Kannur and Kasaragod, the UDF has benefited from the consolidation of Muslim votes. The most significant aspect of the elections is the inroads that the

UDF has been able to make into the Grama Panchayats, cornering nearly 55 per cent of them.

Impressive Performance of the BJP

Early preparations and united work have paid off for the Bharatiya Janata Party (BJP) in the elections to local self-government institutions in the State, though marginally. The party had started its preparations ahead of the ruling and opposition fronts and had managed to choose relatively better candidates this time than in the last elections. Not many social or political factors could be reckoned as the reasons for the party's improved performance in the polls. But party sources say that it could tap its social base better this time.

The people's disenchantment with the ruling front and the development agenda put forward by the party would have contributed marginally to the party's performance. However, the impact of local factors and local development issues is more significant. The biggest break for the party this time is in the Thiruvananthapuram Corporation where it could recover lost ground. The party had experienced a heavy erosion in its support base in the by-election to the Lok Sabha from the Thiruvananthapuram constituency just a month after the elections to local bodies in 2005. The BJP's campaign had been undermined from within, following dissensions in the party. Five years since then, the party could make a concerted effort and translate its support base into six seats in the city Corporation. An Independent representing the Dheerva Sabha and supported by the party has also won the polls. The BJP had only one seat in the outgoing Corporation council.

However, the party's performance is poorer in Kasaragod district and Palakkad municipality where it has a political base. In Kasaragod district, the BJP had its presidents in six Grama Panchayats, and five of the Panchayats were under its control This time, it has to be satisfied with majority in two Panchayats and possible control of two other Panchayats with support of Independents. In the district Panchayat, its tally has come down from two to one. In Palakkad municipality, its seats have dropped from 17 in 2005 to 15.

At the same time, the party could expand it reach to other parts of the State. It has fielded candidates for 9,922 out of 21,456 seats and could win in new areas. In the Grama Panchayats, it has won about 450 seats, compared to 236 in 2005. This figure excludes Independents supported by the party, which exceed 50. It may go up further when the results from Kozhikode district are added up after the counting on October 31. Its score in the Block Panchayats at the moment is the same as last time, seven. In municipalities, the party has expanded its representation. It has won 79 seats in 28 municipalities against 71 in 23 municipalities in the last elections. Besides, 11 Independents supported by the BJP in different municipalities have got elected.

The BJP has improved upon its tally compared to the previous local body polls. The party has got significant representation in Thiruvananthapuram Corporation — six seats, two in Kochi, one in Thrissur and 76 seats in various municipalities, the highest of 15 in Palakkad municipality. The party candidates finished runners-up in eight wards in Thiruvananthapuram Corporation. The party will play a crucial role in deciding the rulers in four municipalities. The SDPI has also opened its account fray securing one seat each in Kannur and Thodupuzha municipalities. A distinct feature of the local body elections this time is that 50 per cent of the over 21,000 seats are reserved for women in the multi-tier local self-government bodies.

The UDF wrested the Kochi Corporation from the LDF after three decades, winning 46 out of the 74 seats. The LDF won 23 Wards and the BJP 2, and Independent 3. The UDF also emerged victorious in the Thrissur Corporation, winning 44 out of the 55 seats. Here, the LDF got six seats, the BJP one and Independents four seats. The LDF has retained the Thiruvananthapuram Corporation winning 51 out of the 100 seats, leaving 41 to the UDF, six to the BJP and two to Independents. The LDF won the Kollam Corporation for a third successive term bagging 34 out of the 55 seats. The UDF got 18 seats and others, three seats.

The SDPI Factor

An unexpected SDPI (Socialist Democratic Party of India) factor, which managed to garner a considerable number of votes, has raised an alarm bell forcing the Indian Union Muslim League (IUML) and the People's Democratic Party (PDF) to deliberate on the circumstances that led to a large scale flow of Muslim votes from their base to the SDPI. Though the IUML had strongly opposed the SDPI right from its inception, it never considered it as a threat to its vote base in the Block Panchayats and Grama Panchayats in Ernakulam district.

Nevertheless, the IUML had cashed in on the opportunity, resulting from the attack on Thodupuzha Newman's College teacher T.J. Joseph by alleged SDPI activists, to lacerate the SDPI as a 'communal organisation with bad credentials'. However, the results of the local body polls has come as a shocker to both the IUML and the PDF as the SDPI has managed to attract quite a number of Muslim votes contesting alone against the IUML and the PDF. While SDPI candidate Prof Anas, an accused in the lecturer attack case, won the Vanchinad division of the Vazhakkulam Block Panchayat by garnering 3,992 votes, the PDF candidate could manage only 223 votes. The SDPI made considerable inroads into the vote base of the IUML and in most of the divisions, the PDP was pushed to fifth and sixth positions. The Blocks where the PDP was relegated to lower positions included Malleppalli (SDPI-111. PDP-66), Cheravalloor (SDPI-573, PDP-76) and Koteepeedikka (SDPI-57, PDP-40).

The SDPI, which had fielded candidates in all the seats where the IUML had contested, was able to gain some votes but not enough to defeat the League candidates. At Kunjunnikkara in Aluva where the SDPI and the League had clashed head on, the former was able to get 379 votes, which was same as that garnered by the League candidate. The other major Panchayats where the SDPI garnered votes pitting against the League included Eramam South (IUML-658, SDPI-331), Kadavuppadam (IUML-629, SDPI-201), Edayyappuram West (IUML-366, SDPI-182) and Mulavoor North (IUML-489, SDPI-112).

The LDF retained Kozhikode

The LDF had escaped without any grievous hurt in the civic Election in Kozhikode district. The poll results were announced on 31st October. With its 39 councillors, the CPI (M) alone secured simple majority in the 75 member Kozhikode Corporation Council and had the support of two members representing its ally, the Nationalist Congress Party (NCP). The Congress led UDF won 34 seats. The LDF has retained power in the Vadakara municipality 27 out of the total 47 seats. The UDF bagged 17 seats. Three independent candidates, including a Congress rebel also got elected. In the Koyilandy municipality, the LDF secured 27 out of the 44 seats. The UDF won 14 seats eight more than what it had in the previous council. The BJP secured three seats.

Front-wise and District-wise Picture

Compared to the previous local body polls held in 2005, the UDF got 15.65 lakh more votes this time. The United Front has received 46.09 per cent of the total votes polled in the State. Out of 1,83,26,367 votes polled, the UDF captured 84,47,977 votes. In the year 2005, the UDF got 68,82,314 votes out of total 1,69,84,236, i.e. 40.52 per cent. In 2010, the UDF has received 6,84,482 more votes than the LDF. In total, the LDF has received 77,63,495 votes in 2010. In 2005, the LDF had won the electoral support of 45.32 per cent voters and in 2010, it had reduced to 42.36 per cent. Compared to the previous poll, there was an increase of 13,42,131 voters in 2010. It shows that majority of the new voters extended their faith and confidence in the UDF. Compared to the UDF and LDF, the position of the BJP has increased drastically. In 2005, the party got

Table 5.2: Total and Percentage of Votes of Various Political Parties

District	*Total votes polled*	*UDF*	*LDF*	*BJP*	*Others*
Thiruvananthapuram	16,82,099	7,11,869 (42.32%)	7,20,286 (42.82%)	1,34,039 (7.96%)	1,15,905 (6.89%)
Kollam	14,34,817	6,26,318 (43.65%)	6,88,545 (47.98%)	67,095 (4.67%)	52,859 (3.68%)
Pathanamthitta	6,78,132	3,12,327 (46.05%)	2,74,565 (40.48%)	56,417 (8.31%)	34,823 (5.13%)
Alappuzha	12,58,095	5,63,417 (44.78%)	5,71,612 (45.43%)	68,424 (5.43%)	54,642 (4.34%)
Kottayam	11,26,151	5,61,723 (49.87%)	4,35,016 (38.62%)	49,211 (4.36%)	80,201 (7.12%)
Idukki	6,43,231	3,42,078 (53.18%)	2,58,413 (40.17%)	19,617 (3.04%)	23,126 (3.59%)
Ernakulam	18,42,321	8,96,072 (44.29%)	7,54,313 (40.94%)	89,037 (4.39%)	1,02,899 (5.58%)
Thrissur	17,98,343	8,20,412 (45.62%)	7,61,114 (42.32%)	1,26,337 (7.02%)	90,480 (5.03%)
Palakkad	15,54,728	6,81,317 (43.82%)	6,92,017 (44.51%)	98,616 (6.34%)	82,778 (5.32%)
Malappuram	20,79,413	11,08,349 (53.30%)	6,99,973 (33.66%)	1,08,514 (5.21%)	1,62,577 (7.81%)
Kozhikode	17,34,212	7,82,047 (45.09%)	7,49,428 (43.21%)	1,21,642 (7.01%)	81,095 (4.19%)
Wayanad	4,34,912	2,15,414 (49.53%)	1,74,983 (40.23%)	24,213 (5.56%)	20,302 (4.66%)
Kannur	13,78,964	5,49,217 (38.82%)	7,24,016 (52.50%)	71,418 (5.17%)	34,313 (2.48%)
Kasargod	6,80,949	2,77,417 (40.72%)	25,921 (38.06%)	1,12,712 (16.55%)	31,609 (4.64%)
Total	1,83,26,367	84,47,977 (46.09%)	77,63,495 (42.36%)	11,47,297 (6.26%)	9,67,598 (5.27%)

9,64,133 votes and in 2010 it had gone up to 11,47,297, i.e., an increase of 1,83,164 votes. The LDF had suffered bitter experiences from Malappuram, Ernakulam and Kottayam districts. In these districts, UDF has increased or strengthened its mass base by capturing over 4 lakh, 1.5 lakh and 1.25 lakh votes respectively. Table 5.2 further reveal the massbase of various political combinations in the state politics – front wise, district-wise and percentage-wise.

Ward-wise Picture

The ward-wise evaluation of the poll shows that the Congress has made a spectacular performance in the Poll, compared with 2005 poll. The party has captured 3,161 more Wards this time, It is an exemplary performance shown by the Congress Party in the recent past in the State politics. In 2005 Poll, the Congress Party came victorious only in 4,454 Wards. In 2010 it has gone up to 7,615.

Table 5.3: Ward-wise performance

Grama Panchayat		*Block*	*District*	*Municipality*	*Corporation*
UDF	8501	1230	194	1097	178
LDF	6607	828	134	803	155
BJP	384	7	1	79	9
Others	1183	30	3	202	17

The second leading partner of the UDF, Muslim League performed this time. In 2005, the League had established elected Electoral control in 1919 Wards. In 2010, it has gone up to 2,235. The other leading UDF

Table 5.4: Performance of the UDF

Party	*GP*	*Block*	*Dist.*	*Mun.*	*Corpn.*
Congress	5729	873	123	746	144
Muslin League	1717	220	35	248	15
KC(M)	643	95	21	55	4
Socialist Janata	127	19	8	11	9
KC (B)	31	4	2	0	0
KC (J)	30	9	1	2	0
INL	32	4	3	7	0
JSS	27	1	0	2	2
CMP	18	5	1	7	3
KRSP(B)	12	0	0	0	1
UDF (Independent)	135	0	0	19	0

partner, Kerala Congress (M) too performed well. In 2005, KC (M) had 411 Wards. It has gone to 818 in 2010. The Socialist Janata Dal, who left LDF and joined hands with UDF, just before the poll won in 174 Wards. The INL captured control in 45 Wards. *In toto*, the UDF has won on 11,200 Wards whereas the LDF confined in 8,527 Wards and BJP in 480 Wards.

Compared to the Congress, the CPM has suffered heavy losses. The party has lost 1,055 Wards, compared to 2005 poll. In 2005 poll, the CPM has captured 8,056 Wards. It had decreased to 7,001 in 2010. Its partner, CPI too suffered humiliating defeat. In 2005, CPI has won in 1,392 Wards. In 2010, it came down to 1,017. The seat share of RSP, another partner in the LDF came down to 70 from 77.

Tables 5.5 and 5.6 illustrate the details regarding front-wise, Ward wise and Party-wise performance.

Table 5.5: Performance of LDF

Party	*GP*	*Block*	*Dist.*	*Mun.*	*Corpn.*
CPI (M)	5431	680	106	661	123
CPI	778	122	24	77	16
RSP	51	5	4	2	9
NCP	34	8	0	2	2
JD(S)	14	3	0	2	0
KC (Thomas)	14	3	0	2	0
Con (S)	6	0	0	4	1
LDF (Indep)	279	7	0	51	4

Table 5.6: People's Verdict 2010 - At A Glance

	Total	*UDF*	*%*	*LDF*	*%*	*BJP*	*Others*
Grama Panchayats	978	565	57.77	348	35.58	2	63
Block Panchayats	152	92	60.52	60	39.47	0	0
District Panchayats	14	8	57.14	6	42.85	0	0
Municipalities	57	40	70.17	17	29.82	0	0
Corporations	5	2	40.00	3	60	0	0

UDF Established Control over 90 Assembly Segments

Another remarkable feature of the Poll was that the UDF had established a clear lead over LDF in 90 assembly segments. As per as vote share is concerned, the UDF has captured only 40.52 per cent votes in the 2005 poll. It has gone up to 46 per cent in 2010. Compared to the UDF, the LDF had won 49 per cent votes in 2005. It has decreased to 42 per cent in

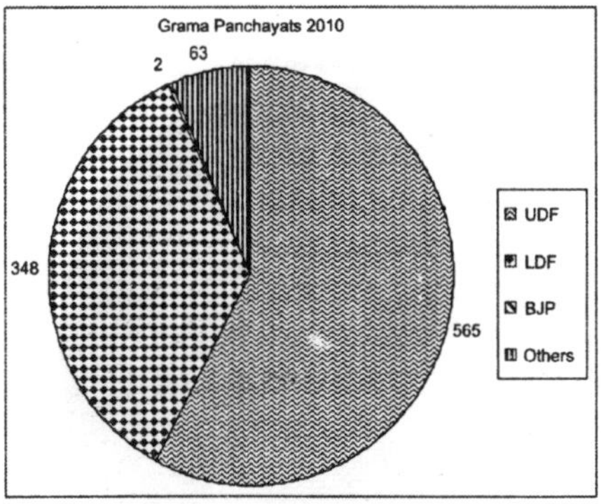
Grama Panchayats 2010
2
63
348
565
UDF
LDF
BJP
Others

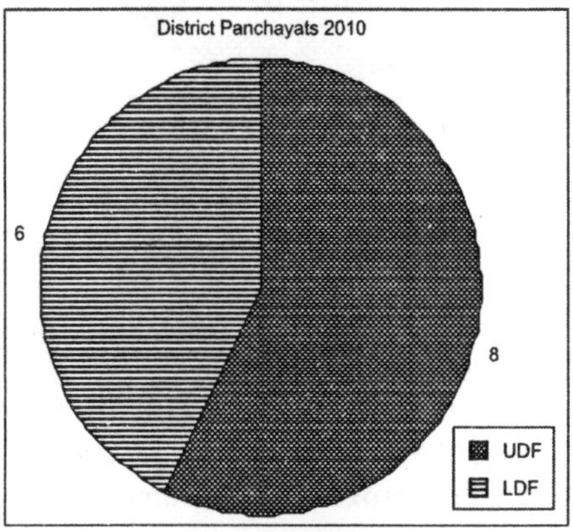
District Panchayats 2010
6
8
UDF
LDF

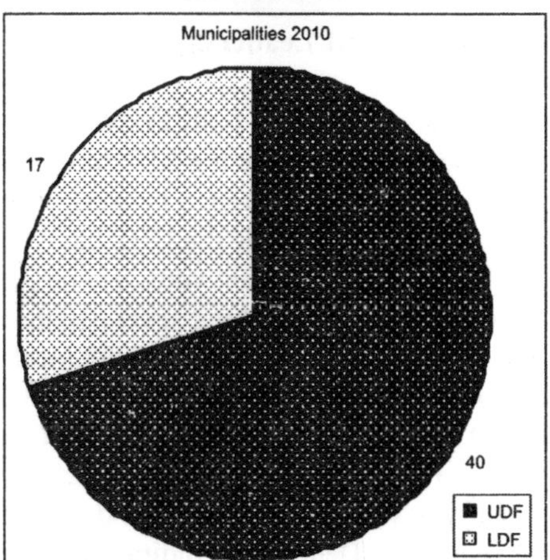
Municipalities 2010
17
40
UDF
LDF

(Contd.)

(*Contd.*)

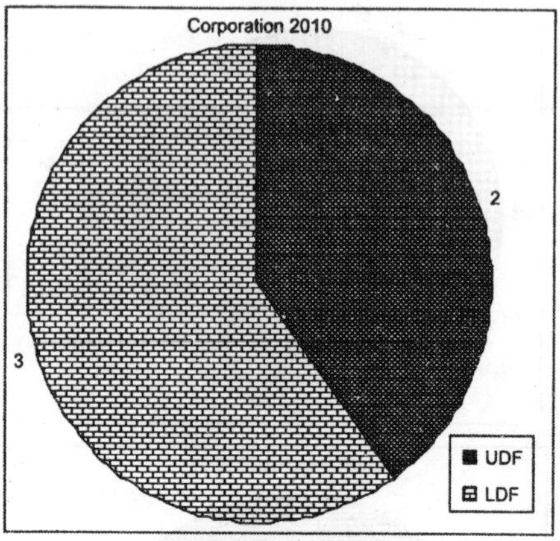

Fig. 5.1: Performance of Grama and District Panchayats as well as Municipalities and Corporations

2010. In 2005, the LDF got a total votes of 84,90,258. It came down to 77,67,888 in 2010. The front had lost over 4 lakhs votes. The only solace for the LDF is that it has made a slight better performance compared to the 2009 parliament poll. In total, the front has increased its vote share of about one per cent. In the 2006 assembly poll, the LDF captured 48.63 per cent votes. The BJP has captured 5.68 per cent votes in 2005. The party has made a slight improvements this time

Post-Poll Claims by the CPM Leadership

The CPM state Secretary in his post-poll review claimed that the UDF has secured 84,55,193 votes, whereas the LDF has garnered 77,67,888 votes. Percentage-wise too the difference between the two fronts was 3.69 per cent. According to him, while the UDF has won 46.01 per cent of votes and the LDF got 42.32 per cent votes. He further stated that the LDF had contested the 2010 polls without several of the allies who were with it – [KC (J), INL, JDS] — during the 2005 local body polls and 2009 Lok Sabha polls. According to the Party Secretary in 2005, the LDF has secured 49.22 per cent of votes. Since the alliance had got only 42.32 per cent votes in 2010. It would mean that the LDF had suffered a loss of 6.9 per cent votes. The allies and outside-backers of 2005 has secured 9.18 per cent votes. Democratic Indira Congress (Karunakaran) DICK had 4.67 per cent; Janata Dal (Secular) had 2.30 per cent, Kerala

Congress (Joseph) had 1.79 per cent and Indian National League 0.35 per cent. He also added that, "If it were an automatic subtraction of their share, the percentage this time would have been only 40.04 per cent".

The actual percentage on the contrary, showed a 2.2 per cent increase in the vote share of the LDF. In 2000 local body polls, the LDF had got 42.64 per cent votes which would mean that the erosion into 1000 time was only 0.32 per cent as he claimed. Further, the LDF's total share of votes has also gone up as compared to 2009 Lok Sabha elections. In the Lok Sabha Polls, the LDF had captured only 38.40 per cent vote share against 40.23 per cent in 2005 and 41.47 per cent in 2000. The actual increase from 2009 in terms of votes came to 10.64 lakh from 67,47,438 to 77,81,671.

V

What went wrong for the LDF?

(1) Anti-incumbency Factors

The poll outcome, showing a clear advantage for the Opposition United Democratic Front (UDF) in both urban and rural local bodies, indicate that the Opposition was successful in whipping up a wave in its favour across the State and that the poll strategy of the Communist Party of India-Marxist (CPI-M) had little in it to carry the ruling front to safety, and worse, had a lot in it to harm its cause. Given the nature of the verdict, it will be hard to rule out a strong anti-incumbency mood among the electorate across the State.

The UDF's success in unleashing a focussed campaign over State level issues, such as the lottery scam, may be one of the major reasons for this, but there will be others such as the inability of the CPI (M) to put its own house in order and the way it virtually drove out parties with local-level clout out of the alliance. On issues such as the lottery scam, the government was seen to be pulling in opposite directions with Chief Minister V.S. Achuthanandan being seen as proactive even as the rest of the government and the alliance seemed far from decisive in their response to the whole issue. The State government's argument that the onus of controlling the other State lottery mafia rested with the Centre fell flat with each new development.

(2) Welfare Measures failed to Catch Votes

The UDF has already bagged 544 Grama Panchayats, 89 Block Panchayats, 39 municipalities, eight district Panchayats and two municipal corporations. The trend would very likely be the same when the votes polled in the 75 or so Grama Panchayats and other local and civic bodies in Kozhikode district too are counted. The UDF could not have scored so emphatic a victory if the LDF campaign managers were right, which means that welfare pay-outs and benefits did not create a politically educated category but only an easily swayed, largely consumerist mass.

(3) Row with Church

The strong showing by the UDF in the central districts suggest that the CPI (M) bid to take on the Church was counterproductive. It did not win the LDF the votes of the majority community and resulted only in hardening of Christian votes. The crushing defeat that the LDF suffered in the Thrissur Corporation and the loss of the Kochi Corporation, which it had been controlling for the past three decades, could be the direct fallout of this. It could even be the case that the real beneficiary of the anti-Church campaign of the CPI(M) was the Bharatiya Janata Party (BJP), which has put in a noteworthy showing in some of these districts.

Chief Minister V.S. Achuthanandan and CPI(M) State secretary Pinarayi Vijayan have described the setback temporary, but CPI State secretary Veliyam Bhargavan has, in his initial response to the poll outcome, admitted that an anti-incumbency mood might also have influenced the outcome to a certain extent. When the UDF routed the LDF in the 2009 Lok Sabha elections, the Opposition had led in 100 Assembly segments. This time, it should be a matter of relief for the LDF that the number of constituencies where the UDF has sway will be less than that figure, when the counting of votes in Kozhikode is completed.

(4) Communal Votes

The LDF leadership is, however, right on one point: that there was a massive consolidation of communal votes across the State. If it was a consolidation of Christian votes in the former Central Travancore, in the north and in many pockets across Kerala, it was consolidation of Muslim votes. With Communist Party of India (Marxist) rebels and former allies hitting back at the alliance with a vengeance, the LDF's share and votes of woes just overflowed. It was, in many ways, a backlash that the LDF did not deserve as a government, but could not avoid as a political formation. And, in that sense, it is tough to see the outcome as a verdict on the performance of the LDF government. The reason why and how the Christian consolidation came about is complex, but the way the CPI(M) strategy of taking on the Church contributed to it is there for everyone to see. The whole debate over mixing religion and politics, an old theme used to its full potential by none other than E.M.S. Namboodiripad, obviously did not win it any new friends. Coming as it did on the heels of the incidents at CMS College, Kottayam, it also further alienated the Church of South India (CSI), though not acutely in the coastal belt of south Kerala.

Only the Latin Catholic community appears to have taken a relatively neutral position in the whole debate. In the case of the Muslim community too, the CPI(M) appears to have failed to look closely at the nuances of the developments within the community and its organisational representations, the beneficiary being the Bharatiya Janata Party. In the event, the debate did not remain what it should have been and the LDF paid a heavy price for it as it did not have the means or ability to reach out to the other side of the political divide with cogent arguments.

However, though figures to prove anything are yet to come by, the Kudumbasree initiative appears to have done some good for the LDF, particularly in Grama Panchayats. But, even here, there could be some surprise in store. Preliminary indications are that the Congress also might have benefited from the participation of Kudumbasree activists in the elections. Only the final figures would tell the whole story. Equally interesting would be the way women have, if at all, performed in general wards. All the relevant figures could be pointers to the way women's politics evolves in the new political situation at the grass roots and the UDF's responsibility is much greater here than it ever was.

At a purely organisational level the CPI(M) and other LDF constituents would also have to see how their inability to put up a joint fight in many places contributed to their collective failure; Kottayam, where the CPI (M) and CPI were openly at each other's throat, being an example. And, within the CPI (M), though factionalism as a pan-Kerala, centrally driven, phenomenon has been snuffed out to a very large extent, much appears to have come unhinged at the time of the elections on account of various local factors. All this just means that the LDF collectively and its constituents individually have their tasks cut out.

Concluding Observations

As cited earlier, it can be stated that in the 2010 polls for the first time the UDF has stormed grass root citadels that were hitherto monopolised by the Left. UDF's muscular showing has decimated the myth that Grama

Panchayats and Block Panchayats are the bastions of cadre-based political parties. The Congress, finally, has bridged the urban-rural divide. The Congress war cry, which was generally considered suited only for the Assembly and the Lok Sabha polls, percolated right down through the three tiers of the Panchayati Raj system. Taking even the Congress leadership by surprise, the party has put up an unprecedented performance in the local body polls almost sweeping the entire Central Travancore and even some of the Marxist bastions in the southern districts.

The UDF captured absolute control over corporations in Kochi and Thrissur. Similarly, the UDF captured absolute control over Grama Panchayats, Block Panchayats and district Panchayats throughout the State. In Block Panchayats the UDF got 89 and the LDF captured 49. The Grama Panchayats, perhaps, threw up the biggest surprise. The UDF got control in 525 while the LDF got 301. The BJP had established control over 2 and others in 75. Among the municipalities, the UDF got 34 and LDF got 12. In 11 municipalities none got absolute majority. Among the district Panchayats, the UDF got 8 and LDF got 5. This is the first time that the UDF has secured such a massive lead in all the sectors irrespective of the rural and urban areas of the State. Kollam, Alappuzha, Palakkad and Kannur are the only districts where the CPM-led LDF could put up a good show. In all the other districts, the UDF has given a tough fight for the CPM. In the districts of Thiruvananthapuram, Pathanamthitta, Idukki, Kottayam, Ernakulam, Thrissur, Malappuram, and Wayanad, the Congress-led UDF has dominated the show.

If a mandate is a slice of social psychology, then the Left in the State has failed to read the mind of its people. The miscalculation that development agenda would eclipse all political controversies have poorly failed. The deliberate attempt to show case development and steer public mind from politics and communal factors only brought them to the forefront.

Long before the UDF zeroed in on its candidates or even thought of the word campaign, the LDF was taking the development activities undertaken by local bodies to the far and wide of the State. Its grass root machinery had jumped into the election scene much before others had even given it a thought. Seminars, exhibitions, Kudumbasree *melas*—every possible idea was utilised. Rice for ₹ 2, EMS Housing Scheme, Asraya project and a lot more for the welfare of the poor was projected. But all went in vain.

The ballot has shown that it is a misconception of the Left that half the voting population are beneficiaries of their various welfare schemes. If the beneficiaries form a mere 20-30 per cent, it is to be assumed that the rest of 60-70 per cent decided the fate of the Left this time. For the latter, it is not rice or house that matters. But improvement of living conditions, roads, undisrupted water supply and better facilities. Even the behaviour of politicians in public sphere matters for this group.

Table 5.7: List of Candidates in Civic Polls 2010 in Kerala

District	*Grama Panchayat*	*Block Panchayat*	*District Panchayat*	*Munici-pality*	*Corp.*	*Total*
Thiruvananthapuram	4689	500	115	489	642	6435
Kollam	4163	460	106	332	276	5337
Pathanamthitta	2712	350	77	351	–	3490
Alappuzha	3866	499	84	697	–	5146
Kottayam	3941	458	98	536	–	5033
Idukki	2518	324	58	116	–	3016
Ernakulam	4425	579	122	1213	378	6717
Thrissur	5092	701	127	799	251	6970
Palakkad	4800	540	125	589	–	6054
Malappuram	6251	763	145	919	–	8078
Kozhikode	4408	552	123	276	410	5769
Wayanad	1407	197	78	88	–	1770
Kannur	3336	411	95	603	–	4445
Kasargod	2009	338	69	329	–	2745

Table 5.8: Civic Polls 2010 in Kerala – Detailed Results

Corporation
Total - 5
UDF – 2
LDF – 3
BJP – 0

Table 5.9: District Panchayats

District	*Total*	*UDF*	*LDF*	*Hung*	*Others*
Thiruvananthapuram	26	14	12	0	0
Kollam	26	8	18	0	0
Pathanamthitta	17	9	8	0	0
Alappuzha	23	19	4	0	0
Kottayam	23	19	4	0	0
Idukki	16	16	0	0	0
Ernakulam	26	22	3	0	1
Trissur	29	17	12	0	0
Palakkad	29	11	18	0	0
Malappuram	32	30	2	0	0
Wayanad	16	13	2	0	1
Kannur	26	6	20	0	0
Kargode	16	6	9	1	1
Kozhikode	27	12	15	0	0

Table 5.10: Block Panchayats

District	*Total*	*UDF*	*LDF*	*Hung*	*Others*
Thiruvananthapuram	11	6	4	1	0
Kollam	11	3	8	0	0
Pathanamthitta	8	7	0	1	0
Alappuzha	12	7	5	0	0
Kottayam	11	10	1	0	0
Idukki	8	8	0	0	0
Ernakulam	14	13	1	0	0
Trissur	16	9	7	0	0
Palakkad	13	5	8	0	0
Malappuram	15	14	1	0	0
Wayanad	4	4	0	0	0
Kannur	11	0	11	0	0
Kargode	6	3	3	0	0
Kozhikode	12	4	8	0	0

Table 5.11: Grama Panchayats

District	*Total*	*UDF*	*LDF*	*Hung*	*Others*
Thiruvananthapuram	73	36	25	12	0
Kollam	70	24	37	9	0
Pathanamthitta	54	36	14	4	0
Alappuzha	73	32	37	4	0
Kottayam	73	58	10	5	0
Idukki	53	41	10	2	0
Ernakulam	84	66	6	12	0
Trissur	88	45	33	10	0
Palakkad	91	36	51	4	0
Malappuram	100	88	8	4	0
Wayanad	25	21	3	1	0
Kannur	81	27	54	0	0
Kargode	38	15	13	8	2 (BJP)
Kozhikode	75	34	40	0	1

Table 5.12: Municipalities – District-wise

District	*Total*	*UDF*	*LDF*	*Hung*	*Others*
Thiruvananthapuram	4	1	1	2	0
Kollam	3	1	1	1	0
Pathanamthitta	3	2	0	1	0
Alappuzha	5	2	0	3	0
Kottayam	4	3	0	1	0
Idukki	1	1	0	0	0
Ernakulam	11	10	1	0	0
Trissur	6	2	4	0	0
Palakkad	2	0	2	0	0
Malappuram	7	6	0	1	0
Wayanad	1	1	0	0	0
Kannur	5	1	4	0	0
Kargode	3	2	1	0	0
Kozhikode	2	0	2	0	0

Table 5.13: Tally of Municipalities — Municipality-wise

Municipality	*Total*	*UDF*	*LDF*	*BJP*	*Others*
Thiruvananthapuram					
Niyyatinkara	44	20	20	0	4
Nedmangad	39	16	18	2	3
Attingal	31	13	17	1	0
Varkala	33	18	11	1	3
Kollam					
Karunagappally	35	21	14	0	0
Paravur	32	15	16	1	0
Punalloor	35	11	24	0	0
Pathanamthitta					
Adoor	28	17	9	0	2
Pathanamthitta	32	17	10	2	3
Thiruvalla	39	17	5	0	0
Alappuzha					
Alappuzha	52	25	26	0	1
Cherthala	35	18	10	0	7
Kayamkulam	44	21	16	2	5
Mavelikkara	28	13	8	2	5
Chegannur	27	14	10	1	2
Idukki					
Thodupuzha	35	22	6	4	3
Kottayam					
Kottayam	52	27	18	3	4

(Contd.)

Table 5.13 (*Contd.*)

Municipality	*Total*	*UDF*	*LDF*	*BJP*	*Others*
Pala	26	18	1	0	7
Vaikom	26	17	8	0	1
Changanassery	37	14	12	0	11
Eranakulam					
Eloor	31	14	13	3	1
Maradu	33	22	10	0	1
Thripunithura	49	25	22	1	1
Aluva	25	22	2	0	1
Angamaly	30	15	13	0	2
North Paravur	29	14	13	0	2
Kalamassery	42	22	17	0	3
Perumbavoor	27	15	9	1	2
Thrikakkara	43	28	13	0	2
Kothamangalam	31	23	8	0	0
Muvathupuzha	28	10	14	0	4
Thrissur					
Guruvayur	43	17	25	1	0
Chavakkad	32	11	21	0	0
Kunnmangalam	37	14	15	2	6
Chalakkudy	36	23	4	0	9
Irinjalakuda	41	28	9	1	3
Kodungalloor	44	11	26	5	2
Palakkad					
Palakkad	52	23	9	15	5
Chottur	29	26	3	0	0
Ottappalam	36	11	15	4	6
Shoranur	33	8	13	3	9
Malappuram					
Malappuram	40	30	8	0	2
Manjeri	50	38	8	0	4
Perinthalmanna	34	17	16	0	1
Tirur	38	28	7	0	3
Ponnai	51	25	22	1	3
Kottakkal	32	24	5	2	1
Nilambur	33	21	8	0	4
Wayanad					
Kalpetta	28	20	7	0	10
Kannur					
Kannur	42	33	8	0	1
Thalassery	52	14	35	2	1
Koothuparamba	28	4	24	0	0
Taliparamba	44	13	31	0	0
Payyannur	44	16	28	0	0

(*Contd.*)

Table 5.13 (*Contd.*)

Municipality	*Total*	*UDF*	*LDF*	*BJP*	*Others*
Kasargod					
Kasargod	38	24	2	11	1
Kanhangad	43	22	16	5	0
Neelaswaram	32	10	20	0	2
Kozhikode					
Koilandi	44	14	27	3	0
Vadakara	47	17	27	0	3

The Left often forgets that it can be a centralised and closed party but it cannot impose its character on the people. The party needs to converse with the upper levels of society just the way they communicate with the grass root. Before it is concluded, the LDF particularly the CPI(M) needs to educate politically its grass root cadred and not feed them on development activities which have gained acceptance.

References

The Hindu, Thiruvananthapuram.
The Kerala Kaumudi, Kollam.
The Kerala Sabdam, Kollam.
The Malayala Manorama, Kollam.
The Mathrubhumi, Kollam.
The New Indian Express, Thiruvananthapuram.

6

e-Panchayat Initiatives

A Review of Policy and Measures in Bihar

Dr. Arjun Sharma

The political and administrative structure of India is largely inherited from the British. The British introduced local democracy in India by constituting municipal councils and the municipal corporations in the last quarter of the nineteenth century.[1] They also provided a federal structure to the country with the Government of India Act 1935.

The independent India today has a quasi-federal structure[2]. Apart from the Government of India in New Delhi, there are 28 states with their own state Governments. The Seventh Schedule to the Constitution of India divides the subjects of State activity between the Union and the State Government. The Union as well as state governments in India both have a Parliamentary form of Government based on the Westminster pattern. The executive powers of the Central Government are vested in the Council of Ministers with the Prime Minister at its Head. Similarly, the executive powers in the State governments are vested in its Council of Ministers with the Chief Minister at its head.[3]

The Constitution of India provides for the government (subject of the State Governments) to make a special provision for setting of Panchayati Raj to fulfil the dream of 'Ramraj', 'Gramraj', 'Swaraj' for that the Father of the Nation Mahatma Gandhi dreamt and fought for.[4] The makers of the Constitution of independent India were not much satisfied with the existing legislation and the working of these local bodies as institutions of popular government and, therefore, a Directive was included in the Constitution of 1949 in Art. 40 as follows:

> "The State shall take steps to organize Village Panchayats and endow them with such powers and authority as may be necessary to enable them to function as units of self-government[5]".

But notwithstanding this Directive in Article 40, not much attention was given to hold elections in these local units as a unit of representative democracy in the country as a whole. During the time of Mr. Rajeev Gandhi, it was considered necessary to further the organization of these local units by inserting specific provisions in the Constitution itself on the basis of which the legislatures of the various States might enact detailed laws according to the guidelines provided by the constitutional provisions.

The ideas so evolved, culminated in the passing of Constitution 73rd and 74th Amendment Act 1992 which inserted Parts IX and IXA respectively in the Constitution. While Part IX related to the Panchayats containing Articles. 243 to 243-O (11th Schedule), Part IXA relates to the Municipalities containing Articles 243P to 243ZG (12th Schedule). The provisions in Parts IX and IXA are more or less parallel or analogous. Now these amendments make it obligatory for the State Governments to organize local bodies to hold regular elections to them and to give them appropriate finances.

The motto of Panchayati Raj Institutions is human welfare and it is possible only through good governance. Governance refers to the systems of directing and controlling the actions, affairs, policies and functions of a political unit, organizations or nation.[6] It has been defined by the UNDP in 1997 as 'the exercise of political, economic and administrative authority in the management of a country's affairs.[7] It has been used in several ways such as corporate governance, local governance, national governance and international governance. Although governance is the mechanism to implement a nation's development plan, yet it implies to provide feedback into planning and to ensure judicious management of the nation's resources.[8]

But with the emergence of concept of public management in the early 1990s, the scholars of America have advocated the need of structural changes in the process of governance by the statecraft in order to involve the beneficiaries themselves and seek the better results at the lowest level.[9] This has the genesis of good governance. It accomplishes governance in a manner essentially free of abuse and competition and with due regard for the rule of law. The test of good governance is the degree to which it delivers on the promise of human rights – civil, cultural, social, economic and political. It implies effective political institutions and the responsible use of political power and management of public resources by the state. The e-governance is the outcome of Good Governance.

e-governance is a short form of electronic governance. It is also called a digital governance. It is the effective use to IT (Information Technology) to improve the system of governance that is in place and thus provides better services to the citizens.[10] IT is a multidisciplinary field emerging from computer technology and internet technology. IT and communication technology now popularly referred to as ICT (Information and Communication Technology) embody satellite broadcasting network, television, video, digital radio, internet, extranets, wireless communication, devices (mobile phones), DVD (Digital Video Disk), CD-ROMS, video or voice mail, e-mail, e-commerce, e-conferencing and so on. We have moved into IT to ICT and now are advancing towards IS (Information society).[11] Truly speaking, e-governance is an attempt of government to harness ICT to improve the efficiency of the executive function to the government including the delivery of public services. The application of electronic means in the interaction between government and citizens, between government and business and between government and government. It is to simplify and improve democratic government and business aspects of governance. It is all about how government business and citizens interact on an ongoing basis.

The system of e-governance is supported by the C^5 Computer, Connectivity, Content, Consumer and Confidence. Computer refers to all the hardware and software requirements of government. Connectivity refers to all the information carriers system, bandwidth, etc. Content refers to the information that is exchange between 'Consumer' of the system. Consumer refers to the entire human and human substitutes system that access and uses the 'Content' in the e-governance system. Confidence building refers of such these measures that help the citizens develop a confidence in the e-governance and encourage them to take to e-transformation.

'Sushasan' has become an integral part of administration and democratic system in Bihar today, so e-governance has been accepted as a tool to accomplish good governance. It focuses in bringing improvements in the service delivery, dissemination of information, transparency, public and private partnership, efficiency and accountability. Government and its numerous agencies being the largest service providers in Bihar specially in rural areas feel the need to make extensive use of ICTs for its major services.[12]

To achieve the targets of good governance in Bihar, the government has taken bold steps to implement e-governance at the grass root levels of Panchayati Raj Institutions. And this effective use to ICT in the affairs of local administration has been termed as e-panchayat. So, e-panchayat has become synonym of e-governance in rural Bihar. e-panchayat is now concerned with the new form of e-governance.

We know that our economy is based on agriculture and people in one way or the other depend on agriculture. A large chunk of our population is poor and socio-economically deprived. More than one-third population lives below poverty-line. So, the state has to take such steps that development of ICTs reaches the deprived section of society. e-panchayat or e-governance is a very bold step taken in this regard. In this context, poor need 'intelligent intermediaries' for using the ICTs who can be drawn from the NGOs working at the grass root level. ICT has become vehicles of enrichment of democratic outlook among the people as the scientific ethos and democratic spirit have the similar nature, viz., not prejudiced with caste, class and regional feelings.

The rural leadership forms an important fabric of rural-socio and political system. Their perception of the local institution goes a long way in improving and delivering the appropriate service to the village community. e-panchayat refers to the application of ICTs by government agencies intending to transform relations with citizens. It deals with the attempts made in the remote areas to implement e-governance in various areas of administration including food, nutrition, health, environment, education, energy, water, electricity, revenue, civil supplies, agriculture, irrigation, civil services and others.

A brief scenario of Bihar needs to be mentioned here. Out of 94,163 sq. km. area of Bihar 92,258 sq. km. belongs to rural Bihar containing 8471 Village Panchayats, 534 Panchayat Samitis and 38 Zila Parishads. This area covers nearly 80 per cent of our population depending on agriculture and traditional occupations.[13] The participation of the rural people in grass root democracy like PRIs will make them efficient in rural environment but their educational backwardness, social-settings, lack of infrastructure, power-shortage, financial crunch, less e-readiness, etc., will make them handicapped. Until or unless they are not equipped properly for the meeting of challenges of the global economy, they will not succeed in achieving the aims of 'Sushasan' through 'e-panchayat'. They not only have to change the traditional modes of living but also have to adopt the new ICTs. They have to be empowered in the area of problems and prospects of use of ICTs and proper management of knowledge.[14]

Keeping in mind all the facts stated above I have attempted in this Research Article to analyse the very conceptual intersections of terms involved for e-panchayat such as governance, good-governance and e-governance. The role of ICTs today in the era of globalization has also worth mentioned. e-panchayat Policy adopted by the Government of Bihar has been illustrated. Initiatives and measures have been reviewed in this regard. Constraints on the ways of ICT revolution have been focused with prospects to remove them and to meet the challenges of the twenty first century. Solutions have been suggested to make Bihar ready for radical change and sustainable development.

Use and Application of ICT

The Worldview

The world is in the midst of a knowledge revolution, complemented by opening up to entirely new vistas in communication technologies. Recent developments in the fields of ICT are indeed revolutionary in nature. Hundreds of million of dollars are being spent on ICTs reflecting a powerful global belief in the transformatory nature of these technologies. ICTs are a diverse set of technological tools and resources to create, disseminate, store, bring value-addition and manage information. Interestingly, ICT when used as a broad tool for amalgamating local knowledge incubated by the communities with information existing in remote data bases and in public domain heralds the formation of a new class of society of the knowledge society.[15] Knowledge thereby becomes the fundamental resource for all economic and developmental activities in the knowledge society of which rural people form an equal part.

The process of synthesis of knowledge possessed across communities, by men and women, with the global pool of knowledge with the scope for further enrichment lays the genesis for knowledge networking.[16] It opens up a new way of interactive communication between government bodies, NGOs, academic and research institutions, and the civil society. It helps communities, both men and women, to take appropriate steps to recognize and document the knowledge they possess and in reflecting this knowledge in a wider social domain for directed change through the use of ICTs.[17]

Knowledge is indeed turned out as a single most important area we need to concern with. If we mean development, we must deal with the issue of knowledge.[18] It is not an overstatement at all when our distinguished scientist and ex-President of India A.P.J. Abdul Kalam pointed out that in the twenty first century, a new society is emerging where knowledge is the primary production resource instead of capital and labour.[19] A new society is emerging and that society's primary source is knowledge[20].

ICT does not include only the internet but a gamut of other tools which could be used individually or in convergence with each other to catalyse the process of change in a manner which reduces the skew in knowledge distribution between rich and poor, educated and uneducated rural and urban, and men and women. The convergence technologies include community radios, internet radios, local areas networks, tele-centres, information kiosks, mobile phones, WAP applications, etc. They often enhance the reach and penetration of the ICT.

ICTs open up a direct window for rural people to the outside world.[21] It entails building up of capacities of women—almost half of the population to overcome social and institutional barriers and strengthening their participation in the economic and political process for an overall improvement in their quality of life. It plays a vital role in empowering them through employment. It creates women entrepreneurs. It gives value-added services to them. It changes their stereotypic roles. It excites them to participate in governance and monitor it. It helps them for service delivery, mobilization and public advocacy.[22]

A view widely held is that science as we know it today is 'the science' which holds the key to the secrets of nature and the modern ICTs are the direct outgrowth of this science. It is this idea that identifies modern technology with highest point of human development and induces among people the fear that not to keep up with the latest of this technology amounts to being left behind in the race of human progress and to wallow in barbarism.[23] Truly speaking, societal empowerment can only manifest from an informed public and the widening use of ICTs can potentially evolve knowledge and power structures that enhance transparency in governance. Public access to alternative information sources through ICTs also means that the public can circumvent government censorship.[24] When governments are ineffective and governance chaotic rather than disciplined, people find their own solutions. Other groups like NGOs and civil societies step in to take the slack and void. ICTs are powerful tools that can engender stronger civil society networks that are better informed and brought together and empower these groups to be more effectively engaged in national development.[25] Dr. Richard Heeks, an e-governance expert based at Britain's Manchester University has gone a step forward to argue that the ICT can facilitate the poor to voice their grievances as well as influence the decision-making process not only as information receiver but also as information provider.[26] It has been argued that good governance is e-governance.[27]

Social applications tend to integrate information technology into large socio-technical systems that involve people, organizations and other technologies and that derive their functionality from the complex interaction of Information Technology with non-technical system elements.[28] The world has shrunk within the 'www' of ICT. No society can afford to go without it. ICT revolution has changed the character of not only the economic world order rather it has affected the social change in its own way.

National Perspective

During the colonial period, much brute physical force and little scientific rationality or technological sophistication were used to prove the machines of capitalism, the decided advantage against other forms or modes of industry. After political independence, it would have been extremely difficult to continue such destructive development as a matter of course.[29]

India began her period of political independence on a note of inadequacy, inferiority and deficiency. Her government decided that something had to be done to bring people and country into the modern age. The state therefore took on the role of developer, of creator of a new civilization, with its own new version of 'temples' and other symbols of modernity for this science became the key. Science proved attractive, for science also remakes.[30] Science recreates definitions, concepts, laws etc. It manufactures new knowledge rather than discovers it and a state which saw itself in terms of a factory for overwhelming production, found in science a most congenital mate in its search for 'progress'. Even the people were sought to be remade as copies of their western counterpart. Ever since the independence, all our developmental efforts have central around industrialization adopted from the modern science and technology of the West. Democracy was defined as participation. The people participated in a pre-conceived design of development set up for their benefit by informed leaders and qualified technocrats.

People became the part of the great adventure of science by consuming its technological wonders. The modern Indian State has rigorously adhered to this specific mode of development in every area of human endeavour, whether it is the making of sugar, furthering of agriculture based on chemicals, the expansion of white revolution, the elaboration of nuclear energy programme or the making of textiles on rotary machines.[31]

The Indian society from time immemorial has nurtured a thinking civilization. It never lived an isolated existence and never displayed xenophobic tendencies.[32] Techno-scientific tradition in India has largely been a synthetic tradition continuously evolving as a result of each politico-cultural interaction with the outside world and social change within the region.[33] In pre-modern times, India was known for its contribution to astronomy, medicine and mathematics. Our society, being one of the oldest civilizations of the world, has been sensitive and responsive to science and technology since ancient times evident from teachings of *Vedas* and discourses of Acharya Charak, Aryabhatta, Varahmihir, Bhaskaracharya, Acharya Kanad and many others.[34] In ancient India medical men, in spite of their scripture orientation, insisted on the supreme importance of direct observation of natural phenomena and on the technique of a rational processing of the empirical data. The ***Charaka Samhita***, an ancient medical text, says, "To one who understands, knowledge of nature and love of humanity are not two things but one.[35] Nothing could illustrate better the links between sciences and developing society like ours. In relatively recent times the relevance of science for the society was not lost either on the colonizers or the colonized. In its very first issue ***The Calcutta Review*** wrote, "the history of science is itself a science and one of the most interesting and important of them all is to trace the stream of discovery from its lofty well head, to follow its various windings, mark its frequent disappearances, its rapids and its stagnancies. It is a work at once of the greatest interests, the greatest importance and the greatest difficulty. The interest of investigation is derived from our very nature and constitution as members of the great human brotherhood".[36]

In India the push for public reforms has brought in its wake the pervasive harnessing of ICTs to achieve declared administrative and social goals. The implementation of e-governance began with National Informatics Centre's efforts to connect all the district headquarters through computer in 1980s. This has typically included connectivity, networking and technology upgradation, selective delivery systems for information and services and an array of software solutions. It is expected that the use of ICT in governance would not only improve the delivery of public services but will also bring into the public domain the issues that have so far been shrouded in secrecy, mitigating corruption in public life. It can also help in improving the systematic deficiencies that allowed the wanton elements both within the government and outside, to selfishly use them for narrow objectives. Civil society, NGOs and professional associations to mobilize opinion and influence decision-making process that affect them are also using ICTs. Government is also using ICTs for electronic publication of draft legislation and statements of direction for public feedback.[37] Government has paid its attention towards ICTs and established various organizations like ICAR, ICMR, CSIR, ISRO, etc., under full-fledged. Science and technology policy 2003 has been formulated and later followed by the others. According to NASSCOM, an apex industry association of software and service companies in India, the e-governance market in India is witnessing year-on-year growth and was estimated to be ₹ 1400 crore in size in 2001-02 and ₹ 2200 crore in 2002-03. The e-governance market grew by 18 per cent in 2002-03 and is the highest growing vertical in the domestic ICTs markets.[38]

Regional Context

We know that our economy is based on agriculture and people in one way or the other depend on agriculture. A large chunk of our population is poor and socio-economically deprived. More than one-third population line below poverty line. So, the state has to take such steps that development of ICTs reaches the deprived section of society. e-Panchayat or e-governance is a very bold step taken in this regard. In this context poor need 'intelligent intermediaries', for using the ICTs who can be drawn from the NGOs working at the grass roots level.[39] ICT has become vehicle of enrichment of democratic outlook among the people as the scientific ethos and democratic spirit have the similar nature, *viz.*, not prejudiced with caste, class and regional feelings.[40]

The rural leadership forms an important fabric of rural socio and political system. Their perception of the local institution goes a long way in improving and delivering the appropriate service to the village community.[41] e-panchayat refers to the application of ICTs by government agencies intending to transform relations with citizens. It deals with the attempts made in the remote areas to implement e-governance in various areas of administration including food, nutrition, health, environment, education, energy, water, electricity, revenue, civil-supplies, agriculture, irrigation and others.

The first principle of good governance is citizen centricity.[42] Bapu, the Father of the Nation, had used the word 'customer' rather than 'citizen'. In that sense, it also applies equally to good 'globalization' because the ultimate objective of promoting globalization is not just to increase wealth of the nations by augmenting the profits of corporate entities and improving the revenues of the governments but to enrich and enhance the quality of life of the citizens.[43] Globalization has also affected the people of the Panchayat through ICTs. 'The poorest and the most helpless man' of Mahatma Gandhi must realize that e-Panchayat is served in the best interest of him.[44]

Bihar: IT Policy, 2008

IT vision of Bihar is that by the end of 2012, Bihar became one of the top five e-governed, IT enabled, e-literate States in the country and is regarded as a preferred destination for IT businesses and is a major supplier of skilled IT manpower. The aforesaid goal would be realized by building core IT infrastructure in the State, ushering in e-governance, providing extensive citizen centric services, promoting an IT education, incentivizing IT business setting up units in the State, regulating IT services and putting in place institutionalized arrangements for implementation and monitoring of IT activities in the State.[45]

The State government has set upon itself the following objectives to implement the strategy outlined above:

(i) **IT infrastructure**
   a. To create world class IT infrastructure and connectivity for e-governance in the State linking its offices from the State headquarters down to districts and Blocks;
   b. To ensure connectivity for Panchayati Raj institutions;
   c. To facilitate setting up of broad band digital networks; and
   d. To encourage NLDOs (National Long Distance Operators) to build robust fibre optic network in the State.

(ii) **e-governance**
   a. To use e-governance to implement government's agenda of good governance;
   b. To improve the internal processes to the government through deployment to IT, administrative reforms, re-engineering and modernization with a view to providing an efficient, responsive, transparent and cost-effective government; and
   c. To take all necessary steps to gain the maximum advantage under the National e-governance plan and the resources available therein for ushering in e-governance in the State.

(iii) **Citizen Services**
   (a) To use IT to bring various services to the people at minimum cost on anywhere anytime basis;
   (b) To bridge the digital divide between urban and rural areas by implementing the scheme of CSC (Common Services

Centre) to provide G2C and B2C services to the citizens at their door steps; and

(c) To undertake computerization of government officers to enable them to respond to citizen's electronic requests for services and information.

(iv) **e-Literacy and IT Education**

(a) To promote measures for in government offices as well as among the masses;

(b) To ensure IT education in schools and colleges; and

(c) To set up dedicated institution for IT Education in public and private sectors.

(v) **IT Industry**

(a) To create a favourable climate in the State for investment in the IT, ITES and knowledge based industries with a view to generating employment and earning income through exports; and

(b) To encourage e-commerce, thereby significantly increasing the contribution of the IT sector to the State GDP.

(vi) **Regulatory Issues**

(a) To devise appropriate legal and regulatory framework for efficient administration of IT and ITES;

(b) To prevent misuse of IT; and

(c) To protect IPR (Intellectual Property Rights), patents and trademarks.

(vii) **Implementation and Monitoring:** To build appropriate administrative framework for implementation and monitoring of IT activities in the State.[46]

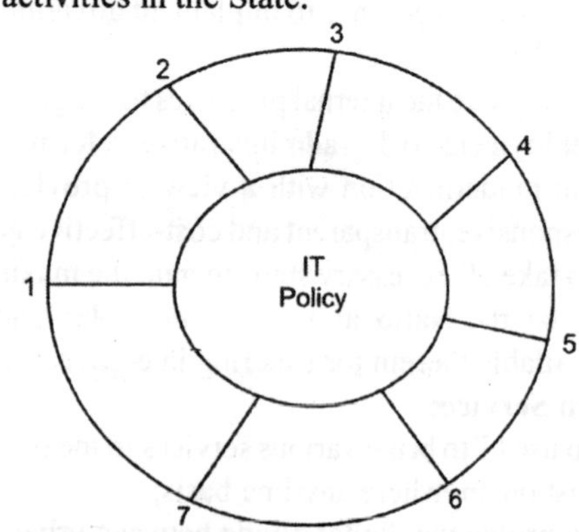

Fig. 6.1: IT Policy: Bihar Road Map[47]

1. Building Core IT Infrastructure in Bihar

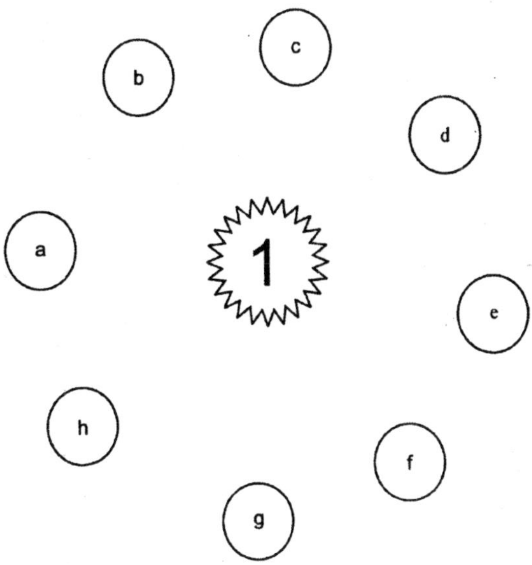

Based on Satelletic Behaviour

(i) BSWAN—Bihar Statewide Area Network under National e-governance Plan core infrastructure initiative, aims at providing 2Mbps (initially) vertical connectivity across the State up to Block level right from the State Headquarters. The SHQ PoP would be located in Patna in conjunction with the State Data Centre.

(ii) Horizontal connectivity—Department of Information Technology is also taking steps to connect all the department offices across Bihar to the nearest BSWAN PoP through Horizontal Connectivity.

(iii) SDC – The other core infrastructure project under NEGP is State Data Centre. The Government of Bihar has already taken initiatives regarding site availability and other pre-installation work such as availability of source power, legal clearance, etc., as per the government of India guidelines and is in a position to immediately take up this task.

(iv) Sec-LAN—DIT has initiated Secretariat Local Area Network Project to connect all government offices in and around the State secretariat through gigabit fibre connectivity backbone.

(v) CSC – Government of Bihar has already taken action to create a network of Common Services Centre, christened 'Vasudha' in all Panchayats of the State as outlets for various services.

(vi) PLC – DIT has planned in its Eleventh Five Year Plan to provide Panchayat Level Connectivity across in all Panchayats in Bihar. This would be a crucial element to facilitate Panchayat level governance and delivery of services in remote corners of the State.

(vii) BIC – The State government would pursue with BSNL, Government of India and USOF an aggressive plan (Broadband Internet Connectivity) to connect rural areas under the National Broadband Plan.

(viii) Departmental Computerization – DIT is taking initiatives to computerize the State departments across the State.

2. e-governance

(i) e-governance framework – The conceptual framework of the State e-governance architecture is provided below:

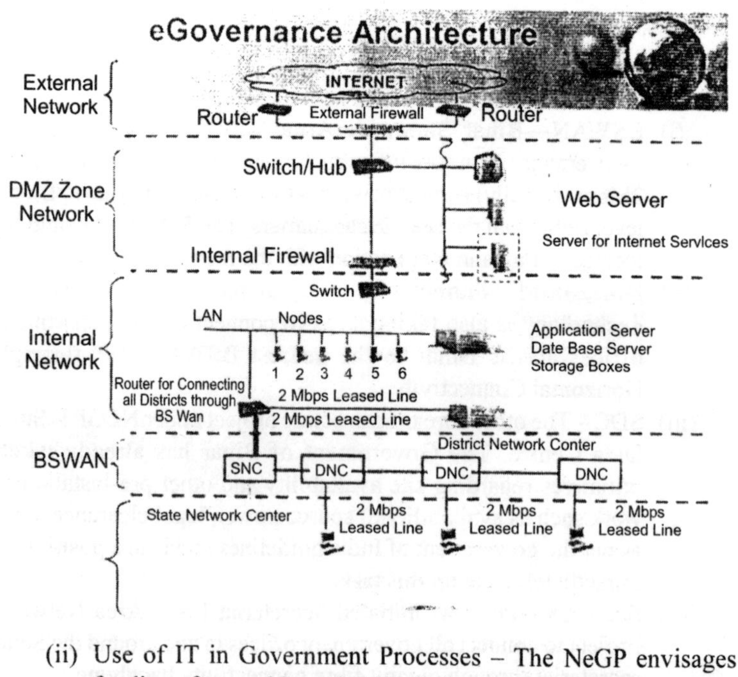

(ii) Use of IT in Government Processes – The NeGP envisages funding of several State-MMPs (Mission Mode Projects) as well as Integrated MMPs. The State would take steps to make full use of these:

(a) State MMPs;
(b) Integrated MMPs;
(c) Other services take ICT at schools, jail computerization, e-muster, Co-Operative Bank computerization, etc.;
(d) Government Process Re-engineering;
(e) Common Standards; and
(f) Capacity Building and Change Management.

(iii) Budgetary and other support –
(a) Each department. shall prepare a 3 years IT Plan.
(b) 3 per cent of the total plan outlay will be earmarked for IT Sector; and
(c) Other provisions.

(iv) Geographical Information System GIS has emerged as powerful tool which has potential to organize complex spatial environment with tabular relationships.

3. Citizen Service

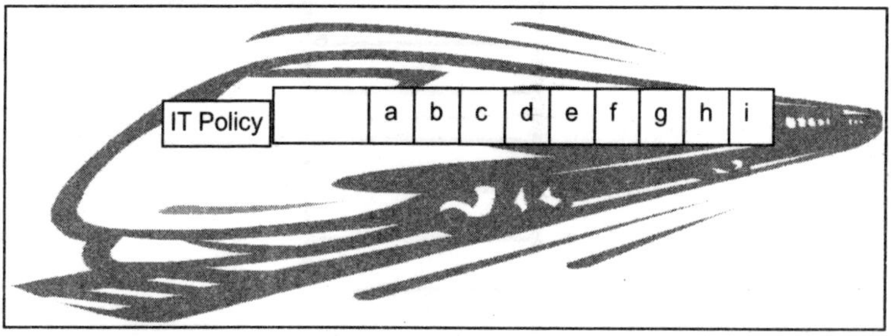

a. Bihar Portal
b. Electronic Delivery of Services through Leverage of IT.
c. e-District
d. CSCs
e. RTI
f. T elemedicine
g. Distance Learning
h. Tourism
i. Wi-Fi City

4. e-Literacy and IT Education

The State government would implement an IT Literacy Plan (ITLP) at the following levels:

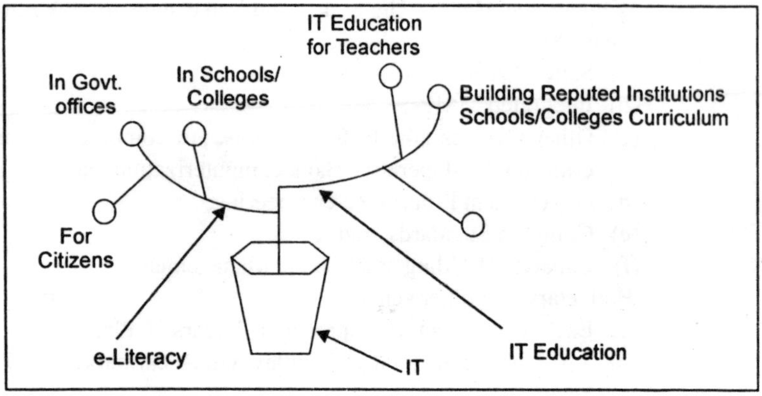

5. *IT Business and Industry*

The policy initiatives in this regard have been structured in the following manner:

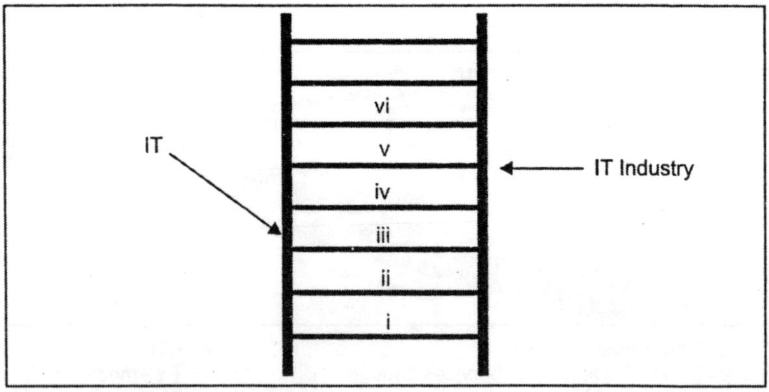

I = Approval and Facilitation measures
II = Fiscal measures
III = Subsidies and Incentives
IV = Procedural Reliefs and Concessions
V = Promotional Measures
VI = Improving Business and Social Infrastructure

6. Regulatory Issues

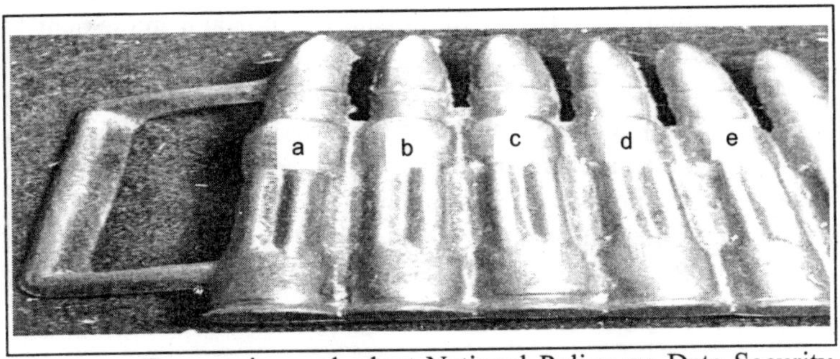

a = To examine and adopt National Policy on Data Security, Privacy and Data Protection and other legal frameworks.

b = To provide a transparent simple and enforceable set of laws.

c = To protect IPR, Patent, copyrights, trademarks etc.

d = To increase awareness of antipiracy and initiate move towards setting up of compliance infrastructure.

e = To set up a high powered IT Security Task Force.

7. Implementation and Monitoring

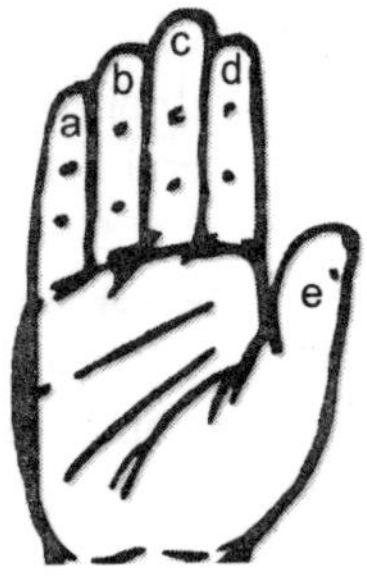

a = BITA (Bihar Information Technology Authority) as the apex body to oversee the comprehensive development of IT sector under the chairmanship of the Chief Minister.

b = DIT (Department of Information Technology) has been created by the State government with effect from 01-04-2007 to act the nodal agency for implementation of the IT policy and computerization within the State.

c = DeGS (District e-Governance Society) shall be constituted in each district. Under the chairmanship of the District Magistrate with representation of various departments. including NIC to formulate, monitor and implement IT scheme or Programmes at the district level.

d = BSEDC (Bihar State Electronics Development Corporation Ltd.) is a Government of Bihar undertaking notified as the State Procurement Agency for IT goods and services.

e = Monitoring and Evaluation, a High Level Committee, shall be constituted and it will be assisted by all departments. BeST (Bihar e-Governance Services and Technology Ltd.) would be the consultant supporting this committee.

e-Panchayat Initiatives: Important Measures taken so far

The Government of Bihar has given its go ahead to implement a ₹ 25.2 crore e-governance project to cover all its 8,479 Panchayats.[48] The Bihar State Electronics Development Corporation (BSEDC) will design the software for the e-governance project in co-operation with the Tata Consultancy Services (TCS). The Infrastructure Leasing and Financial Services (ILFS) will monitor its implementation. Under the project, Panchayat information centres or Panchayat portals called 'Vasudha Kendras' will be set up. This will enable villagers to connect with the outside world and provide affordable and easy access to information about the government and its policies 'Vasudha Kendras' will be connected to all State depots. Through the internet, the government will provide computers and internet connections at the Panchayat level centres. The project aims to establish direct contact with villagers and making the functioning of the government more transparent. According to the plan, eight government departments including the Chief Minister Secretariat will be linked to the State-Wide Area Network (SWAN). Video conferencing facility has also been set up in the State's 38 district headquarters. The State had provided top administrative officials and Ministers with laptops as part of its e-governance initiative recently. Besides, it has also connected all its 38 district headquarters.[49]

In a bid to further hasten its e-governance initiatives as also to usher in greater transparency in its functioning, the State government would hence further inform all the 8,479 Mukhiyas and Panchayat Rozgar Sevak through Internet and SMS, the status of their requests for fund for implementation of projects under the NAREGA (National Rural Employment Guarantee Act).

Besides saving time, the decision is expected to further prod the Panchayat representatives to hasten the pace of the projects implementation as also making the system of fund sanction more transparent and easier.

Today if a villager in a remote Bihar Village wishes to inform himself about say, the price of wheat in the country's wholesale grain 'mandis' or the proper manner of using a particular fertilizer, all he has to do is to key in his query in his Panchayat's Vasudha Kendra CSC (Community Service Centre). This is quite a programme since just three years ago when Bihar was at the bottom in the list of States that had introduced e-governance.[50]

'JANKARI', a Bihar Government initiative to empower people living in the remotest corners of the State to submit applications for information under RTI by using Private or public telephone by dialling 155311, has won the National e-Governance Award, 2008-09 on February 12 this year at the National Conference on e-governance in Goa.[51] JANKARI, the ICT based facilitation centre under RTI Act is a monitoring mechanism for RTI and public grievances. It is another first for the State which happens to be the only one whose RTI applications can be filed on the phone by the entire population of 85 millions scattered over 1162 BSNL exchanges in 19 telecom districts covering 38,475 villages. Authorization was given to review all arrangements including monitoring as well as qualitative analysis on regular basis in all the stakeholders – facilitation centre, Telecom Department, the PIOs, BELTRON (Bihar State Electronics Development Corporation Ltd.), the admission departments NGOs and most importantly feedback from common man. The State government has also set up an independent office of the State Information Commission (SIC) having the powers and the final responsibility to monitor compliance of public authorities to the RTI Act. Chief Ministers Secretariat, Chief Secretary and Department bosses have to keep tabs on babus' responses to public requests and complaining. A cell has been created in the CM Secretariat to monitor movement of complaints[52]. Recently Ministers were provided laptops of I-Dm Lenova comp. each costing the State exchequer ₹ 60,000. State is also providing computers and necessary software to each district and Block officers in order to bring the ICT revolution in the States. The Science and Technology Department has also approved the purchase of over 250 servers, 100 desktop computers and 40 projectors to give a massive boost to the state-non-existent in infrastructure. The State government has also given away brand new luxury SUVs to all its Ministers and (MLAs) at a whopping cost of ₹ 3.8 crores.

After 'Jankari', the Right to Information Call Centre which Bihar pioneered, e-Shakti Call Centre is another initiative of Bihar Government

Chief Minister Nitish Kumar had earlier on February 24, 2009 launched the e-Shakti project in Patna. Around 8.76 lakh village labourers of 14 Blocks have so far been registered under it. The registered labours have been issued e-Shakti biometric cards containing all relevant information about them. Later, payments through bank would be made using the smart card[53].

Chief Minister launched e-Shakti call centre in Patna on October 14, 2009. The centre would help the beneficiaries avail quick and accurate information about work. They can also lodge complaints. The labours just have to make a call on the toll-free number 18003452244. The objective of the call centre is to help the genuine beneficiaries of NREGA (National Rural Employment Guarantee Act) scheme with updated information about work and schemes, identify and solve the problem areas in running the scheme.

e-Panchayats: Certain Constraints

According to NASSCOM, "Now this is time to accept that IT in isolation cannot bring the projected changes in governance under certain constraints are removed".[54] Some of these constraints[55] can be described in the following points:

Social Constraints

In realizing the goal of e-panchayats by using ICTs, there are some social constraints mentioned below which must be removed:

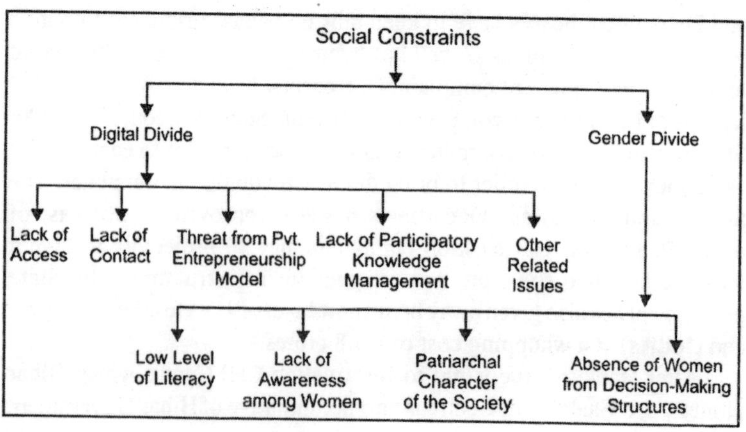

Political Constraints

The will of the actors who control, guide and affect the political process is a determining factor in ensuring '*Sushasan*' through e-panchayats. Where political will exists, e-panchayats can significantly catalyze the reform process towards good governance. In absence of political will, the impact of e-panchayat models will be weak and may not lead to qualitative change in governance process.[56] Today we accept the significance of the role of political leadership in bringing about the required changes. The need of the hour is to change the present brick and mortar governance to e-panchayat by the political leadership at the top. For e-panchayat to succeed, a strong political will and commitment are necessary.[57] Thus, some political barriers[58] mentioned below on the path of progress to e-panchayats must be broken and destroyed.

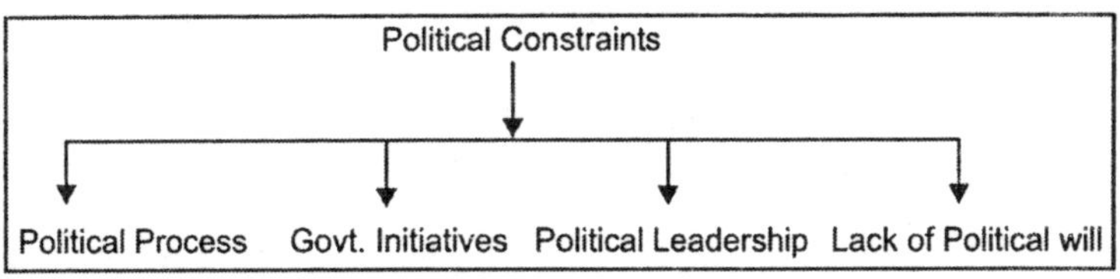

Administrative Constraints

A good administration is prerequisite of e-panchayats. It means the administration must be corruption free, transparent, responsive, moral and accountable.[59] To meet the challenges of e-panchayats today some administrative obstacles[60] mentioned below must disappear:

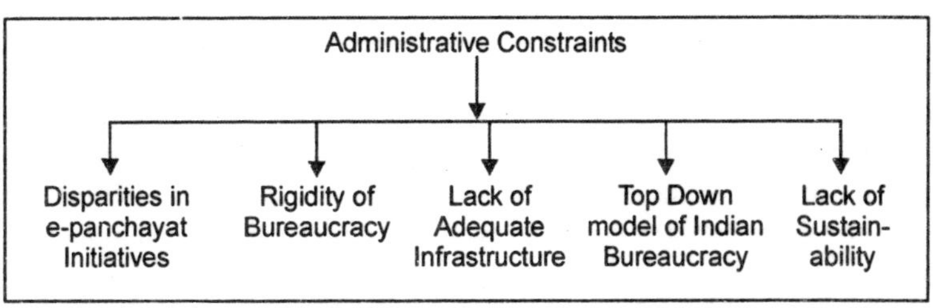

Concluding Remarks

Though to fulfil the 'Swaraj-dream' of 'Bapu' the 'Makers' of the

Constitution of India introduced Article 40 for setting up Village Panchayats, it failed to achieve its required targets. Later, by inserting Part IX (73rd Amendment) and Part IXA (74th Amendment Act 1992) in the Constitution it has been made obligatory for the States to organise local bodies, to hold regular and timely elections to them and to give them appropriate powers and financers to run them well. But the motto of PRIs is human welfare and it can be possibly achieved through '*Sushasan*', an exercise of political, economic and administrative authority in the management of a State's affairs. Public management has rightly brought structural changes in the process of governance in order to involve the beneficiaries themselves and also to seek the fruitful results at the lowest cost.

The outcome of '*Sushasan*' in e-governance and e-panchayat is a forwarding step in this regard. Digital governance, equivalent to electronic e-governance, is the effective use of IT to improve the system of governance. e-governance is an attempt of government to harness ICTs to improve the efficiency of the executive function to the government including the delivery of public series. The application of electronics in the interaction between government and citizens, between government and business and between government and government It is to simplify and improve democratic government and business aspects of governance. It is all about how government, business and citizens interact on an ongoing basis. So, it is same with the system of e-Panchayats. The system of e-governance as well as system of e-panchayat is supported by C^5-Computer Connectivity, Content, Consumer and Confidence.[61]

Bihar Government has taken bold steps to implement e-governance at the grass root level of PRIs. e-Panchayat has become synonym of e-governance and is the new form of '*Sushasan*' in Rural Bihar (Covering 92,258 sq. km. out of total 94,163 sq. km. and containing 8,471 Village Panchayats, 534 Panchayat Samitis and 38 Zilla Parishads) covers nearly 80 per cent population depending on agricultural and traditional occupations. They are empowered in the area of problems and prospects of use of ICTs and proper management of knowledge. ICTs open up a direct window for rural people to the outside world. It can facilitate the poor to voice their grievances as well as influence the decision-making process not only as information receiver but also an information provider. The push for public reforms in India has brought in its wake the pervasive harnessing of ICTs to achieve declared administrative and social goals. e-Panchayat refers to the application of ICTs by government agencies intending to transform relation with citizens. It deals with the attempts made in the remote areas to implement e-governance in various areas of administration including health, food, nutrition, agriculture, water-resources, irrigation, revenue, electricity, energy, education, civil supplies and other services.

Bihar IT Policy 2008 has its own vision. It aims to make Bihar one of the top five e-government and e-literate States by the end of 2012. To make IT-enabled State it has its own IT roadmap. It has to focus on its infrastructure, e-governance, citizens services, e-literacy, IT education, IT industry, regulatory issues and implementation and monitoring issues. Bihar government initiative 'Jankari' won the 'National e-Governance Award 2008-09 in February 2009. Bihar is the first State to start the 'Jankari Project', a brainchild of Chief Minister Nitish Kumar, enables people living in remotest corners of the State to submit applications for information under RTI by using private or public telephone by dialling 155311. The operators receiving the calls in Call Centres draft the application under RTI and send it to the public authorities for providing requisite information to applicants. During the two years, the Call Centres received 22,600 Calls of which 7,070 were to submit applications under RTI, 3,016 calls for filing first appeal and 1,400 calls for filing second appeal before the SIC (State Information Commission).

e-Shakti Project, launched by the CM in Patna on February 24, 2009, covered 8.76 lakh village labourers of 14 Blocks so far been registered under it. e-Shakti biometric cards of these labourers contain all relevant informations about them. It will also cover their payment, work and other schemes including NREGA.

The Government of Bihar has given its go ahead to implement a ₹ 25.2 crore e-governance project to cover all its 8,479 Village Panchayats. The BSEDC will design the software for the e-governance projects in cooperation with TCS. The IL and FS will monitor its implementation. Under the project, PIC or Panchayat Portals called 'Vasudha Kendras' will be set up. This will enable villages to connect with outside world and provide affordable and easy access to information about the government and its policies.

It is true that '*Sushasan*' stands for SMART (Small, Moral, Accountable, Responsive and Transparent) governance. But despite the islands of excellence, e-panchayats have not been able to make rapid progress due to several operational, economic, personnel, planning and implementation issues. Unless certain constraints — social, political administrative and others — are removed, e-panchayat in isolation can not bring the projected changes in governance Policy review and other effective measures must be taken further to strengthen e-panchayat system in Bihar and in the country as a whole.

Refeerences

1. A.K. Mukhopadhyay, *Panchayat Administration in West Bengal* (Calcutta, World Press Pvt. Ltd., 1980).
2. K.C. Wheare, *Modern Constitutions*, 2nd Edition, 1966.
3. D.D. Basu, *Introduction to the Constitution of India* (New Delhi, Prentice-Hall of Indian Pvt. Ltd., 1997).
4. V.T. Patil (ed.) *Studies on Gandhi* (N. Delhi, Sterling Publisher, 1983).
5. Basu, *Shorter Constitution of India* (N. Delhi), Prentice-Hall of India, 1987).
6. E. Vayunandan & D. Mathew (ed.), *Good Governance Initiative in India* (N. Delhi, Prentice-Hall of India, 2003).
7. N. Long & A. Long (ed.), *Battlefield of Knowledge: The Inner-Locking of Theory and Practice in Social Research and Development* (New York, Routledge, 1992).
8. Sumanjeet, "e-Governance: An Overview in the Indian Context". *The Indian Journal of Political Science,* Vol. LXVII, No. 4, Oct.-December, 2006, pp. 857-66.
9. Y.G. Lee & R. Singh "Knowledge Management: Some Theoretical Consideration", *Bihar Journal of Public Administration*, Vol. 1, No. 2 & Vol. 2, No. 1, New Series combined, 2005, pp. 26-37.
10. A. Saxena "e-Governance and Good Governance: The Indian Context", *The Indian Journal of Political Science*, Vol. LXVI, No. 2, April-June, 2005, pp. 313-27.
11. A.P. Yadav, "Information Technology and our Society: An Overview in Context of Poor", n. 9, pp. 91-95.
12. Arjun Sharma, "Good Governance and E-Governance: Prospects for Rural Bihar", *South Asian Journal of Socio-Political Studies*, Vol. 9, No. 1, July-Dec., 2008, pp. 25-28.
13. Sumanjeet, "Contribution of IT Sector in Indian Economy", *Third Concept*, Vol. 209, 2004, pp. 176-81.
14. Eric Schoeniger, "The Future of e-Commerce", *e-Commerce*, January 2002, pp. 45-50.
15. B.K. Dey, "e-Governance in India: Problems, Challenges and Opportunities—A Future Vision", *Indian Journal of Public Administration*, Special No. on e-Governance.
16. C.Malhotra, "Raising Competence of Indian Administration—Role of IIT Training", n. 15.

17. Alvin Toffler, "Tomorrow's Economy: India has to Leverage its Strength in IT to Cross the Final Frontier", *India Today*, 17 March 2003.
18. J. Liebowitz & T. Beckman, *Knowledge Organisation: What Every Manager Should Know* (N.York), St. Lucie Press, 1998).
19. A.P.J. Abdul Kalam, "Vision for 2020: It is the Knowledge Society that will Transform India in to a Developed Nation", *India Today*, 17 March 2003.
20. Peter Drucker, *Post-Capitalist Society* (N. York, H. Collins Publishers, 1993).
21. W.H. Reineke, "The Other World Wide Web: Global Public Policy Networks", *Foreign Policy*, No. 117, Winter, 1999-2000.
22. R. Letha Kumari, *Women in Politics* (Delhi, Authors Press, 2006).
23. Sachchidanand Sinha, "Science, Technology and Appropriate Technology" in G.K.C. Reddy (ed.) *Science, Technology and Transformation* (N. Delhi), Samata Era Publication, 1987), pp. 85.
24. A. Arce & N. Long, "The Dynamics of Knowledge" in N. Long & A. Long (ed.), n. 7.
25. S.P. Bate & G. Robert, "Knowledge Management and Communities of Practice in the Private Sector: Lessons for Modernizing the National Health Science in England and Wales", *Public Administration*, Vol. 80, No. 4, 2002.
26. Richard Heeks, "Information and Communication Technologies, Poverty and Development", *Development Informatics*, <www.man.ac.uk> Institute of Development Policy and Management, Manchester.
27. T.H. Chowdary, "Information Technology for Development: Necessary conditions", *Economic and Political Weekly*, Vol. 37, No. 38, 21 Sep., 2002.
28. V.P. Varma, "Some Aspects of Science and Political Organisation", *Journal of Administrative Sciences*, Vol.VIII, No. 3, Sep.-Dec.-1963.
29. Rajesh Jain, "Emerging Technologies, Enterprises and Markets TECH TALK: Transforming Rural India", *http://www.emergic.org*.
30. Claude Alvares, "Human Rights: The Threat from Modern Science and Technology", n. 23, pp. 28-45.
31. R.K. Sinha, "The Myth of Technology", n. 23 pp. 19-27.
32. Bijanand Prasad, "Relevance of History of Science, Technology, Environment and Medicines (HISTEM) in South Asian Studies", *Review of Politics*, Vol. XVI, No. 2, July-Dec., 2008.
33. A. Rehman (ed.), *Science and Technology in Indian Culture: A Historical Perspective* (N. Delhi, NISTAADS, 1984), pp. 22-23.

34. M.S. Khan, Quadi Said-al-Audalu's Account of Ancient Historical Society (XLO, 1997), pp. 1-31.
35. D. Chattopadhaya, *Science and Society in Ancient India* (Calcutta, 1997), p. 7.
36. *The Calcutta Review*, Vol. 1, 1844, p. 247.
37. M. Moni & N. Vijayaditya, *Convergence and e-Convergence: National Informatics Centre-An Active Catalyst and Facilitator in India (2002)*, http://waterinfo.nic.in News/egover convergence. html
38. NASSCOM, e-Governance in India (Jan. 17, 2003), accelerating, ***http://***
/www.ispai.com/express computer 07 Feb 2003.html
39. Devika Paul, "Rural Development, Panchayati Raj and Burreaucracy in India: A Study in Context of Informatics", n. 9, pp. 65-79.
40. M. Karuppaswamy, "Information Technology and Infrastructure Development: The South Asian Context", *South Asia Survey*, Vol. 7 No. 1, Jan. 2000, pp. 37-41.
41. S.S. Sreekumar, "e-Governance—The Case of Andaman & Nicobar Islands, *The Indian Journal of Political Science*, Vol. LXVI, No. 2, April-June, 2005.
42. D. Nayyar (ed.), *Governing Globalization: Issues and Institutions* (N. Delhi, Oxford University Press, 2002).
43. K. Mamkoottam, *Labour and Change: Essays on Globalisation, Technological Change and Labour in India* (N. Delhi, Response Books, 2003).
44. Alok Ray, "Globalization: Challenges Before India", in P. Bhattacharya & A.R. Chaudhuri (ed.), *Globalisation and India: A Multi Dimensional Perspective* (N. Delhi, Lancer's Books, 2000).
45. Deptt. of Information Technology, Government of Bihar, Patna
46. Information Technology Policy, 2008.
47. Draft, DIT, Government of Bihar, Patna.
48. Published on 10.1.2007, 5:03:00 PM.
49. Government Bureau.
50. Rakesh Verma, "Mukhiyas to get info through SMSes, e-mails", *Hindustan Times*, Patna, 27 May, 2009.
51. Principal Secretary (personnel) Amir Subhani informed the media about the award.
52. Arjun Sharma, n. 12.
53. *htpletters@hindustantimes.com*
54. http://www.ispai.com
55. http://www.emergic.org.
56. http://www.cinsa.info/portal/index
57. http://www.doitpunjab.gov.in/egspeech3.asp
58. http://www.ispai.com/expresscomputer07feb2003.html

59. http://www.infochangeindia.org/features120.jsp
60. http://www.ciol.com/content/news/trends
61. R.K. Verma & N. Sinha, "Good Governance and Rural Development: A Study in Context of People's Participation", *Bihar Journal of Public Administration*, Vol. 1, No. 2 & Vol. 2, No. 1 (Combined). 2005.

7

Technology as an Effective Tool to reduce Mass Poverty

A Study of 'GramSat' e-governance Programme and KBK Districts, Odisha

Ashok Kumar Karna

Introduction

In terms of economic and social sphere, one of the chief features of the KBK regions is that of increasing mass poverty. Poverty continues to be widespread in almost all parts of the KBK districts, Odisha and threatens the very stuff of common men existence in these regions. Indeed, pervasive poverty, destitution and migration have become the plight of the broad masses of the KBK regions. Hence, reducing poverty is presently one of the most challenging problems facing KBK regions of Odisha. Thus, within the backdrop of above stated statements, in one hand this chapter attempts to investigate the anxiety of policy makers in tackling the problems of poverty in KBK districts of Odisha and the other hand examines the problem of poverty, and demonstrates how technology can be applied as an effective tool to alleviate mass poverty in KBK regions.

As we approach the age of science and technology, a major challenge for not only the KBK districts, but also for the whole developing countries is to tackle and find permanent solutions to the pervasive problem of mass poverty which in recent years has reached alarming proportions.

Even, at present[1], the situation has not improved in KBK regions and in many ways it has become worse as evidence by the drop in both rural and urban incomes with higher rate of migration. Hence, in this case we do believe that technology has a leading role to play for poverty alleviation in KBK regions of Odisha. Thus, this chapter scrutinizes how technology can be applied effectively to encounter the growing number of problems[2] caused by the poverty. This chapter has also wrapped the dangers and vulnerabilities of applying technology without due regard and restraint. The necessity for proper and effective acquisition and utilization of technology in developing countries (forget about the KBK regions of Odisha) is becoming more and more evident. This is because technology is not neutral and can be used for different aims and objectives.

> "While technology can be used to promote and enhance social and economic development thereby reducing poverty, the same technology can and is often used as an instrument of exploitation, domination and underdevelopment by those[3] who own and control the technology" (Kopoka : 1996 : 3).

Prospects of ICT as a Technology for Poverty Reduction

ICT (Information and Communication Technology) by its very nature of an operation which are functional in the cyber world and which works with the click of a mouse or a button on a telephone equipment can transcend geographical regions, remoteness of locations and segregated and alienated societies and communities. Its varieties of usages have been a very fascinating experience. The most commonly used components of technology in poverty reduction strategies are the State Wide Area Networks (SWAN), Integrated Voice Recording Systems (IVRS), Internet and Intranet e-mail devices, mobile conferencing and the video conferencing. As services for the poor go online they also become time based and, therefore, their time bound disbursal is part of their very nature. Wherever technology has been properly and appropriately integrated with the communities they have shown increased accountability and transparency of performance. A large number of e-procurement programmes of government have brought down rent seeking and corruption thereby making more funds available for poverty reduction programmes. However, the challenge is for district and State governments to use technology appropriately.

Poverty and Technology: Bridges and Barriers

Once the two situations are understood separately their links are likely to emerge clearly. The concept 'poverty' is very complex. According to World Bank, poverty broadly conceives as the "inability to attain a minimum standard of living" (World Bank : 1990: 26). The World Development Report 2000/2001 states that poverty is a pronounced depriyation in well-being. To be the poor is to be hungry, to lack shelter and clothing, to be sick and not to be cared for, to be illiterate and not schoolcd. Even, at its basic level; poverty can be explained in terms of lack of the means of providing material needs such as food and shelter. Poverty is not just measured by income and consumption. Health, life expectancy, access to clean water and housing are also indicators of human poverty. In this context, the KBK regions are considerably worse off than other parts of Odisha. The situation of access to health service, to sanitation and to safe water, adult literacy and percentage of primary school enrolment to total school age, population and daily calorie supply is miserable.

In these circumstances, technology has been used in all societies throughout history. It allows both individuals and countries either to become more efficient or to do things that were not possible before. One way technology is the sum of knowledge, skills and methods related to production, distribution and consumption of goods and services including the organization thereof (Nyakotey and Adei: 1983:1). Technology has a direct link with the essential segments of the entire fabric of national development or a particular underdeveloped region's development. Hence, it can be argued that if technology can be successfully implemented to the process of overall national development, it can become a potent tool to accelerate development and alleviate mass poverty in the world. Unfortunately this has not happened in Odisha (particularly in KBK regions of Odisha) like Punjab, Rajasthan and Haryana. Especially, in these regions technology has yet to be successfully linked with development objectives and applied to solving social and economic problems. Thus, poverty remains a dominant and terrifying feature of the KBK regions despite the increasing use of modern technology. There is, therefore, urgent need for effective acquisition and application of technology.

> "Technology should be adapted to local conditions and draw on knowledge held by the poor people."[4]

ICTs as a Determinant of the Sustainable Growth of Individuals, Communities and Nations

Many people are there who do not see access to and use of ICTs (Information and Communication Technologies) as a luxury, but instead see them as determinants of the sustainable development of individuals, communities and nations. So, it is a necessity to access and use technology (McNamara: 2000). ICTs are viewed as crucial in the development agenda because they can be used in public administration, business, health and environment.[5] Specifically, it has been argued that ICTs assist in poverty alleviation (Duncombe: 2001) and expand opportunities for economic development.[6]

Access to information provides people with the opportunity "to undertake production, engage in labour markets and participate in reciprocal exchanges" with other people.[7] The growing share of ICTs in world economic output is also cited as evidence of their importance. As evidence, a recent study found that relationship between access to mobile phones and economic growth with its impact is more significant in developing than developed countries (Waverman & Foss: 2005b).

> "Successful projects are led by grass roots based organizations that have the appropriate incentives to work with marginalized groups and are characterized by the use of appropriate technology, local ownership and participation of the community."

In the other hand, an opposing view about ICTs warns that they "will only increase existing inequalities and power relations".[8] Evidence of this is seen from cases showing that areas that have long benefited from excellent physical access and have been dominant politically and economically are the ones benefiting from greater access to information technologies (Niles & Hanson: 2003). The idea that development results from linking the poor nations to ICTs, the internet in particular, is considered a myth (*The Economist*: 2005a:9). There are questions regarding the real effects of ICTs on national development considering the limited evidence regarding its correlation (Heeks: 1999).[9] For instance, while ICTs have been instrumental in the development of India's information technology industry, this has not helped reduce the inequality between the rich and the poor in India's society.[10,11] Finally, for many countries, the utopian ideals of an information society that require investment in ICTs are supplanted by more pressing basic needs (Mahan and Misnikov: 2004). Hence, the view from the middle-ground considers that ICTs can play a role in a country's development if applied appropriately.[12] There is anecdotal evidence that show access to the telephone, for instance, can have a dramatic effect on the quality of life of the rural poor. Historically, however, telecommunications roll-out has generally increased inequality, benefited mostly the wealthy and had little impact on quality of life.[13] Whether ICTs are useful for development, therefore, is dependent on overcoming the same socio-economic barriers that contribute to underdevelopment (Kirkman: 1999). Strategies for using ICTs should, therefore, consider their fit in the global and local context.[14] It also implies the need for innovative public policies to make sure that technologies are not only tools for progress, but are also socially inclusive (UNDP: 2001 and Labelle: 2005).

Capability of Technology on Reduction of Poverty

Technology, the theoretical and factual knowledge of science promises not only to solve those problems which have plagued mankind, but also very possibly to trigger new ones. So, more science with technology is recommended as the probable cures for the new malady. Regardless of whether the problems are poverty, disease, illiteracy or cultural deprivation, science and technology are believed capable of creating those conditions under which peace and equality can rule. Reduction of poverty through technology as a tool of poverty reduction does matter in terms of technology application, sustainability, participation and empowerment of people. Hence, in terms of the capability of technology in reduction of poverty, the conclusions touch upon the importance of indigenous, transparency, participation of people and simultaneous interventions from a number of quarters. However, technology as a tool has led to improvement of plight of large number of people on one hand, and in the other hand it has led to marginalization of large segments of society. Here, this statement put the question mark on the capability of technology in reduction of poverty. Take the example of the continent Africa, where almost the entire continent of Africa (except South Africa) has been bypassed by the flows of the global economy. Although poverty has been dramatically reducing in many parts of the world, a quarter of thc world's people remain in severe poverty (forget about the KBK districts of Odisha). So one way, it is reflecting shameful inequalities and inexcusable failures of national and international policies. Even, in some of the industrial countries, such as the United Kingdom and the US, poverty has risen considerably.[15]

> "If we accept that technology is 'a species of social structure' then it would be easier for us to proceed with its implication on the poor in society."

Anyway, technology has the strength or capability to make a difference to this world and the region like KBK districts of Odisha. The problem is not the tool (technology) but the direction in which it can be utilized. There is a need to evolve a new paradigm in which technology not only produces increase in manufacturing productivity but also touches the lives of downtrodden and those living in the abyss of poverty. So, in this context, it won't be worthless to say that technology on its own is not capable of reducing poverty. Few programmes that have been implemented have rarely reached the intended beneficiaries, especially in the manner required. Reservations, representations and various fiscal benefits have either been fraudulently diverted to ineligible individuals or have been restricted to very narrow elites of the economically weaker and minority communities. Government of India has implemented several schemes and programmes for poverty alleviation, such as IRDP (Integrated Rural Development Programme), TRYSEM (Training of Rural Youth for Self Employment), JRY (Jawahar Rozgar Yojana), PMRY (Prime Minister's Rozgar Yojana), and so on, still there is a large gap between targets set for those schemes and the achievement. In many cases, it is even less than 50 per cent. In such a state of affairs, the desired objectives are difficult to achieve. Hence, there is a need for people themselves getting involved in the poverty alleviation programmes. Particularly, where we do think so that, in e-governance programme the technological operations being controlled by the technological specialists (technological specialist, who keep priority on their own interest rather than the common people). So, one way considering the case of technological specialist, we should not ignore and underestimate the local people's knowledge.

Opportunity, empowerment, and security are the three crucial elements of poverty reduction and these can be accomplished by the use of information and communications technology (World Development Report: 2000/2001). Normally, opportunity makes markets work for the poor and expands poor people's assets, empowerment makes state institutions works better for poor people and removes social barriers, and helps poor people to manage risk. For instance; the case of Gujarat computerized of milk collection centre is worth investigating here. More often than not, these centres are helping ensure fair prices to small farmers who sell milk to dairy cooperatives. Even, this computerized system has increased transparency, expedites processing, and providing immediate payments to farmers. So, we can say technology can change the lives of poor people, but only if policies and projects are designed to exploit its potential. Hence, here it raises the susceptibility of technology on reduction of poverty on its own. People in Odisha have very limited access to information and communication technology. A recent survey of three districts (KBK) in Odisha interpret that only few families have access to a computer or internet connection and some have never viewed television, read a newspaper, or used a telephone.[16] Normally, they get information from family, friends and local leaders—but these informal networks do not satisfy their information needs. So, this can be addressed by policies that increase connectivity and by projects that take into account the constraints facing poor people.

Empirically, innovation is a distributed process generated through interactions among heterogeneous agents (Consoli and Patrucco: 2008). In such a perspective, economic development or poverty reduction is driven by the inter play between the individuals initiatives of specialized actors and the collective processes that are created to harmonize their tasks and align their incentives. So, in another context, technology or innovation on its own cannot reduce poverty alone. So, realizing the potential of poverty reduction for development, technology on its own seems to reach nowhere. It requires attentive public policy formulation and careful project design (innovations) where e-governance, in one way the substitute of good governance have been backfired by higher cost and low returns to ordinary people. Challenging the capability of technology on reduction of poverty on its own, the need of innovations has come out. Here, the point of argument is that without innovations there is no poverty reduction. Recently, various implemented technological based programmes on reduction of poverty have failed to reduce poverty, whereas innovations have succeed. For instance the case of ***'Mahiti Shakti'***[17] based in Panchmahal district, Gujarat and ***'TARAHAT'*** innovation in Bundelkhand, Uttar Pradesh.

Indeed, the thrust of economic development and poverty reduction is the combine outcome of increasing variety in the knowledge base and the creation of specific coordination mechanism. Technology infrastructures are strategic tools to orchestrate inter-organizational coordination within systems of innovation. So, it can be argued that innovation platforms are a particular instantiation of technology infrastructure. Even, somewhere, technology is most effectively deployed in pursuit of some predefined developmental outcome, rather than as an outcome itself. Accordingly, development problems and the strategies to overcome them should be clearly articulated before technological solutions are determined. In many cases, the reverse actually happens; technology is decided upon and then a development opportunity is sought to which it can be applied. Often this leads to the deployment of inappropriate technologies, like computers and internet, when simpler alternatives such as radio and television would have been more appropriate. In addition, computers and the internet tend to deliver maximum output when they are appropriate by the organization and the community to provide assistance with problems that they themselves have identified. One way awareness of technology among the users of the centres is essential.

The Unapproachable Landscape of KBK

Despite concerns and legislative debates poverty remains pervasive in the KBK regions of Odisha. A number of studies reveal that the majority of KBK inhabitants are very poor. For instance, as per the estimates of the 55th round of NSS Survey conducted in 1999-2000, the incidence of rural poverty was as high as 87.14 per cent. Even, at the world level KBK regions is known for its mass poverty. Crores of rupees have already spent for development, still KBK is backward. That is why KBK in twenty first century is still known as an unfortunate landscape of the country (India). Crores of rupees have allotted to the KBK regions in terms of

Table 7.1: Plan outlay of₹ 120 crores under Biju KBK Plan for the Year 2007-08
(₹ 1.5 crores per Block)

Sl. No.	*KBK Districts*	*No.of Blocks*	*Plan Outlay (₹. in crore)*
1.	Koraput	14	21.00
2.	Malkangiri	07	10.50
3.	Nabarangpur	10	15.00
4.	Rayagada	11	16.50
5.	Bolangir	14	21.00
6.	Subarnapur	06	9.00
7.	Kalahandi	13	19.50
8.	Nuapada	05	7.50
	Total	80	120.00

Source: Government of Odisha Planning and Coordination Department, 2006-07.

development and poverty reduction, but maximum amount of that has not reached to the hands of those target groups. For instance, allocated funds to KBK regions in terms of development are shown in Tables 7.1 to 7.4.

Table 7.2: Fund allocated by State and District Sector

Sl. No.	*KBK Districts*	*Biju KBK Fund allocations (₹ in crore)*		
		State Sector	*District Sector*	*Total*
1.	Bolangir	14.00	7.00	21.00
2.	Kalahandi	13.00	6.50	19.50
3.	Koraput	14.00	7.00	21.00
4.	Malkangiri	7.00	3.50	10.50
5.	Nawarangpur	10.00	5.00	15.00
6.	Nuapada	5.00	2.50	7.50
7.	Rayagada	11.00	5.50	16.50
8.	Subarnapur	6.00	3.00	9.00
	Total	80.00	40.00	120.00

Source: Government of Odisha Planning and Coordination Department, 2007-08.

Table 7.3: Biju KBK Plan: 2006-07

Sl. No.	*KBK Districts*	*Amount Allocated (₹ in crore)*	*Expenditure as on 31.03.2008 (₹ in crore)*
1.	Koraput	3.00	2.84
2.	Malkanagiri	2.00	1.84
3.	Nabarangpur	2.50	2.11
4.	Rayagada	2.50	1.92
5.	Bolangir	3.00	2.18
6.	Subarnapur	2.00	2.00
7.	Kalahandi	3.00	2.04
8.	Nuapada	2.00	1.90
	Total	20.00	16.83

Source: Government of Odisha Planning and Coordination Department, 2007-08.

The motivation behind the Tables 7.1 to 7.4 is to highlight the issues of the diversion and misuse of funds and indulge into unaccounted expenditure in which crores of rupees have been spent in KBK regions without making a substantial dent in underdevelopment. The poor people are getting nothing out of that as the corruption rate is high and the

Table 7.4: Biju KBK Plan: 2007-08

Sl. No.	*KBK Districts*	*Amount Allocated (₹ in crore)*	*Expenditure as on 31.03.2008 (₹ in crore)*
1.	Koraput	21.00	5.71
2.	Malkanagiri	10.50	4.64
3.	Nabarangpur	15.00	2.65
4.	Rayagada	16.50	0.63
5.	Bolangir	21.00	0.00
6.	Subarnapur	9.00	0.71
7.	Kalahandi	19.50	1.40
8.	Nuapada	7.50	4.25
	Total	120.00	19.99

Source: Government of Odisha Planning and Coordination Department, 2006-07.

governance system itself is responsible for that. According to Table 7.4, total of 120 crores rupees were granted by the government (since 2006-07) for KBK regions development, but till 31st March, 2008 only 19.99 crores has been utilized. Here it expose the capability of the government on its proper fund utilization and development planning. Hence, though KBK regions is getting crores of rupees (like Biju KBK Plan's 120 crores) as government support for development, still unable to capitalize that for the development of KBK regions. It may be due to bureaucratic malpractices and their unaccountability. So, there is need of proper processing and planning for development, rather than flowing of crores of rupees.

Causes of poverty in KBK are complex and often reflected in the socio-economic situation of a society. The inability of Odisha (KBK in particular) to transform its economy is one of the factors contributing to the state of growing poverty and destitution in the country. Within the rural areas, poverty is severe in regions with unreliable rainfall, poor infrastructural development and the poor access to markets. Many of the young men and women from rural areas of KBK districts are moving in increasing numbers to urban areas and even out of the State with the hope of escaping the ever widening poverty trap that is engulfing rural areas. In many respects, poverty is becoming more and more severe leading to hunger, starvation and even death. At present poverty continues to be widespread in both rural and urban areas in KBK districts with devastating consequences. The persistence of mass poverty in KBK is to a large extent aided by the dwindling economic resources, miss-usage of natural resources and decrease in agricultural productivity. Hence, in this context the introduction and use of modern and improved technologies has in various views a leading role in the alleviation of poverty and human destitution.

Reducing Poverty through 'GramSat' e-governance Programme

According to the data of fund flowing to KBK regions given in the earlier section of this chapter, crores of rupees have been spent in the name of development in KBK regions, but the outcomes towards ordinary people has been very minimal. People of KBK regions are still suffering from starvation, death and so on. Hence, as a solution, the government of Odisha in collaboration with the Central Government has implemented various e-governance programmes to reduce poverty and rural development, for instance, implementation of the 'GramSat' e-governance programme in KBK districts. Theoretically, technology has the potential for reducing mass poverty, so technological based programme like 'GramSat' has the capability for rural development and poverty reduction. But, in reality, its contradictory in KBK regions, the 'GramSat' e-governance programme is just like a cosmetic use for the ordinary people of KBK regions and the outcome is nothing. Still there is corruption, red tapism, lack of accountability and transparency in KBK regions. So, it is obvious that the 'GramSat' e-governance programme has the weaknesses for development and poverty reduction in KBK regions. More often than not, 'GramSat' e-governance programme is completely a technological based programme and there is lack of participation of local or ordinary people of KBK regions. The technological specialists have the monopoly in the operation of such kind of programme. It is totally a failure of proper processing of such type of e-governance programme. Here, the justification is that there is need of proper processing, local peoples participation and appropriate use of technology behind the successful implementation of an e-governance programme (especially which introduce for rural development and poverty reduction, because an e-governance programme succeed in a region may not succeed in another region).

'GramSat' e-governance programme was launched as a technology driven device or strategy for rural development. It reached villages without making a dent in their underdevelopment. Intriguing aspects is that e-governance which should be increasingly participatory has become a tool to distance people and deepen divides in societies, hence have proved to be neither sustainable nor replicable. Practically, such types of e-governance programmes have backfired with higher costs and low returns to the ordinary people and have become an end itself through a coterie of complacent bureaucracy and vendor driven ICT companies. So, here the argument is that technological interventions (especially in underdeveloped and backward regions like KBK, Odisha) also need a support structure to facilitate the process of the implementation and result in fruitful outcomes. One way, the need of participatory e-governance giving importance to local people's knowledge is indispensable. Otherwise the incomplete implementation of such kinds of e-governance programmes may be hazardous or perilous to poverty regions like KBK districts of Odisha.

The level of technology in the KBK regions (especially in rural areas) is rudimentary. The technological based programme has failed to deliver good services for the ordinary people residing in KBK regions and becomes an end itself. Practically, it is because of inappropriate application of technology, lack of innovation and participation and the monopoly of technological specialists (normally, who control those technological based e-governance programmes). So, it is clear that technology on its own is not capable of reducing poverty. There is an argument that information and communication technology is creating new opportunities that can be seized to support human development and poverty reduction strategies.[18] However, at the same time, it also clarifies that ICT on its own cannot leapfrog the old institutional and organizational weaknesses of a region (for instance; KBK regions of Odisha).[19] So, there is need of appropriate use of technology for rural development and poverty reduction.

Appropriate and Effective Use of Technology for Poverty Reduction

The challenge for KBK as well as for other regions of the world is to find means and ways of tackling the diverse and complex problem of poverty and destitution, particularly in rural areas. One way of achieving this objective is by the introduction and use of appropriate technologies. The extent to which technology is appropriate can only be determined by an examination of the degree to which it is serving to meet the basic needs of the rural population. Transforming technology into a potent tool with which to fight poverty and human destitution should centre on such question as: how best and by what means can relevant technology be transformed and adopted by the rural poor (which have the potential of reducing poverty). How can technology be fascinated and integrated into the local economy such that it can be effectively used to alleviate poverty and how can build up indigenous/local technological capabilities (both human and material). Understanding of these key questions will shed light on how technology can effectively be applied to solve the ever-increasing problem of poverty and human destitution.

If technology is to become an effective weapon against mass poverty, a clear development of a comprehensive technology policy is essential. In other words, a policy which will be able to address specific requirements/problems and needs of the rural poor sector and to co-ordinate them to a much focused national science and technology policy is essential. The technology that can be effectively applied to alleviate poverty in KBK regions must be technology that does not marginalize the people, impose unbearable burdens on them or alienates rather than mobilizes them. It meant to say that the application of technology to the problem of poverty or pro-poor governance required human centred holistic strategy.

Concerning the case of 'GramSat' e-governance programme and rural development in KBK districts of Odisha, it is clear that the use of technology alone is not sufficient to overcome the growing problem of poverty. Technological development has to be supported by corresponding political processes that assure human rights, political stability, political empowerment and public accountability. In reverse, this will ensure that the rural population has some say in the choice of technology that they think is most appropriate to their needs. Hence, the task of rural development and reducing poverty in KBK regions can be advanced by simultaneously acquiring and using appropriate technologies. Also by attending to the creation of an indigenous technological capability that would be able to respond to the needs and requirements of those suffering most from poverty. The problems and needs of the rural poor must first be identified and understood before any plan or strategy for introducing or using modern technology in the rural sector is adopted. Clean understanding of the causes and manifestation of poverty in rural areas as well as identifying the needs of the rural poor is, therefore, essential if technology is to be applied successfully to solve the problem of poverty and human destitution.

Indeed, mere application of technology is not sufficient to alleviate poverty in KBK. A local technological capability has to be established so as to ensure effective use of both traditional and modern technology. To realize the pro-poor potential of ICT requires attentive public-policy formulation and careful policy design. Insufficient information and communication infrastructure, high access costs and low levels of education have so far bestowed the benefits of ICT on the better off, urban segments of the population rather than on the poor and rural areas. In order to reach the poor, policies that foster the supply of low cost and accessible telecommunications and information technology infrastructure are needed. Even, the success of ICT projects and programmes for development also depend on policies that promote the demand of ICT. These policies include the provision of locally contextualized information and pro-poor services, as well as investment in ICT training and awareness rising campaigns.

Furthermore, it is also argued that successful projects are led by grass roots based organizations that have the appropriate incentives to work with marginalized groups and are characterized by the use of appropriate technology, local ownership and participation of the community, financial sustainability and the use of monitoring and evaluation techniques.[20] The careful formulation and design of national strategies to promote the information society is essential for countries to realize the potential of ICT for human development.[21] Specifically, an effective mix of public policies to foster both the supply and the demand of ICT is required to improve the poor people's lives and to contribute to equitable development. Supply side policies focus on increasing connectivity and lowering information infrastructure costs and are crucial prerequisite for the poor people to be able to access ICT. Low cost access to information infrastructure is the basic necessity, but insufficient condition to reach the poor, as inadequate or absent connectivity, expensive hardware and software and unstable power supply reduce the economic viability of ICT projects (Kirkman: 1999). In the process of increased globalization, economies of the world have become more integrated whereby information technology plays a major role in it (Odedra and Straub: 1995). In that perspective, information technology play a part in development with modernization, it can be seen as a potential to close the gap among nations (Goldstein and O'Connor: 2000).

Complacent Bureaucracy and Participatory Systems

Usually, it is a matter of concern to raise the debate of complacent bureaucracy and vendor driven ICTs companies, when we do talk about the weaknesses and unsuccessful implementation of e-governance programmes. Basically, this section of the chapter deals with the case, how complacent bureaucracy and vendor driven ICTs companies have been being the root cause of failure of e-governance programmes (especially implemented for rural development and poverty reduction). In reality, maximum of e-governance programmes have been an end itself, due to the complacent bureaucracy and vendor driven ICTs companies (for instance, the case of Odisha, Punjab and Haryana). Particularly in rural areas bureaucrats are ignoring the local peoples' knowledge and their interests, giving priority to their own interests. Hence, as a result, in one hand the bureaucrats and the technological specialists who are controlling the technological based programmes are completely controlling such kind of development programmes denying ordinary peoples' participation. So, it is a natural fact that such kind of technological based programmes are becoming an end itself, rather than an effective tool for reducing poverty and rural development. Here, the case of lower returns of 'GramSat' e-governance programme towards ordinary people development of KBK regions will be the best example to defend the aforesaid statement.

In fact, though the concept of 'governance' is changing day-by-day in terms of development and socio-economic well-being of common people, the age old natures of government still exists. Hence, first of all there is a need to change those traditional natures of government to realize the complete sense of the changing concept of governance. Otherwise, with the existence of such kind of 'government pathology', technology would never be a successful tool for reducing poverty in rural areas. So, there is need to check the complacent bureaucracy and vendor driven ICTs companies to make e-governance programme successful. And as a solution, there is need of participatory approach to realize the benefits of e-governance or technological based programmes in the context of poverty reduction and well-being of ordinary people. Here it means to say that the need of participatory e-governance is essential, as because technology on its own is not capable for reducing poverty. Technology to be an empowering tool for poverty reduction and development, knowledge networks have to be truly open, participatory and demand-driven (Scarf and Hutchinson: 2003:3). In this context, there is an argument that empowerment is achieved by the people developing their own solutions, rather than having them imposed or imported from outside.[22] The rationale to give this argument is to remind the monopoly of technological specialists and to say that, the technological based programmes should be processed by the participation of the local peoples, rather than by the domination of technological specialists (because those technological specialists are like imported from outside). Participatory approach put the knowledge, voices and rights of users at the centre of the design process.[23] Hence, it is important to create a positive context for participatory design by supporting and enhancing communication between actors and by actively involving users from the beginning to the end.

Issues related to the Role and Impact of ICTs in Development

Of the many issues related to the impact and role of ICTs in development, the "digital divide" has gained much attention. The digital divide refers to "situations in which there is a marked gap in access to or use of ICT devices".[24] There is the view that the idea of a digital divide is passé or irrelevant because those who need ICTs in the more developed countries already have them and those who do not have access do not really need them.[25] There are anecdotal evidences however, that access to ICTs can make a difference to people who have been deprived of it (Goldstein & O'Connor: 2000, and Chiung: 2003). Furthermore, there is clear evidence that such a divide exists between and within countries (Campbell: 2001, UNDP: 2001). It has also been argued that while access to ICTs has increased in all parts of the world, the pace of diffusion in the developed countries has occurred at a faster rate than in the developing world, thus increasing the divide between them (Rodriguez & Wilson: 2000, Campbell: 2001). Even, the contribution of new technologies does not necessarily address the divide that exists within societies, such as the differences in the level of access between men and women, the rich and the poor, urban and rural areas, and people with different levels of education (Keller: 1977 and Martin: 1991).

Finally, if we do think technology as an effective tool for development and poverty reduction, then the issue of whether the digital divide is increasing or not, is less important than the question of how to bridge the divide.

> "The issue of whether the digital divide is increasing or not, is less important than the question of how to bridge the divide."

Hence, providing access to basic services should be universal. In the same spirit, policies that deal with bridging the ICT divide should be more commonly referred to as universal service/universal access policies. Universal service and universal access policies mean the sense of affordability, accessibility and quality of service. At the same time, when we speak about access, what we really mean is access to information, knowledge, and communications opportunities, not access to one specific service or technology.

The Capability Approach, Human Development and Universal Access to ICTs

Human development is about much more than the rise or fall of national incomes. It is about creating an environment in which people can develop their full potential and lead productive, creative lives in accordance with their needs and interests. Development is thus about expanding the choices people have to lead lives that they value. And it is thus about much more than economic growth, which is only a means—if a very important one—of enlarging people's choices (UNDP: 2001:9). Embarrassing the statement given by UNDP, Sengupta[26] (2000) says, if improvement of people's well-being is the objective of development, then economic growth.... would not be an end in itself. It can be one of the ends, and it can also be a means to some other ends, when 'well-being' is equivalent to the realization of human rights" (Sengupta: 2000:568). At the same time, the same argument can be made about universal access to ICTs. Access to ICTs, just like economic growth, can expand people's choices, be an end or a means to another end and can be linked to other human rights. For instance, access can be seen as adding to people's capability to participate in the potential benefits that the information society brings.[27] In particular, it is also a prerequisite for peoples' participation in 'digital democracies' (Catinat & Vedel: 2001) and is also needed to protect people's rights to communicate and access information and knowledge (Hamelink: 2003).

In a similar manner, the way development and the information society have been traditionally measured have certain similarities: development, as usual is measured in terms of Gross National Products (GNP) and Gross Domestic Products (GDP). While on the other hand, access to information and communication technologies has been traditionally measured in terms of the growth in the infrastructure through number of Internet Service Providers (ISPs), number of computers per capita, etc. However, in the light of above those statements the human development and the capability approach, traditional measures of development and the information society should also change and be more human-centred (rather than technology oriented). For instance, economic conceptions of development have begun to acknowledge a more people-centred approach. This came as a result of evidence that showed how economic growth did not necessarily lead to poverty reduction.

As with the human development index, it is increasingly becoming apparent that policies must coordinate the construction of both human and technological capabilities in order to benefit from the potential applications of new ICTs. In measuring indicators for sustainable information societies, the United Nations Commission for Science and Technology for Development (UNCSTD) for instance, includes, experience, skills and knowledge as critical components in the development of information societies aside from infrastructure (Mansell and Wehn: 1998).[28] These capabilities are needed to function effectively in today's information society. It means that society also has to move beyond techno-economic measure and understanding of ICT and development (Van: 2000) and beyond access and focus instead on people and how they use ICTs (Norrish: 1998, Soeftestad & Sein: 2003). That's why some intellectuals believe that Sen's capability approach is useful for understanding people's use of ICTs for development (Mansell: 2002).

The situations people find themselves in (i.e., age, wealth, gender, education, location) affect their freedom.[29] Their freedom, in turn, is a factor in their capability to make use of ICTs. Hence, some people from the outset could not afford to use a telephone even when it is provided, or some people cannot get to a telephone because of where they are. Also, even when people are capable of using ICTs, they have the freedom to choose whether to apply it in their lives or not. These are sometimes a function of their own perceptions of its value and utility in their home-life and work. Hence, only when people are truly free, capable and choose to apply ICTs in their lives will the use of ICTs be realized.

Rationale behind the Need of Participatory e-Governance

Technology which combines authoritative controls over both knowledge storage and communications cannot bring any fundamental change in society such as radical poverty eradication drive unless it is democratically transformed. One way ICT has redrawn the map of democracy and participation across the world. So, there is need to rethink about e-governance in terms of participatory approach.

According to Roger Harris[30]:

- Technology alone is insufficient for significant benefits to emerge.

- Technology alone does not have the capability to transform bad development into good development, but can make good development better.
- An effective application of technology needs proper processing, participation and innovations.

In rural settings in developing countries where the vast majority of poor people live, it is always a challenge to install the technological infrastructure, but the task is relatively simple. Hence, for the following points we are in need of participatory e-governance:

- To challenge the autocracy of technical specialists deployed in e-governance programmes.
- For the proper or complete access of poor people of those existing kiosks or e-governance programmes implemented in their local region (this is so because, even if e-governance programme like 'GramSat' implemented in rural areas, there is no guarantee that the poor will access, and its happening).
- To raise the awareness about the potentiality of technology (basically ICTs) among the poor because unawareness among the poor about the potentiality of ICTs is an obstacle on the way of failing of e-governance programme.
- To upgrade the technological skills of common people who are the beneficiaries of those e-governance programmes.
- To reduce the gap (digital divide) between the rich and the poor people with a balance outcomes.

Indeed, participatory e-governance is inevitable in the present imbalance world for the effective outcomes of technological applications. In other words, when we talk about the technological based or e-governance programmes in the context of pro-poor governance for the socio-economic well-being of the common people, the participation of those local peoples should be taken into consideration. So in reality, there is need of participatory e-governance for pro-poor governance. Last but not the least, in the context of pro-poor governance simultaneously technology, innovations and people's participation has a greater role in poverty reduction from grass roots level as successful e-governance projects characterized by local ownership and the participation of the community. Grass roots intermediaries and the involvement of the community are the key factors that foster local ownership and the availability of content and services that respond to the most pressing needs of the poor.[31]

Conclusion

Indeed, technology may not be capable on its own for reducing poverty, but have the capacity to reduce poverty. The only thing, we need to do, to realize technology as an effective tool to reduce mass poverty is to promote and enhance technology with proper processing and peoples' participation. As a result then there will be promotion, and enhancement of socio-economic development in the society through technology as an effective tool of reducing mass poverty. Otherwise technology will be an end itself, rather than as a means to alleviate mass poverty. And, in one hand, the technological based programme will be still incapable to reduce poverty on its own, and other hand there will be a question mark on the sustainability of innovations. To be sure, new trends in technology and high tech machines are not always synonymous with poverty alleviation and development. Adapting and improving on pre-existing, traditional ways is often more effective than using the newer technologies. Infusion of capital or technology is not a solution to the problem of poverty. As earlier mentioned, it is a multifaceted issue and requires at various level. Merely putting in computers in the villages is not a complete solution. The reality is that there are a large number of people who are illiterate, are unemployed and need to be employed meaningfully so that they can earn their livelihoods. Last but not the least, the solutions should be generated by proper processing and the communities themselves rather than from the outside.

Notes

1. This is a personal observation of (January-February, 2009) the field assessment of KBK regions; Odisha and an intuition being an inhabitant of that region.
2. Problems like hunger, starvation, death and so on.
3. Basically, here the term 'those' would like to expose that the e-governance programmes (those technological based programmes) are normally controlled by technological experts and they keep their interests in priority over the interests of common men.
4. World Bank. June 2002. *Using Information and Communication Technology to Reduce Poverty in Rural India,* p. 4.

5. This is a statement given by the World Summit on the Information Society, held on December 2003, URL: www. WSIS-03/GENEVA/DOC/4-E (Accessed on 20th of January, 2012).
6. World Bank.1998. *World Development Report 1998-99: Knowledge for Development.* The World Bank: Oxford University Press.
7. Ellis F. 2000. *Rural Livelihoods and Diversity in Developing Countries.* Oxford: Oxford University Press, p. 31.
8. Nulens, G. 2000. "Information Technology in Africa: The Policy of the World Bank" *in Information Technology in Context: Studies from the Perspective of Developing Countries,* Avgerou, C. & Walsham, G. (eds), Ashgate. England, p. 64.
9. *Heeks, R.* June 1999. "Information and Communication Technologies, Poverty and Development." *Development Informatics.* Working Paper No. 5.
10. United Nations Development Programme (UNDP) 2001. *Human Development Report 2001: Making New Technologies Work for Human Development.* Oxford University Press.
11. Warschauer, M. 2004. *Technology and Social Inclusion: Rethinking the Digital Divide*. Cambridge Massachusetts: The MIT Press.
12. Soeftestad, L. T. & Sein, M. K. 2003. ICT and Development: East is East and West is West and the Twain may yet Meet. *The Digital Challenge: Information Technology in the Development Context,* Krishna, S. & Madon, S. (eds), Ashgate, pp. 63-82.
13. Forestier, E.; Grace, J. and Kenny, C. 2003. "Can Information and Communication Technologies be Pro-Poor?" Telecommunications Policy 26 : 623-646.
14. Volkow, N. 1995. *The Role of Information Technology in Developing Countries in the Process of Globalisation.* Odedra-Straub, M.; Okot-Uma, R. & Cyranek G. (eds.). 1995. *Information Technology and Globalisation: Implications for Developing Countries.* Commonwealth Secretariat.
15. UNDP.1997. *Human Development Report.* New York: Oxford University Press.
16. This is a personal observation during the field survey of KBK districts, Odisha in January-February, 2009.
17. Mahiti Shakti innovation is known as the power of information. It is a Government to citizens' project with an aim of empowering people. It involves creation of a website in local language (Gujarati) and establishment of kiosks in villages with properly trained people. The kiosks' owner is responsible for everything. It also aims at reducing the community and hassles of rural masses associated with availing of various schemes related benefits, certificates and so on.

18. Harris, Roger, and Rajesh Rajora. 2006. *Empowering the Poor: Information and Communication Technology for Governance and Poverty Reduction: A Study of Rural Development Projects in India.* New Delhi: Elsevier Publications Pvt. Ltd.
19. Cecchini, Simone, 2007. *Digital Opportunities, Equity, and Poverty in Latin America.* Latin America: United Nations Economic Commission, p. 1.
20. *Ibid.*, p. 3.
21. *Ibid.*, p. 8.
22. O'Malley, D., and O'Donoghue, G. 2001. *NGOs and the Learning Organisation.* London, UK: British Overseas NGOs for Development.
23. Muller, M. 1993. *Participatory Design: The Third Space in HCI, IBM,* URL:http://domino.watson.ibm.com/cambridge/research.nsf/0/56884f3de38f806285286aaf005a45ab//$FILE/muller%20chapter%20v1-2.pdf (Accessed on 22nd of February, 2012).
24. Campbell, D. 2001. "Can the Digital Divide be Contained? The Digital Divide: Employment and Development Implications." *International Labour Review* 140 (2) : 1.
25. Warschauer, M. 2004. *Technology and Social Inclusion. Rethinking the Digital Divide.* Cambridge Massachusetts: The MIT Press.
26. Sengupta, A. 2000. *Realizing the Right to Development.* Institute of Social Studies: Blackwell Publishers 31: 553-578.
27. Mann, C.L. 2003. "Information Technologies and International Development: Conceptual Clarity in the Search for Commonality and Diversity." *Information Technologies and International Development* 1(2): 67-79.
28. Mansell, R. and U.Wehn. 1998. *Knowledge Societies: Information Technology for Sustainable Development.* Oxford: Oxford University Press, URL: http://idl-bnc.idrc.ca/dspace/handle/123456789/14888 (Accessed on 3rd March, 2012).
29. Sen, A. 1999. *Development as Freedom.* Oxford: Oxford University Press.
30. Harris, Roger, and Rajesh Rajora. 2006. *Empowering the Poor: Information and Communication Technology for Governance and Poverty Reduction: A Study of Rural Development Projects in India,* New Delhi: Elsevier Publications Pvt. Ltd.
31. Cecchini Simone, and Christopher Scottb. 2003. "Can Information and Communications Technology Applications Contribute to Poverty Reduction? Lessons from Rural India." *Information Technology for Development* 10: 73–84.

References

Campbell, D. 2001. "Can the Digital Divide be Contained? The Digital Divide: Employment and Development Implications." *International Labour Review* 140 (2): 1.

Catinat, M., and T. Vedel. 2001. "Public Policies for Digital Democracy." In *Digital Democracy: Issues of Theory and Practice*. Hacker, K.L., and Dijk, J. Van (eds.). Sage Publications: 184-208.

Cecchini, Simone. 2007. *Digital Opportunities, Equity, and Poverty in Latin America*. Latin America: United Nations Economic Commission, p.1.

Cecchini Simone, and Christopher Scottb. 2003. "Can Information and Communications Technology Applications Contribute to Poverty Reduction? Lessons from Rural India. " *Information Technology for Development* 10: 73–84.

Chiung, C.S. 2003. *Gender Governance: An Empowering Tool for e-communities*? Singapore: Paper Presented in the AMIC Annual Conference.

Consoli, Davide; and Pier Paolo Patrucco. 2008. "Innovation Platforms and the Governance of Knowledge: Evidence from Italy and the UK." *Economics of Innovation and New Technology* 17(7-8). URL: http://www.tandfonline.com/doi/abs/10.1080/10438590701785694. (Accessed on 7th of January, 2012).

Duncombe, R.A. 2001. *Information, Technology, and Small, Medium and Micro Enterprise Development in Botswana*. Doctor of Philosophy Thesis, Institute for Development Policy and Management.

Ellis F. 2000. *Rural Livelihoods and Diversity in Developing Countries*. Oxford: Oxford University Press, p. 31.

Forestier, E.; Grace, J. and Kenny, C. 2003. "Can Information and Communication Technologies be Pro-Poor?" *Telecommunications Policy* 26: 623-646.

Goldstein, A. and O'Connor, D. 2000. *E-commerce for Development: Prospects and Policy Issues*. Technical Papers No. 164, OECD Development Centre,

URL: http://ideas.repec.org/p/oec/devaaa/164-en.html (Accessed on 2nd January, 2012).

Government of Odisha. Planning and Coordination Department, Development Report, 2006-07/08.

Hamelink, C. 2003. "Human Rights for the Information Society." In *Communicating in the Information Society*. O' Siochru, S., and Girard. B. (eds) UNRISD, URL:http://www.crisinfo.org/content/view/full/231/ (Accessed on 28th January, 2012).

Harris, Roger, and Rajesh Rajora. 2006. *Empowering the Poor: Information and Communication Technology for Governance and Poverty Reduction: A Study of Rural Development Projects in India.* New Delhi: Elsevier Publications Pvt. Ltd.

Heeks, R. 1990. "Technology Policy Making as a Social and Political Process: Liberalizing India's Software Policy." *Technology Analysis and Strategic Management*, 2(3): 275-291.

Heeks, R. June 1999. "Information and Communication Technologies, Poverty and Development." *Development Informatics*. Working Paper No. 5.

Kirkman, G. 1999. *It's More Than Just Being Connected: A Discussion of Some Issues of Information Technology and International Development*. Massachusetts: Massachusetts Institute of Technology, Cambridge.

Labelle, Richard. 2005. *ICT Policy Formulation and e-Strategy Development: A Comprehensive Guidebook.* UNDPAPDIP : Elsevier Publications, URL:www.apdip.net/publications/ict4d/Comprehensive Guidebook.pdf (Accessed on 18th January, 2012).

McNamara, K.S. 2000. "Why be Wired? The Importance of Access to Information and Communication Technologies." *TechKnowLogia.*

Mann, C.L. 2003. "Information Technologies and International Development: Conceptual Clarity in the Search for Commonality and Diversity." *Information Technologies and International Development* 1(2): 67-79.

Mansell, R., and Wehn, U., (eds.) 1998. *Knowledge Societies: Information Technology for Sustainable Development.* Oxford: Oxford University Press.

Muller, M. 1993. *Participatory Design: The Third Space in HCI, IBM,* URL: http://domino.watson.ibm.com/cambridge/research.nsf/0/56884f3de38f806285286aaf005a45ab//$FILE/muller%20chapter%20v1-2.pdf (Accessed on 22nd of February, 2012).

Niles, S., and S. Hanson. 2003. *A New Era of Accessibility.* URISA Journal 15. APA I, URL:www.urisa.org/files/nilesvol15apa1-4.pdf (accessed on 2nd February, 2012.)

Nulens, G. 2000. "Information Technology in Africa: The Policy of the World Bank" in *Information Technology in Context: Studies from the Perspective of Developing Countries*, Avgerou, C. & Walsham, G. (eds), Ashgate. England, p. 64.

O'Malley, D., and O'Donoghue, G. 2001. *NGOs and the Learning Organisation*. London, UK: British Overseas NGOs for Development.

Sen, A. 1999. *Development as Freedom.* Oxford: Oxford University Press.

Sengupta, A. 2000. "Realizing the Right to Development." *Institute of Social Studies*: Blackwell Publishers 31: 553-578.

Soeftestad, L. T. and Sein, M.K. 2003. "ICT and Development: East is East and West is West and the Twain may yet Meet." *The Digital Challenge: Information Technology in the Development Context*, Krishna, S. & Madon, S. (eds), Ashgate, pp. 63-82.

The Economist. 12 March 2005a. "The Real Digital Divide." *The Economist*: 9.

UNDP.1997. *Human Development Report*. New York: Oxford University Press.

United Nations Development Programme (UNDP). 2001. *Human Development Report 2001: Making New Technologies Work for Human Development.* Oxford: Oxford University Press.

Van Audenhove, L. 2000. "Information and Communication Technology Policy in Africa: A Critical Analysis of Rhetoric and Practice." In *Information Technology Context: Studies from the Perspective of Developing Countries*. Avgerou, C. & Walsham, G. (eds.). England: Ashgate: 277-289.

Volkow, N. 1995. "The Role of Information Technology in Developing Countries in the Process of Globalisation." In *The Information Technology and Globalisation: Implications for Developing Countries*. Odedra-Straub, M.; Okot-Uma, R. & Cyranek G. (eds.) Commonwealth Secretariat.

Warschauer, M. 2004. *Technology and Social Inclusion. Rethinking the Digital Divide.* Cambridge Massachusetts: The MIT Press.

World Bank.1998. *World Development Report 1998/99: Knowledge for Development.* The World Bank: Oxford University Press. World Bank, 2001.

World Development Report.2000/01: *Attacking Poverty*. Oxford University Press, URL: www.worldbank.org/poverty/wdrpoverty (Accessed on 5th February, 2012).

World Bank. June 2002. *Using Information and Communication Technology to reduce Poverty in Rural India*, p. 4.

8

Panchayati Raj and People's Participation

A Special Focus on North-East India

Nazmul Hussain Laskar

The basic principles behind the adoption of Panchayati Raj as a system of local[1] self-governing bodies in the rural areas of the country was that of taking democracy back to the grass root level. This, at length, was also meant to promote people's participation in the management of local affairs in a manner that will lead to self-sufficient and self-reliant village communities of responsible villagers. In other words, the significance of the Panchayati Raj Institutions (PRIs) was to be seen not only in that it seeks to build up a system of local government, however well organised and decentralised it may be, but also in that it seeks to tackle the problems of building democracy and mobilizing the entire potential manpower resources of the country for purposes of economic and social progress at the grass roots level[1]. Indeed, it was the lack of people's participation in the community development programmes that made the Balwant Mehta Committee suggests initiation of PRIs in the country. The committee realised that the popular participation in the community development programmes enlisted through advisory bodies was not adequate. As such, it felt the need for a separate set of statutorily created institutional arrangement to make the popular participation meaningful and effective. The committee observed that there was need to discover or create a representative and democratic institution which will sustain the local interest, supervision and care, necessary to ensure that expenditure of money upon local objects conform with the needs and wishes of the locality, invest it with adequate power and assign to it appropriate finances, which would evoke local interest and excite local initiative in the field of development. Accordingly, the committee insisted that such a body should be statutory, objective, and comprehensive in its duties and functions, equipped with the necessary executive machinery and in possession of adequate resources. The committee also suggested that it should not be loaded with too much government control. Thus, the requirement for real decentralization and meaningful popular participation was very emphatically stressed by the Mehta study team.[2]

Historical Background

The credit for bringing Panchayati Raj into focus as a most potent mechanism for bringing out democratic governance in modern India through popular participation at the local level, however, goes to Gandhiji. While reflecting on the future of an independent India, Gandhiji never wanted to be developed "as a third class or even a first class copy of the dying civilization of the west."[3] Instead he wanted lakhs of villages in India to become a well-living republic in which there are no illiterates, in which no one is idle for want of work, in which everyone is usefully occupied and has nourishing food, well ventilated dwellings and sufficient *khadi* for covering the body, and in which all the villagers know and observe the laws of hygiene and sanitation.[4] It was with this end in view that Gandhi propagated the rejuvenation of self-sufficient and self-governing village republics as the nucleus for a continuously progressing India. Yet, it is interesting to note that the idea of Panchayati Raj did not find a place in the Draft Constitution of India. This happened because the Congress Constitution Committee rejected the idea 'believing that the Congress could neither forgo its political role nor become so utterly decentralized' as envisaged in the Gandhian concept of Gram Swaraj.[5] B.R. Ambedkar, the Chairman of the Drafting Committee himself did not have much faith in the Panchayats of village communities, describing them as the cause of "ruination of India" and that they were nothing but "stink of localism and ignorance and communalism".[6] He even said that he was "glad that the Draft Constitution has discarded the village and adopted the individual as its unit".[7] While such an attitude of Ambedkar towards the Village Panchayats might have been based on his apprehension that these Panchayats shall be dominated by the upper castes, Nehru also chose to remain silent on this issue as he favoured "a centralised polity for making a modern and developed state".[8]

However, owing to passionate pleas from many prominent Gandhians, a directive to set up Village Panchayats and endow them with the authority to function as units of self-government was included later as one of the Directive Principles of State Policy. Though this led to the enactment of Panchayati Raj Acts by various States, these remained only half-hearted attempts to create rural local government institutions and overall these developments did not lead to the evolution of a healthy system of local self-governing bodies in the rural areas. Later attempts including that of the Ashok Mehta Committee (1978) to revitalize the system were made. In 1989, the then Prime Minister of India, late Rajiv Gandhi made an earnest effort to revitalize the Panchayats by moving the 64th Amendment Bill in Lok Sabha. Though the Bill was passed by the Lok Sabha by a two-thirds majority, it was rejected in the Rajya Sabha. The vision for PRIs as local self-governing bodies in rural areas got subsequently institutionalized in the form of the 73rd Amendment Act (1992). This led to the establishment of the new system for Panchayati Raj in the States through the enactment of conformity legislations.

State of Panchayati Raj Institutions in North-East India

North-East India consists of eight States—Assam, Arunachal Pradesh, Manipur, Meghalaya, Mizoram, Nagaland, Tripura, and Sikkim covering more than eight per cent of the total area and four per cent of the total population of the country. A large part of the North-East India is governed by the Fifth and Sixth Schedules of the Constitution of India. The Panchayats (Extension to the Schedule Areas) Act 1996 extends to the Fifth Schedule areas whereas Autonomous District Councils have been envisaged as the system of local self-government in areas covered by the Sixth Schedule of the Constitution.[9] At present five of the eight non-Sixth Schedule States of North-east *viz.* Assam, Arunachal Pradesh, Manipur, Sikkim, and Tripura have introduced Panchayati Raj as the system of local self- government for rural areas except certain areas within their respective territories where they have opted for Autonomous District Councils.

Regarding Assam, the State's tryst with a formal system of Panchayati Raj goes back as early as the promulgation of the Assam Local Self Government Act 1915. The Act provided for the establishment of village Panchayats for the first time on a formal and legal basis. It also provided for an elective non-official majority in the Panchayat and for the election of non-officials as chair persons and vice-chairpersons.[10] In 1926, another Act was passed to further experiment with a more meaningful system of

Panchayats. However, the Panchayati institutions under the British proved to be a failure as these measures were more of nominal gestures rather than genuine efforts to empower the local bodies.[11] In the post-independence period, Assam was one of the pioneering States to introduce Panchayati Raj when it enacted the Assam Panchayati Raj Act 1948. Following the recommendations of the Balwant Rai Mehta Committee, another Panchayati Raj Act 1959 was passed replacing the earlier one. The new Act provided for a three tier system of Panchayati Raj consisting of the Gram Panchayat at village level, Anchalik Panchayats at the intermediate level and Mahakuma Parishad at the sub-divisional level.[12] It may be noted that the Act covered only the plain district of the State and Hill Autonomous Districts and villages in the tea gardens were excluded from the purview of the Act. The Assam Panchayati Raj Act 1972 later opted for a two tier system of Panchayati Raj for the State – Gaon Panchayat at the village level with a population of 15,000-20,000 and Mahakuma Parishad at the apex level. It also brought the villages located in tea gardens areas within its purview.[13] The Act of 1972 was replaced by another new Act introduced in 1986 but became operative only from 5 September, 1990. With it, the State reverted to a three tier system of Panchayati Raj. With the coming of the 73rd Amendment of the Constitution, the State enacted another Panchayati Act in 1994 covering almost all the features of the 73rd Amendment including that of a three tier system and 33.3 per cent reservation for women. The Act extends to the whole of Assam in the rural areas except the autonomous districts under the Sixth Schedule of the Constitution of India.[14]

Regarding Tripura, the Panchayati Raj system inside the State was initially guided by the United Province Panchayati Raj Act, 1947 which provided for a single tier system of PRIs. Later, the Panchayati Raj Act 1983 was brought into force in January 1984 replacing the earlier Act of 1947. The Tripura Panchayat Act of 1993 provided for three tier system of Panchayats for the State with Gram Panchayats at the village level, Panchayat Samitis at the Block level and Zilla Parishads at the district level. The Act also provides for a Gram Sabha which shall meet annually to consider matters relating to accounts, budget and report of development works in the Gram Panchayat. It is significant to note that Gram Sabhas are there in Tripura irrespective of schedule or non-schedule area. Hence, Tripura's local self-government is quite unique.[15] The first general elections for the Panchayats were held in 1997. At present there are four Zilla Parishads, 23 Panchayat Samitis and 511 Gram Panchayats in Tripura.[16]

In Arunachal Pradesh, Panchayats have been in existence from very old days in the form of traditional village institutions which got the status of Gram Panchayats later on. Under the provisions of the North East Frontier Agency (NEFA) Panchayati Raj Regulation Act 1967, a four tier system of local self-governing bodies with Gram Panchayats at the village level, Anchal Samiti at the circle level, Zilla Parishad at the district level and Agency Council at the agency level was inaugurated on 2 October, 1968.[17] Following the enactment of the 73rd and 74th Amendments of the Constitution, the State government passed the Arunachal Pradesh Panchayati Raj Act 1997. The Act provided for a three tier system of Panchayati Raj for the State in the form of Gram Panchayats at the village level, Anchalik Samitis at the circle level and Zilla Parishad at the district level. The first Panchayat elections in Arunachal Pradesh as per the new system were conducted in April 2003.[18]

Coming to Manipur, from time immemorial the State had its own traditional system of local self-governing bodies in the form of Khunja Mipham which was an organized institution to provide justice to the villagers by the elders of the village.[19] At present, the State has adopted Panchayati Raj as the system of local self-governing bodies in the rural areas of the four valley districts. Otherwise, it is not there in the five other districts in the hills of the State where there are Autonomous District Councils. Prior to the enactment of the 73rd Amendment of the Constitution, Manipur implemented the Panchayati Raj System of governance under the adopted United Province Panchayati Raj Act 1947.[20] The second general elections to the Panchayats were held in 1971, also under the same Act. Subsequently, in 1975 Manipur enacted its own Panchayat Act providing for a three tier system of local self-governing bodies—Gram Panchayats, Panchayat Samitis and Zilla Parishads. Though the elections to the Gram Panchayats and Panchayat Samitis were held, the Zilla Parishads were never constituted.[21] With the coming of the 73rd Amendment, the State government passed the Manipur Panchayati Raj Act 1994. The Act came into force w.e.f. 24 July, 1994. It provides for a two tier system of Panchayati Raj inside the State Panchayat at the village level and Zilla Parishads at the district level in place of the three tier system earlier envisaged by the 1975 Act. Altogether the State has 4 Zilla Parishads and 165 Gram Panchayats. The first Zilla Parishad and Gram Panchayats elections were held in 1997. Since then, general elections to the Panchayats have been held for every five years with the last elections held in September 2007.[22] At present the State has a total of 61 elected Zilla Parishad and 1,707 elected Gram Panchayat members.[23]

In Sikkim, the Sikkim Panchayati Raj Act 1993 in keeping with the 93rd Amendment was enacted to establish a two tier system of PRIs — Gram Panchayats at the village level and Zilla Parishads at the district level. The Act extends to whole of Sikkim except for 12 small towns. As on March 2010, there were 4 Zilla Parishads and 163 Gram Panchayats in the State.[24] All these developments were meant to be significant steps to secure people's participation in the management of local affairs in such a manner so that it may lead to the all-round development of the rural areas and people living there.

The State of PRIs and People's Participation at Present

When one talks about PRIs and people's participation, one has to look at the issue in a holistic manner. It is of utmost importance that there should be participation from all the different cross-sections of the rural population, including women, poor and other marginalized sections of the society, and it has to be in a continuous and consistent manner. When one looks at the state of PRIs and people's participation from this point of view, a number of things come to the mind. The need for conducting Panchayat elections at regular intervals can never be overemphasized. Equally important will be that of conducting these elections in a democratic and free and fair manner. Because it is not so much the election results but the process of electoral politics through the results are arrived at that will decide the democratic features of the elections, legitimacy of the institutions established and the real meaning of people's participation. What is essential is a system of Panchayat elections which will accord equality of opportunity to all irrespective of their caste, religious, linguistic and gender considerations. Besides proper vigil over election time expenditure has to be there. It should be a system in which the poor and underprivileged sections of the society have the same prospects of contesting as well as winning the Panchayat elections like those of the rich and privileged sections of the society on the basis of their own individual merit. Whether this has become a distinctive feature of Panchayat elections in the region needs to be closely examined.

So far as the participation of women in the PRIs is concerned, reservation of seats for them, 33.3 per cent or more, has already facilitated their entry into the PRIs as elected members. While Assam, Arunachal Pradesh, Sikkim and Manipur have gone for 33.3 per cent for women in the PRIs, Tripura has gone ahead further by providing for 50 per cent reservation for women making her one of the 12 States of the Union which have 50 per cent reservation for women in these institutions. It is also significant to note that when it comes to their participation in the local self-governing bodies, women in areas covered by the system of Panchayati Raj are in a much more advantageous position than their counterparts in those areas coming under the Sixth Schedule where there are Autonomous District Councils. This is due to the fact that in case of the latter there is no reservation for women. Besides, the traditional village council in most of the Sixth Schedule areas do not have women representatives. The recent developments regarding the Municipal Council Act of Nagaland is a very pertinent case here. It took more than eight years since the 73rd Amendment for the Nagaland Government to enact the Nagaland Municipal Act 2001. But this Act did not have any reservation provision for women. So it took another five years and a law suit filed in the High Court before the State added 33 per cent reservations for women in the Nagaland Municipal (First Amendment) Act 2006. Another three years passed before the wards to be reserved for women could be allotted in 2009. Even after that elections for the councils have been suspended by the cabinet till now. This has been seen as "a ploy to avoid giving women their constitutionally mandated seats".[25] Finally when the State government decided to hold the Municipal and Town Council elections in the month of April, several Naga organizations led by the Naga Hoho came out strongly against the 33 per cent reservation for women.[26] The Naga organizations maintain that reservation would infringe on Article 371(A) of the Constitution that has given absolute power to the Naga people and that no act of Parliament can infringe on the article without the consent of the Nagaland Assembly.[27] Women in the hills of Manipur also suffer from a similar predicament. While the traditional administrative system of the village as represented by the village councils has no place for women, the village authorities and Autonomous District Councils also provide no scope for reservation of women. These features of Local Self-Government in the hills of the State impede political empowerment of women there.[28] PRIs along with meaningful participation of the people can remove a number of flaws in the present trend of implementation of programmes meant for the development of the rural areas and people living there. For instance, many studies have pointed out flaws in the selection of beneficiaries for these programmes. It has been reported that people living above the poverty line have also been selected as beneficiaries for schemes meant for people living below the poverty line. This leads the deprivation of the target group of people of these schemes. Non-adherence to national guidelines meant for the implementation of the programmes has also been another problem that plagues the implementation of these programmes. In connection with wage employment schemes also, there have been many reports of people being provided with reduced number of work days. For instance, in Manipur it has been reported that while implementing Employment Assurance Schemes, the maximum number of man-days actually provided was only 45 per annum as against 100 to be provided as per the provisions of the scheme.[29] Besides there have also been many instances of wage employment programmes failing to create durable assets which are needed for rural development.[30] A healthy system of Panchayat Raj Institutions and meaningful involvement of people in its activities will go a long way in keeping vigil over these problems.

Studies carried out in number of States all over India have also found that by and large, PRIs have not yet become the real institutions of self governance largely due to lack of people's participation, especially women, the poor, and other marginalized groups because of ignorance, poverty and lack of distributive justice. Reluctance on the part of the higher tiers of the government to devolve financial and administrative powers to control the planning and implementation of developmental schemes to the PRIs is another factor contributing to it. Apathetic attitude of bureaucrats and politicians is another serious hurdle. Besides, insufficient capacity and resources of the PRIs in running their activities effectively, and lack of organic linkages among the different tiers of PRIs also adversely affects the emergence of these in situations as meaningful agencies of self-governance.[31] If the Panchayats are to function as effective as well as meaningful institutions of self-governance at the grass root level, then they have to fulfil three basic conditions, namely (1) institutional existence in the sense that the decisions are taken by the people's representatives, (2) institutional capacity in the form of empowering institutions to make their rules independently, and (3) financial viability in terms of sufficiently empowering Panchayats in raising resources to meet their responsibilities.[32] In other words, the Panchayats should enjoy administrative and financial autonomy. However, these things are easier said than actually realised, and we have to find the ways and means to actually realise these things.

The need for sensitising the members of the PRIs as well as the public to the multi-dimensional issue of rural development is another thing which requires proper attention. PRI personnel as well as the people in rural areas have to be made really aware of the different rural development programmes so that these may be meaningfully implemented. In many cases gaps in implementation process and observance of basic guidelines have been due to the lack of awareness among the concerned people at various levels. Apart from their just sensitization to the urgent needs of the rural people, there is also need for a real sense of commitment and sincerity on the part of the PRI personnel while discharging their duty in the course of implementing various programmes. For the people in rural areas also, they are often ignorant of the opportunities offered to them by the various schemes that are there for their development. Once they are not aware of their entitlements, it becomes easy for persons with vested interests to misappropriate the benefits thereby depriving the target group of the various schemes.

Conclusion

Panchayati Raj and people's participation cannot be separated from one another. There is an organic relationship between the two in the sense that there can be no meaningful and healthy existence of one in the absence of the other. The PRIs are basically meant to promote self-governance and self-sufficiency on the part of the people. This obviously requires that people should come forward and participate in the management of their own affairs. Similarly, the people also require certain basic institutions through which they can participate in the management of their own affairs. The PRIs facilitate this requirement. However, the present state of PRIs and people's participation in North-East India is far from being fully satisfactory. Even after almost two decades of the 93rd Amendment, meaningful implementation of rural development programmes through PRIs and people's participation remains an unfinished agenda, a dream yet to be realised. Lack of political will on the part of the most of the State governments to really devolve power into the hands of the PRIs, lack of awareness on the part of the PRI personnel as well as the rural people at large, etc., obstruct effective participation of the people in the rural development programmes through these institutions. The conflict between the State government and the PRIs over the issue of devolution of power is another basic issue that needs to be properly addressed.

Notes

1. http://www.preservearticles.com/2011100514718/useful-notes-on-balwant-rai-mehta-committee-report.html.accessed on April 1, 2012.
2. *Ibid.*

3. *Source:* R. Prabhu and U.R. Rao (eds.), *Village Republics: The Mind of Mahatma Gandhi*, pp. 246-247, http://data.undp.org.in/hdrc/dis-srs/challenges/DecentralisationCO.pdf,accessed on April 1, 2012.
4. *Ibid.*
5. Granville Austin, *The Indian Constitution : Cornerstone of a Nation*, 1996, p. 29.
6. Ranbir Singh, *Unfinished Agenda of Gandhi's Gram Swaraj*: *Fifty Years of Panchayati Raj, in Mainstream*, Vol. XLVII, No. 3, October 10, 2009.
7. *Ibid.*
8. *Ibid.*
9. Dipanjan Roy Choudhury, Autonomous District Councils and Panchayati Raj Institutions in North East India, *Dialogue*, July-September, 2005, Volume 7, No. 1.
10. *Ibid.*
11. *Ibid.*
12. *Ibid.*
13. *Ibid.*
14. P.R. Bhattacharjee and Purusottam Nayak, "Panchayati Raj in Assam", paper presented in the National Seminar on *Local Self Governance and Rural Development: The Indian Experience*, at Utkal University, Bhubaneshwar, 2-25 February, 2001.
15. Dipanjan Roy Choudhury, *op. cit.*
16. Technical Inspection Report on Panchayati Raj Institutions and Urban Local Bodies, Tripura, for the year 2009-2010, http://saiindia.govt.in/English/home/our products/Audit Report/Government wise/local bodies/issued state government/Tripura.html, accessed on April 1, 2012.
17. http://arunachalpradesh.gov.in/panchayat/html/panchayat.htm, accessed on April 1, 2012.
18. *Ibid.*
19. G.S. Oinam, *State of Panchayati Raj in Manipur* Part-1, http://e-pao.net/epSubPageExtractor.
Asp?src=leisure.Essays.Gitchandra Oinam.state of panchayat Raj1, accessed on April 1, 2012.
20. N. Vijylakshmi Brara, "*Brushed under the Carpet:Inclusion and Exclusion in Local Governance*, Sage Publications, New Delhi, 2009, p. 288.
21. *Ibid.*
22. Technical Inspection Report on Panchayati Raj Institutions and Urban Local Bodies, Manipur, for the.year 2008-2009 http://saiindia.govt.in/English/home/our products/Audit Report/Government wise/local

bodies/issued state government/Manipur/Manipur.html, accessed on April 1, 2012.

23. G.S. Oinam, State of Panchayati Raj in Manipur Part-2, http://iesenvis.nic.in/database-panchayat-elections.htm, accessed on April 1, 2012.
24. Technical Inspection Report on Panchayati Raj Institutions and Urban Local Bodies, Sikkim, for the year 2009-2010 http://saiindia.govt.in/English/home/our products/Audit Report/Government wise/local bodies/Tabled Legislature/Sikkim/2009 10/Chap 1.pdf, accessed on April 1, 2012.
25. Naga women file writ petition in high court regarding women's reservation in Nagaland Municipal Councils, http://www.hrln.org/hrln/womens-justice-/pils-a-cases/732-naga-women-file-writ petition-in-high-court-regarding-womens-reservations-in-na, accessed on April 3, 2012.
26. Nagas oppose women quota, http:??www.telegraphindia.com?1120319?isp/northeast/story 15265745 isp#.T3s2vPClfqE
27. *Ibid.*
28. Maireiwon Ningshen, *Political Participation of Tangkul Naga Women in Manipur: 1972-2005*. Ph.D. Thesis, Department of Political Science, Manipur University.
29. Khuraijam Khogen Singh, *District Rural Development Agency and Rural Development in Manipur: A Study of Thoubal District During 1993-2002*, p. 238.
30. *Ibid.*
31. R.N. Murdia, *Participatory Rural Governance in India: A Myth or Reality*, Paper presented in the workshop on Enlarging Citizen Participation and Increasing Autonomy of Local Government in Achieving Social Harmony, organised during the Network of Asia Pacific Schools and Institutes of Public Administration and Governance Annual Conference, Beijing, 2005.
32. *Ibid.*

9

Decentralized Governance in Rural West Bengal during the Left Front Rule

Dr. Ayub Mallick

Decentralization means statutory authority of decision-making power by an elected body or bodies with regard to local matters. Here, in this process of decentralization the concepts of 'power' and 'authority' are important. Power is the capacity to influence others or others' actions. Authority is the legitimization of power. Legitimization comes when the power of the decision-maker is accepted by the people or by the subjects. Then, there is the question of balance between consent and control, of democracy and also of responsibility. Decentralized governance is the process of decentralization, where the processes of both democracy and development are inter-related, when the latter cannot progress without power and responsibility and the former needs meeting of local needs and interests with regard to local matters and development. In the decentralized process there is democracy, full authority of decision-making, autonomy, legitimacy and development. To meet the demands of both democracy and development a golden mean is to be struck between models of Rajasthan and Maharashtra by strengthening Zilla Parishads at the district level as units of Plan and programme formulation and by maintaining Block as the nucleus for Plan and programme implementation on the one hand and people's participation on the other, where the former model treats Block as the unit of decentralization, appears more conducive to the cause of democracy than that of development and the latter treats district as the unit of development, appears to serve the cause of planned development than that of democracy. The evolution of Panchayati Raj is the discovery of golden mean as the medium of planned development and as a system of local government.

Local government or decentralized governance means autonomy and autonomy designates and simplifies local government. There is a direct correlation and powerful link between localism and self-government. Local Self-Government is to make its communitarian contributions arousing the common people to enthusiastic and purposeful activities as a body of selfless individuals. The essential ingredient of a satisfactory democracy is that a considerable proportion of local people should have experience of active participation in local government institutions. In this process 'the induction of the mobilized persons into some relatively stable new patterns of group membership, organization and commitment' (Deutsch, 1961: 494) is central to the aspects of local self-government institutions. There should be a proper balance between institutionalization and participation. At this stage, government and administration should be responsive to local needs and expectations, all the preferences of the people should be treated equally, and all must have unimpaired opportunities to 'formulate their preferences', 'signify their preferences' and 'have their preferences weighted equally in the conduct of government.' (Dahl, 1972: 2). 'Our problem ... is to find democratic ways of living for little men in big societies ... Democracy can work in the great States ... only if each State is made up of a host of little democracies, and rests finally, not on isolated individuals but on groups small enough to express the spirit of neighbourhood and personal acquaintance.' (Cole, 1960: 64). There is a positive correlation between participation in the local government institutions and institutionalization of participation. 'How institutions work depends to a large extent upon the leadership ... the emerging leadership has a more direct bearing on aspects of institution building ... (Shiviah *et al.*, 1980: 104). In fact, 'mere revival of the institution' (Sathe, 1989: 16) would not help proper institutional and rural development. 'Indeed, rural progress depends entirely on the existence of an active organization in the village which can bring all the people including the weaker sections ...' (Department of Rural Development, 1986: para 3.4)

In 1957, Balwantray Mehta Committee was formed to report on Community Projects and National Extension Services and to assess the application of local leadership in community development, its economy and efficacy. The Committee said that unless local interests are created (mobilized) and supplied to provide new blood to representative and democratic institutions, money expenditure on local objects and local development according to local needs and aspirations would be doomed into failure (Committee on Plan Projects, 1959: 5). The competence for self-government and self-management has to be developed by a process of training, and power would not have to be given from the above, it would be taken from below, even from unwilling hands (Narayan, 1962). Ashok Mehta Committee (1977) said that Panchayati Raj Institutions should be fully involved in the process of development. The Committee also recommended political reinforcement of the authority of PRIs to enable them to dominate bureaucracy and to make closer contact with the electorate. To the Committee, it is imperative to decentralize power, planning process and developmental activities below the State level. Development programmes for rural areas call for closer co-ordination at levels below the State. Popular supervision over official machinery has the potential to become an effective instrument of co-ordination. Horizontal pressures are exerted by people's representatives (Mehta Report, 1978). Mehta Study Team recognized 'development management' in place of 'development administration' and stressed on 'functional necessity of management of rural development'. According to this Committee, Panchayati Raj institutions are called upon to take up 'location-specific programmes' along with 'functional necessity' of decentralization and 'open participation' of political parties in the affairs of the Panchayati Raj Institutions.

The Acts of 1957 and 1963 did not make contributions to social change and socio-economic development. Candidates fought the Panchayat elections without party symbols and without proper politicization of the leaders. 'This reflected a politically naïve view of village politics as, in practice, those elected as well as being drawn from among the dominant economic and political elite in the village tended to be the real power brokers of the Congress Party.' (Webster, 1992: 111). The delayed birth of local level institutions in West Bengal received a further setback due to changes in the State government. '... democracy in no country of the world ... can survive unless there is a continuous flow of leadership from bottom upwards, leading to the emergence of linkage politics and strengthening of linkage administration in the country ... This makes the revival of Panchayati Raj once again necessary.' (Narain, 1987: 4). Decentralized governance needs proper interplay between institutionalization and participation. Proper institutionalization of Panchayats needs participation at the local level, at 'every village' (Ramswamy, 1964: 36) and political stability at the national and State levels. In 1967, United Front Government came to power in West Bengal and put forward its approach to Panchayati Raj Institutions. This scheme was not materialized. After that, People's Democratic Front came into being and was dismissed by President's Rule very shortly in 1968. Once again, the United Front Government came back to power in 1969 with a hope to further materialization of people's power and will. A Panchayat Bill was passed under this Government. Once more, the Government was dismissed by President Rule in 1970. For that, the Bill was not formulated in terms of Act. After that, Congress Government took over the charge of government in this State in 1972 and passed West Bengal Panchayat Act 1973 with a provision of three-tier Panchayat structure: Gram Panchayat at the Anchal/Village level, Panchayat Samiti at the Block level and Zilla Parishad at the District level. The micro unit Gram Sabha was abolished thereby with a view to ensure greater democracy with development. A resurgence of Panchayats had taken place during 1970s and 1980s under Left Front rule in West Bengal. This resurgence in West Bengal was preceded by mass movements for changing land-owning pattern in rural West Bengal during 1967-70. Later on, it was accompanied by land reforms, particularly distribution of ceiling surplus land, registration of share-croppers, *i.e.,* Operation *Barga* and distribution of land inputs to the beneficiaries of land reforms (Bandyopadhyay, 1981). The 'two legs' theory (Mishra, 1991) of rural development, land reforms and democratic decentralization is the hallmark of the Left Front Government, which weakened the 'hold of big landlords' (Mukherjee and Bandyopadhyay, 1993:3) over Panchayati Raj institutions. The Constitution (73rd Amendment) Act 1992 came into being providing constitutional guarantees to the Panchayats. The need is to develop a power structure for the rural poor and have-nots as a counter balance against all forms of exploitation and oppression by the rural haves (Kurian, 1980). To ensure effective participation of the people in the process of development, West Bengal Panchayat Acts 1992 and 1994 were enacted, making the institutional innovations like Gram Sabha and Gram Sansad, where all the electors of the Gram Panchayat area are involved in the development process. It has provided the village people of the Gram Panchayat area the power to advice the Gram Panchayat with regard to the identification of schemes to be taken for economic development of the village, to the selection of beneficiaries of various poverty alleviation programmes and constitution of Beneficiary Committee for ensuring people's involvement in the identification, implementation and follow-up of various development projects and overall equal distribution of developmental benefits from multiple community welfare schemes. The

Amendment Act 1994 tries to make room for autonomous political space and workability of mass mobilization, promotion of harmony and solidarity among the people. The Act has empowered the people to record the illegal actions and miscarriage of duties with regard to the implementation of various development schemes on the part of the Pradhan of Gram Panchayat or any Gram Panchayat member. Under this Act, Gram Panchayat is the unit of self-government. The Amendment Act of 1992 also empowers the Gram Panchayats with the tasks of identification, preparation and implementation of various schemes for economic development and social justice.

In West Bengal popular participation has not taken the form of Gram Sabha or village assembly meetings. Decisions about expenditure are rarely based on prescribed forms; rather decisions are reached through informal discussion. It is mainly through the electoral process that popular participation has been practiced in West Bengal (Sengupta and Gazdar, 1997). Echeverri-Gent (1992) and Westergaard (1986) have found electoral competition as avenue to broad-based popular participation. However, little changes have taken place in the rural power structure in villages through Panchayat elections. The Panchayats have brought the middle category of people into key positions. However, power has yet to travel down the lower levels. The middle category people will remain in firm control of the Panchayats (Mukherjee and Bandyopadhyay, 1993). 'Since the efforts of the Left parties have been confined largely to the question of the choice of appropriate representatives, and not so much to the tasks of conscious organization to over through existing relations of power, the evidence of support to the Left does not necessarily reflect a corresponding demolition of the structure of false consciousness among the people.' (Chatterjee, 1997: 86)

The representation of SCs and STs to the Panchayati Raj institutions does not correspond to their proportion of the total population. The representation of the poor and disadvantaged has been increased in Panchayati Raj Institutions, but this representation has not resulted in any significant increase in their control over these institutions. Due to the lack of this class organization, the poor and disadvantaged groups, *i.e.*, Scheduled Caste and Scheduled Tribe members seldom speak up in Gram Panchayat meetings. The real problem is the lack of organizational effort on class lines among the poor and disadvantaged groups. ' ... the CPI(M) and the Left Front mobilized the rural masses by appealing to their class identities, these parties have neither seriously advanced the class struggles in the countryside, nor, apparently, do they mean to do so in the next round.' (Roy, 1983: 1141). In fact, the whole situation is judged by the Left Front 'not in terms of classes but in terms of party affiliations' (Rudra, 1981: A-68). The party does not vigorously oppose the vested interests for pre-occupation to secure votes in spite of its desired objectives of 'grass roots democracy, mass initiative and involvement, and enhancement of right' (Chowdhury, 1988: 6-7). Often vested interests do 'manage to extract support from a substantial proportion of the poorer sections among the rural poor ... in their fight against reform measures' (Dasgupta, 1984: A-90). 'The political leadership of the party is established only when people ... accept the political perspective of the party as their own.' (West Bengal State Committee, 1994: 3). The party has drifted from its tasks of making people conscious about the existing exploitative system and of developing the 'revolutionary spirit' (West Bengal State Committee, 1994). It is the party which 'imposes its prior decisions which violate democratic right of the members of the elected bodies ... The common people have not been involved in the functioning of Panchayat.' (West Bengal State Committee, 1995: 23). In fact, '... 45 per cent of the CPI (M) members belong to the agricultural labourer and small peasant families. 25 per cent comes from the middle peasants and small businessmen.' (Lieten, 1996: 135). Though the agricultural labourers and small peasants form the majority in the Panchayats, the middle peasants control the power pool, in spite of the professed goal of the Panchayats in bringing about an 'equilibrium of class force in favour of the people' (West Bengal State Committee, 1994: 1). '... Panchayats are heavily dependent on the Pradhans' (Burdwan District Committee, 1991: 20), who are party men. The issue of mass initiative has been neglected. People are not involved in the development process. People and Panchayat members are less interested in the decision-making process. The rationality of decisions is not explained before the people and the elected members of the Panchayats (Burdwan District Committee, 1985, 1988 and 1991). 'There is an indifference to involve the people in the decision-making process of the Panchayat ... It is quite impossible to activise for implementing the decision by those who do not take part in decision-making process ... We noticed the indifference of the elected members and ordinary people in running the Panchayats.' (Burdwan District Committee, 1991: 9, 11 and 13). This overpoliticization process is the 'unpolitical science' of the Panchayats (Bhattacharyya, 1996).

The institutions have provided opportunities for the power elite to manipulate benefits in their own interests; in the interests of their relatives and friends as to the scope of manipulability and weakness of the legislation the elite even overcome some of the legal impediments. The informal power elites influence the decision making process. They have an understanding with the formal power elites for resources and benefits, money and wealth. If there is a conflict between the political and economic elites, then it results into twin possibilities of denigration of economic elites and making them appear exploiters in the eyes of the people, and of withdrawal of economic support extended to political elites by the economically dominant. The economic elites try to spend money on the people to make them antithetical to political power elites (Sharma, 1979). Popular participation is a myth. The Panchayat system in West Bengal has spawned a new privileged class in the rural areas which is reaping large benefits from the funds being pumped for the uplift of the poor. The Panchayats have failed to build any infrastructure worth the name (Biswas, 1989). There is an understanding between politicians and bureaucrats. The principal factor causing this is the lack of new initiatives by the Panchayats towards developmental activities. People are aware of this loss. To recuperate this loss, Panchayats 'have involved themselves in trans-developmental activity ... They mediate in disputes and try to solve a variety of people's problems ... at the request of district magistrates Panchayat leaders join in defusing communal and other public order situations.' (Mukherjee and Bandyopadhyay, 1993: 9). '... political power and politics have entered the village recently in a new shape ... the shape being that of fight for gaining power through identifying one's self with the ruling party in the country.' (Chattopadhyay, 1964: 56). Elections to Panchayats have become peaceful and democratic ways to 'political contest for the roots of power' (Sen Gupta, 1979: 118) rather than the avenues to developmental programmes and their implementation. The developmental programmes have become the institutional arrangement for defusing the tensions in agrarian relations. 'Emphasis is more on representation and enlightened leadership than on participation. ...' (Tornquist, 1991: 68). The developmental programmes have become the *de facto* abandonment of the concern with viability (Baruah, 1990) of the peasants and landless peasants. Alignments among factions for power and prestige and control over these institutions have become the realities since the coming of political parties into village politics. The prime goal is accumulation of power, when factions represent not the interests of the superordinate against the subordinate or other counterpoised. 'Rivalries and tensions for power are generally among the families of the same caste and class. It is not that competition for power is between the higher and the lower castes and classes.' (Sharma, 1974: 201). Factions develop to realize personal interests of factional leaders and their followers, and try to maintain cohesiveness by distributing patronage and benefits. 'Factions in Indian Panchayats have seldom been led by the members of the lowest castes.' (Franda, 1979: 126)

The leaders control the village Panchayats on account of their better economy, 'higher educational levels, and better linkages with urban areas' (West Bengal State Committee, 1982: 91). '... the bulk of our leading Kisan activists come from rich and middle peasant origin, rather than agricultural labourers and poor peasants.' (Sundaraya, 1973: 2). Therefore, 'involvement of the people in all governmental process and development activities' (Chaudhuri, 1989: 37) is a myth in this context. Webster and Rao find that the patron-client relations do not clearly represent 'increased popular participation' (Westergaard, 1987), but do serve to reproduce a structure of inegalitarian and conflictual agrarian relations and underlying structures of exploitation (Webster, 1990). The experience on the working of the Panchayati Raj Institutions has revealed that under this exploiting social structure and property relations, the rural elites have come to dominate these popular institutions and appropriated a major share of benefits from development so that the improvement in the living conditions of the downtrodden has become negligible (Rao, 1989). The transformation of power, both institutional and social has taken place in the form of control of power from the grip of dominant landlords to a group of lower middle stratum linked with landowning classes and landed interests (Kohli, 1983). They are not like the 'same old class of rural vested interests' (Chowdhury, 1988), but more than the lower middle class dominant group. The 'red Panchayats' (Sen Gupta, 1979) have not been able to mobilize the rural people along class political lines and for development purposes. The token membership of the landless poor and lack of ideological commitment to the mobilization of the poorest classes among the members have made the rural middle class dominant in the area and representation of the interests of the poor by the dominant middle class minimum. With the help of Panchayats the party represents two inter-linked patterns of political change, *i.e.*, the organizational penetration of party 'centre' into the 'periphery' and simultaneous shift in the class basis of institutional power. Though it is a party of lower middle income group, the party is electorally supported by the poor, and in turn they do get benefits from the government policies (Kohli, 1990). The poverty alleviation programmes remain a narrow management subject to manipulation by those who enjoy the monopoly of social knowledge and power (Rahman, 1984). What I am saying is that the rural power structure has little more changed with the reorganization and institutionalization of Panchayats. The rural elites stand as nets between the poorer people and the well-to-do sections or the outer world, in the sense that they consume resources and benefits. And the Panchayats act as buffers so as not to make any collision between the poorer classes and rural elites. 'There is a sense, however, in which a change from "class mobilization" to a more conciliatory approach is inevitable. While the rise of the Left Front was associated with the sharpening of class conflict in rural West Bengal and the shifting of class alliances, its consolidation has necessitated a more conciliatory approach. Consequently, an important role of PRIs has been that of mediation between conflicting claims in matters such as terms of lease and agricultural wages.' (Dreze snd sen, 1997: 161-162)

The Panchayats are still dominated by small and marginal farmers (Dutta, 1993). Panchayats are not effectively providing 'power to the people' and there is every danger of bureaucratic ills and political nepotism (Krishna, 1993). A process of socialization through a movement of education based on autonomous model of literacy campaign is the new challenge before the West Bengal left (Acharya and Bhattacharya, 1993). Registering the names of the share-croppers (Bhatia, 1979) and giving few reliefs to them through the institution of Panchayats, the Left Front has subdued the intensity of politicization of a huge chunk of the deprived population in West Bengal. Panchayats have been used by the CPI(M) as institution in order to penetrate into the masses, to incorporate the masses in the democratic process through 'electioneering and various developmental programmes' (Kohli, 1987). However, Panchayats have become successful in bringing about a change in the living conditions of the SCs and STs and downtrodden through various development programmes, political mobilization and decentralized planning and in giving power and privileges to the poorest sections of society (Webster, 1992; Lieten, 1992). N. Bhattacharya, M. Chattopadhyay and A. Rudra in their study on the levels of living in terms of private consumption, housing conditions, social consumption, consumer durables, perceptions of the people, etc., have found that mild improvements have occurred in the overall level of consumption of private goods in the period between 1972-73 and 1985-86. Consumption of clothing, footwear and consumer durables showed improvement and housing conditions also showed improvement on an average. The rural poor consumed more food items than that of non-food items. The mild improvements in non-food consumption affected only the upper strata (Bhattacharya, Chattopadhyay and Rudra, 1987, 1988). There were substantial improvements in the distribution of expenditure between 1977 and the late eighties. The Gini co-efficient which was around 0.31 in 1972-73, as well as in 1977-78, fell to around 0.29 in 1983 and to 0.25 in 1989-90. The comparison with other States that experienced agricultural from around 1983 onwards is also enlightening. Between 1983 and 1989-90, the Gini co-efficient for consumer expenditure in rural areas registered a decline for West Bengal and Bihar. 'The decline (i.e., improvements in the distribution of expenditure) was most pronounced in West Bengal.' (Sengupta and Gazdar, 1997). With regard to the people's consciousness of their own rights there has occurred a revolutionary change with the activation of decentralized governance through Panchayati Raj Institutions. Economic dimension has become more important than that of caste dimension, which has not taken deep inroads into the socio-economic fabric of the rural society. 'Caste has stopped being a factor in politics, and even in social intercourse, there is a free mixing of castes. No longer is there any inhibition on sharing food and tea from the same plate, a habit which only a decade ago was not practiced.' (Lieten, 1988: 2072) and '... a thing that was not so dominant in the past now become obvious, and that is, a bond between the men of the same economic class of neighbouring villages as well'. (Chattopadhyay, 1964: 258)

In West Bengal, the social relations are acted upon the notion of a community, a prior collective authority from which all rights and entitlements flow. Caste here does not become a fundamental organizing principle in terms of which the social division of labour is conceived. Castes have disappeared from the political consciousness of the people (Chatterjee, 1997). A study of electoral mobilization in some Midnapore villages has shown that the upper and middle sections of the peasantry would be divided in their support to various parties and the poorest sections of the peasantry, the Scheduled Castes and Scheduled Tribes would be spontaneously mobilized through self-generation during election campaign (Mukherjee, 1983). This support is the result of a particular choice of linkage with the structure of organized politics of a group identifying itself as an exploited peasant community rather than its absorption into the organized structure of politics as a group conscious of itself as constituting part of a class. Hence, there can be no *a priori* ruling out of the possibility of political mobilization on appeals to caste or tribal or religious loyalties (Chatterjee, 1997). Huntington says, 'No social group is more conservative than a landowning peasantry, and none is more revolutionary than a peasantry which owns too little land or pays too high a rental'. (*op. cit.*, Prosterman and Riedinger, 1987: 7). But, class consciousness among the peasantry has not yet developed in rural West Bengal. The growing rural unemployment and underemployment, inadequate surplus land distribution, and increasing population have had tended to increase the two related aspects: 'poverty of the labouring classes and relative surplus of labour' (Ghosh, 1983: 11), even after the relative disappearance of the landlords-traders-moneylenders nexus.

Prof. Sen and Gazdar (1997) remarks that wages did increase in the 1980s as a result of an increase in the demand for labour, increase in cropping intensity, introduction of technological innovations in agriculture, and use of labour inputs added with the accelerated growth in output. Further, improvements in agricultural wages have been made as to the increased bargaining power of agricultural labourers and Panchayats' role in mediating labour disputes. This is one-sided picture of the story. In contrast with the early days of Left Rule in West Bengal when strike actions did raise the wages in the bargaining process, the recent trend of strike threat and strike actions have become the ritualized part. Labour organization, wage strikes and Panchayat mediation did not make important contribution in substantial wage setting. In contrast with Bihar, Orissa and the all-India averages, where wages crossed the growth of output, West Bengal's experience was the opposite, where the growth of wages and growth of output were quite similar. 'Between 1980 and 1991, the trend annual growth rate of real wages in West Bengal was 5.7 per cent while output grew at 5.6 per cent per year. The corresponding rates were 4.8 and 2.7 in India as a whole, 4.8 and 2.8 in Bihar, and 5.5 and 3.3 in Orissa.' (Sengupta *et al.*, 1997: 177). Recent trend in wage rates is not an adequate explanation of improved distribution of income in West Bengal. Theoretically,

(i) improvements in distribution of income = (is equal to) improvement in the consumption of the poor : (is proportional to) improvement in the consumption of the non-poor.
(ii) improvements in distribution of income = (is equal to) economic returns > (is greater than) labour assets/wage increase.
(iii) improvements in distribution of income = (is equal to) transfer of income to the poor/land redistribution.
(iv) improvements in distribution of income = (is equal to) wage increase + land redistribution.

In *Economic Review*, 1980-81, there is 20 per cent increase in the agricultural labour wages rate from 1976-77 to 1979-80. This was an improvement. 'This improvement in wage rate has been as much a result of additional production programmes undertaken in agriculture as of an increase in the bargaining power of the agricultural labourers.' (Government of West Bengal, 1981). Though the number of landless persons has decreased, capitalist relations with regard to the ownership and operation of land remained intact (Dutta, 1974: 34). Dutta (1974) opines that in the rural areas equalitarian distribution of land is accompanied by inequalitarian income distribution and increased exploitation, when the 'contradiction between the rich and the poor will not be solved so long as capitalism exists'. (Dutta, 1974: 39). In the rural class structure, the landowners remain at the top and landless labourers at the bottom within the framework of patron-client relationship.

Panchayats have been involved from the start in the agrarian reform programmes of the Left Front. However, the reform programmes are not so spectacular. The CPI (M)-led Front had incorporated the small and middle peasants into its organization than the lower ones, provided security of tenure to the share-croppers, to politicize them through Panchayats outmaneuvering bureaucrats, and to register them 'aiming at the limited goal of recording the tenancy right of the *bargadars*' (Khasnabis, 1986: 178). Due to organizational failures and uneven development, the Operation *Barga* Programme and registration drives were not implemented well. On the average, 5 to 6 members of a family had to struggle hard against poverty and starvation over 1-1.5 acres of land in mono-crop areas (Mukhopadhyay, 1979). However, compared with the past performance of the Congress, the Left Front made a spectacular success with regard to the recording of the share-croppers. But in 1982, it was recorded as 1,198,000 which reached 1,329,087 by September, 1985. It showed that the programme had virtually come to a halt, experiencing 'an average landholding of 0.97 acres with a total state-wide area of 2.5 million acres under *barga* cultivation' (Mallick, 1993: 56). Besides, the *bargadars* were evicted from the possession of their lands for maintaining order and safeguarding the existing property relations. Mr. Ratan Khasnabis opined that the Left Front Government under the leadership of the CPI (M) had to compromise with class divided and conflict ridden State structure, and sacrificed revolutionary steps to reformist ones (Khasnabis, 1981). The Pradhans of the Panchayats have introduced a parallel administration in the rural areas. Some of them have allegedly misappropriated public funds and not yet submitted accounts (Mukhopadhyay, 1979). 'The Left Front suggested that by its decentralizing of the political process, and placing more power in the hands of village councils, reform implementation would be more effective. However, the experience has been that decentralization without prior displacement of local elites only enhances the local elites' power. West Bengal decentralization, as reflected in revitalization of village councils, did not enhance the power of the old elite, but created a new one, a classless wealthy than the old pro-Congress elite, but nevertheless better off than the majority of the rural population. It is this middle class that has delivered to the Communists repeated electoral victories with the support of the lower classes.' (Mallick, 1993: 76-77)

In spite of land reforms growing mobilization of the landless labourers and cultivators 'growing class consciousness remains localized within the framework of the old patron-client system. Potentially revolutionary antagonisms are thus disarticulated by the preservation of old forms'. (Miller, 1979: 14). The old forms of landowner-tenant structure were present even after land reforms. There were only marginal changes. The old forms of landowner-tenant and landowner-labourer relations remained as 'dominant landholders ... used the destitute position of labourers to tie them with loans, later deducted from their meagre wages; they combined productive capital investment with money-lending to poorer peasants; some combined intensive capitalist production with wage-labour on a part of their land with leasing the remainder out at very high rents'. (Joshi, 1975: 241). Moreover, 'tenancy reforms to reduce rents, gives security against eviction, and give tenants an opportunity to acquire permanent rights over land by payment of fixed compensation subject to landlord's right to resume cultivation of a certain area for his personal cultivation' (Desai, 1969: 773) were designed 'to create a class of prosperous peasants out of substantial tenants' (Desai, 1969: 775). The transformation of land into commodity, introduction of private property in land, payment of revenue in cash and the need for money have forced the landowning cultivators to part with their produce and to follow a semi-feudal and semi-capitalist market relations. The Indian bourgeoisie with the help of state power had pursued an economic policy, which was to shift power from 'consumption-oriented semi-feudal and interest-oriented money-lending strata' (Desai, 1984: 149) to profit-oriented and market-oriented strata, to provide some concessions to the deprived masses within the matrix of exploitative-capitalist system with the help of political-ideological offensive and subtle caste mechanism. Syamalkanti Sengupta (1979) in studying Kotaigarh village comes to the conclusion that power comes from two sources: control over land and support of large sections of the people in the villages. Landownership in the rural areas stabilizes economic and political power. Those who are at the top of ownership and control are at the top of power stratification. The positions of castes or tribes are determined according to their position in the power structure. The landowners by means of their control over land prevent the growth of class consciousness among the landless. The other factors which contribute to the erosion of class consciousness are 'indistinct class position and double affiliation of persons' and 'the incoming of non-agriculturist castes and tribes into paddy cultivation creates competition and rivalry among themselves for lands'. (Bouton, 1985: 46).

In West Bengal, in short, it is the

> ... class structure is characterized by the presence of the differences in legal privileges and style of life. The legal privileges of the class members of the *Mahajan* and the *Chasi* or the *Krishan* classes is the same but when the *Chasi* or *Krishan* become related with the production simultaneously as the *Bhagchasi* or the *sanja Krishan*, the legal privilege differs. The style of life of the *Mahajan* is distinct and different from the *Chasi* or *Krishan*. The intra-class differences are not visible in *Mahajan* class but noted in the *Chasi* or the *Krishan*. The technical culture is borne not by the *Mahajan* but by *Chasi* or the *Krishan* on whom the *Mahajan* depends. The intra-class differences in style of life, multiple affiliations of the members of the *Chasi* or the *Krishan* class to two or more other classes prevent political activation. (Sengupta, 1979: 150)

The increasing commercialization and monetization have brought about rural indebtedness, land transfer, eviction of tenants and significant rise in rural migration from Midnapore, Bankura and Birbhum to Calcutta, Howrah, Hooghly, Burdwan and 24-Parganas, *i.e.*, from agricultural field to industrial field (Dasgupta, 1987: 282). At present the landed upper classes rely more on land ownership and control than distribution of income from property, do not permit political power to the landless cultivators and tend to use expanding profit from technological change to subvert social movements and divert the movements into reformist channels. The rich peasants and land owners took the control of the Panchayats throughout their lives. They are dominant castes in the village. In studying the Tusugaon and Birbhum villages, Pradip Kumar Bose has come to the conclusion that the landlords and the rich peasants are presented in the Panchayat bodies to muddle the interests of the weaker sections, tribals and untouchables. In the village Tusugaon two rival factions are led by two well-to-do Mahato rich peasants. They are more or less economically the same and similar in caste background. Conflicts often take place over the issue of control of village affairs. In Birbhum villages, the conflict is more on class line and the combined political function is controlled by the concentration and accumulation of wealth by the upper class. The Mahatos in Tusugaon have manipulated the Panchayat system, to gain the control over the lower castes (Chattopadhyay, 1992: 650). The high caste village elites who are economically and politically powerful also controlled the village life, nominated their clients for Panchayat and Assembly elections as their representatives, and mobilized the poor peasants against the 'headman'. And 'a local well-to-do Brahmin who was so far not recognized in the village as a man of importance is now trying to become the headman with the support of the poor peasants, who are not pleased with existing headman'. (Chattopadhyay, 1964 : 44). The Panchayat system was dominated by rural elites, leaders of dominant class or caste, when the Panchayat administration had the instrument of dominant rural elite, power had been transformed 'from the hands of the dominant propertied groups to a lower middle stratum' (Kohli, 1983: 794). The higher upper strata of the society controlled the village institutions, Panchayat and government officials, when the mass of the villagers participated least in the village affairs. Suraj Bandopadhyay and Donald Von Eschen have pointed at both 'generating power out of class' and 'generating class and caste out of power' (*op. cit.*, Gupta, 1992: 357-358). They point out that there was a close interpenetration between power, class and caste, when high class and caste had brought about power on the one hand, and power, on the other hand, provided the individuals wealth in the short-run and high class and status position in the long-run.

A new class configuration of rich, not-so-poor and poor has emerged in rural West Bengal. This has ushered in intense competition among various sections of the propertied classes for larger slices of benefits and facilities provided by the government. For possible benefits and making their interests protected, the not-so-poor class, middle class and lower middle class formed alliances with professional politicians and came to be sided with the landless (Roy, 1978 and Mukherjee, 1978). There are two kinds of coalition in operation. Each of these 'big-men' attempted to gather support among the wider population of the village in order to compete with other 'big-men' for controlling the Panchayati Raj

Institutions. Apart from these vertical coalitions, there were horizontal coalitions between some of these 'big-men' in order to fight others (Chattopadhyay, 1992: 647). These new rural elites generally represent caste groups in the midway between the highest and lowest ranks, who generally engage in manual labour and personal cultivation having a degree of mobility. They have bettered their positions by gaining access to Panchayats and other rural institutions. These rural influentials or 'expansive elites' (Rosenthal, 1977: 15) represent a shifting coalition of interests between various local elite groups and factional alliances for political ambition and economic benefits from various governmental inputs in rural development through Panchayati Raj Institutions. 'As a result, support among established or aspiring persons from locally dominant socio-economic and political strata was readily forthcoming, especially once the new institutions began to show signs of carrying both political and personal material value.' (Rosenthal, 1977: 316). The elite groups in association with party Panchayat leaders do not want any 'fundamental structural change in the form of radical land reforms' (Bandyopadhyay, 1981: 4). They always try to maintain a *status quo*, a modicum of unequal distribution of the means of production reducing a 'highly personalized dependency relationship' and a 'remnant of feudalism' (Dasgupta, 1984: A-145) in terms of 'functional linkages with the bureaucracy, elected rural self-growing institutions and peasant organizations' (Ghosh, 1981: A-50). However, employment generation and wage increase have liberated the landless agricultural labourers from the 'highly personalized dependency relationship' (Bandyopadhyay, 1981).

The Panchayati Raj Institutions in West Bengal were revitalized through various rural development programmes, for example, IRDP, JRY etc. Panchayati Raj Institutions in West Bengal are important arenas of political activity and these institutions represent themselves as effective loci of power and governance. Realization of local self-government would be incomplete without an active programme of development. In essence,

> The decreasing emphasis on political activism on the part of the PRIs and the increasing emphasis on limited routine functions ... the scope for further agrarian reforms is restricted by legal as well as political considerations and, therefore, programmes like the JRY and IRDP provide the mainstay of the Panchayats' activities ... the scope for activism on the part of the Left Front organizations and PRIs ought not to be limited, however, to

> agrarian reforms alone. In post-reform West Bengal, PRIs can act as instruments of public policy much more efficiently than they are able to do over most other parts of the country. Their role in the implementation of IRDP and JRY is simply an example of the potential they represent. Other interventions, such as the policy of positive discrimination in favour of the political representation of women and people belonging to Scheduled Castes and Scheduled Tribes, and the recent literacy campaign in the State, have been implemented through the PRIs. The fact remains, however, that such actions have been piecemeal, and that after the exhaustion of the agrarian reforms agenda, the PRIs are left without a clearly defined programme ... the potential created in West Bengal due to the institution of effective governance remains largely unfulfilled. (Sengupta and Gadzar, 1997: 162-163)

Underutilization of funds and poor monitoring of the schemes have had reduced the possibility of employment potentialities and employment generation in rural West Bengal. A spokesman of the Zilla Parishad himself said that in Murshidabad ₹ 1.04 crores were spent against the allotted money of ₹ 1.42 crores for the year, 1985-86, which went down to the spending of ₹ 85.5 lakhs for the year 1986-87 and created only 2,16,000 mandays of employment (Report, 1986: 16). However, Jahar Sarkar, the District Magistrate of Burdwan district said *The Statesman* that 'in Burdwan district ₹ 1.66 crores were spent under NREP during 1984-85. The figure rose up to ₹ 2.57 crores during 1985-86, which represented an increase of 54 per cent in a year. In RLEGP sector ₹ 63 lakhs were spent during 1984-85 and the figure rose to ₹ 1.93 crores during 1985-86.' (Report, 1986: 16). There were regional variations in rural development within the State of West Bengal. With regard to the performance rating of the government in IRDP, West Bengal's performance along with Sikkim, Tripura, Meghalaya, Nagaland, and Jammu and Kashmir was below 70 per cent (Sattar, 1987). West Bengal Government's performance in the RLEGP was more successful than that of the NREP with regard to the percentage of employment generated or mandays created to the resource utilized; but not more hopeful to alleviate poverty and reduced rural employment and restrict it under control (Government of West Bengal, 1987: 18-19). A mention here may be made that in West Bengal the percentage of family members employed for the period 1987-88 under the NREP and the RLEGP was 31.7 per cent which was highest in comparison with other

State's performances (NRID, 1988, 1989). The Scheduled Castes and Scheduled Tribes population were benefited least, badly placed economically and socially, and would in future fall further behind the general population of West Bengal. Most of them are below the poverty line as stipulated by the government.

Infrastructural developments, full employment and surely not supplementary employment during the periods of seasonal unemployment are needed for upgradation of the poor. 'A large-scale programme of assured wage employment for the rural poor will make the relevant part of what is IRDP today productive and worthwhile.' (Rath, 1985: 245). In West Bengal, the co-efficient of variation in wage rates was below than that of other States during the period of 1974-75 to 1984-85 (Mukhopadhyay, 1979; Dasgupta, 1984; Bose, 1981; Jose, 1988), though a moderate and gradual increase had to take place with some socio-economic constraints: the labourers did not sell their labour as commodities in the market, rather take only subsistence wages and they did not constitute 'class-for-itself' among themselves, restricted by male-female disparity in wage rates; patron-client relationship between labourers and employers; economic dependence of labourers on employers due to low per capita income and hostility among workers in adjacent villages. There remained a large and wide-scale disparity in wages within different districts. Labourers had to suffer from 'class-for-itself' and Bengal Unit of All India Kisan Sabha did not rise above mere 'economism'. The average wage increase in 1979-80 was only ₹ 1.10. 'The minimum wage levels fixed by the government have helped to define a target, and to strengthen the case of the labourers in their bargaining with the landowners. But the outcome of such bargains has been determined by the factors like the aggregate level of demand for labour, the strength of the organization of agricultural labourers, and the extent of intervention by the panchayat through its public works programme in the labour market.' (Dasgupta, 1984: A-146).

As the means of production is concentrated in few hands and supply of labour in excess of demand, so the rate of wage cannot go up as fast as the rate of profit from land. This has to be combated by enhancing the bargaining power of the rural poor through mobilization under the organization of the labourers (Bose, 1981: 2057). The village Panchayats lacked administrative expertise and did not take decision with regard to policy implementation, and hence, Food-for-Work Programme, IRDP and other schemes remained unimplemented in reaching the target. Though the poor were benefited, the CPI(M) controlled Panchayats provided benefits to consolidate their political and economic control over the villages (Mallick, 1993). The major difficulties confronting the Panchayats have to do with 'attitudes and organization rather than money' (Franda, 1979: 140-141). In fact,

> The village Panchayats lacked administrative expertise, and found the task of decision making tough. Since the bureaucracy was prevented from taking any part in the Panchayats' activities as a matter of policy, the implementation of anti-poverty programmes ground to a halt. Besides, the Panchayats in the States were entrusted with many other activities and made responsible for implementing a variety of schemes and programmes. Under the burden of these numerous responsibilities, lack of bureaucratic support, communication gap, etc., the whole set-up nearly collapsed. No decisions could be made, no activities could be undertaken and no programme was implemented. This explains the poor performance of the State in IRDP. (Sundaram and Tendulkar, 1984: 154-155).

References

Bandyopadhyaya, Nripen. 1981. 'Operation Barga and Land Reforms Perspective in West Bengal', *EPW* (June 20).

Baruah, Sanjib. 1990. 'The End of the Road in Land Reform?', *Development and Change* (Vol. 21).

Bhatia, B.M. 1979. 'Rural Unrest: Irrelevance of Land Reforms', *The Statesman* (Calcutta: Feb. 22).

Bhattacharya, N.; M. Chattopadhyay; and A. Rudra. 1987. 'Changes in the Level of Living in Rural West Bengal – Private Consumption', *EPW* (July 11).

Bhattacharya, N.; M. Chattopadhyay; and A. Rudra. 1987. 'Changes in the Level of Living in Rural West Bengal – Social Consumption', *EPW* (Aug. 15).

Bhattacharya, N.; M. Chattopadhyay; and A. Rudra. 1987. 'Changes in the Level of Living in Rural West Bengal – Housing Consumption', *EPW* (Sep. 5).

Bhattacharya, N.; M. Chattopadhyay; and A. Rudra. 1987. 'Changes in the Level of Living in Rural West Bengal – Consumer Durables, Clothing and Footwear', *EPW* (Oct. 31).

Bhattacharya, N.; M. Chattopadhyay; and A. Rudra. 1987. 'Changes in the

Level of Living in Rural West Bengal – Perceptions of the People', *EPW* (Nov. 28).

Bhattacharya, N.; M. Chattopadhyay; and A. Rudra. 1988. 'Changes in the Level of Living in Rural West Bengal – Variations across Socio-economic Groups', *EPW* (May 28).

Bhattacharya, Harihar. 1996. 'Unpolitical Science of West Bengal', *Socialist Perspective* (Vol. 24; Nos. 1-2).

Biswas, Jayanta (RSP). 1989. Speech delivered at West Bengal Legislative Assembly on 16.03.89 (Calcutta: West Bengal Legislative Assembly).

Bose, Buddhadeb. 1981. 'Agrarian Programme of the Left Front Government in West Bengal', *EPW* (Dec. 12).

Bouton, Marshall M. 1985. *Agrarian Radicalism in South Asia* (Princeton: Princeton University Press).

Burdwan District Committee, CPI(M). 1985. *Political-Organizational Report* (Burdwan: 14th Conference).

Burdwan District Committee, CPI(M). 1988. *Political-Organizational Report* (Burdwan: 15th Conference).

Burdwan District Committee, CPI(M). 1991. *Political-Organizational Report* (Burdwan: 16th Conference).

Chatterjee, Partha. 1997. *The Present History of West Bengal* (New Delhi: OUP).

Chattopadhyay, Gouranga. 1964. *Ranjana: A Village in West Bengal* (Calcutta: Bookland Pvt. Ltd.).

Chattopadhyay, Sujit Narayan. 1992. 'Historical Context of Political Change in Rural West Bengal', *EPW* (March 28).

Chowdhury, B.K. 1989. 'Panchayati Raj: Perspective and Prospect', *Yojana* (Vol. 33: Nos. 1-2).

Chowdhury, Binoy. 1988. *Paschimbanga Tristar Panchayat Nirbachan* (in Bengali) (Calcutta: West Bengal State Committee).

Cole, G.D.H. 1960. 'Democracy Face to Face with Hugeness' in *Essays in Social Theory* (London: Macmillan).

Committee on Plan Projects. 1959. *Report of the Team for the Study of Community Projects and National Extension Service, Vol. 1* (Delhi: Manager of Publications).

Dahl, Robert A. 1972. *Polyarchy: Participation and Opposition* (New Haven: Yale University Press).

Dasgupta, Biplab. 1984. 'Agricultural Labour under Colonial, Semi-capitalist and Capitalist Conditions – A Case Study of West Bengal', *EPW* (Sep. 29).

Dasgupta, Biplab. 1984. 'Share-cropping in West Bengal – From Independence to Operation Barga', *EPW* (June 30).

Dasgupta, Biplab. 1987. 'Urbanization and Rural Change in West Bengal', *EPW* (Feb. 14).

Datta, Pravat. 1993. *Prasanga: Panchayat* (Calcutta: National Book Agency).

Department of Rural Development. 1986. *Draft Concept Paper on Revitalization of Panchayati Raj Institutions* (Nov. 28).

Desai, A.R. 1969. 'Impact of Governmental Measures on Rural Society' in A.R. Desai (ed.). *Rural Sociology in India* (Bombay: Popular Prakashan).

Desai, A.R. 1984. *India's Path of Development: A Marxist Approach* (Bombay: Popular Prakashan).

Deutsch, Karl W. 1961. 'Social Mobilization and Political Development', *American Political Science Review* (Vol. LV: No. 3).

Dutta, Kalyan. 1974. 'Class Structure in Rural India' in Amal Kumar Mukhopadhyay (ed.), *Society and Politics in Contemporary India* (Calcutta: Council for Political Studies).

Franda, M.F. 1979. *India's Rural Development* (Bloomington: Indiana University Press).

Ghosh, Ajit Kumar. 1983. *Agrarian Reform in Contemporary Developing Countries* (New York: Martin's Press).

Government of West Bengal. 1981. *Economic Review* (Calcutta: West Bengal Government Press).

Government of West Bengal. 1987. *Economic Review, 1986-87.*

Gupta, Dipankar (ed.). 1992. *Social Stratification* (New Delhi: Oxford University Press).

Jose, A.V. 1988. 'Agricultural Wages in India', *EPW* (June 25).

Joshi, P.C. 1975. 'Agrarian Social Structure and Social Change' in K.M. Kurian (ed.). *India: State and Society* (New Delhi: Orient Longman).

Khasnabis, Ratan. 1986. 'More on West Bengal Tenancy Reforms', *EPW* (Jan. 25).

Kohli, Atul. 1983. 'Parliamentary Communism and Agrarian Reform', *Asian Survey* (Vol. XXIII: No. 7).

Kohli, Atul. 1987. *The State and Poverty in India* (Cambridge: Cambridge University Press).

Kohli, Atul. 1990. 'From Elite Activism to Democratic Consolidation' in Francine R. Frankel and M.S.A. Rao (eds.). *Dominance and State Power in Modern India, Vol. II* (New Delhi: OUP).

Krishna, Sudhir. 1993. 'Panchayati Raj', *EPW* (Sep. 25).

Kurian, M.K. 1980. 'Rural Development: Approaches and Programmes', *State and Society* (Vol. 1: No. 3).

Lieten, G.K. 1988. 'Panchayat Leaders in a West Bengal District', *EPW* (Oct. 1).

Lieten, G.K. 1992. *Continuity and Change in Rural West Bengal* (New Delhi: Sage Publications).

Lieten, G.K. 1996. *Devolution, Development and Democracy* (New Delhi: Sage Publications).

Mallick, Ross. 1993. *Development Policy of a Communist Government in West Bengal* (Cambridge: Cambridge University Press).

Miller, D.B. 1979. 'Introduction' in D.B. Miller (ed.). *Peasants and Politics: Grass Roots Reaction to Change in Asia* (London: Edward Arnold).

Misra, Surya Kanta. 1991. *An Alternative Approach to Development: Land Reforms and Panchayats* (Calcutta: Government of West Bengal Press).

Mukherjee, Mihir. 1978. 'Panchayat Poll: Keen Interest in Rural Areas', *The Statesman* (Calcutta: June 2).

Mukherjee, Nirmal and D. Bandyopadhyay. 1993. *New Horizons for West Bengal's Panchayats: A Report for the Government of West Bengal* (February).

Mukherjee, Partha Nath. 1983. *From Left Extremism to Electoral Politics* (New Delhi: Manohar).

Mukhopadhyay, Ashim. 1979. 'Share-croppers: A Long Story-III', *Frontier* (Aug. 25).

Narain, Iqbal. 1987. 'Revival of Panchayati Raj', *ICSSR News Letter* (Vol. 18: July-Sep.).

Narayan, Jayaprakash. 1962. 'The Role of Political Parties in Panchayati Raj', *Indian Journal of Public Administration* (Oct.-Dec.).

National Institute of Rural Development (NIRD). 1988/89. *Rural Development Statistics*.

Prosterman, Roy L. and Jeffrey M. Riedinger. 1987. *Land Reform and Democratic Development* (Baltimore and London: Johns Hopkins University).

Rahman, Anisur. 1984. *Grassroots Participation and Self-reliance* (New Delhi: OUP).

Ramaswamy, A.S. 1964. 'Decentralized Democracy or Despotic Democracy', *Kurukshetra* (Vol. 17: No. 4).

Rao, C.H. Hanumantha. 1989. 'Decentralized Planning: An Overview of Experience and Prospect', *EPW* (Vol. 24: No. 8).

Rath, Nilakanta. 1985. 'Garibi Hatao: Can IRDP do it?', *EPW* (Feb. 9).

Report. 1986. 'CPI(M)-Cong(I) Battle Over Rural Development', *The Statesman* (Dec. 3).

Roy, Ajit. 1983. 'Panchayat Elections – Class Mobilization without Class Struggle', *EPW* (June 25).

Roy, Ranjit. 1978. 'Panchayat Poll: Infighting between Left Parties', *The Statesman* (Calcutta: May 31).

Rudra, Ashok. 1981. 'One Step Forward, Two Steps Backward', *EPW* (June: Review of Agriculture).

Sathe, Vasant. 1989. 'Panchayati Raj: Its Validity', *Yojana* (January 26).

Sattar, Abdus. 1987. *Speech* (May 18), *Assembly Proceedings* (File No. nil, Page No. nil).

Sen Gupta, Bhabani. 1979. *CPI (M): Promises, Prospects and Problems* (New Delhi: Young Asia Publications).

Sengupta, Sunil and Haris Gazdar. 1997. 'Agrarian Politics and Rural Development in West Bengal' in Dreze and Sen (eds.). *Indian Development* (New Delhi: OUP).

Sengupta, Syamalkanti. 1979. *Caste, Status Group Aggregate and Class* (Calcutta: Firma KLM).

Sharma, K.L. 1974. *The Changing Rural Stratification System* (Simla: Indian Institute of Advanced Study).

Sharma, K.L. 1979. *Rural Society in India* (Jaipur: Rawat Publications).

Shiviah, M.; K.B. Srivastava and A.C. Jana. 1980. *Panchayati Raj Election in West Bengal, 1978* (Hyderabad: NIRD).

Sundaram, K. and Suresh D. Tendulkar. 1984. *Integrated Rural Development Programme in India* (Kuala Lumpur: The Asian and Pacific Development Centre).

Sundarayya, P. 1973. *An Explanatory Note on the Central Committee on Agrarian Issues* (Calcutta: Communist Party of India-Marxist).

Tornquist, Olle. 1991. 'Communists and Democracy: Two Indian Cases and One Debate', *Journal of Concerned Asian Studies* (Vol. n.f.: No. n.f.).

Webster, Neil. 1990. 'Agrarian Relation in Burdhwan District, West Bengal', *Journal of Contemporary Asia* (Vol. 10: No. 2).

West Bengal State Committee, CPI(M). 1982. *Political-Organizational Report* (Calcutta: 13th Conference).

West Bengal State Committee, CPI(M). 1994. *Panchayat Parichalona Prosange Nirdeshika* (in Bengali) (Calcutta: 17th Conference).

West Bengal State Committee, CPI(M). 1995. *Political-Organizational Report* (Calcutta: 18th Conference).

Westergaard, Kristen. 1987. 'Marxist Government and People's Participation', *Journal of Social Studies* (No. 38).

10

Local Governance and Empowerment of Elected Women: A Case Study of Karnataka

Chandrashekar. E.

Introduction

Since independence, various initiatives have been undertaken for improving the socio-economic conditions and empowering women in India. In this context, the Constitution guarantees socio-economic and political equality and the provision of equal rights for availing different opportunities to all social groups of population, especially women. Increasing emphasis has also been placed on initiating variety of development schemes and welfare programmes for maximizing the participation of women in different activities. Various legal reforms and resolutions in the form of social Acts have also been introduced to improve the social status and empowerment of women in the Indian social system. However, little progress has been visualized in the participation of women in different activities.

Recognizing the unsatisfactory progress, that has been achieved in improving the socio-economic status of women, it has increasingly been felt desirable that involving rural women in any political system and ensuring their participation in the activities of such institutions, including in matters related to certain decision-making process, would be instrumental in improving the socio-economic status and political empowerment of women. In view of these assumptions, the introduction of reservation policy is in favour of women in the Panchayati Raj Institutions. This has been an important Government intervention for maximizing the participation of women in different activities at village Panchayat levels.

This study relates to Panchayati Raj Institutions with particular reference to the 'Gram Panchayat (Local governance) and Empowerment of elected women representatives in rural Karnataka. Though in Karnataka the Panchayati Raj System is based on three tier system, this study is focused on the basic tier, i.e., Gram Panchayat. This is done with a view to explain the basic units of Local Government in Karnataka. Here there is scope for people's participation and particularly for women's representation. It is very difficult to study in detail the whole system of Panchayati Raj, as the subject covers vast area. In this study an attempt is made to analyse the empowerment of women representatives in Gram Panchayat – A case Study of 10 Gram Panchayats in Shimoga district.

Review Literature

Biduyt Mohanty's (2000) recent study on the impact of 73rd amendment in Orissa through field experience analyses that about 80-90 per cent of women attend the Panchayat meeting regularly. Given the sure number, one might conclude that the democracy has become participatory than before at least at the grass roots level. In her study of taking interview of elected women leaders from Karnataka, observed that the socio-economic background of these women which showed that majority of them come from the lower income group particularly at the village Panchayat level. The micro studies also show that the working culture of the Panchayat has changed because of the presence of the women. Finally, a part of the increase of the female literacy rate can be attributed to the presence of the women in Panchayat and their willingness to get educated. She also found that the standard of political institution at the grass roots level has not been lower because of women reservation and to some extent; the development process has become engendered. It is alleged that since many of the women are first timers and are illiterate, they depend upon their menfolk for conducting the Panchayat activities first; the husbands for other male representatives will shield them from the Panchayat secretary, B.D.O. if they try to harass the women. In fact, some of the State governments have passed a rule that their male relatives could accompany the women elected representative to the Panchayat. This is because in some cases, the Secretary of the Panchayat tries to implicate the inexperienced women by asking them to sign on blank cheques, etc. Some of the women chiefs went to jail because of those acts. An interesting finding came out from the above field experience. Even if women representatives depend on relatives, the power relations between husband and wife has already changed due to the reservation for women, the woman's husband gets a chance to come to the public sphere because of the wife and particularly no longer monolithic structure is seen in family relation. Studies point out the emergence of proxy women in Panchayat where the husbands or brothers look after her official activities. Mohanty however states that the first one or two years of the tenure, the proxy women are seen. Gradually, they become independent so finally Mohanty concludes 73rd Amendment has an empowering impact on women.

S. Govinda Gowda[1] and others (1996) in their study of Karnataka women elected Panchayat leader found that the women members of developed taluks were found to play a better developmental role that their counterparts in the backward taluks. The study reveals that among the socio-economic attributes such as age, education, caste, annual household income and landholding of women leaders, only education and annual household income had a highly significant and positive relationship with their developmental role performance. The findings of the study states that women members of the Panchayati Raj Institution could play an effective developmental role if they are given adequate recognition and encouragement.

O.P. Bohra (1997) in his case study of a Tamil Nadu Panchayat observed that even though women electorate constitute half of the voters, candidates including female candidate do hardly have interest in campaigning to seek the women' support. Rashmi Arun[2] (1997) in a case study of Madhya Pradesh found that in most of the cases women are housewives, first time entrants into politics and most of them are illiterate or educated up to primary level. Indian Institute of Social Science[3] (2000) in a study of Panchayati Raj in Haryana has reviewed the progress of some hundred elected women in four districts; majorities of the elected women Panches including younger women were illiterate when elected to office. After two years in office, they demanded literary skill and generally feel the need of education for their daughters. K. Jayalakshmi[4] (1997) A.P. based on the field study conducted in the Nalgonda district states that reservation in Panchayat ensures entry for all sections and thus visualizes as the harbinger of equality and social justice. Further, it is found that reservation has merely brought in a quantitative change in the gender participation rather than ushering a qualitative developmental efforts.

P. Manikyamba, in her study of Andhra Pradesh found that socio-economic background in general and political backgrounds in particular are important determinants of shaping the nature and level of participation of members in political institutions. The study reveals that education and participation are interrelated. In general, women members having secondary educational qualification are more participated well in the meetings. Next, economic status gives a sense of confidence and encouragement to participate. The participation of the poor women members is found mostly insignificant. The middle class and rich members showed greater degree of participation. Then, age has its impact on participation. The extent of participation of the young and the middle aged is generally more than that of old aged. Next, women members with experience in politics played active roles in the institution under study.

Focus of the Present Study

The view of women's empowerment as emerged from the above is a multi-dimensional one. It involves social equality through redefinition of women's status in existing patriarchal and social power structures that can offer them freedom from impediments imposed by age old customs, beliefs and practices governing status and treatment towards them and ensuring them greater say in social and political spheres. The present study has taken note of such a broader view of empowerment of women, which receives little or no attention in most studies restricting themselves to mere presence in PRIs. This study laid stress on the role women played in and the resultant change occurred in their knowledge, skills and attitudes. As the main objective of the present study is to find out as to how women's 'participation' in PRIs proves to be 'empowering'; the term 'participation' was conceptualised in three ways subsuming in some form the broader view of empowerment as outlined above: symbolic or physical presence in Panchayat meetings, substantive contribution, and development of women members themselves. Thus, the study represents a departure from the earlier trend.

The present study has attempted to examine various issues related to the implementation pattern of reservation policy and its awareness among women, the nature of participation of women members in different meetings, activities and various development programmes of Gram Panchayats, social reform and welfare activities.

Objectives of the Study

- To understand and report the socio-economic, educational background of the elected women representatives to Gram Panchayats of the area under study.
- To study and assess the level of awareness of the elected women members about their roles and responsibilities and various development programmes.
- To study the involvement of elected women members in decision making.
- To study the problems and difficulties faced by the elected women representatives of Gram Panchayats.

Methodology

For the purpose of the study ten Panchayats in Bhadravati Block of Shimoga district in Karnataka was purposefully selected. The fundamental reason behind my selection of the Panchayats for the study deserves two answers, first in these Panchayats women from backward class won important post like president and vice president. And I proceed with the contention that women are not only for women's development. For that, to study in my work that how far women leaders are responding to the general problem? In 2008 PR election 61 women members were elected from these ten Panchayats. I took all the elected women members of those Gram Panchayats as my samples. In this study one ex-president, secretary of a Panchayat, a senior citizen, and a present president and one woman graduate came as my samples including one husband of a woman ward member.

Comprehensive interview schedule was the primary technique to gather necessary information as to women's participation and performance. Sample of 60 women members of Gram Panchayats was randomly drawn from the member's list of 10 Gram Panchayats. Another sample of 40 male members and 20 officials was also randomly drawn from the same member's list to study the attitude of men towards women. In this connection select the JRY programme to study a roadwork to evaluate the performance of women leaders. In that area and it is to be clear that women members have been regarded as one separate category. Women members's subject of the inquiry and their Panchayat participation and performance have been analyzed in the overall social, political and functional context of Panchayat.

Socio-economic and Political Profile of the Respondents

Socio-economic and political status of women depend much upon their basic background, characteristics pertaining to their own personality and the society in which they live. The socio-economic profile is vital to any study as it helps in building a comprehensive and complete picture of the respondents. The individual profile is derived by looking at factors such as age, caste, religion, marital status, type of the family, educational level, occupation and annual income of the respondents. The education and occupation level of the respondent's husband is also taken into account to gauge the economic status of the family.

Table 10.1: Age, Caste and Educational Characteristics of the Respondents

Aspects	*Distribution of the Respondents*		
	Age group	*Number*	*Per cent*
Age(1.1)	<25	03	2.50
	26-35	33	27.50
	36-45	51	42.50
	46-55	29	24.17
	56+	04	03.33
	Total	**120**	**100.00**
Education (1.2)	*Status of Respondents*		
	Illiterate	06	05.00
	Primary	27	22.50
	Secondary	54	45.00
	Pre-University	15	12.50
	Graduate	14	11.67
	Post-Graduate	04	03.33
	Total	**120**	**100.00**
Caste (1.3)	*Caste-wise classification*		
	Scheduled Caste	18	15.00
	Scheduled Tribe	12	10.00
	Backward Castes	35	29.17
	Forward Castes	55	45.83
	Total	**120**	**100.00**

An analysis of the age of women members as presented in Table 10.1 reveals that about 42.50 per cent of women were below 45 years of age, 24.17 per cent of women were above 45 years and 3.33 per cent of women were above 55 years of age. About 27.50 per cent of women were below 35 years of age, and 2.50 per cent of women were less than 25 years of age. This shows that marriage and motherhood do not seem to inhibit women from seeking a political career. The mean age of women in Gram Panchayat is 37 years, which indicates that the younger generations of women have realized the value of political participation. They are more mobile in comparison with the older generation and have broken the traditional barriers.

This illustrates that the educational level of the women members is lower. It clearly indicates that the participation of respondents with below secondary education tends to be more in a decentralized democracy. It is an accepted fact that the overall educational status of female is quite low in all the Gram Panchayats. In the case of educational background of the women Gram Panchayat members illustrated in Table 10.2 shows that the 45.5 per cent had education up to secondary level, 22.50 per cent had primary level education, while 11.67 per cent were graduates, 12.50 per cent had education up to pre-university level, while 5.0 per cent were illiterates and 3.33 per cent were post-graduates.

Table 10.2: Religion, Marital Status and Occupation of the Respondents

Aspects	*Religion-wise Classification of Respondents*		
Religion (2.1)	*Religion*	*Number*	*Per cent*
	Hindus	105	87.50
	Christians	08	06.67
	Muslims	07	05.83
	Total	120	100.00
Marital status (2.2)	*Marital Status of Respondents*		
	Married	97	80.83
	Unmarried	17	14.17
	Widow	03	02.50
	Separated	03	02.50
	Total	120	100.00
Occupation (2.3)	*Husband's Occupation of the Respondents*		
	Agriculture	84	70.00
	Service	03	02.50
	Labour work (Cooli)	31	25.83
	Petty business	02	01.67
	Total	120	100.00

The one-third representation of Scheduled Caste and Scheduled Tribe women in the Gram Panchayat clearly indicates that the reservation of seats for them in general and women in particular ensured the participation of women. It may be pointed out that 73rd Constitutional amendment introduced reservation of seats for women in Gram Panchayats. This reservation was based on population of Scheduled Castes, Scheduled Tribes and Backward Classes. It is instrumental in bringing the socially and economically backward sections of the people to the mainstream of politics. Caste structure of respondents has been depicted in Table 10.3 reveal that about 45.83 per cent of the members belonged to the forward castes/communities. The representation for the Scheduled Castes is 15.00 per cent, while Scheduled Tribes is 10.00 per cent and 29.17 per cent for the backward castes.

Table 10.2 presents religion-wise structure of respondents. The religion-wise data shows that majority of women members were Hindus who numbered 87.50 per cent. While Christian women members were 6.67 per cent and Muslim members were 5.83 per cent. This result is an outcome of population structure of the villages. It may be observed that the Christians had a better representation than Muslim members in the Gram Panchayats. Table 10.2 reveals that majorities are married women and they are able to balance their roles as Gram Panchayat members/vice presidents/presidents with their role in the family. The participation of more number of widows indicates their faith in the political empowerment of women through grass roots level democratic institutions. Data on the marital status of women members are given in Table 10.2 shows that 80.83 per cent of women members were married. Only 14.17 per cent of the members were unmarried. Among the married respondents, three were widows and three members of the sample study were separated. The occupational status of the spouses of the women Gram Panchayat members illustrated in Table 10.3 reveals that the primary occupation of the majority of them, *i.e.*, 70.00 per cent was agriculture, 25.83 per cent was labour work, 1.67 per cent was petty business. It revealed that a majority of Gram Panchayat members' spouses were engaged in the agricultural activities as cultivators.

The occupational skills of respondents in all selected panchayats are also uniformly low. This is also reflected in the income levels of the respondents. The occupational status of the respondents presented in Table 10.3, the majority 55.83 per cent of them were engaged in the household related non-economic activities as housewives, 18.33 per cent of the gram panchayat women members were working as agricultural labourers. 15.83 per cent of them were working as (factory) industrial workers, 3.33 per cent of members were working as Beedi-rolling and 6.67 per cent of them were engaged in self-employment. This is because many seem to be engaged in home-based occupations, which are not perceived as profession. It was found that large number of respondents fell in the low income group. Table 10.3 presents income distribution across members. The majority 51.67 per cent of the respondents has annual income of less than ₹ 11,000. This is due to the higher number of respondents engaged as agricultural labourers and house wives. Income groups—₹ 11,000 to ₹ 25,000 covered 23.32 per cent and ₹ 25,000 to ₹ 50,000 covered 11.67 per cent and ₹ 50,000 to 75,000 covered 7.50 per cent and ₹ 75,000 to 1,00,000 covered 4.17 per cent and remaining 1.67 per cent families had income above ₹ 1,00,000.

Table 10.3: Occupational-wise Classification of the Respondents

Aspects	*Classification of the Respondents*		
Occupational (3.1)	*Occupational*	*Number*	*Per cent*
	House wife	67	55.83
	Agricultural labour	22	18.33
	Beedi Rolling	04	03.33
	Industrial labour	19	15.83
	Self-employed	08	6.67
	Total	**120**	**100.00**
Annual income (3.2)	*Income-wise classification of the Respondents*		
	Less than ₹ 11,000	62	51.67
	11,000-25,000	28	23.32
	26,000-50,000	14	11.67
	51,000-75,000	09	7.50
	76,000-1,00,000	05	4.17
	Above 1,00,000	02	1.67
	Total	**120**	**100.00**

It was well visualized that very little opportunities and freedom have been provided to women to participate in educational systems, social and cultural activities and in seeking employment in rural areas of selected 32 sample Gram Panchayats due to traditionally developed and prevailing backward social and cultural system. Inequalities in work participation were highly prevalent among the women of different castes and income groups. The women among the upper castes and those belonging to economically sound households were hardly participating in different economic activities even in the family enterprises and agricultural operations. The existence of some strict practices in Muslim communities restrict the ladies to participate in different social and religious functions. However, the unmarried girls had little more opportunities than the married women to participate in different activities and to move outside households. The proportion of literate women representatives was significantly higher than in the previous years.

The economic activities of different categories of respondents show that agricultural operations were generally performed by the women members belonging to low-income groups. The women members belonging to upper castes and higher economic background participated more in other economic activities apart agricultural work. By and large some women members of Gram Panchayat had relatively higher level of freedom to move outside households and to participate in different economic, social, cultural and political activities. At the same time, various studies also postulate the fact that poverty is not the sole cause; other socio-cultural factors also influence the phenomena of women respondents' participation in work.

Elected Women Members' Empowerment through Panchayats

The empowerment of women is becoming an increasingly popular term in development discourses. Women's empowerment is a process, and the outcome of the process, by which women gain greater control over material and intellectual resources, and challenge the ideology of patriarchy and gender-based discrimination against women in all the institutions and structures of society. Empowerment is concerned with power, particularly with changing the power relations between individuals and groups in society. The outcome of empowerment should manifest itself as a redistribution of power between individuals, genders, groups, classes, castes, races, ethnic groups. Empowerment means the transformation of structures of subordination, through radical changes in law, property rights, control over women's labour and bodies, and the institutions, which reinforce and perpetuate male domination. Therefore, empowerment means making informed choices within an expanding framework of information, knowledge and analysis of available options.

Women's empowerment is not against men, but against the system of patriarchy and all its manifestations. The empowerment spiral transforms every person involved – the individual, the collective and the environment.

The method of measuring and evaluating women's empowerment and progress is by looking at:

- Whether women status has improved as a result of being in Panchayats?
- Whether awareness levels of women in Panchayats has increased?
- Whether the ability of effective participation in Panchayats has increased?
- Measure whether the women have been raising problems in Panchayat meetings.

The issue of women's empowerment, which enables women to assert their political power, has been on the anvil of discussion at many levels in India. The Beijing conference (1995) drew particular attention to the neglect of women in political structures all over the world and the importance of bringing women into political arena. In the present study, measurement and evaluation of empowerment has been looked into based on several important dimensions, *viz*., awareness, participation, decision-making, perception, etc.

Table 10.4: The Sources of Inspiration

Sources of inspiration	*Number*	*Percentage*
Family members	38	31.67
Husband	67	55.83
Political party	74	61.67
Village leaders	18	15.00
Self	41	34.13

**Note*: Percentage is not equal to 100 due to multiple choices.

Table 10.4 indicates the sources of inspiration of respondents into the public life due to the influence of varied factors, such as self-interest, compulsion of family members and party encouragement. It is evident from Table 10.4 that party encouragement was the chief factor responsible for large scale induction of women into Panchayats, which constitutes 61.67 per cent, while 34.13 per cent had self-motivation with a deep urge to serve public. 31.67 per cent were motivated by their family members. Only 15.00 per cent of the respondents were made to enter politics by village leaders. It is clear that political parties, husband and family members played an important role in motivating women to enter politics.

Table 10.5: Present Position of the Respondents in Gram Panchayats

Present position	*Number*	*Percentage*
Member	102	85.00
Member of standing committee	06	05.00
Vice President	09	07.00
President	03	02.00
Total	**120**	**100.00**

Table 10.5 explains the present position of members in their respective Gram Panchayats. An overwhelming majority of 85.00 per cent are just the members in Gram Panchayats, whereas meagre 2.00 per cent enjoy the position of presidents. Slightly less than 7.00 per cent of the respondents enjoy the position of vice presidents. From this, it follows that a majority of the Gram Panchayats are headed by male presidents and minority number of Gram Panchayats are headed by female presidents.

Table: 10.6: Number of Times Respondents elected to Panchayats

No. of times elected	*Number*	*Percentage*
First time	93	77.50
Second time	24	20.00
Third time	03	02.50
Total	**120**	**100.00**

Thus majority of the members are first entrants to Panchayats and hence are less experienced. From Table 10.6, it can be inferred that majority 77.50 per cent of the respondents are representing their ward for the first time, only a moderate number 20.00 per cent are representing their wards for the second time and a small percentage of 2.50 per cent are representing their wards for the third time.

Table 10.7: The awareness of the 73rd Constitutional Amendment Act by Respondents

Awareness of 73rd amendment	*Number*	*Percentage*
Very well aware	18	15.00
Just aware	73	60.83
Ignorant of it	29	24.17
Total	**120**	**100.00**

From this, it is concluded that most of the respondents knew that reservation of seats has been made for women as per the Amendment Act. This illustrates that the awareness levels of women in Gram Panchayat is quite high. Table 10.7 showing the awareness of the 73rd Constitutional Amendment Act by respondents, in which a provision has been made for 33.33 per cent women's reservation in Gram Panchayat. Of the total 120 respondents, 41 are elected from the reservation category. It shows that a majority of 60.83 per cent are just aware of the 73rd Constitutional Amendment Act, 15.00 per cent are very well aware and 24.17 per cent are ignorant of it.

Table 10.8: Training imparted to Newly Elected Women Representatives

Training imparted	*Number*	*Percentage*
Yes	109	90.83
No	011	09.17
Total	**120**	**100.00**

Training is important for better participation of women in political processes. The study reveals that majority of the members have received training in political participation which has increased their awareness. Table 10.8 indicates that 90.83 per cent respondents had undergone some sort of training, while 9.17 per cent did not get any training.

Table 10.9: Opinion expressed by the Respondents on the Women's Political Reservation Bill

Opinion on Women's Political Reservation Bill	*Number*	*Percentage*
Absolutely essential	12	10.00
Essential	81	67.50
Not essential	23	19.17
Not at all essential	04	03.33
Total	**120**	**100.00**

It can be concluded that an overwhelming majority of the respondents are in favour of the Bill, because, this has enabled a large number of women to enter into politics. Similarly, the reservation for SC/ST, OBC and women has provided opportunities to become members and participate in the development process. Table 10.9 explains about the awareness of respondents on the women's political Reservation Bill. Among them 67.50 per cent of respondents say that it is essential, 10.00 per cent of respondents are of the opinion that it is absolutely essential, 19.17 per cent of women expressed the opinion that it is not essential and a meagre proportion of 3.33 per cent argued that it is not at all essential.

Table 10.10: The Affiliation of Respondents to other Social Organisation

Member of Local Organization	*Number*	*Percentage*
Self-help group	96	80.00
School development committee	13	10.00
Any other	11	09.17
Total	**120**	**100.00**

Table 10.10 reveals that 80.00 per cent of the respondents are the members of self-help group. 10.00 per cent of respondents are the members of school betterment committee and sizeable number of respondents are the Members of Mahila Mandal. The participation of respondents in various social organizations shows this enhances the empowerment of women members in Gram Panchayats.

Table 10.11: Nature of Participation by Respondents in Panchayat Proceedings

Nature of participation	*Number*	*Percentage*
Always	15	12.50
Very often	51	42.50
Often	34	28.33
Less often	13	10.83
Not at all	07	05.84
Total	**120**	**100.00**

Table 10.11 explains participation of respondents in the proceedings of Panchayat meeting and speaking about Ward related issues. 42.50 per cent of the members take part in the proceedings very often and 12.50 per cent of them always speak in the meetings. 28.33 per cent of the members participate in the proceedings often and 10.83 per cent less often. 5.84 per cent of the members did not take any part in the proceedings. Majority of the respondents thus take part actively in the proceedings of Panchayats.

Table 10.12: Frequency of Visit by the Respondents to their Wards

Visit the ward	*Number*	*Percentage*
Always	22	18.33
Very frequently	46	38.33
Frequently	37	30.83
Less frequently	13	10.84
Never	02	01.67
Total	**120**	**100.00**

It can be concluded that majority of the respondents have the awareness of their roles and responsibilities in Panchayats. They visit the Ward and interact with people to identify the problems of the Wards. Table 10.12 illustrates the frequency of visit by the respondents to their Wards. An overwhelming majority of 38.33 per cent very frequently and 18.33 per cent always visit their wards, 30.83 per cent members frequently visit their Wards, while 10.84 per cent and 1.67 per cent respondents less frequently and never visit their wards, respectively.

Table 10.13: The Nature of Participation by Respondents in Ward Sabha and Panchayat meetings

Nature of participation in meetings	*Number*	*Percentage*
Very actively	14	11.67
Actively	68	56.67
Less actively	24	20.00
Passively	14	11.67
Total	**120**	**100.00**

It is observed that majority of the members take active participation in Ward Sabha and Panchayat meetings. Table 10.13 shows participation of women members in Ward Sabha and Panchayat meetings. 56.67 per cent of the members take part in the meetings actively and 11.67 per cent have reported very active participation. The participation of 20.00 per cent of the members is found to be less active while 11.67 per cent of the members reported only passive participation.

It follows that, in general respondents in most of the Gram Panchayats seem to play an active role in discussing village problems in Ward meetings, interacting with people to identify the needs of the community etc. Table 10.14 illustrates that the frequency of presentation of problems

Table 10.14: The Frequency of Presentation of Problems by Respondents in Ward/Panchayat Meetings

Frequency of presentation of problems	*Number*	*Percentage*
Always	13	10.84
Very often	33	27.50
Often	44	36.67
Less often	23	19.17
Not at all	07	05.84
Total	**120**	**100.00**

by respondents in Ward and Panchayat meetings. A majority of 36.67 per cent are often presenting the problems, whereas 27.50 per cent very often present the problems in Panchayat meetings; 19.17 per cent of the respondents present problems less often, while a meagre percentage of 5.84 did not present the problems.

Table 10.15: Opinion expressed by the Respondents on Women Empowerment through 73rd Constitutional Amendment Act

Empowerment with 73rd Constitutional Amendment Act	*Number*	*Percentage*
Yes	57	47.50
No	38	31.67
Can't say	16	13.34
Not Known	09	07.50
Total	**120**	**100.00**

It can be concluded that majority of the respondents expressed the opinion that after the advent of 73rd Constitutional Amendment Act, the

Table 10.16: The Specific Problems faced by Women in Politics

Specific Problem	*Number*	*Percentage*
Gender discrimination	37	30.83
Family iife and Work life balancing	64	53.33
Male members dominant attitude	43	35.83
Lack of previous political experience	41	34.17
Lack of knowledge of the Panchayat Act and other Govt. circulars sent from time to time	94	78.34
Male dominated society	46	38.33
Lack of awareness, inferiority complex and self confidence	28	23.33

**Note*: Percentage is not equal to 100 due to multiple choices.

women had been empowered in politics to a greater extent. Table 10.15 illustrates the opinion expressed by the respondents on women empowerment with 73rd Constitutional Amendment Act. Majority of the respondents, i.e., 47.50 per cent are in favour of women empowerment through 73rd Constitutional Amendment Act, 31.67 per cent of respondents are neither in favour of the Act nor in disfavour of it, 13.34 per cent in disfavour of the Act and only 7.50 per cent of respondents have shown their ignorance of the Act.

Table 10.16 shows that overwhelming majority of the respondents argued that they face various problems in politics. For 78.34 per cent of the respondents' problem is the lack of knowledge of Panchayat Act and other Government Circulars sent from time to time. 53.33 per cent of the respondents are finding it difficult to balance their family life and political career. For 34.17 per cent of the respondents, the problem is lack of previous political experience. 35.83 per cent and 30.33 per cent of the members admitted male domination and gender discrimination in the society as their major problems. For 23.33 per cent of the members the problem is lack of awareness, inferiority complex and self-confidence. Domination by male members in the Panchayats was considered as a problem by 38.33 per cent of the members.

Table 10.17: Opinion expressed by the Respondents on Continuance in Politics

Continue in politics	*Number*	*Percentage*
Yes	43	35.83
Cannot say	28	23.33
No	49	40.84
Total	**120**	**100.00**

Table 10.17 explains about the respondents on continuance in politics. Of 35.83 per cent of respondents expressed their desire to continue in politics and an equal proportion of respondents were unwilling to continue their political career. 23.33 per cent of the respondents could not give any opinion. From this, it can be analysed that a majority of the female members have interest in politics and minority of female members have no interest in politics.

Table 10.18 illustrates that opinion expressed by the respondents about the enhancement of status in society after the membership. 34.17 per cent of the respondents were of the opinion that membership of Panchayats had enhanced a lot, their status in society. For 40.00 per cent

Table 10.18: Opinion expressed by the Respondents about the Enhancement of Status in Society after the Membership

Opinion	*Number*	*Percentage*
Enhanced a lot	41	34.17
Moderately increased	48	40.00
Somewhat increased	19	15.83
Neither increased nor decreased	12	10.00
Decreased	Nil	—
Total	**120**	**100.00**

of the respondents it was moderate enhancement and for 15.83 per cent it was small increase, 10.00 per cent expressed the opinion that there was neither increase nor decrease in their status in society due to Panchayat membership. No respondent indicated decrease in social status. It can be concluded that Panchayat membership has given better status to women in public spheres.

Table 10.19: Opinion expressed by the Respondents on Extra Responsibilities of Women Leaders towards Women

Opinion on Extra Responsibilities	*Number*	*Percentage*
Yes	69	57.50
No	51	42.50
Total	**120**	**100.00**

Table 10.19 analyses the opinion expressed by the respondents on extra responsibilities of women leaders towards women. An overwhelming majority of 57.50 per cent of the members expressed the opinion that they had extra responsibilities towards women. But 42.50 per cent of the members did not think so. Thus it can be inferred that majority of the women members believed that they had extra responsibilities towards women.

Table 10.20: The Nature of Involvement in the Process of Decision-making by the Respondents

Involvement in Decision making	*Number*	*Percentage*
Actively involved	32	26.67
Involved to a moderate level	43	35.83
Less involvement	31	25.83
No involvement	14	11.67
Total	**120**	**100.00**

There is a lot of scope and potential for women to emerge as decision-makers. Involvement of women in decision-making roles is an important tool for empowerment. Better understanding of rules, regulations and procedures of the Panchayats and the various schemes are equally important for the women members to take proper decision at the Panchayat level. Table 10.20 explains the nature of involvement of respondents in the process of decision-making. It was reported by a majority of respondents (35.83%) that they involve moderately in decision-making. 26.67 per cent were actively involved in decision-making process of Panchayats. 25.83 per cent women members just involved in the process of decision-making, while a very small number of respondents 11.67 per cent were not involved in the process of decision-making. From this, it follows that a majority of the respondents are moderately and actively involved in the decision-making process of Panchayats.

Table 10.21: Respondents handling Issues Independently

Handling Issues independently	*Number*	*Percentage*
Yes	63	52.50
No	57	47.50
Total	**120**	**100.00**

From this analysis, it is understood that majority of the respondents are very strong in the consciousness of their role in Panchayat. They are capable of handling issues independently. Table 10.21 explains the respondents handling issues independently. An overwhelming majority of 52.50 per cent are handling issues independently in Wards and Panchayats, while 47.50 per cent of respondents are not having the capacity to handle issues independently in their constituencies.

Table 10.22: The Responsibilities discharged by the Respondents

Responsibilities	*Number*	*Percentage*
Identification of the present problems of the Ward	31	25.83
Presenting the problems in the meeting and getting the approval	72	60.00
Presenting the problems identified by the people of the Ward	37	30.83
Taking initiative to complete the half done projects	24	20.00
Taking initiative to see that Govt. projects and schemes reach the people	41	34.17

Note: Percentage will not be equal to 100 due to multiple choices.

From this, it follows that majority of the respondents are aware of their responsibilities and independently discharge their functions in Panchayats. Table 10.22 analyses the fact that a large proportion of respondents 60 per cent were discussing the problems in meeting and get the approval, 25.83 per cent of women identify the present problems of the Ward, while 30.83 per cent of respondents discuss the problems identified by the people of the Ward in the meetings. 34.17 per cent take initiative to see that Government projects and schemes reach the people. Only few 20 per cent take the initiative to complete the half-done projects.

Table 10.23: Specific Contribution made by the Respondents to their Ward

Specific Contributions	*Number*	*Percentage*
House for houseless	19	15.83
Water connection for the Ward	69	57.50
Initiations to open Anganwadi	04	03.33
Propaganda to prohibit alcoholism	31	25.84
Initiation to provide basic infrastructure	51	100.00

Note: Percentage is not equal to 100 due to multiple choices.

It can be concluded that women members have better knowledge of their roles and responsibilities and knew the functions of the Gram Panchayats. From the analysis of the data, it is inferred that 57.50 per cent of the respondents provided water connections in their Wards, 25.84 per cent were engaged in propaganda against alcoholism, 15.83 per cent provided houses for the houseless and 3.33 per cent took initiative in opening up of anganwadis.

Table 10.24: The perceived Level of Satisfaction of Power and Position of Respondents in Gram Panchayats

Level of satisfaction	*Number*	*Percentage*
Excellent	21	17.50
Very good	34	28.33
Good	39	32.50
Neither good nor bad	16	13.33
Bad	10	08.34
Total	**120**	**100.00**

As a result of their outdoor participation in the delivery of welfare services, these respondents have acquired a new identity full of self-satisfaction and self-respect. They are getting much awaited social recognition from the community people. Moreover, it is not only that their status changed within the family but even the very status of the family has changed in the community. It is quite evident from Table 10.24 that nearly 28.33 and 32.50 per cent expressed their opinion on power and position as very good and good respectively. Only a minority of the respondents expressed their opinion on power and position as bad and disappointing.

Table 10.25 : The perceived Level of Dominance by Male Members in the Meetings as reported by the Respondents

Dominance by male	*Number*	*Percentage*
Dominance to a greater extent	18	15.00
Dominance to a moderate extent	31	25.83
Dominance to a minimum extent	26	21.67
No dominance	45	37.50
Total	**120**	**100.00**

However, the analysis reveals that traditionalisation still exists and some, particularly illiterate and ignorant members were subject to domination in Panchayats by male members. Table 10.25 explains that 37.50 per cent observed that women were in no way dominated by men. 25.83 per cent of respondents opinion is dominance to a moderate extent. 21.67 per cent respondents expressed the view that there was dominance to a minimum extent and only 15.00 per cent reported dominance to a greater extent. Majority of the women reported no or limited dominance by male members.

Conclusion

In all the thirty-two Panchayats, it has been found that women are fairly young in age, which indicates that the younger generation of women have realized the value of political participation. It has been observed that the participation of respondents with below secondary education tends to be more in a decentralised democracy. Regarding the caste profile, one-third of the representatives belonged to Scheduled Castes and Scheduled Tribes. The reservation of seats for these groups ensured their participation in Gram Panchayats. It is found that the Christians had a better representation than Muslim members in the Gram Panchayats. It reveals that majority of the respondents are married and are able to balance their roles in family life and political life. An overwhelming majority of the respondents come from joint family background. The occupational status of the respondents shows that, majority of them were housewives engaged in the household related activities. A majority of the respondents belonged to low income groups. Most of the women are from non-political background and entered politics due to the pressure of political parties, husband and family members. Social status of the family tends to bear a strong influence in determining women empowerment in Gram Panchayat than the economic status of the family. Majority of the respondents are only the members in Gram Panchayats. It is found that a majority of the Gram Panchayats are headed by male presidents. Majority of the respondents have represented their Wards for the first time. It indicates the lack of experience, skill and ability of participation on the part of members. The members have secured self-satisfaction and self respect and also acquired a new identity because of their participation in welfare services. Most of the respondents knew that reservation of seats had been made for women from the 73rd Constitutional Amendment Act and they were in favour of the Bill. This shows that the awareness level of women in Gram Panchayat is quite high. Majority of the respondents have awareness of their roles and responsibilities. They always visit the Ward and interact with people to identify the problems of the Wards.

The nature of participation by the respondents in Panchayat proceedings and the Ward Sabha are quite encouraging. Involvement of women in the public activity is important for empowerment of women. Majority of the respondents have strong consciousness of their role in Panchayats and are capable of handling issues independently. The respondents in most of the Gram Panchayats discuss village problems in meetings, interact with people to identify the needs of the community and implement developmental programmes. Majority of respondents have made specific contributions in the form of taking initiative to provide basic infrastructure and water connection for Ward.

Decision-making role is important for empowerment. Majority of the respondents have involved themselves actively in decision-making process. They have also exhibited potentiality to emerge as decision-makers. Large proportions of respondents present the problems in the meetings and get the approval. They are aware of their responsibilities and discharge their functions in Panchayat independently. Dominance by male members still exists in the Panchayat. The respondents think that only illiterate and ignorant members are dominated by male members. A majority of respondents have shown interest in continuation in politics. A large proportion of the respondents' opinion is that women leaders have got extra responsibilities towards women. Most of the respondents are of the opinion that training should be imparted to newly elected representatives. The problems faced by majority of the women in politics are balancing family life and professional career, lack of previous political experience, lack of knowledge of the Panchayat Act, lack of awareness, inferiority complex and lack of self-confidence.

Notes

1. Gowada, S. and Others, 1996, "Developmental Role of Women members of Panchayati Raj institutions : A study in Karnataka", *Journal of Rural Development*, Vol. 15(2), pp. 249-259, NIRD, Hyderabad.
2. Arun, Rashmi, 1997, "Role of Women in Panchayati Raj", *Administrator*, Vol. XII, April-June.
3. Status of Panchayati Raj in the States and Union Territories of India, 2000, Institution of Social Science, New Delhi.
4. Lakshi, 1993, *Women and Politics: A Study in Political Participation*, Book Link Corporation, Hyderabad.

References

Gupta, K.R. (Ed.), *Rural Development in India*, Atlantic Publishers and Distributors, New Delhi, 2003.

Heptulla, Najma, *Reforms for Women*, Oxford and IBH Publishing Co. Pvt. Ltd., New Delhi, 1992.

Iltiza H. Khan, *Government in Rural India*, Asia, Bombay, 1969.

Institute of Social Sciences (ISS), *The New Panchayati Raj in Karnataka: An Evaluation*, New Delhi, 1994.

Jana Everett, "Women and Political Leadership" in Joyce Lebra and Others (eds.)., *Women and Work in India : Continuity and Change*, Promilla & Co., New Delhi, 1984.

Jasprit Kaur Soni, *Women Empowerment: Exploring the Facts*, Author Press, New Delhi, 2006.

Jha Uma Shankar (Eds.), *Status of Indian Women: Crisis and Conflict in Gender Issues*, Kanishka Publishers, Distributors, New Delhi, 1998.

Kaushik Susheela, (ed), *Women's Participation in Politics*, Vikas Publishers, New Delhi, 1993.

Kelber, M. (ed.), *Women and Government: New Ways to Political Power*, Westport and London, Praeger, 1994.

Khanna, B.S., *Rural Local Government in India and Asia*, Deep & Deep Publications Pvt. Ltd., New Delhi, 1999.

Kumari Letha R., *Women in Politics: Participation and Governance*, Author Press, New Delhi, 2006.

11

Growth and Development of the Framework of the Panchayati Raj Institution in Karnataka

Munikrishna

Introduction

The local government system, commonly referred to in India as Panchayati Raj is believed to have been popular and widely prevalent in India from ancient times. During British times, an attempt was made to introduce some legislation but the imperial masters preferred to allow the local government system to run in the manner that the locals wished as long as it did not adversely impact on the Raj.

The Constitution of India in its original form, referred to Panchayati Raj only as part of the Directive Principles, wherein the States were asked to promote these institutions as instrument of self-government. At best it represented a belated after thought, at worst it represented the tokenism and lack of seriousness about local government that reflected the mood in the Constituent Assembly. Four factors need to be kept in mind while reading the original provisions in the Constitution relating to Panchayati Raj. Firstly, it represented the 'unitary mindset of the Constitution makers., Secondly, the issue of State and local rights was accorded a 'secondary status' by the founding fathers. Thirdly, the leadership in the Assembly was convinced that the 'sociology of local politics' inevitably encouraged divisiveness rather than unity. Finally, the constitutional provisions on local government appeared to be a minor concession extended to the 'Gandhians', many of who made a passionate plea for incorporating the Gandhian dream of '*Rama Rajya*' in Constitution.

Three important landmarks need to be flagged in the progress of Panchayati Raj Institutions in India after the inauguration of the Constitution. The impact and implications of the Balwantray Mehta Committee Report (1957), the Asoka Mehta Committee Report (1978) and its ramifications and finally the amendment of the Constitution and the guaranteeing of a Constitutional status to local bodies (73/74 Amendment). This chapter would focus on local government from the window of women's empowerment. The focus would be on the role and contribution of local government structures, institutions and processes to the empowerment of women.

Article 40 of the Constitution of India provides that the State shall take steps to organize village Panchayats and endow them with such powers and authority to enable them to function as units of local self-government. However, even after the recommendations of the Balwant Ray Mehta Committee and Asoka Mehta Committee on Panchayats had been put into force, several ills continued to afflict the Panchayati Raj System in the country in the post-independence period. There were long delays in holding of Panchayat elections, frequent suspension/suppression/dissolution of the Panchayat bodies, lack of functional and financial autonomy, inadequate representation of marginalized and weaker sections and meagre, occasional and tied Government grants. This crippled the functioning of Panchayats and did not allow them to function as institutions of local self-government as had been envisaged in the Constitution. An imperative need accordingly emerged to enshrine in the Constitution of India, certain basic and essential features of local self-government so as to enable local bodies to function as institutions of self-governance both in planning and implementation of development programmes. Consequently Constitution (73rd Amendment) Act 1992 was passed and was brought into force with effect from 24.4.1993. The Act does not apply to Schedule V and VI Areas of Assam, Tripura, Meghalaya and Mizoram, State of Nagaland, hill areas of the State of Manipur for which District Councils exist and the Panchayati Raj Gram Panchayat meeting goes in progress.

Constitutional Amendments – 73rd and 74th

The 73rd and 74th amendment of the Constitution was in 1992. As a result Panchayati Raj Institutions (PRIs) gained constitutional status and came to be regarded as the third level of governance.

The 73rd and the 74th Constitutional amendments came into effect on 20 April, 1993. All State governments had to enact laws to conform to the broad framework enunciated in the Constitution. The Constitutional amendments heralded major departures with regard to the authority and powers of the local bodies. The amendments gave each local body a constitutional right to prepare its annual plans, subject to the revenues made available and to the guidelines given by the State government. The Constitutional amendments have thus created an enabling framework for the State Legislatures to determine the scope and extent of actual decentralisation to local bodies.

The 73rd amendment to the Constitution envisages setting up of local governance structures with the intention of deepening democracy at the grass roots. This was to be achieved by bringing the marginalized groups to the mainstream political process through affirmative action. Positive discrimination in the form of reservation of seats in the local governance structures resulted in spaces being created for better and increased participation by various politically marginalized groups.

Panchayati Raj Institutions in Karnataka

The forerunner of the present State of Karnataka, the princely state of Mysore, also had a long and somewhat chequered history of decentralisation. Commencing as far back as 1881 it went through several phases up to independence. Given the stage of political development and the infancy of democratic institutions and traditions, it was inevitable that these initiatives were able to register only limited success. Shortly after Independence three committees examined and reported on measures to strengthen local government. They were the Venkatappa Committee (1949), Chandrashekaraiah Committee (1954) and Kondajji Basappa Committee (1962).

Policies, which were evolving at the national level, also had an impact on developments in the State. Following the report of the Balwant Ray Mehta Committee (1957), the Mysore Village Panchayats and District Boards Act 1959 was enacted and continued to be in force until 1983.

In contrast to many States, in Karnataka the Panchayati Raj Institutions functioned quite effectively under the 1959 Act. Its limitations came to be registered in the course of time. In 1978, the Asoka Mehta Committee submitted its report. One of the major recommendations of the Asoka Mehta Committee was that there should be a two tier local government structure with *Zilla Parishads* at the district level and *Mandal*

Panchayats at the lower level. The Committee suggested that where *Panchayat Samitis* were already in existence they could continue without direct elections. This report was the basis for the Karnataka Zilla Parishads, Taluk Panchayat Samitis, Mandal Panchayats and Nyaya Panchayats Act 1983, which came into effect in 1987.

Prior to the 73rd Amendment, a reasonably well-functioning PR was in place in Karnataka. Since the constitutional amendment, grass roots institutions empowering local populations have been weakened. It still constitutes one of those few States where grass roots institutions have been strengthened.

Present day Karnataka was formed in 1956. The Village Panchayats and Local Boards Act, passed in 1959, followed the BRMC recommendations for PRI. Major restructuring of PRI on the Asoka Mehta model occurred again in 1987, following a second Act passed in 1983. The Act created an institutional arrangement for planning and management at local levels. It reserved 20 per cent of the seats for BCs and 25 per cent reservation for women. The authority of local elected representatives was recognized by officials. PRIs performed well in diversified sectors of development: health, education, and poverty alleviation. During five years of functioning (1987-92) the Mandal Panchayat and Zilla Parishads successfully strengthened local democratic development processes.

With changes in State-level political leadership, the new government began dissolving the powers of PRI towards end of 1991. In the meantime, the Karnataka PR Act 1993, was adopted, which was a step backward since it provided for administrators to take over responsibilities of elected representatives. The Government of Karnataka appointed Nayak Committee to review controversial promotion of this Act. Accordingly, the Act was amended in March 1994. It has made CEO, EO and other officials of superintendence and control of chairperson of these bodies who have now been designated executive heads. The Act has differentiated functions (though there is overlap also) for the three tiers base on the principle.

The State of Karnataka has a fairly impressive record in terms of decentralization. The first major landmark in recent times is the 1983 Act [The Karnataka Zilla Parishad, Taluk Panchayat Samiti, Mandal Panchayats and Nyaya Panchayat Act 1983]. This Act, influenced by the Asoka Mehta Committee's recommendations (1978) at the national level, went further in some respects. It established a two-tier structure with the Zilla Parishad (ZP) and Mandal Panchayat (MP), both elected and a Taluk Panchayat Samiti which was ex officio. A notable feature was 25 per cent reservation for women in ZPs and MPs even before this was mandated by the Constitution. Elections under this Act were held in 1987.

This Act was substituted by a new legislation in 1993 (**the Karnataka Panchayat Raj Act 1993**). This was due partly to the need to accommodate the mandatory provisions brought in by the 73rd and 74th amendments to the Constitution. By virtue of these amendments Panchayat Raj Institutions (PRIs) obtained a constitutional status. Further a three tier elected structure was also made mandatory (with a few exceptions). As a result the 1993 Act provides for the following three tier structure—Zilla Panchayat (district level), Taluk Panchayat (Block level) and Gram Panchayat (village level).

Given this long history, extensive research has been conducted on the Karnataka decentralization model. However, research on local governments in Karnataka has not focused sufficiently on the interface between the customary institutions and formal structures of governance. The reasons for this are many. One is the assumption referred to above that the Customary Panchayats are shrinking in the face of competition from formal structures and that Grama Panchayats have filled the vacuum left by these shrinking customary institutions. However, field research indicates otherwise. Contrary to popular belief, there has not been a unilinear displacement of Customary Panchayats by the formal structures of governance such as Grama Panchayats. Rather there is some evidence to suggest that customary institutions themselves both influence and adapt to the existence of formal governance structures.

This evidence/finding raises a number of critical questions as to what happens to the existing informal institutions at the village level when formal governance structures are introduced, particularly to those that are part of village governance?

- Do they get subsumed by the newly created formal structures of governance?
- Do they continue to function as parallel bodies?
- Do they try to influence the formal structures?

Constitutional provisions relating to the establishment, powers, and responsibilities of the Panchayats were introduced through the 73rd Amendment in 1993. Under Article 243B of the Constitution there shall be constituted in every State, Panchayats at the village, intermediate and district levels in accordance with the provisions of Part IX. In States with a population not exceeding twenty lakh, Panchayats at the intermediate level may not be constituted. Article 243C empowers States to make provisions through law for the composition of Panchayats, subject to the provisions of Part IX of the Constitution. Reservation of both seats and leadership positions for the Scheduled Castes, Tribes, and women are provided in Article 243D. Article 243E provides for a normal duration of five years for Panchayats and a gap of not more than six months between the expiry of the period and the conduct of the elections for the next term of the Panchayats. Article 243K invests the authority of preparing the electoral rolls and conducting elections in the State Election Commission. Article 243F empowers the State government to make laws providing criteria for disqualification of candidature from Panchayat elections. Under Article 243J, the State can legislate with respect to maintenance of accounts by the Panchayats and their audit. Constitutionally mandated Panchayati Raj prescribed reservations for deprived classes and women in Panchayat seats and leadership positions.

'Subject to the provisions of this Constitution, the Legislature of a State may, by law, endow the Panchayats with such powers and authority as may be necessary to enable them to function as institutions of self government and such law may contain provisions for the devolution of powers and responsibilities upon Panchayats at the appropriate level. Subject to such conditions as may be specified therein, with respect to—

(a) The preparation of plans for economic development and social justice;
(b) The implementation of schemes for economic development and social justice as may be entrusted to them including those in relation to the matters listed in the Eleventh Schedule.'

Article 243H speaks of the funds of the Panchayats and their powers to impose taxes. Here too, the Legislature of a State may by law, authorize and set out procedures for Panchayats to levy, collect and appropriate such taxes, duties, tolls, and fees. The State legislature may assign to a Panchayat such taxes, duties, tolls, and fees levied and collected by the State government for such purposes. Subject to certain conditions and limits, it may provide for making such grants-in-aid to the Panchayats from the Consolidated Fund of the State. The State can also provide for constitution of such Funds for crediting all such moneys received, and for its withdrawal.

Article 243I states that every five years a State Finance Commission shall be constituted to review the financial position of the Panchayats and to make recommendations to the Governor as to the principles which should govern :

(i) the distribution between the State and the Panchayats of the net proceeds of the taxes, duties, tolls, and fees leviable by the State, which may be divided between them under this Part and the allocation between the Panchayats at all levels of their respective shares of such proceeds;

(ii) the determination of the taxes, duties, tolls, and fees which may be assigned to, or appropriated by the Panchayats;

(iii) the grants-in-aid to the Panchayats from the Consolidated Fund of the State :

(a) the measures needed to improve the financial position of the Panchayats; and

(b) any other matter referred to the Finance Commission by the Governor in the interests of sound finance of the Panchayats.

Article 243ZD creates Committees for District Planning at the district level, which shall consolidate the plans prepared by the Panchayats and the municipalities in the district and prepare a draft development plan for the district as a whole.

This committee has a composition that gives representation to both members of Panchayats and municipalities in the district. In preparing the draft development plan, the District Planning Committee (DPC) shall clearly spell out the way forward for the integrated development of infrastructure and environmental conservation and the extent and type of available resources, whether financial or otherwise, in matters of common interest between the Panchayats and the municipalities including spatial planning, sharing of water, and other physical and natural resources. The duty of the DPC is to forward the development plan, as recommended by such Committee, to the government of the State.

Article 243N sets a one year limit to the continuance of any provision of any law relating to Panchayats that is in force in a State immediately before the commencement of the Seventy-third Constitution Amendment Act 1992 (73rd CAA), which is inconsistent with the provisions of Part IX.

In Article 243N the premise is implicit that after one year of coming into force of the 73rd Amendment, no provision of any law that relates to Panchayats can exist. In other words, the Panchayat law enacted under the provisions of Part IX of the Constitution would gain precedence over any provision of any law. It is thus clear that legislations empowering Panchayats with powers and responsibility have a special and predominant status. The spirit of Part IX of the Constitution is that the Panchayats are expected to be constituted and to function as units of rural local self government. The emphasis is to 'empower them with certain functional mandates, give them a significant degree of autonomy and impart to them an element of self-reliance and self-sufficiency through fiscal transfers, taxation powers and tax assignments' (MOPR, 2006). The expressions in Article 243B relating to the Constitution of Panchayats are very similar to those in Article 79 relating to that of Parliament and Article 168 relating to that of the Legislatures in States. Article 243L, which speaks of the creation of the State Finance Commissions, has a wording similar to Article 275 related to the Constitution of the Finance Commission regarding recommendations to the President as well as the distribution of the net proceeds of taxes between the Union and the States and other related matters. The expressions used in Article 243K with respect to the State Election Commission are similar to those used in Article 324 relating to the Election Commission. In fact, it is not far-fetched to suggest that the relationship between the State and the Panchayats is designed on lines similar to that of the Centre and the State, with the notable difference being that there are no legislative powers conferred on Panchayats, but a representative list of functions that may be assigned to them, in the Eleventh Schedule of the Constitution.

Social justice is an avowed objective of Panchayati Raj. It is important to note that Karnataka experimented with reservations for women in local bodies much before the 73rd and 74th Constitutional amendments were passed. The 1983 Act reserved 25 per cent of the seats in Zilla Parishads for women. Seats were reserved for Scheduled Castes and Scheduled Tribes in proportion to their population but the minimum was fixed at 15 and 3 per cent respectively.

In the wake of the 73rd Amendment to the Constitution, Karnataka enacted a new legislation, the Karnataka Panchayati Raj Act that came into force from 10th May, 1993. This Act, was not fundamentally different from the 1983 Act. With regard to empowering women a few facts need to be stressed. The new Act increased the percentage of reservations from 25 to 33. It also provided for reservations in the positions of Chairpersons of local bodies and reservation for women among various other castes based on social categories of reservation. Karnataka can take pride in the fact that inspiration for the 73rd Amendment to the Constitution (as also the 64th Amendment moved by Rajiv Gandhi) was the state's initiative.

The term of all members in local governments is five years. Adhyakshas and Upadhyakshas of Taluk and Zilla Panchayats hold office for 20 months. This is with the intention that in a period of five years, the rotation of the offices will cover three categories of reservation.

Constitution of Grama Panchayats

Area comprising a village or group of villages having a population of not less than five thousand and not more than seven thousand to be a Panchayat area: Provided that the Government may order that an area with a population of not less than two thousand five hundred may be so declared as a Panchayat area in such areas of the districts of Belgaum, Chickmagalur, Dakshina Kannada, Dharwar, Hassan, Kodagu, Shimoga, Udupi, Haveri and Uttara Kannada as may be specified by the Government:

Provided further that irrespective of population, wherever it is found necessary, the Government, as a special case, may, order that an area within a radius of five kilometres (diameter of ten kilometres) from the centre of a village may be so declared as a Panchayat area in such areas of the districts of Belgaum, Chickmagalur, Dakshina Kannada, Dharwar, Hassan, Kodagu, Shimoga, Udupi, Haveri and Uttara Kannada as may be specified by the Government: Provided, the previous permission of the Government declare any area comprising a village or group of villages having a population of either less than five thousand or more than seven thousand to be a Panchayat area.

Constitution of Grama Panchayat

The Grama Panchayat shall consist of such number of elected members as may be notified from time to time by the State Election Commission, at the rate of one member for every four hundred population or part thereof of the Panchayat area:

> Seat shall, subject to the general or special order of the State Election Commission, be reserved by the Deputy Commissioner in a Grama Panchayat,—
> (a) for the Scheduled Castes; and
> (b) for the Scheduled Tribes;
> and the number of seats so reserved shall bear as nearly as may be, the same proportion to the total number of seats in the Grama

Panchayat as the population of the Scheduled Castes in the Panchayat area or of the Scheduled Tribes in the Panchayat area bears to the total population of the Panchayat area;

Not less than one-third of the seats reserved in each category, for persons belonging to the Scheduled Castes, Scheduled Tribes and Backward Classes and of the non-reserved seats in the Grama Panchayat shall, subject to the general or special order of the State Election Commission, be reserved for women.

Every Grama Panchayat shall be a body corporate by the name of the "*Grama Panchayat*".

Method of voting and procedure for election: Every voter shall have as many votes as there are members to be elected for the constituency. No voter shall give more than one vote to any one candidate. Elections to the Grama Panchayat shall be held by ballot on non-party basis in accordance with such rules as may be prescribed.

Right to vote: Every person whose name appears in the voters list relating to a constituency shall vote at any election which takes place in that constituency. No person shall vote at an election under this Act in more than one constituency or more than once in the same constituency and if he does so, all his votes shall be invalid.

List of voters: Subject to the provisions of sub-section the electoral roll of the Zilla Panchayat for the time being in force for such part of the constituency shall be deemed to be the list of voters for such Grama Panchayat constituency.

Qualification for membership: Every person whose name is in the list of voters of any Grama Panchayat constituency shall be qualified to be elected as a member of the Grama Panchayat: Provided that in the case of seats reserved for the Scheduled Castes or Scheduled Tribes or Backward Classes and women.

Disqualification for members: No person shall be disqualified on the ground that he is less than twenty-five years, if he has attained the age of twenty-one year, if he has been sentenced by a criminal court to imprisonment for a term exceeding three months in respect of an offence under the Karnataka Excise Act 1965.

If an order has been passed against him under section 117 of the Code of Criminal Procedure 1973. If he has been dismissed from service under any local authority; or if he has been removed from membership of any local authority; or if he holds any office of profit under any local or other authority subject to the control of the Central Government, the State Government or the Government of any other State.

Penalty for misconduct at polling station: Any person who during the hours fixed for the poll at any polling station misconducts himself or fails to obey the lawful directions of the presiding officer, may be removed from the polling station by the presiding officer or by any police officer on duty or by any person authorised in this behalf by such presiding officer.

Maintenance of secrecy of voting: Every officer, clerk, agent or other person who performs any duty in connection with the recording or counting of votes at any election shall maintain and aid in maintaining, the secrecy of the voting and shall not communicate to any person any information calculated to violate secrecy.

Breaches of official duty in connection with elections: If any person to whom this section applies is without reasonable cause guilty of any act or omission in breach of his official duty, he shall, on conviction, be punished with fine which may extend to five hundred rupees.

Offence of booth capturing: Whoever commits an offence of booth capturing shall be punishable with imprisonment for a term which shall not be less than six months but which may extend to two years and with fine and where such offence is committed by a person in the service of the Government, he shall be punishable with imprisonment for a term which shall not be less than one year but which may extend to three years and with fine.

Prohibition of public meetings on the day preceding the election day and on the election day: No person shall convene, hold or attend any public meeting, within any polling area within forty-eight hours before the commencement of the poll or on the date or dates on which poll is taken for an election in that polling area.

Disturbance at election meetings: Any person who at a public meeting held in connection with an election under this Act, acts or incites others to act, in a disorderly manner for the purpose of preventing the transaction of the business for which the meeting was called shall, on conviction, be punished with fine which may extend to five hundred rupees.

Restrictions on the printing of pamphlets, posters, etc.: No person shall print or publish, or cause to be printed or published any election pamphlet or poster which does not bear on its face the names and addresses of the printer and the publisher thereof.

Term of office: The members of a Grama Panchayat shall hold office for a term of five years.

Commencement of term of office: The term of office of the members elected at a general election or at a second election shall commence on the date appointed for the first meeting of the Grama Panchayat.

Resignation of member: A member of a Grama Panchayat may resign his membership in writing under his hand addressed to the Adhyaksha and his seat shall become vacant on the expiry of fifteen days from the date of the receipt of such resignation, unless within the said period of fifteen days he withdraws such resignation by writing under his hand addressed to the Adhyaksha. The Adhyaksha shall cause the letter of resignation to be placed in the next meeting of the Grama Panchayat.

Removal of members for misconduct: The Government if it thinks fit, on the recommendation of the Grama Panchayat, or otherwise, may remove any member after giving him an opportunity of being heard and after such enquiry as it deems necessary if such member has been guilty of misconduct in the discharge of his duties or of any disgraceful conduct or has become incapable of performing his duties as a member.

Election of Adhyaksha and Upadhyaksha: Every Grama Panchayat shall, within one month from the date of publication of names of elected members choose two members of the Grama Panchayat to be respectively Adhyaksha and Upadhyaksha. In the event of occurrence of any vacancy by reason of death, resignation, removal or otherwise in the office of Adhyaksha or Upadhyaksha, the Grama Panchayat shall choose another member to be the Adhyaksha or the Upadhyaksha, as the case may be.

Procedure for election of Adhyaksha and Upadhyaksha on the establishment of Grama Panchayat, etc.: The prescribed officer shall after every general election of members of a Grama Panchayat or on its constitution, reconstitution or establishment under this Act and in any case within one month from the date of publication of names of the elected members and so often as there arises any casual vacancy in the office of the Adhyaksha or Upadhyaksha, call for a meeting of the Grama Panchayat and preside over it, without right to vote, and in such meeting the Adhyaksha or the Upadhyaksha or both, as the case may be, shall be elected.

Term of office and conditions of service of Adhyaksha and Upadhyaksha: The term of office of every Adhyaksha and every Upadhyaksha of the Grama Panchayat shall, save as otherwise provided in this Act, be thirty months from the date of his election or till he ceases to be a member of Grama Panchayat, whichever is earlier.

Appointment of Adhyaksha during vacancy in the office: During a vacancy in the office of the Adhyaksha of the Grama Panchayat, the

Upadhyaksha and when there is no Upadhyaksha, an officer appointed by the Deputy Commissioner shall exercise the powers and perform the duties of the Adhyaksha until an Adhyaksha is duly elected.

Resignation or removal of Adhyaksha and Upadhyaksha: The Adhyaksha of the Grama Panchayat may resign his office by writing under his hand addressed to the Assistant Commissioner and the Upadhyaksha of the Grama Panchayat may resign his office by writing under his hand addressed to the Adhyaksha and in absence of the Adhyaksha to the Assistant Commissioner.

Every Adhyaksha or Upadhyaksha of the Grama Panchayat shall vacate his office if he ceases to be a member of the Grama Panchayat.

An Adhyaksha or Upadhyaksha removed from his office under sub-section may also be removed from the membership of the Grama Panchayat.

Motion of no-confidence against Adhyaksha or Upadhyaksha of Grama Panchayat: Every Adhyaksha or Upadhyaksha of Grama Panchayat shall forthwith be deemed to have vacated his office if a resolution expressing want of confidence in him is passed by a majority of not less than two-thirds of the total number of members of the Grama Panchayat at a meeting specially convened for the purpose in accordance with the procedure as may be prescribed.

Casual vacancies: A casual vacancy in the office of the Adhyaksha or Upadhyaksha or member of the Grama Panchayat shall be filled by election of an Adhyaksha or Upadhyaksha or member who shall hold office so long as the Adhyaksha, Upadhyaksha or member in whose place he has been elected would have held office if the vacancy had not occurred.

Meeting of the Grama Panchayat: A Grama Panchayat shall meet for the transaction of business at least once in a month at the office of the Grama Panchayat and at such time as the Adhyaksha may determine.

The Adhyaksha may, whenever he thinks fit, and shall, upon the written request of not less than one-third of the total number of members and on a date within fifteen days from the receipt of such request, call a special meeting.

Seven clear days notice of an ordinary meeting and three clear days notice of a special meeting specifying the place, date and time of such meeting and the business to be transacted thereat, shall be given by the Secretary of the Grama Panchayat to the members and such officers as the Government may prescribe, and affixed on the notice board of the Grama Panchayat.

The officers to whom notice is given and other Government officers having jurisdiction over the Panchayat area or any part thereof shall attend every meeting of the Grama Panchayat.

Quorum and procedure: The quorum for a meting of the Grama Panchayat shall be one-half of the total number of members. If at the time appointed for the meeting a quorum is not present the presiding authority shall wait for thirty minutes, and if within such period there is no quorum, the presiding authority shall adjourn the meeting to such time on the following day or such future day as he may fix. He shall similarly after waiting for thirty minutes adjourn the meeting if at any time after it has begun attention is drawn to the want of a quorum. A notice of the meeting so fixed shall be pasted in the office of the Grama Panchayat. The business which could not be considered at the meeting so postponed for want of quorum, shall be brought before and disposed of at the meeting so fixed or at any subsequent adjourned meeting at which there is a quorum.

Modification or cancellation of resolution: No resolution of a Grama Panchayat shall be modified or cancelled within six months after the passing thereof, except by a resolution passed by not less than one-half of the total number of members at an ordinary or special meeting.

Interpellations and resolutions: Any member may call the attention of the Adhyaksha to any neglect in the execution of the Grama Panchayat work, to any waste of Grama Panchayat property or to the wants of any locality and may suggest any improvements which may appear desirable.

Validity of proceedings: No disqualification of or defect in the election or appointment of any person acting as member or as the Adhyaksha of the Grama Panchayat or the Chairman or member of the committee of the Grama Panchayat constituted under this Act shall be deemed to vitiate any act or proceeding of the Grama Panchayat or any such committee as the case may be, in which such person has taken part whenever the majority who were parties to such act or proceeding were entitled to act.

No resolution of a Grama Panchayat or of any committees of a Grama Panchayat constituted under this Act shall be deemed invalid on account of any irregularity in the service of notice upon any member, provided that the proceedings of the Grama Panchayat or committee were not prejudicially affected by such irregularity.

Conclusion

Representative institutions in a democratic process have often been viewed, as forums for the expression of popular will. John Stuart Mill eloquently outlined the role of such representative institutions. In modern democracies, representative institutions were perceived to be 'pillars of democracy and rule by popular consent (that) mirror the aims, aspirations and sentiments of the people'. From the perspective of a conscientious citizen, the representative assembly is the 'conscience keeper of the nation and the repository of public confidence'. Representative assemblies provide a better and more visible access to positions of power and legislators have an opportunity to make an important intervention on issues that touch the life of common people.

References

"Auctioning of several GP seats", *The Hindu*, 30.4.2010.

Chakrabarty, Bidyut. *Forging Power: Coalition Politics in India*. New Delhi; New York: Oxford University Press, 2006.

De Souza, P. R. 2002. "Decentralization and Local Government: The 'Second Wind' of Democracy in India", in Zoya Hasan, E. Sridharan and R. Sudharshan (eds), *India's Living Constitution:Ideas, Practices, Controversies*, Delhi, Permanent Black, p. 372.

Desai, Vasant. 1990. *Panchayati Raj: Power to the People*, Bombay, Himalaya Publication.

Esther Kar (2010, May 05) "Transform Rural India through Panchayati Raj", Jansamchar.net (online newspaper) Available on www.dalit.eu/india-dalitwomen-in-panchayatraj

Gangrade, K.D. 1991. "Power to the Powerless: Dawn of Participatory Democracy", *Kurukshetra,* April.

Gurumurthy, U. 1987. *Panchayati Raj and the Weaker Section*, New Delhi, Ashish Publishing House, p.168.

Hirway, I. 1986. "Panchayati Raj at Crossroads", *Economic and Political Weekly*, July 22, pp.1663-1667.

Mathew, George and Ramesh C. Nayak. 1996. "Panchayats at Work: What it Means for the Oppressed?" *Economic and Political Weekly*, Vol. XXXI, No. 27, July 6, pp. 1765-1771.

Mathew, George. 2004. "Local Self-Government and Dalits" in Bibek Debroy and D. Shyam Babu (eds.), *The Dalit Question: Reforms and Social Justice,* Globus Books with Rajiv Gandhi Institute for Contemporary Studies, New Delhi, pp. 255-262.

Mehta, Balwantrai. 1957. *Report of the Committee on Panchayati Raj Institutions*, Government of India.

Mishra (eds), "Dreams and Realities", New Delhi, *Indian Journal of Public Administration*, p. 103.

Palanithurai, G. 1996. *New Panchayati Raj System: Status and Prospects*, New Delhi, Kanishka Publication.

Panchayati Raj Institutions and Social Inclusion of Dalits, p. 85.

Shiviah, M. 1986. *Panchayati Raj: An Analytical Survey*, Hyderabad, NIRD.

Singh, A.K. 1996. "Panchayati Raj Legislation in Selected States: A Comparative Study", *Man and Development*, September.

Social Action, Vol. 62 January–March 2012.

12

Random Sample Survey of Habitations in Kerala

Dr. Jose Chathukulam and *Rekha, V.*

PART I
INTRODUCTION AND METHODOLOGY

Background

Availability of basic information about the coverage of rural areas is an essential prerequisite for effective implementation of Rural Water Supply Programme. Rural Water Supply Programme intend to support the State and Union Territory Governments in extending coverage in rural areas as well as to tackle water quality problems. The success or failure of the programme can be assessed statistically by conducting census or sample surveys or obtaining data through implementing agencies. It was in 1991, the first nation wide rural habitation survey to assess the status of the rural drinking water supply coverage was conducted through the respective State Governments. The results were revalidated during 1993-94, verified in 1996-97 and updated in the year 1999-2000. The Department of Drinking Water Supply under Ministry of Rural Development conducted a nation wide rural habitation survey in 2003 to ascertain the exact position of the status of the rural habitation with regard to availability of drinking water. Based on the results of this survey, now the Ministry is in a position to develop future strategies for the programme.

The Monitoring division of the Ministry of Rural Development conducted Random Sample Survey for Habitation in about 17,155 rural habitations of 27 States including 560 habitations in 30 Blocks of all the

Districts (14) in Kerala. In 2006, the Monitoring Division of the Ministry of Rural Development approached the Centre for Rural Management (CRM), Kottayam to find out if it was interested in undertaking a study on Random Sample Survey of Habitations in the state of Kerala. The Centre for Rural Management responded positively. The Ministry approved the proposal on 10th October, 2006 and the study was launched on 6th November, 2006.

Objectives

The main objectives of this survey are to verify the results of the Rural Habitation Survey 2003 and to ascertain the exact position of the status of the rural habitation with regard to availability and quality of drinking water in the State of Kerala. This survey will help in categorization of the habitations into Not Covered (NC)/Partially Covered (PC)/Fully Covered (FC) as per the position in 2003. Based on random sampling, it will be possible to identify the reasons and extent of slippages and emergence of new habitations.

The major objectives of the random sample survey are the following :

1. Whether the categorization of habitations into Not Covered (NC)/Partially Covered (PC) are correct as per Habitation Survey 2003;
2. The position of NC/PC as on date;
3. The reasons for slippage from FC to PC, PC to NC or FC to NC;
4. Type of water quality problem, if any;
5. Whether new habitations have emerged since the last survey; and
6. The sources of drinking water supply, management and maintenance system that exists in the surveyed habitations.

Scope

The study covered the entire State of Kerala. The data has been collected from 5,600 households in 30 Blocks of 14 districts of the State and 30 Block level officers of the rural water supply departments (Kerala Water Authority). The present study seeks to verify the results of the Rural Habitation Survey 2003 and to ascertain the exact status of rural habitations with regard to quantity and quality of drinking water available.

Methodology

(a) Sample Size

A multi-stage stratified random sampling design was adopted to select the districts, Blocks and habitations in the State. The nodal agency provided selected habitations list to CRM for the State of Kerala. The list also provided the following details about the habitation. State name and code, district name and code, Block name and code, Panchayat name and code, village name and code, habitation name and code, habitation population as per 2003 habitation survey, coverage status and water quality status.

(b) Estimation of Sample Size for the Population Proportions

In this survey, the key parameter that needed to be assessed was the actual status of the habitations that have been categorized as NC/PC habitations. And, it was desired that, wherever be the true proportion, a 95 per cent confidence interval extends no further than 0.05 on each side of the sample proportion.

The desired variance $\sigma^2 px$ of the sample proportion has been estimated as follows:

Standard Error at 3 per cent

$$1.96\ \sigma px = 0.03$$
$$\sigma px = 0.0255102$$
$$\sigma^2 px = 0.0006507$$

The number of sample observations (sample size) required has been estimated for each category of habitations and for the State of Kerala using the following formula:

$$n = \frac{Np\ (1-p)}{(N-1)\sigma^2 px + p\ (1-p)}$$

The Block-wise details of sample size for Random Sample Survey of Habitations 2006 are given in Table 12.1.

Table 12.1: Block-wise Sample size for Random Sample Survey

Block	*Number of habitations surveyed*	*Habitation Survey 2003*		
		FC	*PC*	*NC*
Neeleswaram	20	0	20	0
Iritty	17	0	17	0
Kalpetta	19	0	19	0
Balussery	19	0	19	0
Nilamboor	28	0	28	0
Thiroorangadi	20	0	17	3
Perunthalmanna	16	0	16	0
Alathur	19	0	19	0
Kodakara	17	0	17	0
Mathilakam	11	0	11	0
Vadakancherry	23	0	23	0
Angamali	18	0	17	1
Vytilla	2	0	2	0
Azhutha	15	0	15	0
Kanjirappalli	30	0	12	18
Ettumanoor	29	0	8	21
Pallam	17	0	14	3
Pampady	23	0	9	14
Chenganoor	34	0	6	28
Mavelikkara	8	0	3	5
Chambakkulam	8	0	7	1
Konni	11	0	11	0
Ranni	11	0	11	0
Ochira	33	0	0	33
Kottarakkara	12	0	11	1
Karunagappally	29	0	4	25
Chittumala	8	0	8	0
Chavara	38	0	1	37
Vamanapuram	12	0	12	0
Parassala	13	0	13	0
Kerala	**560**	**0**	**370**	**190**

Source: Status as per HS-2003- Block-wise count of NC and PC from the List of Selected Habitations.

(c) Sampling Design

The sampling design proposed for the study is a two stage stratified cluster sampling procedure involving selection of Blocks and habitations.

(d) Selection of Blocks

In order to select the number of Blocks in each State, it was decided to adopt 30- cluster approach, i.e., 30 Blocks from each State. Where number of Blocks was less than 30, all the Blocks were selected. To identify 30 Blocks from each State, following steps were employed.

Firstly, overall weight was calculated by dividing required sample size of a particular category from total number of habitations in that particular category for both the categories, i.e., NC and PC habitations.

Secondly, calculated weight for each of the category (NC and PC) multiplied with the number of available NC and PC habitations in each Block to get the separate weights for each category.

Thirdly, total Block-wise weights were derived by adding NC and PC weights for every Block and cumulative weight was also obtained for each Block.

Lastly, by using Systematic Random Sampling (SRS) technique, 30 blocks were selected from each State.

(e) Selection of Habitation

To select the NC and PC habitations in each Block, total sample size of NC and PC habitations of the State was distributed proportionately in each Block. Finally, habitations were selected from four stratum, i.e., quality affected NC and PC and quality unaffected NC and PC habitations by using Population Proportion to Size (PPS).

(f) Selection of Households

To select the required number of households in every habitation Systematic Random Sampling procedure was adopted. First, the team collected the number of households in the habitations and it was assisted and supported by the Chairperson and Secretary of the respective Gram Panchayat. Second, we divided the total number of habitations by 10 to get the interval. Third, the team randomly selected one household in the habitation and by following right hand rule selected 10 households using the interval.

Example: Say, the total households in the habitation = 400

$$\text{Interval} = \frac{400}{10} = 40$$

After selection of one household randomly, selected every 40th household by using right hand rule.

(g) Research Tools

The Nodal Agency has provided selected Habitations list to the Research Agencies. In consultation with the Ministry, the Nodal Agency has designed research tools to carry out the survey. The tools include the following three types of questionnaires/schedule.

1. Habitation Questionnaire,
2. Household Questionnaire, and
3. Water Supply Department Schedule.

(h) Habitation Questionnaire

Habitation questionnaire was designed to capture the various information related to quantity, quality and distance of water supply sources from the habitation. This questionnaire mainly focused on the following aspects:

- General information of the habitation like population, social groups, total households, BPL and APL households and number of habitations in each village.
- Types and number of available water supply sources, their functional and seasonal status.
- Types and number of water supply sources having water quality problem like Arsenic, Fluoride, Salinity, Iron and Nitrate.
- Types and number of water supply sources located within 1.6 km distance in plains and 100 metre elevation in hilly areas and outside 1.6 km distance in plains and above 100 metre elevation in hilly areas.
- It also captured information about the prevailing management and maintenance system in the habitation, perception of the people regarding quality and quantity of water supply, seasonal variation of the availability

(i) Household Questionnaire

Household questionnaire was designed to get an idea about the consumption pattern of the household, required and available quantity of water, quality of water as perceived by the household member, adequacy of water during different seasons, distance of water supply sources from household and their perception about the availability of water for drinking, bathing, washing clothes/utensils, sanitation and other household chores.

(j) Water Supply Department Schedule

This schedule was designed to collect the information about the status of habitation as per CAP 1999, Habitation Survey 2003 and status as on date. This schedule also captured the reasons for slippage and water quality problem of habitations.

Since the survey involves technical exercise and understanding of technical terms, a three-day intensive training programme was organized for field supervisors and investigators. On the first day, classroom training was arranged and it was followed by field level practices in a few habitations on the second day. The discussion about the problems encountered during the field was taken up on the third day.

(k) Coverage

During the survey of 560 habitations across 30 Blocks in the State, as per the sample design of the study we had to interview 10 households in a habitation. Hence, the total number of the interviewed persons from the households comes to 5,600 in the State.

PART II
PROFILE OF THE SURVEYED HABITATIONS

This part includes two sessions. Session I deals with demographic profile of the surveyed habitations and the surveyed households in the habitations. In addition to this it also gives the socio-economic profile of the households in the habitations and the respondents in the surveyed households. Session II deals with water supply sources in the surveyed habitations. The purpose of these sessions is to understand the correlation of the general environment settings in which the survey has been done and source of water supply and its management.

Demographic Profile of Surveyed Habitations

Type of Habitation Surveyed

Out of the total of 560 habitations selected for the survey from 30 Blocks in the State, 121 habitations (21.6%) were main habitations and remaining

439 habitations (78.4%) were other habitations. It is observed that all the habitations selected for survey in Nilamboor, Thrioorangadi, Chambakkulam were 'other habitations'.

Number of Habitation in Census Villages

The 560 habitations surveyed in 30 Blocks of the State belong to 191 Grama Panchayats and 244 census villages. The number of habitations in 2003 was 7,664. During the present survey it is noticed that there are 9,146 habitations belonging to these census villages, which is more by 1,482 habitations when compared to the total number of habitations in 2003. The change in the number of habitations had been made due to various reasons.

Social Groups in Households

Of the 2,68,619 households in surveyed habitation a total of 36,582 households belongs to SC category, 4,055 households belongs to ST category and 2,27,982 households belong to 'other category'.

SC Household

The total number of SC households in the surveyed habitation is 36,582, which is 13.6 per cent of the total households. The lowest percentage of SC household (2.45%) is found in Iritty Block of Kannur District. It is followed by 4.94 per cent in Kalpetta Block of Wayanad District. The highest percentage (40.48%) of SC household is found in Azhutha Block of Idukki District. It is followed by 31.94 per cent in Mavelikkara Block of Alappuzha District.

ST Households

The total number of ST households is 4,055, which works out as 1.5 per cent of the total households in the surveyed habitations of the State. During the survey, it is revealed that there is no ST family in two habitations of Vytilla Block of Ernakulam District, 16 habitations of Perithalmanna Block of Malappuram District, 11 habitations of Mathilakam Block of Thrissur District, eight habitations of Chambakkulam Block of Alappuzha District, eight habitations of Chittumala Block of Kollam District and 20 habitations in Thiroorangadi Block of Malappuram District. Kalpetta

Block in Wayanad District is having the highest percentage (14.55%) of ST households in the State. It is followed by 5.78 per cent in Azhutha Block of Idukki District and 4.94 per cent in Ranni Block of Pathanamthitta District.

Other Households

A total of 2,27,982 out of 2,68,619 households in the surveyed area of the State belong to 'other category', which comes to about 84.9 per cent. The lowest percentage (53.74%) of 'other households' is identified in Azhutha Block of Idukki District and it is followed 68.09 per cent in Mavelikkara Block of Alappuzha District. The highest percentage (93.85%) of other households, were found in Iritty Block of Kannur District and it is followed by 92.70 per cent in Ettumanoor Block of Kottayam District.

BPL and APL Families

During the survey of 560 habitations in 30 Blocks of the State, out of 2,68,619 households 1,22,676 households belong to the Below Poverty Line (BPL) category and 1,45,943 households belong to Above Poverty Line (APL) category.

BPL Families

It is observed that a total of 1,22,676 households belong to BPL, which is less than half (45.7%) of the total households of the surveyed habitations. The highest percentage (59.73%) of BPL families was found in Vytilla Block of Ernakulam District. Karunagappally Block of Kollam District holds the second position with 58.38 per cent followed by Vamanapuram Block of Thiruvananthapuram District with 57.30 per cent. On the other side, Kodakara Block of Thrissur District having the lowest percentage (32.49%) of BPL families. The other two lowest percentages of Blocks are Mathilakam Block of Thrissur and Alathoor Block of Palakkad having 34.04 per cent and 35.54 per cent respectively.

APL Families

There are 1,45,943 households belonging to APL category, which is 54.3 per cent of the total households in the surveyed area of the State. Kodakara

Block of Thrissur District is having the highest percentage (67.51%) of families belonging to APL category. It is noticed that 65.96 per cent and 64.46 per cent families are from APL category respectively in Mathilakam Block of Thrissur District and Alathoor Block of Palakkad District. The lowest percentages of APL families are in Vyttila Block of Ernakulam District, Karunagappally Block of Kollam District, Vamanapuram Block of Ernakulam District. The percentages of APL families in these Blocks are 40.27, 41.62 and 42.70 per cent respectively.

Status of Water Quality in the Surveyed Habitations as perceived by Villagers

During Random Sample Survey of Habitations, villagers were asked about the water supply sources affected with water quality problem during 2003 and 2006. The response of the villagers was purely based on their perception and their knowledge about the water quality affected sources of the habitation and the analysis is done by adding those habitations who were categorized as FC in Habitation Survey 2003 in No Water Quality Problem habitations because it is presumed that FC habitations are not having any water quality problem or these habitations are served by sufficient number of safe water supply sources.

During the field visit it is observed that in the Reassessment for Habitation Survey 2003, Iron problem is reported by 17.14 per cent (96 habitations) of the total habitations followed by Salinity (12.32 % or 69 habitations), other problems (11.07% or 62 habitations), Arsenic[1] (0.71%) and Fluoride and Nitrate (0.54%). Other problem includes turbidity, bad smell, poor taste, etc. From the State figure from Habitation Survey 2003, 2091 habitations (17.2 %) with Iron problem, 1,382 habitations (11.4 %) with other problem, 1315 habitations (10.8 %) with Salinity problem, 311 habitations (2.6 %) with Arsenic problem, 294 habitations (2.4 %) with Fluoride and 67 habitations (0.5 %) with Nitrate problem were observed. A similar status was observed in the Random Sample Survey of Habitations 2006, Iron problem is reported by 19.11 per cent (107 habitations) of the total habitations followed by Salinity (13.04% or 73 habitations), Other problems (11.61%), Arsenic[1] (1.24%), Fluoride (1.07%) and Nitrate (0.54%).

Other problems include turbidity, bad smell, poor taste, etc. From this we obtained the figures for all State as 2,023 habitations (16.6%) with Iron problem, 1,400 habitations (11.5%) with salinity and other problems,

364 habitations (3%) with Fluoride problem, 340 habitations (2.8%) with the Arsenic problem and 84 habitations (0.7%) with Nitrate problem.

People's Perception about Quantity and Quality of Water available in the Habitation

Availability of Quantity of Water

Of the total surveyed habitations, just 1.61 per cent (9) habitations reported quantity of water as very good, 28.21 per cent (158) good, 56.07 per cent (314) average and 13.21 and 0.89 per cent reported poor and very poor availability of quantity of water respectively. It is observed that 25 per cent of total surveyed Habitations in Chambakkulam Block of Alappuzha District reported very good. The Kanjirappally Block of Kottayam District, which is the most dissatisfied with the quantity of water as 6.67 per cent reported very poor availability of water in the habitation.

Availability of Quality of Water

Of the total surveyed habitations, just 1.8 per cent (10) habitations reported quality of water as very good, 51.4 per cent (288) good, 32.9 per cent (184) average and 10.7 and 3.2 per cent reported poor and very poor availability of quality of water respectively. It is observed that 15 per cent of total surveyed habitations in Thirrorangadi Block of Malappuram District reported very good. The Chambakkulam Block of Alappuzha District, which is the most dissatisfied with the quality of water as 62.50 per cent reported very poor quality of water in the habitation.

Demographic Profile of the Persons Interviewed

During the survey of 560 habitations across 30 blocks in the state, as per the sample design of the study we interviewed 10 households in a habitation. The total number of the interviewed persons is 5600.

Respondents of Interview

During the visit of 5,600 households, a total of 3,192 male respondents (57 %) were covered. Remaining 2,408 (43%) were female respondents. The Vytilla Block of Ernakulam District had the highest percentage of female respondents (60%) and it is followed by Kodakara Block of

Thrissur District with 55.29 per cent. The lowest percentage (25%) of female respondents was interviewed from Mavelikkara Block of Alappuzha District and it is followed by 27.50 per cent in Chambakkulam Block of the same District. The sex composition of the respondents is mainly due to the availability and willingness of the respondents at the time of interview. Other socio-cultural dimensions of the region also contributed to this.

Social Groups of Respondents

From the data collected during the field visit of habitation survey a total of 5,600 respondents were interviewed from 560 habitations. Out of these 916 respondents belong to SC category, 116 belong to ST category, 2,184 belong to OBC and 2,384 respondents belong to other category.

SC Respondents

Out of the total respondents, 916 respondents (16.4%) are from SC category. The lowest percentage (2.35 %) of SC respondents was found in Iritty Block of Kannur District. In Pallam Block of Kottayam District 5.88 per cent of SC respondents were found in the survey. The Konni Block of Pathanamthitta District is with 41.82 per cent of SC respondents and it is the highest percentage of SC respondents followed by 30.67 per cent in Azhutha Block of Idukki District.

ST Respondents

The survey covered 116 ST respondents (2.1%). As mentioned earlier, there is no ST family in surveyed habitations of Vytilla Block of Ernakulam District, Perithalmanna Block of Malappuram District, Mathilakam Block of Thrissur District, Chambakkulam Block of Alappuzha District, Chittumala Block of Kollam District and Thiroorangadi Block of Malappuram District. In our survey no ST respondent is covered in Vadakanchery Block of Thrissur District, Pallam Block of Kottayam District, Mavelikkara Block of Alappuzha District, Konni Block of Pathanamthitta District, Kottarakkara Block of Kollam District and Vamanapuram and Parassala Blocks of Thiruvananthapuram District. The highest percentage of ST respondents (16.84%) is found in Kalpetta Block of Wayanad District. It is followed by Ranni Block of Pathanamthitta District with 11.82 per cent.

OBC Respondents

The survey covered 2,184 Other Backward Community (OBC) respondents (39%). Mathilakam Block of Thrissur District with 68.18 per cent of OBC respondents has the highest share from OBC community respondents. With 66.21 per cent of OBC respondents, Karunagappally Block of Kollam District had the second place in this regard. In Neeleswaram Block of Kasargod District 60 per cent of respondents are from this category. The lowest percentage (16.11%) of OBC respondents are from Angamali Block of Ernakulam District. Azhutha Block of Idukki District followed it with a percentage of 16.67.

Other Respondents

The survey included 2,384 respondents belonging to 'other social groups'. This constitutes 42.6 per cent of total respondents. The highest percentage (67.83%) of other social group respondents is in Pampady Block of Kottayam District. In Angamali Block of Ernakulam District 66.11 per cent of respondents are from other social group. The lowest percentage (5.45%) of other social group is found in Mathilakam Block of Thrissur District, and it is followed by 14.38 per cent of respondents from the same group in Perinthalmanna Block of Malappuram District.

Family Size of the Respondents

During the field visit it is observed that 4,009 respondents (71.6%) belong to the nuclear families (family size of 1 to 5 members), and the remaining respondents are from joint family. The respondents of the joint family have family sizes ranging from six to 20 members.

It is noticed that 1,485 respondents (26.5%) belong to the family size of six to 10 members, 90 families (1.6%) to family size of 11 to 15 members, 14 families (0.3%) to family size of 16 to 20 members. There are two families, belonging to the family size of more than 20 members. It is found that around 80 per cent of the families interviewed in Karunagappally Block of Kollam District, Kottarakkara Block of Kollam District, Kanjirappally Block of Kottayam District, Angamali Block of Ernakulam District and Mavelikkara Block of Alappuzha District could be categorized as nuclear families. The nuclear family size is less than 45 per cent in Thirrorangadi and Perinthalmanna Blocks of Malappuram District. The family size of six to 10 members is more in Thirrorangadi

Block of Malappuram covering 53 per cent. There are only 14 families with family size of between 16-20 members. Out of this, four families are in Thirrorangadi Block of Malappuram District, two each in Kalpetta Block of Wayanad District and Nilamboor & Perintalmanna Blocks of Malappuram District, and one each in Neeleswaram Block of Kasargod District, Vadakanchery Block of Thrissur District, Pampady Block of Kottayam District and Chavara Block of Kollam District. The two families with more than 20 members are located in Thriroorangadi and Perintalmanna Blocks of Malappuram District.

Water Supply Sources as reported by Households

During the survey it is observed that 5,600 Respondents were using 7,194 different sources for their daily use. Out of this 68.89 per cent (4,956) was Dug wells followed by 14.46 per cent (1,040) with other sources, 10.76 per cent (774) with Public Stand Post with Surface Water, 3.50 per cent (252) with Public Stand Post with Underground Water Sources and 1.64 and 0.75 per cent (118 and 54) with Hand Pumps and Spring sources. In Chambakkulam Block of Alappuzha District 45.36 per cent (44) sources were Other sources. The other sources include Rain Water Harvesting Tanks, Ponds and Canals.

Location of Water Supply Sources

From the responses about the distance of water sources we learned that, out of 7,194 sources 4,203 sources (58.4%) are within dwelling yard or plot of the respondent, 2,695 sources (37.5%) are in the same habitation of the user and 296 sources (4.1%) were outside the habitation. In Ranni Block of Pathanamthitta District 28.98 per cent of sources are out of the habitations whereas in the habitations of Ochira Block of Kollam District, 79.68 per cent of the sources are within the plot of the respondents.

Distance of Water Supply Sources from the Households

As far as distance of the sources is concerned, out of 7194 sources almost all sources, that is 6,692 sources (93.02%) are within a distance of 1.6 kms. Another 440 sources (6.12%) are within the distance of 1.7 to 2.5 km distance, 28 sources are within the distance of 2.6 to 3.5 km distance and 34 sources lies in between 3.6 to 5 km distance. There are no sources in the surveyed area at a distance of more than 5 km.

Consumption of Water on the Previous Day of Survey

In order to assess the requirement of the quantity of water of the people of habitations, previous day's consumption of water was recorded. Water consumption pattern of the households reveal that as high as 35.2 per cent of the total surveyed households require up to 200 litres per day, which is adequate as per DDWS norm for a household having a family size of 5.

Around 36.9 per cent households reported previous day's consumption of water between 201 to 300 litres and the rest 27.9 per cent reported more than 300 litres consumption on the previous day of survey.

The Azhutha Block of Idukki District (8.93 %) and Parassala Block of Thiruvanathapuram District (7.82 %), the consumption of water on the previous day is highest in less than 50 litres. In Ranni Block of Pathanamthitta District (43.67 %), Chittumala Block of Kollam District (34.78 %), Mavelikkara Block of Alappuzha District (56.63 %), Balussery Block of Kozhikodu District (34.6%) and Thiroorangadi Block of Malappuram District (19.68 %), the consumption of water on the previous day is highest in 51-100 litres,101-200 liters, 201-300 litres, 301-500 litres and more than 500 litres categories respectively.

Dependency on the Available Water Sources in the Habitation

Out of 7,194 sources, 5,795 sources (80.6%) provide water throughout the year. It is observed that 893 sources (12.4%) can provide water only a few months in a year. There is wide variation in the scarcity of water by quantity between summer and winter. There are 418 sources (5.8%) in summer whereas only 88 sources (1.2%) in winter.

Type of Water Supply Sources

The water supply sources in the surveyed habitations of the State of Kerala are divided into 3 categories:

1. Safe Community Water Supply Sources,
2. Safe Individual Water Sources, and
3. Unsafe Community Water Sources.

Safe Community Water Sources

The following five sources will come under this category:

- Hand pumps;
- Public stand posts with surface water sources;
- Public stand posts with underground water sources;
- Protected spring sources; and
- Protected dug wells.

Out of 2,16,760 sources in the surveyed habitations, 29,243 sources (13.49%) belong to this category of safe community water sources. Protected dug wells is the major portion with 20,715 sources (70.8%) followed by 5,449 public stand post with surface water sources (18.6%), 2,277 public stand post with underground water sources (7.8%) and 802 hand pumps (2.7%). During the field visit, it is observed that there are no protected spring sources in the habitations selected for survey.

Of the total Safe Community Water Supply Sources available in the surveyed Habitations, 13.99 per cent sources in Vyttila Block of Ernakulam District, 11.92 per cent in Pampady Block of Kottayam District were hand pumps.

Public Stand Posts (SW) source is highest in Azhutha Block of Idukki District (66.21 %) followed by Mathilakam Block of Thrissur District (45.06 %).

Public Stand Post (UW) sources are highest in Karunagappally Block of Kollam District (37.84%) followed by Chambakkulam Block of Alappuzha District (29.32%).

Protected Dug Wells are most widely used in Mavelikkara Block of Alappuzha District (95.89%) followed by Ettumannor Block of Kottayam District (91.36%). A similar pattern of Safe Community Water Supply sources is observed during 2003.

Safe Individual Water Supply Sources

Safe Individual Water Supply include the following sources:

- Individual Hand Pumps not accessible to public;
- Individual Piped Water Supply (Source – Surface Water); and
- Individual Piped Water Supply (Source – Underground Water).

There are 32,932 sources under this category. Out of this, 17,423 piped water supply with surface water sources (52.9%) is the major source and it is followed by 11,306 piped water supply with underground water (34.3%) and 4,203 individual hand pumps (12.8%).

Piped Water Supply (SW) sources is the only Safe Individual Water Supply source in Kottarakkara Block of Kollam District followed by 99.42 per cent in Kalpetta Block of Wayanad District.

Piped Water Supply (UW) sources are highest in Ochira Block of Kollam District (84.27%) followed by Karunagappally Block of Kollam District (78.62%). The highest number of individual Hand Pumps (2,603) was reported from Mathilakam Block of Thrissur District. A similar pattern of Safe Individual Water Supply sources is observed during 2003.

Unsafe Community Water Supply Sources

Unsafe community water supply sources include the following sources:

- Unprotected dug wells;
- Unprotected spring sources; and
- Other sources.

A total of 1,54,585 sources of this category are found in surveyed habitations. Out of this, 1,52,767 sources (98.8%) are unprotected dug wells, followed by 1,734 sources (1.1%) belonging to 'other sources'. There are 84 unprotected spring sources. A similar pattern of Unsafe Community Water Supply Sources is observed during 2003.

All the Unsafe community water supply sources in Mavelikkara Block of Alappuzha District and Perinthalmanna Block of Malappuram District are unprotected dug wells. The other source of water includes lakes, ponds, rivers and rainwater harvesting tanks, etc.

Usage of Water Supply Sources for different Purposes

During the survey, it is reported that respondents are using different sources of water for different purposes. The main sources of water in the habitations are hand pumps, public stand post with surface water, public stand post with underground water, spring sources, dug wells and other sources. The other sources include lakes, ponds, rivers and rainwater harvesting tanks, etc.

Usage of Hand Pumps (Private/ Government) for Different Purposes

Hand pumps are used by 51 respondents for all purposes. It is also reported that 26 respondents used hand pumps for drinking, 40 respondents for bathing, 52 respondents for household chores and 11 respondents for cattle.

Usage of Public Stand Posts (SW) for Different Purposes

During the survey it is observed that 267 respondents are using the source for all purposes, 394 respondents for drinking, 366 respondents for bathing, 374 respondents for household chores and 69 respondents for cattle.

Usage of Public Stand Posts (UW) for Different Purposes

This type of sources are used for all purposes by 110 respondents, 99 respondents for drinking, 113 respondents for bathing, 109 respondents for household chores and 12 respondents for cattle.

Usage of Spring Sources for Different Purposes

It is reported that 115 respondents are using water from spring sources for all purposes, 38 respondents for drinking, 86 respondents for bathing, 53 respondents for household chores and 28 respondents for cattle.

Usage of Dug Wells for Different Purposes

It is noted that 2,457 respondents are using dug wells for all purposes, 2,363 respondents for drinking, 2,058 respondents for bathing, 2,064 respondents for household chores and 176 respondents for cattle.

Usage of Other Sources for Different Purposes

The other sources of water like lakes, ponds, rivers, rainwater harvesting tanks etc. are used by 301 respondents for all purposes. Another 434 respondents are using them for drinking, 587 respondents for bathing, 521 for household chores and 88 for cattle.

Scarcity of Water

To capture the scarcity of water in the surveyed habitations during any time of the year, people's perception and experience in their habitations in relation to scarcity of water during one year before the survey was obtained. Investigator was also asked to give his/her own opinion about the same question after having an idea of water supply sources of the habitations and discussions with the community groups and individual households.

As per the perception and experience of the villagers during one year before the survey, nearly 6.6 per cent (37) of the total habitations (560) reported scarcity of water during whole year, 18.6 per cent (104) during summer, 1.6 per cent (9) during winter and 61.8 per cent (346) reported few months in the year. About 11.4 per cent habitations (64) reported no scarcity of water.

About 27.27 per cent of the habitations in Konni and Ranni Blocks of Pathanamthitta District reported scarcity of water for whole year. Scarcity of water during summer was reported in 57.89 per cent of the habitations surveyed in Kalpetta Block of Wayanad District. Scarcity of water during few months in year was reported in 91.67 per cent of the habitations surveyed in Vamanapuram Block of Thiruvananthapuram District. No scarcity of water was reported from 50 per cent habitations in Vytilla Block of Ernakulam District.

Investigator's opinion regarding scarcity of water is similar to the perceptions of the villagers.

Management and Maintenance System of Public Assets

Management and Maintenance system plays an important role in regular supply of water. It has been observed in various infrastructure development programmes that if the management and maintenance is not well defined and do not have sufficient funds, entire money spent on infrastructure development go waste. Every State has its own management and maintenance system of water supply.

The management of public assets under water supply in the surveyed habitations is mainly done by Water Supply Department (Kerala Water Authority). About 37 per cent (207) habitation's public assets are maintained by Department, 36.6 per cent (205) are maintained by Grama Panchayat, 23.9 per cent (134) by user groups and 1.6 per cent and 0.9 per cent by community and others.

Grama Panchayats maintain all the water supply related Public assets in Vyttila Block of Ernakulam District and Mavelikkara Block of Alappuzha District. Water Supply Department maintains 66.7 per cent of the water supply related public assets in Ochira Block of Kollam District.

Mobilization of Resources for Maintenance

At the time of survey, it was ascertained that who is mainly responsible for the maintenance of public water supply assets. In those cases where assets are maintained by Gram Panchayats, User Groups and Community; it was further asked how the resources are mobilized.

Grama Panchayat fund is used as the main resource for maintenance of public assets under water supply system. In 149 habitations (42.8%) Grama Panchayats uses their own fund for maintenance of public assets and 195 habitations (55.9%) Grama Panchayats use the water charges collected from users for this purpose.

Kerala Water Authority collects water charges according to meter reading. In such cases, a fixed some of ₹ 22 per month is for first 10,000 litres, afterwards the charge is calculated according to the slabs in tariff (₹ 3 for every 1000 litres up to 30,000 litres). In some other cases, water charges and other related expenses are equally shared by user groups. A few user groups do not allow for using water more than 10,000 litres per month. In such cases a fixed amount is charged of ₹ 30 for the first 6,000 litres of water and ₹ 50 up to 10,000 litres. At present, there is no charge for using water from public hand pumps and public stand post.

Investigator's Perception

In order to get a fair idea about the maintenance of public assets in the habitation, some observation questions were put in the questionnaire for investigators. Investigator personally visited 3-4 hand pumps or PSPs, as the case may be, and recorded their perceptions on five-point scales.

Status of Hand Pumps Maintenance as perceived by Investigators

In just 3.9 per cent (22) and 24.1 per cent (135) of the total surveyed habitations, investigators reported the maintenance of public water supply sources as very good and good. In about 26.1 per cent (146), 39.6 per cent (222) and 6.3 per cent (35) habitations investigators reported maintenance of Public Hand Pumps as average, poor and very poor respectively.

Status of Public Stand Posts Maintenance as perceived by Investigators

Maintenance of PSPs has been reported as Very Good and Good in around 0.5 per cent (3) and 22.4 per cent (126) habitations. In about 52.7 per cent (295), 20.5 per cent (115) and 3.8 per cent (21) habitations investigators reported maintenance of Public Stand Posts as average, poor and very poor respectively.

PART III
STATUS OF WATER SUPPLY IN KERALA

As per the 2005 Annual Report of MoRD and CAP 1999, and the coverage reported by States/UTs thereafter, there were 5,368 (0.38%) NC, 60,884 (4.28%) PC and 13,56,031 (95.34%) FC habitations in the country. In order to verify the figures reported by various States and to ascertain the exact position of the status of the rural habitations with regard to availability and quality of drinking water, Random Sample Survey of Habitations was conducted. In this survey, people's perception is obtained in relation to quantity and quality of water in the habitation, and distance of the water supply sources from the habitation. Water supply department officers are also contacted to gather status of habitation and to ascertain the reasons for slippage. This part broadly talks about people's perception about the various aspects of quantity and quality of water, status of habitations as per CAP 1999, Habitation Survey 2003 and Random Sample Survey of Habitations 2006 and reasons for slippage.

People's Perception about the Available Water Supply

It has been mentioned earlier that in every habitation, ten households were interviewed to get their perception about the available water supply sources in terms of quantity, quality, colour, taste, smell, adequacy and availability of water for different purposes.

Quantity of Water as perceived by Villagers

In the habitation questionnaire, a group of people was asked to rate the available quantity of water in their habitation on a five-point scale. Just 0.7 per cent (4) of the villagers rate the quantity of water as very good, 27.3 per cent (153) rated the quantity of water as good, 57.3 per cent (321) rated as average, 14.1 per cent (79) as poor and 0.5 per cent (3) as very poor.

Less than three-fourth of the respondents (72.7 %) from Mathilakam Block of Thrissur District reported the quantity of water as good. All the villagers from habitations of Vytilla Block reported the quantity of water available as average.

Quality of Water as perceived by Villagers

In the habitation questionnaire, a group of people was asked to rate the available quality of water in their habitation on a five-point scale. Just 2.3 per cent (13) of the villagers rated the quality of water as very good, 49.3 per cent (276) rated the quality of water as good, 33.9 per cent (190) rated as average, 11.6 per cent (65) as poor and 2.9 per cent (16) as very poor.

All the villagers from habitations of Iritty and Kodakara Blocks reported the quality of water as good. About 62.5 per cent of the habitations from Chambakkulam Block of Alappuzha District reported the quality of water as very poor.

Colour of Water

Colour of water is important to know the presence of iron or any other physiological impurity in the water. If the water is colourless, it is presumed that it is free from iron and physiological impurities. If it is muddy, it indicates that there is some sort of physiological impurity. Respondents were asked about each of the water supply sources being used to get the perception about colour of water. As far as colour of the water is concerned 6,772 sources (94.1%) have no problem for colour of water. However, 308 sources (4.3%) have the problem of reddish colour and 114 sources (1.6%) have muddy coloured water.

Taste of Water

Taste of water clearly reveals the presence of salt in water. Concentration of salt in water makes the water slightly brackish or brackish while good taste of water means that there is no salt content in water. Considering the taste of the water 6,566 sources (91.3%) have no problem. The remaining has the problem due to taste. There are 532 sources (7.4%) having slightly brackish taste and 96 sources (1.3 %) brackish taste.

Smell of Water

As far as smell of the water is concerned, in 6,837 water sources (95.0%) the water is odourless, 293 sources (4.1%) with the slight pungent smell and 64 sources (0.9%) with pungent smell.

Adequacy of Water

During household interview, perception related to adequacy of water was also recorded about the various water supply sources being utilized by interviewers. It is noticed that 5,153 sources (71.6%) can provide 'sufficient' quantity of water. The remaining 2,041 sources (28.4%) provide only 'insufficient' quantity of water.

In Mavelikkara Block of Alappuzha District 88.46 per cent (46) of the sources provides sufficient quantity of water. In Kanjirappally Block of Kottayam District 50.62 per cent (205) of the sources cannot provide sufficient quantity of water to the user.

Status of Habitations as per CAP 1999

The PH division of Kerala Water Authority is the authority for rural water supply in the State of Kerala. The CAP 1999 data was collected from the Executive Engineer of concerned Block in each District taken up for survey. As per the data received from the department, out of 560 habitations selected for survey 496 habitations are 'partially covered' (PC) that is 89 per cent of the total habitation. 43 habitations (8%) are 'fully covered' (FC) followed by 21 habitations (4%) that are 'not covered' (NC).

Looking at Block-wise details of the habitation surveyed it is found that all the surveyed habitation in Neeleswaram Block of Kasargod District, Iritty Block of Kannur District, Kalpetta Block of Wayanad District, Balussery Block of Kozhikode District, Nilamboor Block of Malappuram District, Alathur Block of Palakkad District, Kodakara, Mathilakam and Vadakanchery Blocks of Thrissur District, Angamali and Vyttila Blocks of Ernakulam District, Azhutha Block of Idukki District, Pampady Block of Kottayam District, Konni and Ranni Blocks of Pathanamthitta District and Vamanapuram and Parassala Blocks of Thiruvananthapuram District were of 'partially covered' (PC) status.

Status of Habitations in 2003 as per Present Survey

During the survey the details of the habitations in 2003 were collected from Gram Panchayat officials and through focus group discussions. As per the data collected, the status of the habitations during 2003 was calculated according to distance, quality and quantity.

To calculate the status of habitations in the present survey, only two aspects have been considered, i.e., Quantity and Distance. Quality parameter has not been considered while calculating the status of habitation because in the present survey, water quality is not tested in the laboratory, only perception of the people have been taken which cannot be considered as very much authentic. Hence, on the basis of quantity and distance parameters, number of safe water supply sources is identified and per capita availability of water is calculated in the habitation to categorize habitation as NC, PC and FC. If the available quantity of water from all safe sources in the habitation is less than 10 lpcd, habitation is categorized as NC, if it is in between 10 and 40 lpcd, habitation is categorized as PC and if it is more than 40 lpcd, habitation is categorized as FC.

If water supply sources in any habitation are fulfilling quantity norms of water supply but the distance is more than 1.6 km in plains and 100 metres elevation in hilly areas, habitation is categorized as Not Covered (NC). Hence, a habitation can only be FC habitation, when it meets both the norms, i.e., Distance and Quantity.

Status of Habitations in 2003 as per Present Survey according to Distance Norm

According to the calculations by distance, 245 habitations (44%) were 'fully covered' (FC), 178 habitations (32%) were 'partially covered' (PC) and 137 habitations (24%) were 'not covered' (NC).

All the habitations in Vytilla Block of Ernakulam District are fully covered. In Mathilakm Block of Thrissur District, 91 per cent of the habitations were fully covered by distance. In Mavelikkara Block of Alappuzha District, 75 per cent of the habitations were not covered by distance-wise analysis.

Status of Habitations in 2003 as per Present Survey according to Quantity Norm

According to DDWS norms, one hand pump or one PSP is sufficient for 250 populations. As per this norm, one hand pump can meet the requirement of 250 persons, which is 10,000 litres per day. Considering this norm of DDWS, per capita per day availability of water was calculated and habitations were categorized as NC, PC and FC.

By quantity-wise 62 habitations (11%) were 'fully covered' (FC), 310 habitations (55%) were 'partially covered' (PC) and 188 habitations (34%) were 'not covered' (NC).

In Vytilla and Chambakkulam Blocks 50 per cent of the habitations were fully covered and 85 per cent of the habitations in Parassala Block were not covered by quantity-wise analysis.

Overall Status of Habitations in 2003 as per Present Survey

In order to calculate the overall status of habitation, quantity and distance norms are considered together. If any habitation is FC as per quantity norms and NC as per distance norm, the habitation is categorized as NC habitation. Similarly, if a habitation is categorized as FC habitation, it means that the habitation is categorized as FC as per both the norms, i.e., quantity and distance. There are 30 habitations (5.4%) were 'fully covered' (FC), 296 habitations (52.9%) 'partially covered' (PC) and 234 habitations (41.8%) 'not covered' (NC).

According to the status of re-assessment of 2003, 6 habitations (35%) out of 17 habitations are 'fully covered' (FC) in Pallam Block of Kottayam District and it is the highest of FC habitations in the State. Mavelikkara Block of Alappuzha District has the highest percentage (88) of 'not covered' (NC) category of habitations in the State.

The status of the whole State was calculated as per the re-assessment of habitation survey 2003. According to this, out of 12,165 habitations 5,284 habitations are under 'fully covered' (FC) category, 5,883 habitations under 'partially covered' (PC) and 998 habitations under 'not covered' (NC).

Finally, after adding all the FC habitations of Habitation Survey 2003 with the Re-categorized FC habitations (earlier categorized either NC or PC) of present survey, the status of habitations in the State emerged in the following manner:

Status of habitation	*Habitation survey 2003*	*Re-assessment of habitation survey 2003*
NC	366 (3 %)	998 (8.2 %)
PC	9457 (77.7 %)	5883 (48.4 %)
FC	2342(19.3 %)	5284(43.4 %)

Source: Field Survey by CRM.

As the margin of error at the time of sampling was ±5%, the final figures for the State as a whole during 2003 was estimated as under:

Status of habitation	*Re-assessment of habitation survey 2003*	*Estimated status of Habitation after considering ±5% margin error*
NC	998 (8.2%)	1048–948
PC	5883 (48.4%)	6177–5589
FC	5284 (43.4%)	5548–5020

Source: Field Survey by CRM.

Status of Habitations in 2006 as per Present Survey

Status of Habitations in 2006 as per Present Survey according to Distance Norm

As per the results obtained by distance-wise analysis, 267 habitations (48%) are 'fully covered' (FC), 186 habitations (33%) are 'partially covered' (PC) and 107 habitations (19%) are 'not covered' (NC) category. All the habitations in Vytilla Block were fully covered by distance.

Status of Habitations in 2006 as per Present Survey according to Quantity Norm

The quantity of the water concerned in 71 habitations (13%) are 'fully covered' (FC), 341 habitations (61%) are 'partially covered' (PC) and 148 habitations (26.4%) are 'not covered' (NC) categories. In Pallam Block of Kottayam District 53 per cent of the habitations were fully covered by quantity-wise analysis. No NC habitations were present in Mathilakam and Vytilla Blocks.

Overall Status of Habitations in 2006 as per Present Survey

One of the objectives of Random Sample Survey of Habitations is to know the present status of Habitations. As per this survey, it was observed that there were 33 habitations (5.9%) were 'fully covered' (FC), 336 habitations (60%) were 'partially covered' (PC) and 191 habitations (34.1%) were 'not covered' (NC) categories.

By analysing the Block-wise status of the habitation it is observed that six habitations (35.3%) out of 17 habitation were fully covered in Pallam Block of Kottayam District and it is the highest number in the State followed by two habitations (25%) out of eight habitations in

Chambakkulam Block of Alappuzha District. As far as 'not covered' (NC) category is concerned, no habitations in Mathilakam Block of Thrissur District and Vyttila Block of Ernakulam District was found.

It has been estimated that 4,364 (35.9%) FC habitations, 6,662 (54.8%) PC habitations and 1,139 (9.4%) NC habitations out of 12,165 habitations in the State.

Status of habitation	*No. of habitations in the State in 2006 as per present survey*
NC	1139 (9.4%)
PC	6662 (54.8%)
FC	4364 (35.9%)

Source: Field Survey by CRM.

As the margin of error at the time of sampling was ±5%, the final figures for the State as a whole during 2006 was estimated as under:

Status of habitation	*No. of habitations in the State in 2006 as per present survey*	*Estimated status of Habitation after considering ±5% margin error*
NC	1139 (9.4%)	1196-1082
PC	6662 (54.8%)	6995-6329
FC	4364 (35.9%)	4582-4146

Source: Field Survey by CRM.

Slippage of Habitation

Slippage of habitations mainly occur when the status of habitation slipped down such as FC to PC, PC to NC or FC to NC. Along with the slippage it has also been assessed that how many habitations have improved and how many remained the same as compared to previous survey. Since the CAP 1999 data was not available for all the sampled habitations, therefore, slippage between CAP 1999 and HS-2003 has not been worked out. Slippage between HS-2003 and RSSH-2006 and Re-assessment of Habitation Survey-2003 and RSSH-2006 has been done.

Slippage between HS-2003 and Status as on Date (RSSH-2006)

By comparing the State figures of Habitation Survey-2003 and Random Sample Survey of habitations 2006, it is noticed that there are 773 habitations (6.4 %) slipped back from PC to NC whereas 2,022 habitations (16.6 %) have improved their status from 'partially covered' (PC) to 'fully covered' (FC). The status of the remaining 9,370 habitations have not changed during the period with 366 habitations (3.0%) in 'not covered' (NC) category, 6,662 habitations (54.8 %) in 'partially covered' (PC) and 2,342 habitations (19.3%) in 'fully covered' (FC) categories.

Slippage between Re-assessment of Habitation Survey-2003 and Status as on Date (RSSH-2006)

By comparing the results of Re-assessment of HS-2003 and Random Sample Survey-2006, it is noticed that there are 632 habitations (5.2%) slipped back from 'partially covered' (PC) to 'not covered' (NC). 2,942 habitations (24.2%) has improved their status from 'partially covered' (PC) to 'fully covered' (FC). It is also noted that status of remaining habitations are kept as it is with 2,342 habitations (19.3%) in 'fully covered' (FC) status, 5,883 habitations (48.84%) in 'partially covered' (PC) status and the remaining 366 habitations (3.0%) in 'not covered' (NC) status.

Reasons for Slippage

As per the survey conducted by the research agency there are 632 slipped back habitations from re-assessment for Habitation Survey-2003 to present status as per the Survey-2006. The data furnished by the water supply department also shows slipped back positions. The reasons for the same were also reported by the department and the main reasons for slippage of habitation status are (i) increase in population (27.8%), (ii) decrease in watertable (25.9%), (iii) permanently defunct water sources (20.4%) and (iv) increase in number of habitations (15.7%). Apart from this contaminated water, poor governance of water supply systems are some other reasons for slippage of the status of habitations during this period.

PART IV
REASONS OF VARIATIONS, MAJOR FINDINGS AND CONCLUSION

Reasons of Variations

One of the objectives of the Random Sample Survey of Habitations (RSSH-2006) was to ascertain whether the categorization of habitations into Not Covered (NC) and Partially Covered are correct as per the Habitation Survey-2003. In order to capture the status of habitation in 2003, re-call method is adopted. As per this method, a group of villagers like Sarpanch, Panchayat Members, retired service men, teacher, community leader, village secretary and senior citizens having fare knowledge of the village were gathered at one place to know the various water supply sources including quality affected, seasonal and perennial and functional and non-functional water supply sources during 2003. After completion of the RSSH-2006, the results of Re-assessment of Habitation Survey-2003 compared with the Habitation Survey-2003 (undertaken by the State's water supply department) results. A comparative analysis of both the surveys clearly reveal that in Habitation Survey-2003, in Kerala underreporting of NC habitations and overreporting of PC habitations were observed. Major reasons of variations between Habitation Survey-2003 and Re-assessment of Habitation Survey-2003 for overreporting of PC and underreporting of NC are:

- It is felt that the ability of the respondents to recall the status of their own habitations in 2003 (the situation three years ago) is limited.
- In this study, dug wells have been classified as community water supply sources. Since it is an all-India study the classification has its own justification. The reason is that this is the case in majority of the habitations in different States in India. However, in the case of Kerala, the dug wells are found under the ownership of individuals. This classification resulted in the underestimation of individual water sources in the present study.
- As far as Re-assessment of Habitation Survey-2003 is concerned, we have strictly followed all guidelines and directions, particularly in the case of protected and unprotected dug wells issued for conducting this survey. We have no idea on how the Habitation Survey-2003 was conducted by the department. The concept of protected/unprotected dug wells might have been caused for the variation.
- Increase in the number of habitations (19.3%) might be another reason for variation.
- As more PC habitations status may have shifted to NC due to Definitional problem, actual number of PC habitations may have reduced as a result of which PC habitations status is coming as moderately overreported.

Major Findings of the Survey

Status of Habitation at the time of Habitation Survey-2003 after Re-assessment of HS-2003

According to Habitation Survey-2003, there were 12,165 habitations of which 366 (3%) were categorized as NC, 9,457 (77.7%) habitations were categorized as PC and 2,342 (19.3%) were categorized as FC in the State. After re-assessment of the Habitation Survey-2003, it is found that of the total habitations in the State, 5,284 (±5% or 5,548 - 5,020) were FC, 5,883 (±5% or 6,177 – 5,589) were PC and 998 (±5% or 1,048 – 948) were NC.

Status of Habitations as on Date

- Current Status of habitations in Kerala including already categorized FC habitations in Habitation Survey-2003:
  FC Habitations may lie between 4582 - 4146;
  PC Habitations may lie between 6995 - 6329; and
  NC Habitations may lie between 1196 - 1082.

Major Reasons for Slippage

The main reasons for slippage of habitations are (i) increase in population (27.78%), (ii) decrease in watertable (25.93%), (iii) permanently defunct water sources (20.37%), and (iv) increase in number of habitations (15.74%).

Emergence of New Habitations

Nearly 19 per cent new habitations[2] emerged since the last survey. This is much higher than National Average (3.7%).

Status of Water Quality

Majority of the sources provide good quality water in terms of colour, taste and smell as per the perception of the respondents.

Adequacy of Water Supply Sources

Majority of the sources provide water throughout the year. However, it does not mean that the sources have the capacity to provide 'sufficient' quantity of water, as per the perception of the respondents.

Management and Maintenance of Public Assets

- Water supply department and Grama Panchayats are entitled to manage and maintain the rural water supply in the State. However, in a few habitations the responsibility is handed over to user groups and community organizations (Swajaldhara, Jalanidhi and Sector Reforms Project). Poor operation and maintenance of assets under water supply scheme have been noticed. This is mainly due to the lack of ownership, reluctance to accept the new paradigm shift in governance and lack of skilled personal at the user groups and community based organisation. As a result, delivery points have often become defunct or not functioning. This is more visible in the case of water supply schemes under Swajaldhara, Jalanidhi and Sector Reforms Project. It is found that majority of the 'not functioning schemes' are due to issues related to poor governance.
- Water charges collected from users are quite inadequate to meet the operation and maintenance (O&M) cost of the water supply systems.

Location of Sources

It is found that about 60 per cent of sources are located within the dwelling yard or plot of the respondents. More than 35 per cent of sources are within the habitations. Remaining sources are located outside the habitations. It is also found that more than 90 per cent of the water sources are within the distance of 1.6 km.

Perception about availability of Water

More than 40 per cent of the respondents rated that the availability of water is 'good' for their daily use. About three-fourth of the respondents reported that the availability of water supply in their habitations remained the same as the situation in 2003. Just 10 per cent of the respondents opined that the situation has improved. They expressed their thanks to Sector Reforms Project, Jalanidhi[3] Swajaldhara Schemes.

NOTES

1. It is not a scientifically tested result, only the perception of the people.
2. This is not due to the natural development of habitations. It is because of demarcation of the boundaries of the habitations by administrative order for politico-administrative convenience of the Panchayats. In Kerala, Wards (constituencies) of the Grama Panchayats are considered as habitations.
3. T.M. Joseph and Jos Chathukulam, State-Society Partnership in Drinking Water Management: The Case of Jalnidhi Project in Kerala [Paper presented in the National Institute of Rural Development (NIRD) Foundation Day Seminar on Democratisation of Water held on 10-11 November 2006, Hyderabad].

13

A Study of Micro-Insurance in India

Problems and Prospects

Dr. Lekshmi Rani Kulsheshtra and *Dr. Rupali Satsangi*

Introduction

In most developing countries social protection systems are underdeveloped and generally only cover employees with formal employment. Workers in the informal economy are left to their own devices, or rely heavily on the support of their community. Crises are recurrent features in the lives of the poor, often involve high expenditure and drive a poor family deeper into poverty. They are the most vulnerable ones and are the least capable of withstanding the adversaries and regain strength to normalize. Impact of risk is compounded for the poor due to their financial exclusion from savings, because banks find it unviable to maintain micro-savings account. They are excluded from credit because willingness to lend to informal sector and without collateral is low; and excluded also from insurance (mutual insurance) because standard documents are not available for underwriting risks, e.g., age proof documents, etc. In such conditions poor people protect themselves from risks by taking emergency loans, by depleting savings, by selling productive assets, by defaulting on loans and by reducing spending. Indeed enhancing the ability of poor to deal with various risks is increasingly being considered integral to any poverty reduction strategy. Micro-Finance is the most important socio-economic development of our times for combating poverty. With the concept of micro-credit coming in picture, it had been proved that poor can become creditworthy if they form small groups. In the 1990s, numerous agencies involved in micro-credit operations in India started adding other financial securities including micro-insurance to its micro-credit operations.

Micro-insurance—The Concept

Micro-insurance is a first step in providing social and economic security to the poor, particularly business and livelihood security. Micro-insurance refers to protection of assets and lives against insurable risks of target population such as micro-entrepreneurs, small farmers and the landless, women and low-income people through formal, semi-formal and informal institutions. These groups have to pay specific amounts as regular premiums, proportionate to the livelihood and the cost of risk against which they are insuring their life, those of their family members and property. Micro-insurance is normally offered to that group of people who are not encompassed by the mainstream of commercial and social insurance schemes because these people do not have access to the products offered in the general line. Insurance companies also ignore them because these groups do not have a regular and predictable source of income.

In principle, micro-insurance works like any typical insurance business. But there are several things that differentiate it from normal insurance. It is group insurance that can cover thousands of customers under one contract. (e.g., in India, Allianz covers 42,000 customers under one contract); it requires an intermediary between the customer and the insurance company, e.g., NGO or MFIs, etc.; and it is a low value product (involving modest premium and benefit package) which requires different design and distribution strategies such as premium based on community risk rating (as opposed to individual risk rating) and active involvement of intermediary agency representing the target community and bundling with micro-saving and micro-credit. This way, micro-insurance combines positive features of formal insurance (pre-paid, scientifically organized scheme) as well as those of informal insurance (by using local information and resources that helps in designing appropriate schemes delivered in a cost-effective way). Micro-insurance is a form of health, life or property insurance which offers limited protection at a low contribution (hence micro). It is aimed at poor sections of the population and designed to help them cover themselves collectively against risks (hence insurance).

Micro-insurance in India—The Present Scenario

Historically in India, a few micro-insurance schemes were initiated, either by non-governmental organizations (NGOs) due to the felt need in the communities in which these organizations were involved or by the government. The government on its own and through the nationalized industry brought in several schemes to alleviate the financial losses that the low-income groups in rural areas suffered. Two schemes introduced by the government were: The Personal Accident Social Security (PASS) schemes and the Hut Insurance. The PASS scheme covered persons with income below the poverty line for ₹ 3,000 sum insured against accidental death; the Hut Insurance Schemes covered the destruction of huts by fire and natural calamities to enable rebuilding them up to ₹ 5,000 each. The government had also simultaneously embarked on numerous schemes in the 1970s and 1980s to develop the earning power of the low-income groups in the rural areas and concentrated on loans being made available to them to purchase milch cattle, engaging in horticulture and other economic pursuits. The nationalized General Insurance Corporation (GIC) administered both the schemes for the Government of India on a reimbursable basis. The GIC itself as an instrument of social change, which was the primary purpose of nationalization, brought in a new personal accident scheme in 1975 known as Janata Personal Accident Insurance, making it available at a cost of ₹ 12 for sum insured of ₹ 10,000 against death and permanent disability. This scheme turned out to be very popular and was extensively availed of by a large number of low-income individuals and by Cooperative Banks as a cover for credit-life. Several community based organizations in India have focused on developing Community Based Health Insurance (CBHI) schemes during the last decade. Most of these CBHI schemes are also known as Micro Health Insurance Schemes

The micro-insurance schemes have now gathered momentum partly due to the development of micro-finance activity, and partly due to the regulation that makes it mandatory for all formal insurance companies to extend their activities to rural and well-identified social sector in the country (IRDA, 2000). The Insurance Regulatory and Development Authority (Micro-Insurance) Regulations, 2005 provided that any micro-insurance product issued as per the regulations will qualify for rural and social sector obligations of the insurer. The social obligations are in terms of number of individuals to be covered by both life and non-life insurers in certain identified sections of the society. The rural obligations are in terms of certain minimum percentage of total policies written by life insurance companies and, for general insurance companies, these obligations are in terms of percentage of total gross premium collected. Some aspects of these obligations are particularly noteworthy. *First*, the social and rural obligations do not necessarily require subsidizing insurance. *Second*, these obligations are to be fulfilled right from the first year of commencement of operations by the new insurers. *Third*, there is no exit option available to insurers who are not keen on servicing the rural and low-income segment. *Finally*, non-fulfilment of these obligations can invite penalties from the regulator.

These regulations have generated massive pressure on insurers to sell micro-insurance. In order to fulfil these requirements all insurance companies have designed products for the poorer sections and low-income individuals. Both public and private insurance companies are adopting similar strategies of developing collaborations with the various civil society associations. Many private Insurance Companies have started designing composite micro-insurance product combining life and general insurance covers for the new products to be filed under the new IRDA Regulations for micro-insurance. Recently, State owned LIC decided to enter this segment. LIC announced last year Aam Aadmi Bima Yojana with a view to extended death and disability insurance cover to the unorganized sector. Rashtriya Swasthya Bima Yojna is a health Insurance scheme for below poverty line families and provides benefits of up to ₹ 30,000. The Scheme's premium is to be borne by both the Central and the State government.

In order to reach to the much neglected rural areas and the other underprivileged people, Aviva Life introduces micro-insurance products. These products are basically small premium policies that range between ₹ 5,000 to ₹ 50,000 and includes health, household, fire and motor insurance portfolios. General Insurer IFFCO TOKIO on 21 April, 2008 launched Janta Bima Yojana in micro-insurance which aims to serve the rural population with better products and services to ensure that they are protected from risks of any kind. The scheme provides covers under two sections property cover and critical illness with an assured sum of ₹ 10,000 under both the sections.

Birla Sun Life on August 31, 2007 announced the launch of its micro-insurance product Bima Suraksha Super and Bima Dhan Sanchay. These products are simple transparent and convenient and designed for rural masses as well as for socially weaker sections from semi-urban and urban areas. Birla Sun Life Insurance has been consistently exceeding its rural targets since the first year of its operations. In 2006-07, the company sold 1,00,349 policies in the rural areas, which constituted nearly 21.6 per cent of the total individual policies sold by the company.

Tata, one of the largest business houses in India announced its policy into micro-insurance sector last year through its insurance joint venture—Tata AIG, which is the first insurance company in India to come up with a focused micro-insurance scheme. The new business procured through micro-insurance as on 31-03-2008, has been given in Table 13.1.

Table 13.1: The New Business procured through Micro Insurance

Division	*Absolute Volume for the Year*		
	Policies	*S.A. ('000s)*	*F.P.I. (₹)*
Agra	5436	84984.00	952168.00
Aligarh	6000	78030.34	1297574.00
Allahabad	3011	37395.52	439455.00
Bareilly	8390	99790.20	1287169.00
Dehradun	6729	126613.09	1070311.00
Faizabad	6610	62983.88	1027445.00
Gorakhpur	5893	88328.36	976095.00
Haldwani	3223	55626.11	744018.00
Kanpur	9806	116775.60	1675602.00
Lucknow	12089	123720.06	2004625.00
Meerut	5004	82471.67	1092808.00
Varanasi	4008	52924.58	701380.00
NCZ	76199	1009643.41	13268650.00

Source: Pragati, April 2008 quarterly magzine published by LIC.

Table 13.2: Models and Methods for Micro Insurance in India

Partner-Agent Model	*Full-Service Model*
• Insurers utilize MFIs delivery mechanism to provide sales and basic services to clients. • There is no risk and limited administrative burden for MFIs. • Advantage—Limited control. • Disadvantage—Limited risks.	• The end claims assessment. • The provider is responsible for all aspects of product manufacturing, sales, servicing insurers are responsible for all insurance related costs and losses and they retain all profits. • Advantage—Full control. • Disadvantage—Higher risks.
Provider-Driven Model	*Community-Based/Mutual Model*
• The service provider and the insurer are the same, i.e., hospitals or doctors offer policies to individuals of groups. • Advantage—Full control • Disadvantage—Limitation on product and services.	• The policyholders own and manage the insurance programme, and negotiate with external health care providers. • Advantage—Ability to design market products more easily and effectively • Disadvantage—Small size and scope of operations.

Methods and Models for Micro-insurance vary depending on the organization, institution, and provider involved. In general, there are four main methods for offering micro-insurance in India. Each of these models with their own advantages and disadvantages have been given in Table 13.2. Table 13.3 shows possible delivery channels in India for micro-insurance.

Table 13.3: Possible Delivery Channels in India for Micro Insurance

Self-help groups linked to banks	1,618,476
Non-Governmental Organizations as development facilitators (approx.)	200,000
Non-Governmental Organizations involved in micro-finance	3,024
Rural and Semi-Urban Commercial Bank Branches	33,388
Regional Rural Bank Branches	14,446
Private Fertilizer Dealers	192,000
Primary Agricultural Cooperative Societies	105,735
Post Offices in Rural Areas	138,756

Source: National Bank of Agriculture and Rural Development and Reserve Bank of India, Annual Report, 2006.

About the Study

After having an orientation with the concept of micro-insurance, philosophy behind it, and the present scenario of micro-insurance in India, it is of prime importance that one analyses the micro-insurance segment to know why micro-insurance is needed in India, what are the reasons for companies entering into the micro-insurance; what are the problems and prospects anticipated by the insurers and also to recommend strategies for the success of micro-insurance in India. For the purpose, a minor research has been undertaken on the basis of primary data collected through a self-structured questionnaire. The questionnaire having questions with multiple options was administered upon 25 respondents randomly selected from Agra based insurance companies (Table 13.4). Five-point likert scale was used for obtaining responses on the multiple dimensions. The findings of the study on the basis of their mean scores are given in Table 13.5 and presented graphically in Figure 13.1 to 13.5. The responses supported by at least 75 per cent of respondents have been considered in the study.

Table 13.4: Insurance Companies operating in Agra

Public Sector	*Private Sector*
1. Life Insurance Corporation of India (LIC)	1. Bajaj Allianz Life Insurance Co. Ltd.
	2. Birla Sun Life Insurance Co. Ltd.
	3. HDFC Standard-Life Insurance Co. Ltd.
	4. ICICI Prudential Life Insurance Co. Ltd.
	5. ING Vysya Life Insurance Co. Ltd.
	6. Max New York Life Insurance Co. Ltd.
	7. Met Life India Insurance Co. Pvt. Ltd.
	8. SBI Life Insurance Co.Ltd.
	9. TATA AIG Life Insurance Co.Ltd.
	10. AVIVA Life Insurance Co. Pvt. Ltd.
	11. Bharti AXA Life Insurance Company Ltd.
	12. Kotak Mahindra Life Insurance Co. Ltd.

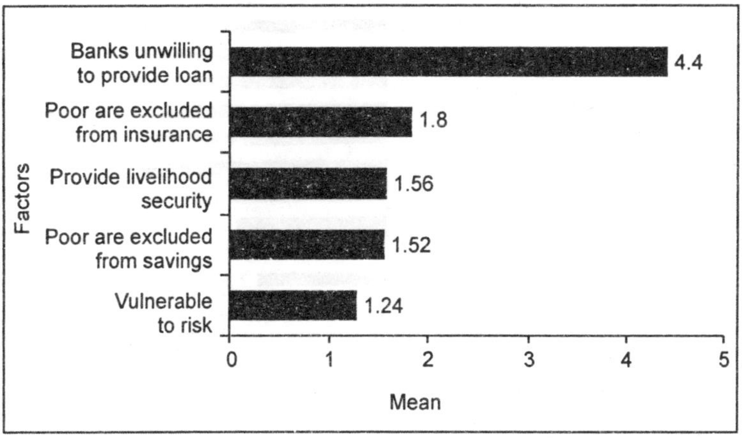

Fig. 13.1: Need of Micro-insurance in India

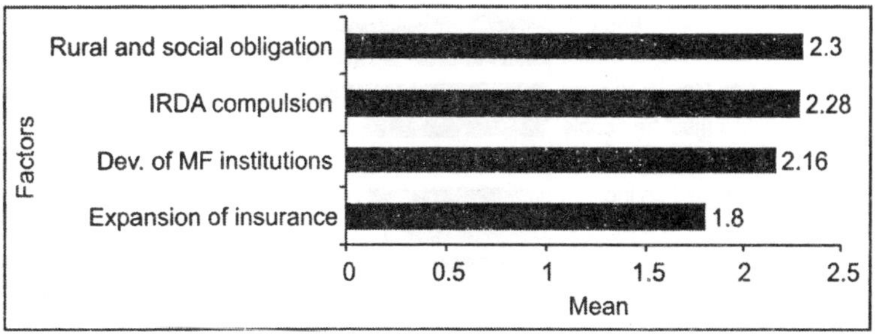

Fig. 13.2: Reasons for Companies Entering Into Micro-insurance

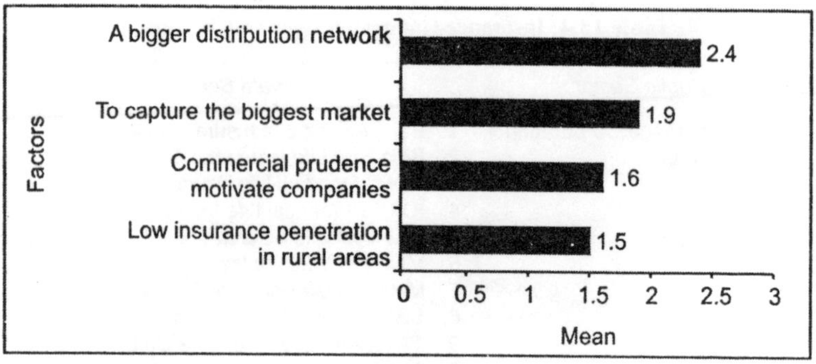

Fig. 13.3: Prospects anticipated by Insurance Companies in Micro-insurance

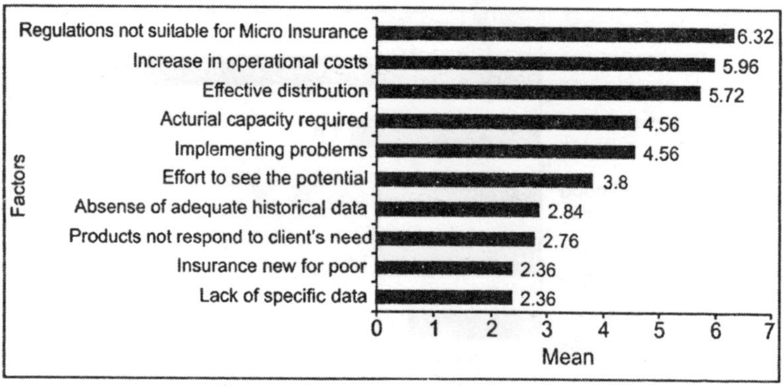

Fig. 13.4: Problems anticipated by Micro-insurance Companies

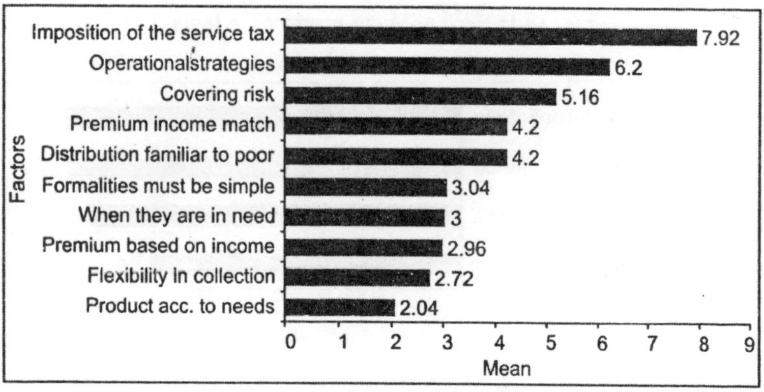

Fig. 13.5: Strategies recommended for Insurance Companies

Table 13.5: The Findings of the Study

Parameters	*Mean*
Need of Micro Insurance	
1. Poor are more vulnerable to risk	1.24
2. Poor are excluded from savings because banks find them unviable to maintain savings	1.52
3. Provide livelihood security to poor	1.56
4. Poor are excluded from insurance because age proof documents are not available	1.80
5. Banks are unwilling to provide them loan without collateral	4.40
Reasons for Companies Entering into Micro Insurance	
1. Expansion of insurance market in rural areas	1.80
2. Development of micro-finance institutions	2.16
3. IRDA compulsion	2.28
4. Rural and social obligation	2.30
Opportunities Anticipated by Companies in Micro Insurance	
1. Micro-insurance initiatives can alter the picture of low insurance penetration in rural areas in India	1.5
2. Commercial prudence which motivate companies to enter into the market	1.6
3. Private insurance companies have opportunity to capture the biggest market	1.9
4. A bigger distribution network	2.4
Problems Anticipated by Insurance Companies	
1. Lack of specific data for micro-insurance target market	2.36
2. For poor people the concept of insurance may be quite new	2.36
3. Standardised products designs may not respond to clients' need	2.76
4. Absence of adequate historical data on risks and claims expenses	2.84
5. It will take time and effort to see the potential	3.80
6. Specialised actuarial capacity required	4.56
7. Implementing organizations require the understanding of their target clients and focused efforts to educate clients on insurance service and products	4.56
8. Quick and fair claim and services is required for effective distribution	5.72
9. Unsuitable procedures can lower service quality and increase in operational costs	5.96
10. Standard regulations may not be suitable for Micro Insurance	6.32
The Strategies Recommended for the Insurers	
1. Product design and pricing should respond to consumer needs	2.04
2. Flexibility in premium collection should be there to enhance the membership size	2.72
3. Premium should be based on the pattern of income stream of the target population and spread of risks for rural poor	2.96
4. Micro Insurance should deal with applicants when they are in need	4.00
5. Formalities and procedures must be simple	3.04
6. Existing infrastructure and distribution system familiar to poor clients can be leveraged to sell insurance	4.20
7. The timings at which the premium need to be paid and the income of the poor should match	4.20
8. The insurance schemes should aim at covering risk that the clients face otherwise it will not attract them	5.16
9. The insurance concept should be disseminated using appropriate and innovative marketing and operational strategies	6.20
10. The government must exempt rural and social insurance covers from the imposition of the service tax	7.92

Conclusion

Although the current reach of 'micro-insurance' is limited, the early trend in this respect suggests that the insurance companies, both public and private, operating with commercial considerations, can insure a significant percentage of the poor. MFIs are playing a significant role in improving the lives of poor households. Linking micro-insurance with micro-finance makes better sense as it helps in bringing down the cost of lending. In his message, the President of India, Dr. A.P.J. Abdul Kalam cautioned that for "micro health insurance to be a sustainable success in the long run, needs to be linked to the Programme for Urban Amenities in Rural Areas (PURA), as employment created through this programme will progressively add more and more people who can afford insurance. In addition, involvement of self-help groups will create avenues for capacity building to further make micro-insurance sustainable. Thus, a virtuous cycle should be created where the cover provided under micro-insurance schemes increases with growth and buying power through employment as well as through development of rural communities".

References

1. Anabil Bhattacharya (2008), "Micro Insurance in India", *The Insurance Times*, Vol. XXVII. No. 5, May.
2. Kaur Jotirmayee (2008), "Microinsurance: Some Key Issues in Protecting the Poor from Adverse Income Shocks", *Insurance Chronicle*, April, pp. 27-30.
3. Rao G.V. (2008) "Microinsurance in Rural India—The Regulatory Challenges", *Insurance Chronicle*, April, pp. 17-26.

Websites

www.microinsurancefocus.org
www.asianinsurance.com
www.bimaonline.com
www.birlasunlife.com
www.allianzbajaj.co.in
www.allianz.com
www.news.moneycontrol.com
www.itgi.com
www.irda.org
www.ensuranceprofessional.com
www.avivaindia.com
www.licindia.com
www.munichre-foundation.org.
www.tata-aig-life.com
www.icrier.org
www.bimabajar.com

14

Financial Inclusion and Rural Development

Dr. V. Sreedevi

Introduction

India, where three fourth of the population resides in rural areas, is needless to say, predominantly a rural economy. Rural development therefore, is the urgent need of the hour for planning in India to facilitate the overall development of the country. Rural development may be defined as a process of bringing about structural change in the socio-economic situation of the poor in rural areas and making the process of development self sustaining.

Rural development became a planning concern because the programs and strategies adopted in India remained largely ineffective in solving the unemployment problem, ensuring distributive justice and alleviating poverty.

Indian economy has witnessed considerable growth acceleration during the post liberalization period. The economy has been growing at an annual growth rate of 9 per cent for the last four years. Our economy now has the potential to become the fastest growing economy in the world in the coming decades. The major factors of the growth acceleration are; demographic dividend, increase in the total productivity, aspirants of entrepreneurship and India's acceptance of globalization. This growth acceleration has substantially reduced in the percentage of people below poverty line. This growth rate is not easily achieved as some inter regional, intra-regional and intra-personal inequalities in wealth and income do exist. India is still home to the world's largest number of poor. (Vijay Kelkar, 2010)

The urban rural gaps are getting wider day by day and sizable sections of the population, particularly the vulnerable groups, continue to remain excluded from even the most basic opportunities and services provided by the various sectors, especially financial sectors.

Finance plays a major role in economic development. Financial development has an impact on the well being of the people. It alleviates poverty apart from contributing to overall economic development. To enhance their income and improve their living conditions, poor people require finance. In most of the countries, however, all financial services are provided to high income people and large enterprises. The people below poverty line who actually require access to the financial services are being excluded from the basic services.

The banking sector, despite the fact that it has 47000 branches, does not lend any financial help to a large section of the people in India. Only 27 per cent of farmers get some of the institutional credit, 22 per cent get credit from money lenders and remaining 51 per cent do not get any credit at all.

Financial Exclusion

Financial exclusion is the result of banker's reluctance to provide comprehensive financial services to the poor and downtrodden in a cost effective way by adopting innovative delivery and business models.

Financial inclusion has to be viewed by banks not only as a mere corporate responsibility but also as a business opportunity. (Sharma R.H., 2007)

Financial exclusion is the lack of access by certain customers to appropriate, low cost fare and safe financial products and services from mainstream providers. The low income people are excluded from the financial services. Access to various financial services helps the bottom of the pyramid to increase their income. (Sujatha & Sushama, 2007)

Financial exclusion can be defined as the process of denying access to financial services to a section of the population. Financial exclusion has become a major concern of many countries today.

The reasons for financial exclusion are:

- Lack of awareness of financial products and services

- Lack of sufficient income
- Unemployment and under employment.
- Denial of access to financial services due to the stringent conditions imposed by agencies providing these services.
- Low savings or no savings.
- Lack of assets.
- Poor financial habits resulting in incriminate spending.
- Psychological disabilities
- Feelings of being out cast from the mainstream of financial services.
- Indigenous and ethnic issue.
- Geographical inconvenience.
- Lack of time.
- Computer illiteracy or lack of access to PC/ internet.
- Availability of alternate product and services
- Alternate Suppliers providing services.

In India RBI has understood the implications of financial exclusion and addressed this vital issue in their annual policy statement for the year 2005-2006. Technological advancement in the financial sector, has kept bank away from the reach of common people due to the cost structure as a well as complexity, sophistication and urbanization of many products and services. The entry of foreign banks and financial institutions has changed the face of Indian banking and replacement of men with machines has taken away personalized services which elderly people may prefer. (Leeladhar V., 2006)

The Government of India has a long history of earnestness to expand financial inclusion. Nationalization of major private sector banks in 1969 was the first step. In 1975 Government established RRBs to expand bank branches in rural areas. As per RBI's guidelines to banks 40 per cent of their net bank credit should be given to priority sector which mainly consists of agriculture, small scale industries, retail trade, etc. (Leeladhar V., 2006)

Need for financial inclusion

Low people are excluded from the formal financial services. The poor are constrained to spend their savings to meet unforeseen expenditure. In certain cases they require credit not only to increase their investment in agriculture and productive activities but also to meet some of their regular expenditure. To meet their needs they require small loans which they would repay in due course. Unfortunately they depend upon informal sources as they are almost prevented from enjoying financial services. The informal sources exploit the poor by changing exorbitant. As a result they are not in a position to clear the debt they have incurred and consequently suffer from poverty always.

Credit from formal financial institutions helps them to diversify their business opportunities and increase their income. As the interest rate is less compared to that of the informal lenders, they can repay the loan without much difficulty and can also save for the future. Rural people are mostly involved in agricultural activities which involve many risks. If they are provided with insurance facilities, they can protect themselves from the loss arising out of such risks. Proper guidance and advice is also necessary for the poor to plan for the future and manage finance efficiently. Their access to financial services will definitely changes the social structure.

Access to various financial services helps the bottom of the pyramid to increase their income. This increase helps to diversify their business activities and implement modernized techniques which in turn augment productivity. Improvement in financial status urges people toparticipate in other social activities. The poor will be able to provide good education for their children and maintain good health and improve their standard of living. Availability of low cost loans would enable the excluded people to possess assets and eradicate poverty. They will develop good financial habits and come to posses sound knowledge of the various products available in the market.

Financial inclusion is also profitable for the financial institutions. They improve their delivery mechanisms by implementing new technology and there is likely to be an increase in the number of customers and their volume of transaction. Banks and other institution will be able to enjoy the benefits of financial deepening.

Efficient financial systems are vital for the prosperity of a community and nations as a whole. To ensure that poor people are included in the benefits of development it is necessary that these vast numbers of the poor have consistent access to financial services, which can translate in to a key element of economic growth and poverty alleviation.

Increase in productivity improves financial conditions; upgradation of technology and generation of employment opportunities accelerate economic growth apart from improving the financial condition of the poor.

India is still home to world's largest number of poor. The urban-rural gap is getting wider. A sizable section of the population, particularly the vulnerable group continues to remain excluded from even the most basic opportunities and services provided by the various sectors, especially, financial sectors. For higher economic growth these vulnerable and weaker groups should be included. Achieving financial inclusion for them is a challenge for the financial sector of a country. It requires collective effort of banking industry, insurance, government and other financial institution and, above all, the people. By realizing the urgent need for bringing the urban and rural poor to the formal financial system, the government has taken proper initiative towards financial inclusion. Both the government and the RBI have been stressing, in recent years, on facilitating banking services to a large section of the society which remains unbanked even sixty years after the country's independence. This will have some desirable effect; yet a lot still needs to be done, given the low level of banking penetration in the country. To put further impetus on improving financial inclusion in the country, the Finance Minister has stated in his budget speech, that in consultation with the RBI, it has been decided to provide by March 2012 appropriate banking facilities to habitation having population in excess of 2000. Besides, it has also been proposed to extend insurance and other services to the targeted beneficiaries. To improve banking penetration, banks are looking forward to engaging the services of local volunteers, deploying latest technologies and using various other models to reach out even the remotest places where setting up banking operations are practically impossible given the infrastructural and logistical bottle necks. Through this arrangement the government aims at covering 60000 habitations. Further the budget also envisages allocating a sum of ₹ 100 crore for each of the financial inclusion fund and the financial inclusion technology fund of NABARD which were set up in 2007-2008. (Amit Singh Sisodiya and Ramana Pemmraj "Budget 2010-2011", XVI No. 4, April 2010.)

The recent national sample survey of 2007 reveals that out of 89 million farmers in our country, more than 40 million will have to acquire access to finance, whether formal or informal. For the remaining 45 million households who have huge outstanding debt of which more than 40 per cent comes from non formal institutions such as moneylenders. Thus in 2006-2007 more than ₹ 1.5 lakh crore was borrowed from traditional lenders and not from the formal financial sector. Some estimate shows that only 60 per cent of the urban households have bank accounts. Remaining 40 per cent of the urban population does not have access to financial services such as savings, credit and payment system. The survey also shows that in recent years the share of the traditional system of credit such as moneylenders, might have increased enormously in rural areas possibly, and also in urban areas. This is, really, a challenge to the financial system. The system needs to be reformed to ensure that everyone can have access to financial goods and services.

Financial Inclusion

Financial inclusion is the delivery of banking services at an affordable cost to the vast section of the disadvantaged and the low income groups. Unrestrained access to public goods and services is the sinus none of the open and efficient society. As banking services are in the nature of public good it is essential that availability of banking and payment services to the entire population without discrimination is the prime objective of public policy (Vimal Priyan B. Suriya Prabha Financial inclusion: A business opportunity; facts for You May 2010, Vol. 30, No. 8).

Financial inclusion shall include the opening of a no-frill account saving bank and offering general credit card on relaxed terms apart from taking over the liabilities of the farmers from non institutional lenders. By Financial inclusion giving people can have an opportunity to build better lives for themselves and their children. Financial inclusion is important for sustaining equitable growth. Economy transmitting from an agrarian system to a part industrial modern society without broad based financial inclusion.

RBI implemented financial inclusion program through the banks and permitted to make use of the services of Non-Governmental Organizations (NGOs/SHGS), micro finance institutions and other civil society for providing banking and financial services. The implementation of this project is analyzed by surveying hundred houses from kattathurai area of kanyakumari district which comes under Indian Overseas Bank.

Objectives

- To find out the number of persons having 'no-frills' account in the selected area.
- To identify the people who are desirous of opening a bank account.
- To open 'no-frill' savings bank account to all the people identified.
- To find out the awareness level of savings and other financial services provided.

Methodology

The researcher used simple random sampling for the study and selected 100 residents of Kattathurai town Panchayat-a small town in Kanyakumari district of Tamilnadu. Both primary and secondary data have been for the study. Primary data is collected by means of well constructed questionnaire and secondary data is collected and gathered from various books, websites, journals, etc.

The study has some limitation due to the non-cooperation of the respondents and their reluctance to give correct information.

Analysis and Findings

The collected data is analyzed through percentage analysis. Table 14.1 shows age-wise distribution of respondents.

Table 14.1: Age-wise distribution of respondents

Age	*No. of Respondents*	*Percentage of no. of respondents*
18-25	3	3
26-33	11	11
34-41	30	30
42-49	38	38
50-57	14	14
58-65	4	4

Source: Primary

The above Table 14.1 indicates that the majority of the respondents are between the age group of 42-49 and 34-41. 51 per cent of the people have only one earning member and 49 per cent of the houses have two earning members (Table 14.2).

Table 14.2: Number of earning members

Earning member per family	*No. of respondents*	*Percentage of No. of respondents*
One	51	51
Two	49	49
Above two	—	—

Table 14.3: Education-wise classification

Education	*No. of respondents*	*Percentage of no. of respondents*
Illiterate	—	—
Matric	91	91
Graduate	5	5
Post graduation	4	4

As per above table out of 100 respondents 5 per cent are graduates and 91 per cent are having education at school level and 4 per cent are post graduates. No one is illiterate.

Table 14.4: Nature of employment

Nature of employment	*No. of respondents*	*Percentage of no. of respondents*
Organized	4	4
Un-organized	96	96

As per above table most of the respondents are working in unorganized sector that is 96 per cent.

Table 14.5: Income-wise classification

Family Income	*No. of respondents*	*Percentage of no. of respondents*
Below 4000	76	76
4001-8000	20	20
8001-12000	—	—
12000 & above	4	4

The above table indicates the level of income affects the motivation to open a bank account reveals income-wise distribution of the respondents.

Table 14.6: Earnings pattern

Earnings Pattern	*No. of respondents*	*Percentage of no. of respondents*
Daily	44	44
Weekly	22	22
monthly	34	34

In the above table most of the respondents (44%) have worked for daily wages, 34 per cent have worked for monthly salaries and 22 per cent have worked for weekly wages.

Table 14.7: Members having savings

Saving habit	*No of respondents*	*Percentage of No. of respondents*
Yes	8	8
No	92	92

In the above table out of 100 respondents only 8 per cent possesses savings habit and remaining 92 per cent does not having any savings habit. Table 14.8 indicates that 15 per cent of the respondents do not have any bank account

Table 14.8: Number of households having bank account

Having Accounts	*No of respondents*	*Percentage of No. of respondents*
Yes	85	85
No	15	15

Table 14.9: Reasons for not having account

Reasons	*No of respondents*	*Percentage of No. of respondents*
No money	9	60
No bank	—	—
No. of difficulty to open	6	40

Due to the formalities in opening the account 6 per cent of the people don't have any account (Table 14.9).

Table 14.10: Awareness regarding No. frills Account

Knowing No-frills Account	*No of respondents*	*Percentage of No. of respondents*
Yes	72	72
no	28	28

In the above table all the respondents who do not have any bank account are desirous to opening an account. 72 per cent of the respondents are aware of no-frills and 28 per cent of them are unaware of that.

Table 14.11: Respondents having No-frills Account

Having No-frills Account	*No of respondents*	*Percentage of No. of respondents*
Yes	6	7
No	79	93

Table 14.11, shows that 7 per cent of the respondents have no frill account in the bank and have the difficulty in introductory 55 per cent, clear address proof (26%) and have other difficulty 4% (Table 14.12).

Table 14.12: Difficulty while opening a Bank Account

Reasons	*No. of respondents*	*% of respondents*
Not having an introductory	55	65
Not having clear address proof	26	30
Others	4	5

Table 14.13: Purpose of having Bank Account

Purposes	*No. of respondents*	*% of respondents*
Depositing and withdrawing	—	—
For getting Loan	15	18
For NREGP	6	7
For other services	64	75

Table 14.14: Awareness about Smartcard

Knowing Smartcard	*No. of respondents*	*%*
Yes	19	19
No	81	81

The main purpose of having bank account by the respondents is availing financial services (64%) rather than for depositing and getting loan (15%) and for NREGP (6%)

Table 14.15: Persons having Smartcard

Having Smartcard	*No. of Respondents*	*%*
Yes	9	47
No	10	53

19 per cent of the respondents have the awareness about smartcard banking facilities (Table 14.14) and only 47 per cent are having smart card (Table 14.15)

Table 14.16: Usefulness of Smartcard

Usefulness	*No. of Respondents*	*%*
Yes	12	63
No	7	37

Most of the respondents say that smart card is very useful (63%) remaining 37 per cent options that it is not much useful Table 14.16 and 32 per cent of them are satisfied about their reachness.

Table 14.17: Reachness of Smartcard

Reachness	*No. of Respondents*	*%*
Yes	6	32
No	13	68

Table 14.18: Perception about bank

Opinion about Bank	*No. of Respondents*	*%*
Time of constraint	76	76
Only for high income group	24	24

Of the 100 respondents 76 per cent expressed their view that this banking facility is time consuming and cost constraint and it is meant for high income group (24%) vide, Table 14.18.

Proceedings and Conclusion

The findings of this study show that most of the respondents are between the age group of 34-49 and have only one earning member in the house/ family. Most of the respondents work in the unorganized sector and have limited source of income. 15 per cent of the respondents do not have access to bank account and are excluded from whole set of financial services saving credit remittances etc. Since most of the respondents are not educated they do not have any identification or proof of address which is a significant barrier to open an account in any bank.

Even though all the banks implement financial inclusion plan successfully its reachness to the public is very low and still majority of the respondents are of the belief that opening of an account in bank is cost consuming and it is for high income group. They are unaware of the banking operations and the financial services provided by them.

Since financial inclusion is an important tool for sustaining equitable growth by bringing the poor sections of society into a formal financial system, the following suggestions may be considered by banks, FIS policy holders and the governments are:

- Establish many customer care and 'may I help' centre's in different areas
- Conduct financial literacy programmes to create awareness.
- Banks may offer no-frill savings account with basic services without terms and conditions which are class/group specified but applicable to all and give wide publicity about this facility.
- Steps may be taken to include financial education in school curriculum.
- Upgrading RBI's financial education website.
- Integrating Unique Identification Number (UIN), the primary reason for respondents being refused of a bank account was that they are not havi9ng UIN.
- Introduce smartcards for opening account with biometric identification. This will help the customer to get banking services at their door steps.
- Banks may redesign their strategy to incorporate specific plans in order to promote financial inclusion of low income groups, as part of their business as well as corporate social responsibility.
- Banks have to make use of Information Communication Technology.
- Banks may make a linkage with micro finance institutions and local communication to achieve financial inclusion in a cost effective manner.

- All the technology in providing access to banking products must be user-friendly for the convenience of the illiterate, the less educated and those who do not know English.

References

1. Amit Singh Sisodiya and Ramana Pemmaraj "Budget 2010-11", *The Analyst* Vol. XVI, No.,4, April 2010.
2. Elian Kempson & Clair Whyley 'Kept out or Opt out; Understanding and Combating" Financial Exclustion Policy Press March 8 (1999).
3. Leeladhar V. "Taking Banking Services to the Common Man— Financial Inclusion" *RBI Bulletin* Jan 2006 RBI Mumbai pp. 73-74.
4. *RBI Bulletin* July 2007.
5. Sasidharan *et al.*, '*Financial Services & Systems*' TATA McGraw Hill Companies, New Delhi 2008.
6. Sharma R.H. 2007, 'Financial Inclusion how to succeed' *Financial Inclusion Concepts and Strategies,* ICFAI University Press.
7. Sujatha *et al.* 2007 "Financial Inclusion – A Step towards Inclusive growth" *Financial Inclusion Concepts and Strategies,* ICFAI University Press.
8. Vijay Kelkar 2010 "Financial Inclusion for Inclusive Growth" *ASCI Journal of Management* 39(1) pp. 55-68.
9. Vimal Priyan B. Suriya Praba 'Financial Inclusion : A Business Opportunity', *Facts for You*, May 2010, Vol. 30 No. 8.

15

SHG Based Micro-finance – The Root for Augmentation of Women

Dr. J. Venkatesh and *K. Kala*

Introduction

It has been found that women tend to make their payments more constantly than men. If a loan comes in to the hands of a woman then she has a better chance to improve her children's opportunities and also she can accomplish her society's richness. Empowering women is the clear goal of micro-finance programmes. There are varying basic motivations for pursuing women empowerment. The most arguing fact is that women are in the midst of the poorest and the most susceptible of the underprivileged. Priority should be in serving them.

Upholding Micro-finance for Women's Empowerment

Micro-finance programmes accomplish millions of people extensive bringing them together in organized groups repeatedly. And moreover it equips women the right of entry to savings and credit. To women's empowerment and gender equality, they are potentially a very remarkable payment. Micro-finance programmes have potential to commence a series of 'worthy spirals' of economic empowerment. And thus it will lead to increased security for women and their family unit. The crash of micro-finance shows that the Millennium Development Goal to promote gender equality is the key for achieving the target of dividing extreme poverty by 2015. Women's micro-finance groups can also be strategic agents for achieving the goals of the Micro-credit.

For the women to acquire improved advantage there have been many important present modernisms in products and services. However the remuneration cannot be understood if gender blind may seriously disempower women. Micro-finance programmes have an extended way to go before making a credible role to gender equality and empowerment. For the reason that of over speedy development, a lot of strategies promoted for financial sustainability may worsen the negative impacts of debt.

The Magic Element

The main promoted contributor for addressing poverty and women empowerment is micro-finance. The programme is a welcome remedy to precede neglect of women's creative position. On behalf of a few women micro-finance programmes have definitely set in motion a course of empowerment. It is the course where all the outside elements have been mutually reinforcing. Many prejudiced case studies has showed in NGO reports of women who have given away historic offer. At hand there has no systematic, cross-cultural comparative study in which micro-finance programmes donate to women's empowerment.

It has been undeclared that high take-up and repayment levels specify positive blow on women by the evaluations which are made by micro-finance institutions. Some have untrustworthy information from participatory consultations and gender workshops. The detailed studies which exist have damaged diverse definitions and methods of empowerment. It has reached slightly assorted conclusions even about the same organizations. The pressure from donors has accompanied the increased funding. This increased funding has been accompanied to adopt a financial systems approach. This approach has been made to prioritize price efficiency and economic sustainability. This prominence has been a feedback previously to deficiency, low repayments and lack of impact on micro-finance programmes.

The Micro-charisma

Why is the blend of micro-finance and women so heady?

Women are decisive not only for their families but also for themselves. When the women keep lifting up themselves out of poverty, they automatically carry their families to an enhanced living. On one occasion they get a leg up, women are expected to spend their earnings on children's medical care and education. The real empowered women are the women who provide for themselves and their families. They have got more preferences and authority in negotiating. Self-esteem and amplified self-belief will be of greater sense in women's abilities. Women who succeed logically also believe in their right to make decisions about their own lives. The enhanced form of a few women benefits the larger society. The studies which we have come across prove that low status for women obstructs a country to economic development. The Micro-finance is the sector which put forwards women the chance to enter the public sphere and thus it makes the women as businesswomen by expanding their roles beyond housewife to breadwinner.

Women develop into more involvement generally and politically by contributing in the economy. They may promote for changes within their communities that will better their own lives. Constantly, the power of example is vital. Most of the families want to get education for their girls and so they will pay for their girls to attend school. Women in various cultures can hold back their efforts to start a business. Women have resorted to participate in micro-finance secretly in some cases. An attempt to educate women has been there about their rights and in involving men and so that the micro-finance process seems less alien.

Guide to Women's Capital

Hard work of women to make money can illustrate consideration to the fact that her husband or father is degenerating to provide for the family. A few numbers of people are worried that whether this could guide to an increase in family fighting. However, the opposite has been true. At last group have discovered the fact that contribution of women in micro-finance has led on the whole decrease in domestic violence in their household. And perhaps lack of education is the major obstacle for women. Illiteracy and accounting skills are ordinary in the middle of women existing in poverty. Possibly this can harm the competitive edge of business.

By way of micro-finance, education expands the business skills of women. Micro-finance women who master reading and writing work in a superior place for themselves. Many micro-finance institutions bring in the following:

- Business training,

- Information access,
- Technology development, and
- Policy and support.

The exciting aspect about women and micro-finance is its positive sphere. By improving their form in the society, they invest in their children's education and health, and raise the status of women in their communities. Women seem to have a magic touch at the time it enters to micro-finance. Organizations such as the United Nations, the World Bank, gives prominence to the field of education as it is the key to more opportunities for girls and women across the board. Perhaps educated girls have a propensity to delay marriage and motherhood. They may possibly become more feasible to look for medical care for themselves and their children. And as they know the value of education they are more apt to inspire their own children to stay in school longer.

Conclusion

Women's livelihood has been prominently empowered by Micro-finance. Serving the women through micro-finance means fighting poverty and promoting gender equality. The weapon of choice can be said as micro finance. There are two special ways to look at this: one is that micro-finance is excellent for women; the other is that women are excellent for micro-finance. The lessons have exposed that women are liable to repay their loans than men. For any micro-finance institution interested in profit it is significant. The methodology used by many micro-finance providers have made the women more inclined to work in the cooperative to reach large number of clients efficiently. Micro-finance is specifically considered as one way to correct some of the broader gender inequalities which are existing around the world. SHGs are the groups where a greater part of groups are linked with the help of NGOs. And it provides support in financial services and specialized training which has a higher scope to create a positive blow on women empowerment.

References

Ackerly, B.A. (1995) "Testing the tools of development: credit programmes, loan involvement and women's empowerment", in *Getting Institutions Right for Women in Development*, *IDS Bulletin*, Vol. 26, No. 3.

Annas, J. (1993). "Women and the Quality of Life: Two Norms or One?" In *The Quality of Life*, edited by Martha C. Nussbaum and Amartaya Sen.

Armendariz de Aghion, B. and J. Morduch (2005). *The Economics of Microfinance*, MIT Press.

Basu P. and Srivastava P. (2005). "Scaling-up Microfinance for India's Rural Poor", *World Bank Policy Research Working Paper* 3646, WB, Washington DC.

Basu, Priya and Srivastava, Pradeep (2005). "Scaling-up Microfinance for India's Rural Poor" *World Bank Policy Research Working Paper* 3646, June 2005.

Chakrabarti, Rajesh (2003). "The Indian Microfinance Experience—Accomplishments and Challenges".

Charitoneko, Stephanie (1998). "Case Studies in Microfinance: Kenya Rural Enterprise Program" retrieved on April 8, 2007.

Kropp, Erhard, W. and B.S. Suran (2002). "Linking Banks and (Financial) Self Help Groups in India–An Assessment", Paper presented at the *Seminar on SHG Bank Linkage Programme* at New Delhi, November 25-26, 2002.

Noponen H. (1990). "Loans to the Working Poor: A Longitudinal Study of Credit, Gender and the Household Economy", *PRIE Working Paper No. 6*, Rutgers University, New Brunswick.

Otero M. and E. Rhyne (Eds.) (1994). "The New World of Microenterprise Finance: Building Healthy Financial Institutions for the Poor", IT Publications, London.

Seibel, Hans D. and H.R. Dave (2002). "Commercial Aspects of SHG Banking in India", Paper presented at the *Seminar on SHG-Bank Linkage Programme* at New Delhi, November 25-26, 2002.

16

Environment Sustainability

M.K. Negi

Introduction

Modern technology is based upon a number of manufacturing units, exploiting the natural resources. Modernisation has led the society with additional comforts and thus is a boon to the mankind. But it is not totally true. Due to rapid industrialization and fast population growth we are suffering from an unwanted danger of environmental problem. At the other hand misuse of technology has also increased sharply. Science has given us atomic energy, comfortable communication systems, etc. These means should have been used only for the betterment of the society and the target has been achieved up to a certain extent but at the same time the life has become uncomfortable and tenseful due to the presence of same devices. Today the lifestyle of human being and surrounding has reached to at its lowest level.

Global Warming

The reason is a lot of atmospheric pollution associated with the production of these devices. This pollution is accompanied by the gradual rise in global atmospheric temperature, which is known as Global warming. Of the 12 hottest years on record, 11 have occurred since 1995, i.e., in last 12 years only. Temperatures have risen by 0.74 degrees over the past century. Studies have suggested that temperature rise of just 2-3 degrees will see fall in crop yields by 30-40 per cent in east and south Asia. Even some African countries are facing increased risk of famine. An unstable climate can also lead to a more unstable world, stoking tensions and feeding conflicts.

Meanwhile, one billion people in south Asia are likely to struggle to get water for themselves and for their crops as the Himalayan glaciers melt monsoon pattern shifts.

If the scale of problem is clear, is there anything we can actually do about it? The answer is yes if we act now, act decisively act together to cut carbon emissions. Everyone loses to stand out from global warming. This is not the problem any country can solve on its own. There is a global imperative for us to co-operate.

The concentration of greenhouse gases in the atmosphere has risen dramatically since the Industrial revolution. Methane has doubled and carbon dioxide levels are up by 30 per cent since 1750. The Intergovernmental Climate Change Panel (ICCP) released the report in the first week of February 2007 on the basic science of climate change and as many had feared, it confirms that the threat is more serious than we had thought. It predicts that within a few years temperature will have risen by 1-6.4 degrees and as a result sea levels will rise by 18-59 cm. The gases that are warming the earth have built up over hundreds of years. They do not disappear or dissipate easily. Even the world's most scientists are of the opinion that the concentration of greenhouse gases will continue to rise for the next few decades. Global warming is already baked into earth's future.

Between India and China, these two countries are currently building 650 coal-fired power plants. The combined carbon dioxide emissions of these new plants is five times the total savings of the Kyoto accords, that is, if the Kyoto accord is followed strictly by western countries, which they are not. We need to think about our policies and actions. Apart from the plans to slow down the global warming adaptation schemes must move forward fast. Constructing flood defenses, banning building close to sea areas are some of such types of measures we can adapt. It is said that prevention is better than cure.

America, who is one of the largest generators of the carbon dioxide, is not ready to co-operate in this regard. Pentagon had clearly mentioned in its report submitted to the President of U.S.A. that if we do not stop/reduce the generation of carbon dioxide and other harmful gases immediately in the near future we will have to combat with such an enemy against which we can neither apply muscle power nor any weapon. And we will have to face the consequences of it helplessly.

Continuous emissions of large quantities of greenhouse gases has caused the depletion of ozone layer, consequently there is an open attack of ultraviolet rays on the earth causing the generation of a number of diseases. Nature cycle has also been disturbed due to increase in pollution the result is we have to face a number of unexpected problems like Tsunami, famine, heavy flood, unseasonal rainfall, etc., in addition to the number of unseen diseases.

Factors contributing Environment Pollution

The main reason behind the increase in pollution and global warming is the increase in number of industries. Number of industries have increased due to increase in demand of materials or devices. Demand is increased due to two reasons: (1) Increase in population, and (2) Greediness—the desire to collect more and more.

Life seems to have become the treasure of impatience and corruption due to loss of self-consciousness and discipline in life.

There is the difference between the requirement and desire. A person unnecessarily collect the materials/devices often misutilises them. This unnecessary extra collection increases the demand of the products in the market thus industries have to increase their production. Another reason for increase in population is the lack of willpower to control sexual desire. Thus, immorality/impurity introduced in our minds is directly responsible for the increased population and global warming.

If we want to get rid of this external pollution we will have to make free our minds from internal/mental pollution and for this purpose self-discipline or adoption of moral values in our lives become an inevitable task.

There is direct relationship between thoughts generated in mind and our attitude/actions. So, naturally if we want to change our actions we will have to change our thoughts. We have to cut short our desires, avoid the misuse. It is the responsibility of every citizen to be firm regarding controlling of thoughts and thus desires.

Most of the industrialists are self-centred that so why they do not think about the possible harmful effects causes to the society arising due to pollution. Now this is the call of time to think globally, to have the well wishes for all, keep aside selfishness. If we do not change our view today, tomorrow it will be too late and then everything will be out of our control. Organising the self-awareness programmes, planning exhibitions in different parts of the countries to be aware of global warming are some of the steps we can initiate. We must show the necessary courage to take these steps and to bring our positive selfless actions to a logical completion.

Need for Sustainable Development

There is a need for sustainable development, the development which focuses on combined needs of environment, economics and society. Present model of development is mainly based on economic development, which has not delivered equity in the society and thus is responsible for impatience of society. It is also an indirect reason of growing intolerance for injustice, corruption and uncaring corporate behaviour.

Measure of level of any country's development is GDP (Gross Domestic Product), which does not indicate the level of sustainable living, i.e., the factors of environmental impact, societal impacts have not been taken into account. Environment should not be degraded in the process of economical growth (in contrast to what has been happening at present). Someone from amongst the demonstrating people gathered near White House in America threw a smoke bomb, which was the result of an irritation against the economical policies of America, due to which their country's economy was regularly declining. Degradation of atmosphere may be viewed in the light of corruption. Corruption does not mean just taking bribe for doing any job but it also includes intolerance for small matters. If work is delayed, call is not responded, some desire/wish is not fulfilled, people becomes short-tempered, which not only pollutes the atmosphere but vitiates/developes crack in the relationship also. In this way, environmental and social circles get negatively charged.

Stabilisation of Memory in Reality is the Solution

We are equally responsible for today's situation of the world. Today it is the need of the hour to have moral values in our lives. We want to see morality in each other's lives but when the question arises to implement it practically, we find ourselves failed on most of the occasions. The reason behind the failure is the resolves (*sanskars*/habits) of our last births. Intensity of these evil resolves is so powerful that the thought of morality becomes feable/weak before it and thus we are forced to commit mistakes/wrong deeds. In this way, we find ourselves away from the path of spirituality and morality. If we pay proper attention then we will come to conclude that due to lack of true knowledge, we are running in an endless blind race and the result is the main purpose of life (self identity, reality about the Almighty, how to adopt morality, how to remain peaceful and satisfied, etc.) remains untouched. How to get rid of our evil resolves/habits? *Gita* says the solution—Be in real memory (soul consciousness), vanishing the illusion, i.e., *Nashtomoha Smritirlabdha.* The root cause of all our troubles is body consciousness and ego. Soul/atma is an eternal power in form of point of light. Whenever, the soul leaves the body, people enlighten the lamp in memory of soul. In temples, churches, on the auspicious moments also people enlighten the lamp to remind the true identity of soul. In this way, soul is the controller/driver of the body (made out of 5 natural elements). The intention/feeling with which the karma/work is performed by the soul, contributes to develop a kind of tendency. When the work is repeated with same feelings for a number of times it becomes the habit/resolve of the soul. Naturally, if we want to get rid of the habit (bad) we need to empower our intellect with true spiritual knowledge in order to change the ill-thoughts/feelings. This process will help to force the organs to do right job at right moment (*satkarma*).

Self-identity or knowing about the self is not sufficient to immediately correct the old habits because of lack of long practice. The soul has the long experience/practice to be in body cosciousness so we get defeated in practical life repeatedly and then we think that why are we so unhappy despite being religious minded. Our intellect will only remain long lasting in the real memory of soul consciousness when we will set free our intellect from the false knowledge/illusion. So far we have been praying to God to provide us pure and perfect intellect, true light of knowledge. Attachment of intellect with the Almighty and the true knowledge given by him is the real process of taking help from the God. As we do set our physical body in comfort at the time of meditation/prayer/worship, as we need to set our mind and intellect in real memory. Make intellect regularly aware of the real nature of body, materials and the circumstances, i.e., these all are changeable and vanishable, these will come across the life as a part of soul's account/*karma bandhan.* Nothing is permanent here except the soul who is secretly sitting in the body, closely watching everything and responsible for all the deeds. In this way when our (soul's) intellect will become freed from the false illusion, will easily be stable in real memory of self-awareness and thus will be helpful to run the organs of body in right direction. Awareness/carefulness in every step with firm belief will certainly open the doors of eternal and final victory.

A Step towards Protective, Preventive and Productive Environment

A coin or currency has two printed sides. Suppose one of the side is not printed then such a coin will not run in the market. Our personality is also like a coin having two sides, one is physical and other is spiritual. At present we do concentrate mainly to protect physical body, i.e., one side of the coin of personality only, other part is almost neglected and that is the most important side in comparison to other.

In the industries, the common measures taken for the protection are: Hand gloves, shoes, safety spectacles, Helmet, mask, earplug, suit/coat for the protection of various parts of the body. Thus, we are very careful about the protection of our physical body but which type of work should be performed through these parts/organs of the body, which kinds of thoughts should be produced in mind enveloped by Helmet protected head, which steps should we take through these protected legs to serve the organization and the society for which we are working round the clock, are not paid much attention.

I had worked in a mini steel plant for more than a year before joining this teaching profession. I still remember the incidence occurred when I was assisting the shift in charge in melting operation. During tapping of liquid metal from the furnace into the ladle, 2-3 red hot slag particles suddenly got dropped near to my shoulder, a person wearing hand gloves immediately removed those red hot particles and thus saved me from getting severely burnt. Similarly, other safety devices are helpful to protect the other organs of the physical body. Main reason behind any mishap/accident is the lack of concentration of mind. If your mind is entangled somewhere else, then chances of committing mistakes and thus mishappenings are maximum because you are only physically attached with your work. So utmost care must be taken to protect this part of the personality.

There are a number of reasons affecting mental stability. Family problems, tension of work load, physical health, personal relationship, pressure of earning more money or to get promoted to meet the needs of family or to maintain the status in the society.

> A person in tense cannot give his 100 per cent efficiency and thus cannot produce best quality in his performance. In this age of professional, commercial attitude/environment, today no one cares about it and expects every time superb performance. This attitude pollutes the working environment and affects the productivity.

How to Maintain Psychology, Productivity, Quality Fruitful

Encourage the spreading of positive and constructive thoughts amongst the people serving in industry like mutual love, cooperation, punctuality, discipline, honesty, regularity. Arrange the series of meetings to allow the people to present their views/problems. Organise various cultural, spiritual programmes to boost up their morality and enforce energy. Simultaneously discourage any kind of indiscipline/immorality in behaviour. It is observed that people while relaxing for a few minutes frequently discuss the matters of here and there or criticize others. This kind of talks create negative energy in minds and working efficiency also gets deteriorated. Slogans based on positive thoughts may be displayed with natural sceneries at various locations to minimize this tendency to feed the positive food for mind.

One thing must be made very clear in the minds that we all are here to serve the organization/society/nation.100 per cent perfection either in working or in facilities provided cannot be expected either from the workers or from the owner. So keep the mind prepared for a compromise. Each and every thing cannot be fulfilled, at the same time we do come across variety of people having different thoughts/ideas so it will be improper to expect positive response always from everyone.

Inclusion of Morality as a Policy Matter

A renowned scientist from India was taking the interview of the candidates gathered at his office for the post of junior scientist. One by one he rejected all the candidates. After winding up Scientist came out of his office and saw that the last candidate was wandering here and there. He told him do not waste your time you are rejected, no influence/request will work here. Candidate replied that Sir, we had been paid TA-DA to attend this interview and I had been given some extra money by mistake so I am waiting for the clerk to return this sum to him. Scientist told him I need the honest people like you in my team, if you are lacking in technical knowledge I may make it up but if you are loose in character, it may act as cancer for the society. You please come tomorrow to collect your appointment letter and to return the extra money because it is 5.30 and everyone has left the office except you and me.

Conclusion

Thus we have to take care of both sides of the coin of our personality. In fact the possession of moral values among all the people right from top to bottom must be included as a matter of policy of the organization to make the environment pollution free (outer as well as inner/mental environment).

References

Maharashtra Environment, Published by Maharashtra Pollution Control Board Officers Welfare Association, Vol.1, July 2007, *Global Warming*, pp. 15 to 17.

Environment Science and Engineering, Vol.6, 2008 March-May, published by Enviro Publishers Pvt. Lt., Thoraipakkam, Chennai, pp. 49 to 50.

Maharashtra Environment, Published by Maharashtra Pollution Control Board Officers Welfare Association, Vol.2, July 2008 *Stabilisation of Memory*, pp. 58 to 60.

Science and Spirituality, Prajapati Brahma Kumari World Spiritual University, Mount Abu.

Globalisation of Indian Foundries, Seminar News, *Foundry*, Sep. 2011, Vol. XXIII, No. 5, page 23.

News in TOI, dt. 20-01-12.

17

Livelihood Security and Socio-economics of Community Based Ecotourism (CBET) in Kerala

Prof. D. Rajasenan and *Dr. Bijith George Abraham*

Tourism Industry is a major source of income and employment which is expected to grow at a considerable pace, because of its buoyant growth. Within the tourism sector, the growth of ecotourism has been phenomenal during the last decade with the increase in tourist inflow and associated activities. In Kerala, most of the Ecotourist destinations are inhabited by the weaker sections of the society including tribes who still lag in the path of development set-up experienced in other parts of the State. 56 potential ecotourism destinations from 14 districts have been generally accepted by Kerala Tourism Department (Government of Kerala, 2006). Ecotourism projects in Kerala are based on the concept of sustainability in the tourism sector where there is a balance between the nature and the people living there. 15 wildlife sanctuaries and 5 national parks form a predominant role in the ecotourism initiative of the State. These projects are successfully undergoing because of popularity and tourist demand. The ecotourism development of Kerala and the simultaneous increase in the flow of tourists to these ecotourist destinations would help in providing livelihood opportunities to the local communities and the betterment of their lives.

The Forest Development Agencies (FDA) scheme aimed at providing employment to the local forest dependent communities through afforestation and conservation programmes, thereby creating valuable forestry assets for the forest dependent communities and other durable community assets for overall eco-development of the target communities.

The FDA thus can be stated as a consortium of the Eco Development Committee (EDC) or Vana Samrakshana Samithi (VSS) institutional settings in Kerala. Ecotourism activities in these protected areas need close monitoring. Tourism in these protected areas should be ecologically sustainable and the visitor should be educated about the environment conservation and biodiversity. Since the members of VSS and EDC's are the inhabitance of the forest, they have intimate knowledge about the wildlife, and their survival instinct could be best used for participating in ecotourism activities. By participating in ecotourism activities in addition to conservation and protection, the benefit they earn from these monitoring should be accumulated to the local population to ensure sustainability (Tisdell, 2003; Ross and Wall, 1999). Hence, tourism in these protected areas should be forest protection-cum-visitor management with active involvement of VSS/EDC members. These VSS/EDC members are trained for conducting ecotourism activities and to manage the destination. The income generated from visitor management will go a long way to meet the livelihood requirements of forest dependent marginalized communities, improve forest protection and satisfy the requirements of serious visitors.

Understanding the socio-economics and opinion of the local community members would help to situate whether the people who matters the most in these initiatives are satisfied with the employment and livelihood options available to them and level of physical and social infrastructure at the tourist spot. Community Based Eco Tourism (CBET) has always advocated involving the local communities in the development initiatives as they are the most affected group during the conservation process. Most of the ecotourism sites are in and around the forest area and are occupied by local/tribal communities. These community members depend on forest for their livelihood as majority are working as guides, watchers and other employees at the tourist sites. Community support is the most important factor for the success of ecotourism projects. Without their support, this whole venture can turn into a failure. Community support can be ensured only if the overall management scheme can be made attractive to local people to adopt it as a long-term livelihood strategy (Thampi, 2005).

Materials and Methods

As the power of decision-making and implementation lies with the local communities, analyzing their perception is essential in designing and deriving strategies and action plans for these projects. Communities are a part of local ecosystem and decision-makers should invest their time in understanding the communities involved. Any analysis in this regard will help to fine tune the ecotourism project ventures in a way to optimize the benefits of the project both to the environment as well as to the local communities. This analysis is an attempt to study the perception of the local communities in ecotourism destinations in the State. It also tries to situate the demographic and financial position of these communities *inter alia* their general outlook on forest conservation and the satisfaction level of the local community. Data of 650 (EDC/VSS) members from three zones, 230 from South Zone (Thiruvananthapuram, Kollam, Pathanamthitta and Kottayam), 220 respondents from Central Zone (Idukki, Ernakulam and Thrissur) and 200 from North Zone (Palakkad and Wayanad) involved in various fields of CBET in Kerala are analyzed for this purpose. The allocation to each zone was on the basis of active EDC's/VSS in the area, population proportion, etc. Socio-economic variables, such as gender, age, education, income, employment, saving pattern, banking habits, debt and standard of living index have been analysed by using statistical tools such as Chi-Square, and Correspondence analysis.

Results and Discussion

Gender-wise Distribution of Samples

As can be seen from Table 17.1, about 75.50 per cent of the respondents are males and the rest (24.50%) are females. Zone-wise break up of data also shows similar results. In the South Zone, 74.80 per cent of the respondents are males and in the Central Zone 79.10 per cent are males and North Zone has the highest proportion of females in the sample (27.50%).

Table 17.1: Gender-wise Distribution of Samples

Zone	*Gender (%)*		*N*
	Male	*Female*	
South Zone	74.8	25.2	230
Central Zone	79.1	20.9	220
North Zone	72.5	27.5	200
Total	75.5	24.5	650

Age-wise Distribution of Respondents

Majority of the respondents (66.5%) are in the age group of 20 to 40 years followed by the age group of 40-50 (20.2%), whereas only 1.20 per cent constitutes the age group of above 60. Analysis within the zones, as can be seen from Fig. 17.1, gives similar results with majority between the age group of 20-40.

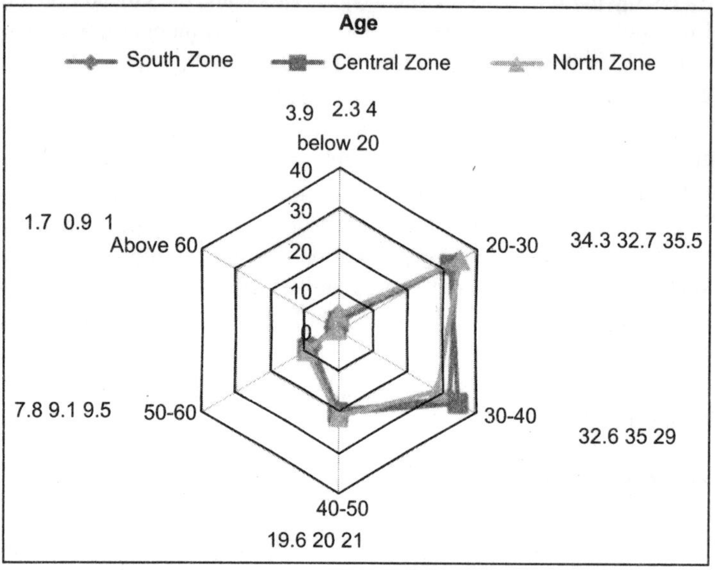

Fig. 17.1: Age-wise Distribution of Respondents.

Educational Qualification of the Community Members

We can infer from the analysis of the educational qualifications in Table 17.2 that majority (i.e., 62.20%) had a formal education of 10th class and below. Most of the locals had only basic school education. 21.40 per cent are undergraduates, whereas 10.20 per cent constitutes respondents having qualification of graduation and 6.20 per cent have qualification of Post-Graduation and above. We can further infer from Table 17.2 that majority of graduates and post-graduates comes from south and central zones (36.60% of the post-graduates are from the south zone and 46.30% are from the central zone and 59.10% of the graduates are from south and 33.30% from the central zone). There is not much difference in percentages when we analyze the sample based on education level of 10th and below and under-graduation. Even though Graduates and Post-Graduates form a meagre part of the total sample, more than 80 per cent of the respondents having these qualifications are from South and Central zones. It is clear from Table 17.3(a) that there is difference in the formal education level between three zones. As can be seen from the cross tab analysis, the zone-wise difference is in the proportion of graduates and post-graduates as there are lesser percentage of graduates and post-graduates in the north zone compared to other two zones. To confirm this, we have done the Chi-square of the zone and educational qualification by taking only South and Central zones which show no significant difference between the same which is shown in Table 17.3(b).

Table 17.2: Formal Education of the Community Members

	Formal Education %				
Zone	*10th and Below*	*Under-Graduate*	*Graduate*	*Post-Graduate*	*Total*
South Zone	34.70	25.90	59.10	36.60	35.40
Central Zone	32.90	33.10	33.30	46.30	33.80
North Zone	32.40	41.00	7.60	17.10	30.80
Total	100	100	100	100	100
% of Total	62.20	21.40	10.20	6.20	

Table 17.3(a): Chi-Square Tests (South, Central and North Zones)

	Value	df	Asymp. Sig. (2-sided)
Pearson Chi-Square	35.250[a]	6	.000
Likelihood Ratio	38.732	6	.000
Linear-by-Linear Association	7.922	1	.005
N of Valid Cases	650	—	—

a. 0 Cells (.0%) have expected count less than 5. The minimum expected count is 12.62.

Table 17.3 (b): Chi-Square Tests (South and Central Zones)

	Value	*df*	*Asymp. Sig (2-sided)*
Pearson Chi-Square	6.388[a]	3	.094
Likelihood Ratio	6.453	3	.092
Linear-by-Linear Association	.064	1	.801
N of Valid Cases	450	—	—

a. 0 Cells (.0%) have expected count less than 5. The minimum expected count is 16.62.

Income, Employment and Saving Pattern

Income and Employment

Nearly ninety nine per cent of the respondents work in tourism sector throughout the year as guides, naturalists, watchers, drivers, eco-shop workers, cook, etc. As can be seen from Fig. 17.2 that 56.20 per cent of respondents' income is solely from tourism related activities. 34.80 per cent of community members have income between 75-99 per cent from tourism whereas the rest (9.10%) have less than 74 per cent of their income from tourism. Zone-wise analysis also shows similar results as is evident from Fig. 17.2.

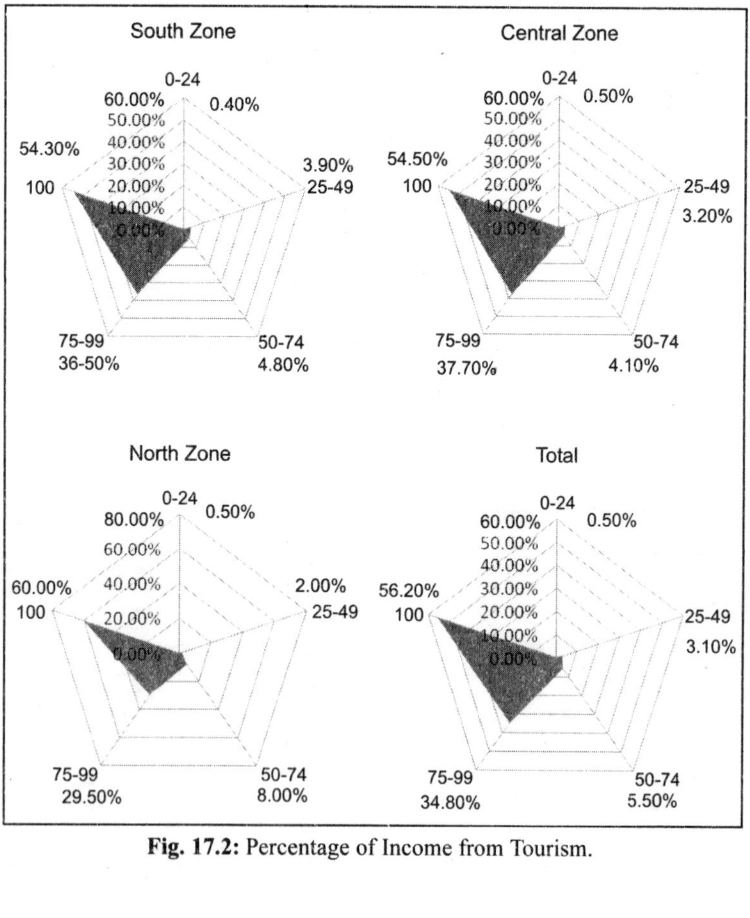

Fig. 17.2: Percentage of Income from Tourism.

Table 17.4: Main Occupation of the Community Members

Zone	*Main occupation in %*		Total
	Tourism	*Other*	
South Zone	95.2	4.8	100
Central Zone	96.4	3.6	100
North Zone	93.0	7.0	100
Total	**94.9**	**5.1**	**100**

94.9 per cent of the respondents have recorded their main occupation as tourism related activity and the remaining 5.10 per cent are involved in activities such as agriculture, private sector jobs, coolies, etc. We can infer this from Table 17.4. Most of the community members around the tourist spots are opting tourism related occupation rather than doing petty business, manual labour, etc. If the community members were not provided with this option of working in the Community based ecotourism (CBET) initiatives, they would have been left with no choice other than depending on forest resources, which, in turn, would have resulted in exploitation of these resources. Regarding the tourism related occupation in which the community members are engaged in, about 40 per cent are working as guides, followed by watchers (22%), other occupation (13.08%) and drivers and business (8.77% and 8.15%, respectively). This is shown in Fig. 17.3 and the zone-wise analysis also give similar results.

It can be inferred from Table 17.5 that majority of the respondents (55.50%) fall under the income group of ₹ 3001-4000. 23.80 per cent has income between ₹ 4001-5000 and 13.20 per cent has a monthly income between ₹ 2001-3000. And the rest (3.10% and 4.30%) has an income of ₹ 1001-2000 and above ₹ 5000 per month, respectively.

Table 17.5: Monthly Income from Tourism Activities – Zone-wise

Zone	*Income (in %)*					Total
	1001-2000	*2001-3000*	*3001-4000*	*4001-5000*	*Above 5000*	
South Zone	3.5	10.4	53.9	29.1	3.0	100
Central Zone	3.2	13.2	56.4	24.1	3.2	100
North Zone	2.5	16.5	56.5	17.5	7.0	100
Total	**3.1**	**13.2**	**55.5**	**23.8**	**4.3**	**100**

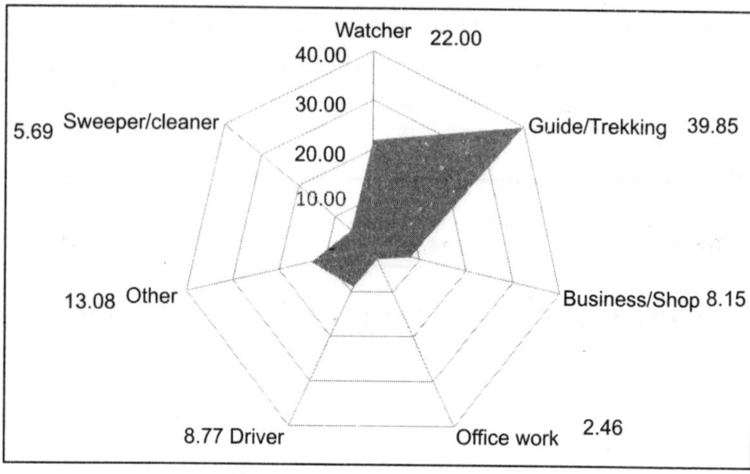

Fig. 17.3: Tourism related Occupation.

Most of the community members are earning more than what they used to get as EDC/VSS workers. Their dependency on forest for their livelihood did not provide any security in income earnings.

Banking Habits

This section analyses the banking habits of the respondents in maintaining a bank account, savings, indebtedness, etc. Table 17.6 shows the total percentage of households having a bank account. It is evident that while 48.60 per cent do not hold a bank account, whereas 51.40 per cent of households have bank account. Education level is an important determinant in the financial habits of the individuals. People with better education have better financial habits than those having less level of education. As can be seen in section (a) of Table 17.6, the level of education has an influence on banking behaviour. People with formal education of 10th and below (38.10%) hold a bank account. As we move to the respondents with higher qualifications, the percentage moves in favour of those who are holding a bank account, i.e., 43.60 per cent of undergraduates hold a bank account. In the case of graduates, 92.40 per cent hold a bank account. All the respondents having qualification of post-graduation have banking habits. Saving pattern shows that 62.90 per cent of the respondents had these habits and out of this 80.4 per cent saved on a monthly basis. (see Fig. 17.4). Education-saving pattern cross tabulation also evinces the same pattern [see section (b) of Table 17.6].

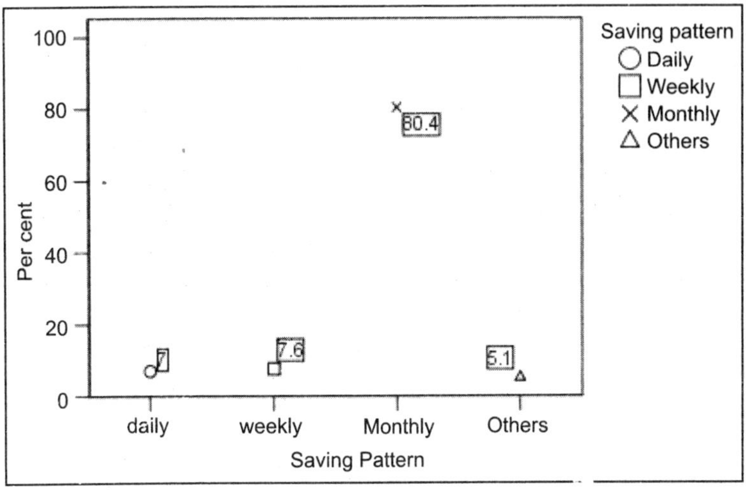

Fig. 17.4: Saving Pattern

Table 17.6: Formal Education — holding of bank account — savings — Indebtedness — Cross tabulation

Formal Education	*(a) Holding of bank account (in percentage)*		*(b) Does your family save (in percentage)*		*(c) Indebtedness (in percentage)*		*Total (a)/(b)/(c) (in percentage)*
	yes	*no*	*yes*	*no*	*yes*	*no*	
10th and Below (1)	38.10	61.90	56.40	43.60	83.90	16.10	100.00
Under Graduate (2)	43.60	56.40	54.30	45.70	63.60	36.40	100.00
Graduate (3)	92.40	7.60	98.50	1.5	66.70	33.30	100.00
Post Graduate (4)	100.00	0.00	100.00	0.00	14.60	85.40	100.00
Total (5)	48.60	51.40	62.90	37.10	73.40	26.60	100.00

Fig. 17.5 depicts the purpose for which the respondents save, i.e., whether they save for future consumption, education, marriage, earn interest or doing business. This category is dichotomized into revenue generating and non-revenue generating purposes. Saving to earn interest or to do business/self-employment can be termed as a revenue generating

affair and as consumption, marriage, for other purposes, etc., do not earn any direct or immediate financial returns and this is termed as non-revenue generating purpose.

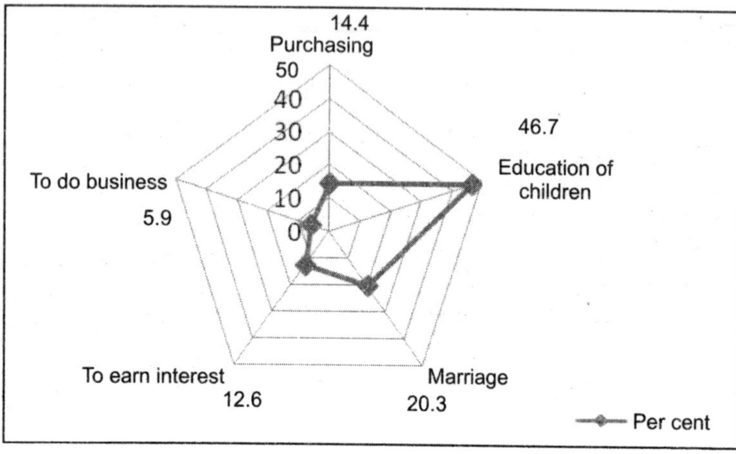

Fig. 17.5: Purpose of Savings

The community member's nature of saving, i.e., whether they save in bank, post office, chit funds, SHGs, home savings, etc. (given in Fig. 17.6), show that 18.20 per cent of the respondents have bank savings, 18.00 per cent have post office savings. 31.10 per cent have other kind of savings. 10.50 per cent of the respondents have savings in chit funds and self help groups. The rest have savings with co-operatives (7.30%) and home savings (4.40%).

In the case of indebtedness [section (c) of Table 17.6] it may be observed that number of people with debt comes down as the education level increases. Combined analysis shows that 73.40 per cent of respondents have indebtedness of some sort. Regarding the source of the debt, 31.60 per cent borrowed from the private money lenders, 19.50 per cent from Kundumbasree, 15.50 depended on the co-operative societies for their borrowing needs and 12.20 had indebtedness with the local shop keepers [see Fig. 17.7].

Fig. 17.8 situates the purpose for which the community members have taken indebtedness. Most of them borrow for day to day expenses, construction of house, marriage, education, treatment, etc.

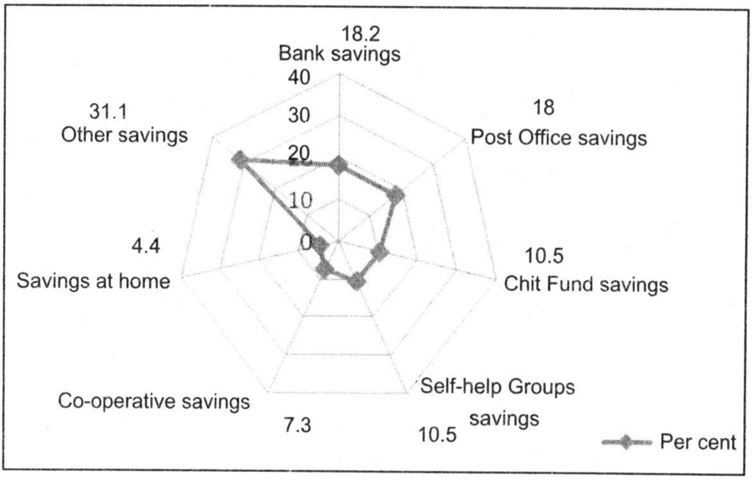

Fig. 17.6: Type of Savings.

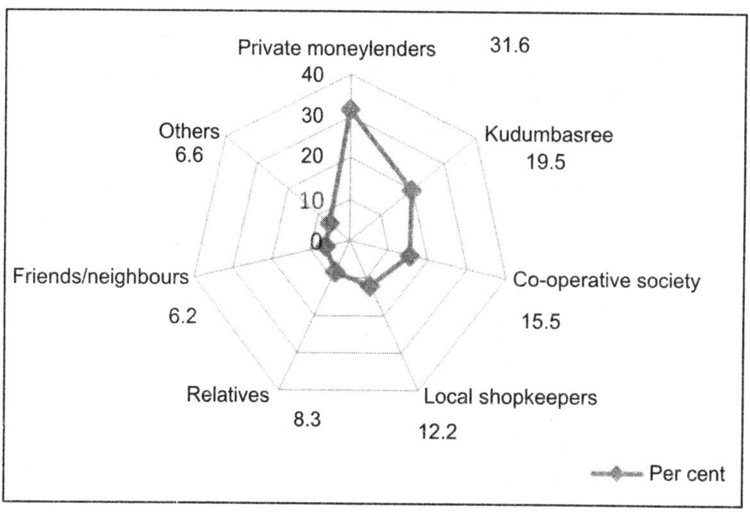

Fig. 17.7: Source of Debt

If we bring together bank account holding tendency, savings and borrowings, we can see that as most of the graduate and post-graduate respondents have bank account and saving habits, they have lesser tendency to borrow compared to the reset of the group. Chi-Square

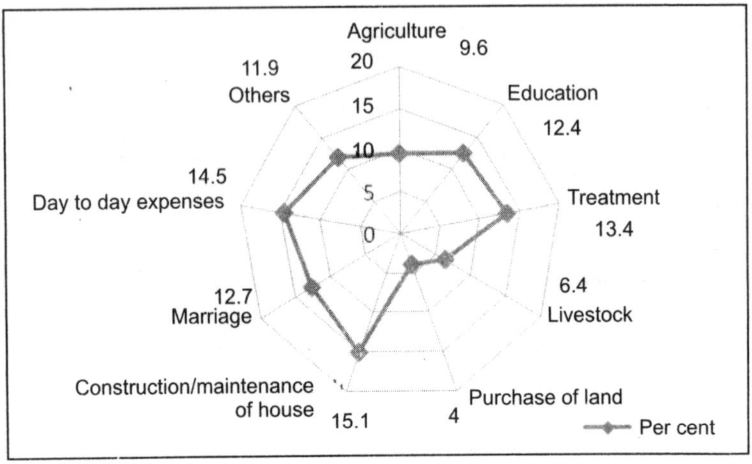

Fig. 17.8: Purpose of Indebtedness

analysis between education-holding of bank account, education-savings and education-indebtedness is given in Table 17.7(a). We can infer from the analysis that there is significant difference between formal education level of the community member and his/her tendency to save, hold a bank account and to take debt.

Chi-square based on zones of these three banking habits, viz., savings, bank account holding tendency and indebtedness [Table 17.7(b)] shows that there is no significant difference between zone and saving habits, while difference exists between zone and bank account holding tendency and zone and indebtedness.

Quality of Life

Factors which represent the quality of living of the community members like ownership of house, source of drinking water, source of power, information source, etc., are analysed in this section. Performance of three zones in providing these amenities is depicted in this section.

Place of Living

Analysis about the ownership of house brings to light that 80.80 per cent of respondents live in their own house, 4.20 per cent in rented house,

Table 17.7(a): Chi-square test (Education-bank account, Education-saving and Education-indebtedness)

	Education-Bank account [1]			*Education-Savings* [2]			*Education-Indebtedness* [3]		
	Value	*df*	*Asymp. Sig. (2-sided)*	*Value*	*df*	*Asymp. Sig. (2-sided)*	*Value*	*df*	*Asymp. Sig. (2-sided)*
Pearson Chi-Square	113.513[a]	3	.000	72.013[a]	3	.000	104.123[a]	3	.000
Likelihood Ratio	138.058	3	.000	101.634	3	.000	95.886	3	.000
Linear-by-Linear Association	96.495	1	.000	51.479	1	.000	86.778	1	.000

Note: 1. 0 cells (.0%) have expected countless than 5. The minimum expected count is 19.93.
2. 0 cells (.0%) have expected countless than 5. The minimum expected count is 15.20.
3. 0 cells (.0%) have expected countless than 5. The minimum expected count is 10.91.

Table 17.7(b): Chi-square test (Zone-bank account, Zone-savings and Zone-indebtedness)

	Zone-Bank account [1]			Zone-Savings [2]			Zone-Indebtedness [3]		
	Value	*Df*	*Asymp. Sig. (2-sided)*	*Value*	*df*	*Asymp. Sig. (2-sided)*	*Value*	*Df*	*Asymp. Sig. (2-sided)*
Pearson Chi-Square	5.975[a]	2	.050	1.121[a]	2	.571	8.921[a]	2	.012
Likelihood Ratio	5.994	2	.050	1.117	2	.572	8.790	2	.012
Linear-by-Linear Association	3.951	1	.047	1.023	1	.312	3.858	1	.050

1. 0 cells (.0%) have expected count lessthan 5. The minimum expected count is 97.23.
2. 0 cells (.0%) have expected count lessthan 5. The minimum expected count is 74.15.
3. 0 cells (.0%) have expected count lessthan 5. The minimum expected count is 53.23.

1.70 per cent in their parent's house and 12.60 per cent of the respondents have other kinds of accommodation facilities, such as staff quarters, etc. (see Table 17.8). This shows that in the matter of accommodation/housing facilities, more than 75 per cent of the respondents are self-sufficient. Zone-wise analysis also gives similar outcomes.

Table 17.8: Place of Living

Zone	*Place of living (in %)*					*Total*
	Own house	*Rented house*	*Relatives's house*	*Parent's house*	*Other*	
South Zone	76.5	6.1	.9	1.3	15.2	100.0
Central Zone	83.6	3.6	.9	1.8	10.0	100.0
North Zone	82.5	2.5	.5	2.0	12.5	100.0
Total	**80.8**	**4.2**	**.8**	**1.7**	**12.6**	**100.0**

Source of Water

It is one of the major determinants of the quality of life of the households. The zone-wise analysis of source of drinking water of the households is given in Table 17.9.

Table 17.9: Source of Water

	Source of water (in %)					*Total*
Zone	*Own well*	*House connection*	*Public well*	*Public tap*	*Canal/river/ pond*	
South Zone	73.20	2.40	17.10	0.00	7.30	100.00
Central Zone	17.10	11.80	22.90	40.60	7.60	100.00
North Zone	30.20	2.40	30.20	37.20	0.00	100.00
Total	28.30	8.70	23.20	33.50	6.30	100.00

From the overall analysis, we can infer that majority, i.e., 63 per cent depend on public source of water. Easy availability of drinking water is still a problem for community members. Inter-zone analysis in Table 17.9 brings to the fact that majority (73.2%) of the community members in the South Zone depend on their own well for water. When we take the case of the respondents in the Central Zone, they depend more on public sources for water [public tap (40.60%) and public well (22.9%)]. Only 28.90 per cent have their own source for water (17.10% have own well and 11.80% have house connection). In North Zone too, more than 60 per cent (30.20% on public well and 37.20% on public tap) depend on public sources for drinking water. Only 30.20 per cent of the respondents have own well and 2.40 per cent have house connection.

Source of Light

Table 17.10 points out that majority of the respondents (76.2%) have electricity connection in their homes, 20.70 per cent use kerosene as their source of light, 6.2 per cent use other sources and 3.70 per cent use oil lamps as source of light in their houses. Zone-wise analysis also gives similar results showing most of the respondents having electricity connection.

Table 17.10: Source of Light

	Source of Light				*N*
Zone	*Electricity*	*Oil Lamp*	*Kerosene*	*Other*	
South Zone	75.5	4.4	19.2	6.1	230
Central Zone	77.6	3.2	21.5	5	220
North Zone	75.4	3.5	21.6	7.5	200
Total N	493	24	134	40	650
Percentage	76.2	3.7	20.7	6.2	100

Source of Information

Community members were asked to mark the sources from which they received news and information. Table 17.11 shows that across zones 29.6 per cent depend on TV, 21.4 per cent on radio as the source of information, followed by newspaper (19.0%), government officials (13.9%), neighbours (6.5%), public leaders (5.7%) and magazines (3.3%).

Standard of Living Index for Community Members

Field survey experience had shown that there was considerable difference in the living standards of different communities. To evaluate this, a standard of living index was constructed from the survey data for respondents and a correspondence analysis was performed. SLI is an index constructed to understand the general living conditions of people taking into account different indicators of lifestyle and living standards. These include socio-economic conditions like ownership of house, drinking water, energy used for lighting, etc. Each indicator was given scores in the band of one to three, where 1 is given for minimum value, i.e., low SLI, 2 for medium value or medium SLI and 3 for maximum value or high SLI. The results of cross tab analysis and Chi-square tests with various parameters like zone, income, educational qualifications, etc., have been considered.

Table 17.11: Source of Information

Zone	*Source of Information*								*N*
	News-paper	*Tele-vision*	*Maga-zine*	*Radio*	*Neigh-bours*	*Govt. officials*	*Public leaders*	*Other sources*	
South Zone	18.1	30.4	1.9	22	7	15.1	5.1	0.5	230
Central Zone	17.8	30.3	3.8	22.3	6.3	13	6	0.5	220
North Zone	21.4	27.9	4.3	19.8	6.2	13.6	6	0.8	200
Total N	228	355	39	257	78	167	68	7	650
percentage	19	29.6	3.3	21.4	6.5	13.9	5.7	0.6	100

The results of the correspondence analysis in Table 17.12 show that North Zone has the highest number of households in the Low SLI category, whereas Central Zone has the least number of households.

Table 17.12: Zone-wise Correspcndence Analysis of SLI

SLI	*South Zone*	*Central Zone*	*North Zone*	*Total*
Low SLI	32.00	29.30	38.70	100
Medium SLI	32.50	28.60	38.90	100
High SLI	37.10	36.60	26.30	100
Active Margin	**230**	**220**	**200**	**650**

Table 17.13 proves that there is a significant difference between zones and the SLI value which is further portrayed in the form of correspondence chart through Fig. 17.9. Majority of households in the high SLI category

are in South and Central Zones whereas the North Zone is closer to the medium SLI and low SLI category.

Table 17.13 Summary Table

Dimension	*Singular Value*	*Inertia*	*Chi Square*	*Sig.*	*Proportion of Inertia*		*Confidence Singular Value*	
					Accounted for	*Cumulative*	*Standard Deviation*	*Correlation*
1.	.131	.017			.999	.999	.040	–.005
2.	.004	.000			.001	1.000	.037	
Total		**.017**	**11.142**	**.025***	**1.000**	**1.000**		

* 4 degrees of freedom.

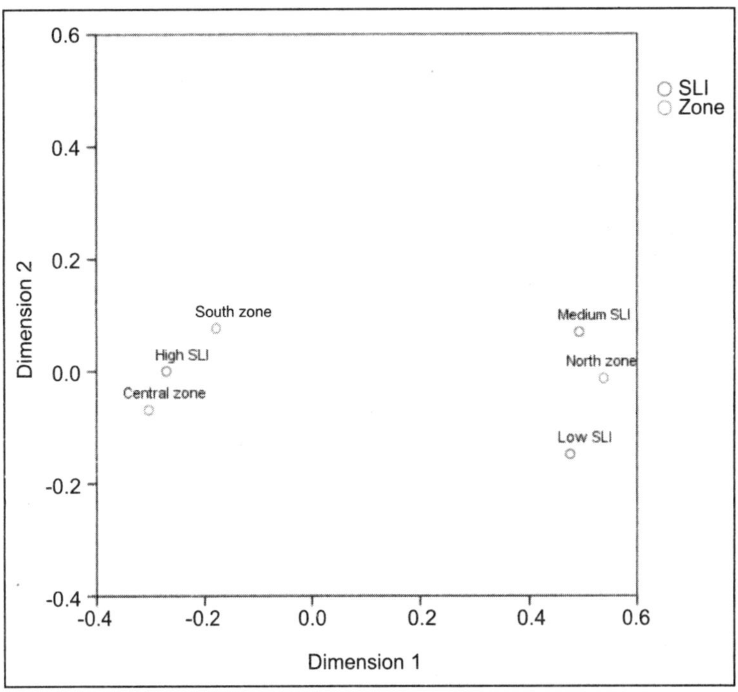

Fig. 17.9: Scatter Plot for Row and Column Points.

SLI-Income Cross Tab

It is inferred that there is significant difference between the Standard of Living parameters and income level of the community members. Community members having low SLI value (57.33%) are in the income group of ₹3001-4000, 18.22 per cent constitutes income levels of 2001-3000 and 14.22 per cent in the income group of ₹ 4001-5000. Only 5.33 per cent of the community members are in the income category of ₹ 5000 and above. In the case of medium SLI category, we can see a similar pattern with slight variations in the percentages of medium SLI in 4,001-5,000 income categories. In the case of high SLI, respondents having an income above ₹ 5,000 (see Fig. 17.10).

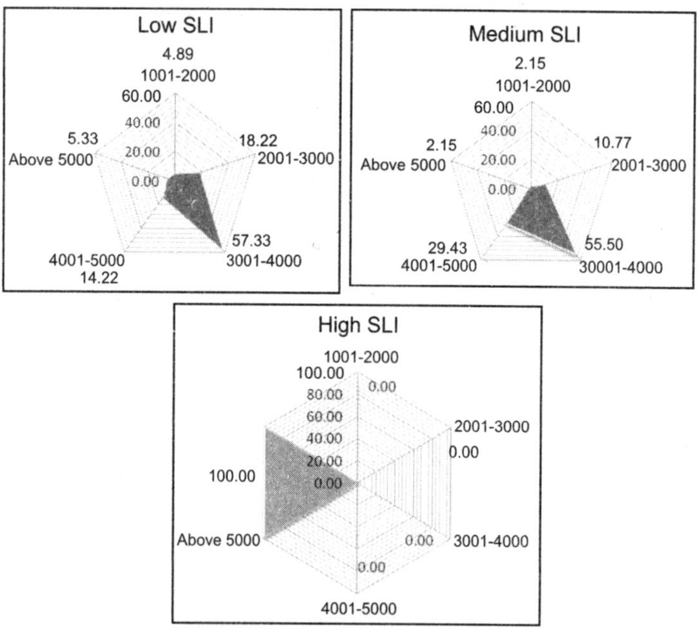

Fig. 17.10: SLI-income Percentages.

From this, it is clear that there is difference in SLI value based on income levels of respondents. This is statistically proved with the Chi-Square test values. The result shows that there is significant difference between income levels and Standard of Living of the community members (see Table 17.16).

Table 17.14: SLI-income Chi-Square

	Value	*df*	*Asymp. Sig. (2 sided)*
Pearson Chi-Square	191.092[a]	8	.000
Likelihood Ratio	76.136	8	.000
Linear-by-Linear Association	23.307	1	.000
N of Valid Cases	649	—	—

[a]. 5 cells (33.3%) have expected count less than 5. The minimum expected count is .22.

SLI-Educational Qualification Cross Tab

When the effect of educational qualification on the SLI of the community members was analysed, considerable variation has been identified based on the educational qualification attained by the individual. The results are shown in Tables 17.15, 17.16 and Fig. 17.11. It can be seen from the Table 17.15 that majority of respondents having low SLI are having the educational qualification of 10th and below (85.78%) and undergraduates (12.89). Graduates and post-graduates form only 1.33 per cent (0.44 and 0.89%, respectively) of the total respondents having low SLI. But, there is an increase in the share of the other two categories with graduate respondents constituting 15.35 per cent and post-graduates 8.63 per cent of the medium SLI category. In high SLI section, majority (52.86%) are post-graduates, followed by graduates (24.28) and undergraduates (14.29). Higher the educational qualification of the community members, the greater will be the tendency to be in the high SLI category and *vice versa*. Chi-Square test also shows that there is significant difference in the SLI value of the respondents based on the educational qualification attained by them.

Table 17.15: SLI-Formal Education Cross Tabulation

	Formal Education (in %)				*Total*
	10th and Below	*Under-graduation*	*Graduation*	*Post-graduation*	
Low SLI	85.78	12.89	0.44	0.89	100.00
Medium SLI	49.88	26.14	15.35	8.63	100.00
High SLI	8.57	14.29	24.28	52.86	100.00

Table 17.16: Chi-Square Tests

	Value	*df*	*Asymp. Sig. (2-sided)*
Pearson Chi-Square	104.624*	6	.000
Likelihood Ratio	116.874	6	.000
Linear-By-Linear Association	88.266	1	.000
N of Valid Cases	649	—	—

* 4 cells (33.3%) have expected count less than 5. The minimum expected count is .44.

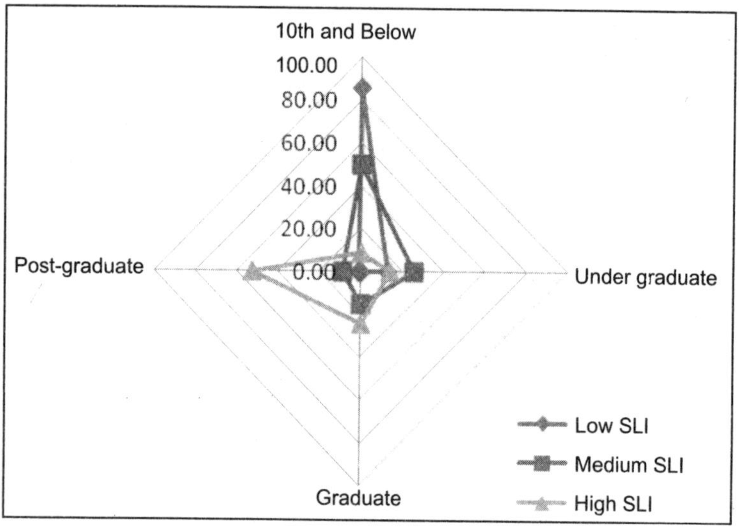

Fig. 17.11: SLI-education Cross Tab

Conclusion

Community based ecotourism initiatives on the part of the government has benefited the community in a big way as 56.20 per cent of the community members in the sample solely depend on ecotourism as their only livelihood. Any setback, either seasonal or random, will have deleterious effect on their income and livelihood options inasmuch as they find it difficult to unearth alternative avocations in this alienated and difficult terrain. Moreover, the community is also striving hard to conserve the forest and ecosystem with a view to attracting more and more ecotourists, which in a way expands their livelihood base. This has been well specified by the respondents when asked about their main occupation, of which about 95 per cent of the community members answered that their primary occupation is only related to ecotourism. Most of the socio-economic indicators of the community in the ecotourist centres show a positive trend once these centres have been active with tourists. This has reflected in monthly income earnings, education attainment of the community, saving habits and related attainments. Chi-Square analyses pertaining to various socio-economic analyses have also confirmed this.

Zone-wise analysis shows that the community members have benefited totally from tourism development in the region as they have got both employments as well as secured livelihood options. This has helped to draw attention to reduce overall exploitation of forest land by these communities which in turn perpetuates sustainable development of ecotourist sites and ecotourism in Kerala. Inter-zone analysis to highlight the differences in the socio-economic aspects brings to the fact that difference between and among zones is marginal. This may be either due to the small geographical area of Kerala and as such the in-bound and out-bound ecotourism happening almost equally with all the ecotourist centres or may be due to different niche ecotourist sites are equally preferable to all the visitors coming over to Kerala for ecotourism activities.

References

Government of Kerala. (2006), "Forest Management- involvement of People-Participatory Forest Management with local communities implementation" in various Orders issued, Kerala Forest Department, Thiruvanathapuram.

Ross and G. Wall (1999), "Ecotourism: Towards Congruence between Theory and Practice", *Tourism Management*, pp. 123-132.

Santosh, P. Thampi. (2005), "Ecotourism in Kerala, India: Lessons from the Eco-Development Project in Periyar Tiger Reserve", *E-Paper Series*, No. 13, June 2005.

Tisdell, C.A. (2003), "Economic Aspects of Ecotourism: Wildlife-based Tourism and its Contribution to Nature", *Sri Lankan Journal of Agricultural Economics*, Vol. 5, No. 1, 2003.

18

Issues of Community Based Ecotourism Development in Sikkim

A Descriptive Analysis

Supriya Dam

Introduction

Ecotourism is a global phenomenon in recent years, especially during the early years of twenty-first century. The early definition of ecotourism was presented by the International Ecotourism Society (IES:1991) which defines it as "responsible travel to natural areas that conserves the environment and sustains the well-being of local people". Ceballos-Lascurain (1996) has given a comprehensive definition on ecotourism which states "ecotourism is environmentally responsible travel to natural areas in order to enjoy and appreciate nature (and accompanying cultural features, both past and present) that promotes conservation have low visitor impact and provide for beneficially active socio-economic involvement of local people". In a similar vein, UN World Tourism Organisation (WTO) defines it as "travelling to relatively undisturbed natural areas with the specific object of satisfying, admiring and enjoying nature and its wild plants, animals as well as existing cultural aspects (both past and present) found in these areas". Thus, ecotourism is understood as purposeful travel to natural areas for understanding and appreciating cultural, natural and ecological environment for not altering the ecosystem; while making allowances for conservation of natural resources which are beneficial to local populace.

Spread of Ecotourism

According to the data released by the World Tourism Organisation (2006), eco-touristic journeys comprised up to 7 per cent (45 million of all journeys), while it is expected that the number will increase up to 70 million per year in 2010. Ceballos-Lascurain (1996) shows that the share of ecotourism journeys reaches 20 to 60 per cent of all journeys.

The diversity in geography in India provides a wealth of natural areas that could support ecotourism activities. The natural reserved areas for the tourists include national parks, biosphere reserves, wetlands, mountain areas and forests, coral reefs and mangrove under ecotourism. In this way, the natural reserved areas have been opened for the tourists that include 13 biosphere reserves (to limited extent in outer buffer zone), 89 natural parks and 490 wildlife sanctuaries (MoIB: 2004).

The Government of India, through policy initiatives, has acknowledged the significance of ecotourism with policy measures. Both the Ministry of Tourism and the Ministry of Environment and Forests have responded to the development in the field of ecotourism. The Department of Tourism issued Policy and Guidelines on ecotourism in July 1998. The policy lays down the objectives for ecotourism and contains operational guidelines for major stakeholders. During 2000, Territorial Forest Divisions recognized ecotourism in protected areas as one of the fifteen thrust areas of the Ministry of Environment and Forests. The Indian chapter of the Pacific Asia Travel Association (PATA) has formulated an action plan for National Ecotourism Policy, which has been forwarded by the Ministry of Tourism for the State Governments for review (Boora: 2005).

In the midst of these developments, several State governments have also taken policy measures to promote ecotourism. The Government of Himachal Pradesh has announced a 'Policy on Development of Ecotourism' in May 2001 with special focus on local people. The Government of Madhya Pradesh has announced an 'Eco and Adventure Tourism Policy' for 2001-02 placing emphasis on the involvement of private sector. The Forest Departments of Kerala, Goa, Karnataka, Himachal Pradesh and Sikkim have designated officials to coordinate ecotourism activities. Several State governments including Madhya Pradesh, Rajasthan, Karnataka and Andhra Pradesh have issued orders for recycling of entry fees from protected areas for conservation and community development. The Forest Corporation of West Bengal and Uttaranchal has initiated ecotourism activities and Government of Kerala has launched the Thenmala Ecotourism Promotion Society to develop a model for ecotourism. Recently, the practitioners and individuals interested in Sikkim tourism established Ecotourism and Conservation Society of Sikkim (ECOSS), with the objective of promoting conservation and ecotourism projects, research and advocacy. In fact, Sikkim Ecotourism Policy envisioned establishing the state as an ultimate and unique ecotourism destination offering memorable and high quality learning experience to the visitors; while contributing towards poverty alleviation and promotion of nature conservation (FEWMD:2011). In the private sector, there are examples of eco-friendly concept hotels such as Orchid Hotel and Project Development by the Casino Group in Kerala. Ecotourism activities occur not only in and around national parks and wildlife sanctuaries but even in the forest areas and other natural areas which have varied attractions and more relaxed legal restrictions (CBN: 2002).

Topography and Biodiversity

Sikkim is a small mountainous State in the Eastern Himalayan Region of India extending approximately 114 kilometre from north to south and 64 kilometre from east to west, having total geographical area of 7096 square kilometre. It is surrounded by vast stretches of Tibetan Plateau in north; Chumbi Valley and Kingdom of Bhutan in the east; Darjeeling district of West Bengal in south and Kingdom of Nepal in the west. The State has four districts, namely east, west, north and south, with a population of 5,40,493, having an average density 76 persons per square kilometre as per 2001 Census. This region is listed among the world's ten most critical centres' for biodiversity and endemism with 150 species of mammals, 550 species of birds, 650 species of butterflies and moths, 33 species of reptiles, 16 species of amphibians, 48 species of fishes, 4,500 species of flowering plants, 36 species of rhododendrons, 9 species of conifers, 450 species of trees, 430 species of orchids, 350 species of ferns and allies and 175 species of wild edible plants.

Objectives

The basic objective of the study is to assess the issues pertaining to community based ecotourism development in select pockets in Sikkim and ways and means of addressing it. The objectives of the study are: to appraise the growth of ecotourism sector in Sikkim; and assess the level of local involvement in ecotourism in the State.

Ecotourism Practices in Sikkim

Ecotourism programme was kicked off in Sikkim during the adoption of 'Sikkim Biodiversity and Ecotourism Project' in the year 1995-98. Yuksam in West Sikkim was the project site for the same where people were sensitized regarding environmental conservation and preservation of natural resources. The project has shown positive impact on the environmental and socio-cultural system of the State. But this form of tourism got momentum in the first decade of twenty-first century in which the tiny Himalayan State has experienced increased amount of tourists' influx. The following discussion will draw attention to select ecotourism practices in Sikkim over the years.

Bhattacharya and Kumari (2004) have done a comparative study of ecotourism practices in Yuksam and Pelling village of Sikkim. During May 1996, participatory community based planning was introduced in Yuksam with the help of local people and it has served the basis for future growth of ecotourism in the State. The rhetoric of Yuksam Community Based Ecotourism (CBE) entirely relies on local peoples' participation with negligible presence of outsiders. The programme has brought enhanced income and employment opportunities for the locals in the area with minimal impact on ecological balance of the destination. Although, there are less number of sophisticated hotels and lodges in Yuksam, primarily because of local financing, but the economic impact of CBE are visible among locales in the area. The CBE is almost absent in Pelling and due to pressure and influence of outsiders, local people participation in ecotourism is significantly low over there.

Sikkim Industrial Development Corporation (SIDICO) in conjunction with Voluntary Health Association of Sikkim (VHAS) promotes ecotourism in two remote villages, Rong in the south district and Lading in the west district. An interesting finding from these projects is that success in involving villagers in the developmental work and effecting changes among the community is inversely related to accessibility to government funding. In Lading, which is more remote than Rong and thus had lower recourse to government resources, the project was able to secure higher level of villagers' participation (GoI: 2008).

In another ecotourism project in Assam Lingzey (near Gangtok) run by project Khedi Ecotourism and Eco-development Promotion (KEEP), an NGO, local residents offer room in their houses for home stays and work as guide for trekkers traversing the Khedi route and for day long hikes through the village and neighbouring areas. By involving visitors in their traditional way of life, the project encourages local Bhutia people to retain the traditional feature of their homes, local customs, and sensitizes village inhabitants and visitors to the importance of environmental preservation (GoI:2008).

Among the PAs, Khanchendzonga National Park and Khanchendzonga Biosphere Reserve are popular among tourists visiting the State. Rest of the PAs have low visitation rate in proportion to total influx of tourists in the tiny hilly State. In fact, only 7 per cent of tourists surveyed (both domestic and foreign) made their trip to PAs of Sikkim while 30 per cent of them have overtly expressed their concern for deteriorating condition of PAs in the State.

Apart from protected areas, there are certain vintage cultural and religious sites where local institutions reserve the operational rights related to tourism. For example, in west Sikkim, the sacred lake of Khecheopalri, a popular tourist destination, is being looked after by the Khecheopalri Holy Lake Welfare Committee (KHLWC). The revenue earned from the visitors visiting the lake is used for the development of the lake area and the local community at large (Sharma, *et al.*, 2000).

Table 18.1: Parks and Sanctuaries in Sikkim (under Protected Area Network)

Sl. No.	*Name of Parks and Sanctuaries*	*Area in sq. kms*	*District*	*Altitude (metres)*	*Date of Notification*
1.	Varsey Rhododendron Sanctuary	104	West	2200-100	08.06.96
2.	Fambonglho Wildlife Sanctuary	51.76	East	1524-749	02.04.84
3.	Kyongnosla Alpine Sanctuary	31.00	East	3292-116	05.12.92
4.	Maenam Wildlife Sanctuary	35.34	South	2300-263	09.03.87
5.	Pangolakha Wildlife Sanctuary	128.00	East	NA	07.11.2000
6.	Shingba Rhododendron Sanctuary	43.00	North	3048-575	05.12.92
7.	Khanchendzonga National Park	1784.00	North/West	NA	26.08.72
8.	Khanchendzonga Biosphere Reserve	2620.00	North/West	NA	NA
9.	Kitam Bird Sanctuary	6	NA	320-875	NA

Source: Tourism Department, Government of Sikkim.

Asian Development Bank (ADB:2010) project also stresses on community based tourism activities focused on culture, ecotourism through promotion of home stays and community supported treks in Sikkim. The objective is to enhance local access to livelihoods based on tourism activities. Rey Mindu, a Lepcha village along the Sajong-Lingdum-Gangtok road, has the potential to be developed as heritage village tourism project, apart from trekking and handicrafts. Rey Mindu, being situated in the periphery of the Gangtok city, has maintained its traditional character; and offer significant potential for development of treks leading to the Fambong Lho Wildlife Sanctuary on the upper reaches of the village. Fambong Lho Wildlife Sanctuary has been identified by the Department of Forest, Environment and Wildlife Management (FEWMD), Government of Sikkim as an ideal destination for ecotourism including the development of one or two days trek. Uttarey and Damthang are the two villages critically located within the Singalila trek and Singalila Ecotourism Zone starting from Hilley to Uttarey for a length of fifty kilometres within the Khanchedzonga National Park. The project comprises of two major components, i.e., capacity building to the communities in development of village products, imparted training for guides, management of home stays, cooking, etc.; and minimal improvement of infrastructure in the village in the form of sanitation, waste management and other amenities such as information centre within the village as well as upgrading other products such as trekking routes, etc.

Table 18.2: Important Bird Areas in Sikkim

Sl. No.	*Bird Areas*	*Area (ha)*
01.	Barsey Rhododendron Sanctuary	10400
02.	Dombang Valley-Lachung-Lema-Tsungthang	600000
03.	Fambong Lho Wild Life Sanctuary-Himalayan Zoological Park-Ratey Chu Reserve Forest	7826
04.	Khanchendzonga National Park and Biosphere Reserve	28500
05.	Kyongnsola Alpine Sanctuary—Tsomgo-Tamze-Chola	3100
06.	Lhonak Valley	5000
07.	Low Land Forest (Melli-Bguwa-Kitam-Jorethang-Namchi-Sombarey)	2000
08.	Maenam Wild Life Sanctuary-Tendong Reserve Forest	3539
09.	Pangolakha Wildlife Sanctuary-Zuluk-Bedong Cho-Nathula	12400
10.	Tso Lhamu Plateau Lashar-Sebula Yumesamdong Complex	5000
11.	Yumthang-Singba Rhododendron Wildlife Sanctuary	43000

Source: Islam and Rahmani (2004).

Yuksam-Dzongri is a popular ecotourism high altitude trek along the Rathong Chu River in West Sikkim passing through dense forest, placid alpine lakes and offering breath taking vistas of the Mount Khandzonga, the third highest mountain peak in the world. The number of tourists visiting the destination has increased manifold over the last fifteen years. March to May and September to November are the two main trekking season with October being the peak month for tourists visiting the site (Tambe *et al.*, 2007). This trail is mainly used by three groups, namely, tourists, mountaineers and local communities such as yak-sheep grazers, etc. In trekking and mountaineering season, high volume of visitors along with the support staff and pack animal crowd the area. (Rai *et al.*, 1998)

In Sikkim, eleven zones are declared as important bird areas (IBAs), which are critical not only for birds but also for providing connectivity to protected area (PA) system. All IBAs satisfy three criteria: (i) the IBA contain significant numbers of globally threatened (endangered, threatened and vulnerable) bird species; (ii) it contains highly restricted range species such as endemics or biome-restricted species; and (iii) there is high congregation of migratory or other birds, especially wetlands species (Islam and Rahmani, 2004). These areas, which have been identified by the Birdlife International and Bombay National History Society can also be used as landscape level stepping stones as well for ecotourism.

Community Participation and Regulations

Government of Sikkim has initiated the process of community participation at different levels of forest management. To implement such measures, Joint Forest Management Committees (JFMCs), Eco Development Committees (EDCs) and Pukhri Sanrakshan Samiti (PSS) (i.e., Lake Conservation Committee) are formed for the purpose of joint management and conservation of forest and biodiversity under the jurisdiction of the FEWMD. Till 2009, there are 158 JFMCs, 57 EDCs and two PSS have been formed in the State of Sikkim (FEWMD, 2009). One PSS is called Changu Lake PSS in the east district which was established in 2007 and registered in April 2008. The other PSS is called Khecheopalri Lake PSS in the west district, has been established in 2008 and is at an early stage of its operation.

These committees are established for the management of different land-use categories: JFMCs are constituted for the management of reserved, khasmal and gorucharan forests; EDCs are for protected areas and PSSs are for lakes. Although Gram Panchayat Ward is the basic unit for establishing these committees, a single Gram Panchayat Ward cannot have both a JFMC and an EDC (FEWMD, 2009).

The JFMCs, EDCs and PSSs consist of a general body and an executive committee. The general body comprised of one member from each household of the Ward whereas executive committee composed of ten members including one Panchayat nominee, six elected representatives of the beneficiaries (one-third of which should have women members), one NGO representative and the concerned range officer. The president of the executive committee is elected by the members of the committee. The specific roles and responsibilities of each of the member of the executive committee of JFMCs and EDCs are not defined; rather it was confirmed by the committee members during stakeholders meeting (FEWMD, 1998). However, in the case of PSS, the ex-officio president is a Panchayat Ward member whereas the president of JFMC or EDC is elected by the executive committee out of the elected members.

The duties of the EDCs includes protection and conservation of forests, environment, wildlife and biodiversity; assistance in forestry works; assistance in eco-development activities; assisting in implementation of various forest legislations; and assistance in ecotourism activities. According to the notification, assistance to ecotourism refers to such activities, like providing quality service to the visitors; and ensuring responsible behaviour of the visitors and ecotourism service providers in PAs (FEWMD, 2002).

The main duties of PSS are to ensure the protection of the lakes, their environment, wildlife and biodiversity in the PSS area and to provide assistance to ecotourism; same as EDCs. Their main activities include (FEWMD, 2002) conducting awareness and education campaigns on lake conservation; adopting garbage control measures; cleaning lakes; managing tourist shops near the lakes; observing the biodiversity around the lakes; and patrolling for illegal activities around the lakes.

Apart from these, there are numerous area based small conservation programmes that dot the entire State through the initiative of NGOs like Ecotourism and Conservation Society of Sikkim (ECOSS), Voluntary Health Association of Sikkim (VHAS), Khancendzonga Conservation Committee (KCC), Sikkim Paryavaran Sanrakshan Sangh (SPSS), Travel Agents Association of Sikkim (TAAS), etc., for tourism promotion in the State. NGOs are also entrusted with the task of imparting education for ecological ethics through workshops, fairs, street plays and modal demonstrations exposing among students about the conservation activities; conducting seminars and quizzes for developing awareness about conservation as well as extending collaboration with agencies like World Wildlife Fund (WWF) for conservation activities. Similarly, different skill development training for porters, vegetable farmers, cooks, pack animal operators and local guides, etc. It also includes training and capacity building of NGOs and stakeholders involved in ecotourism and conservation.

The legal framework for forest management and biodiversity conservation in Sikkim includes national and State Acts, which the FEWMD is responsible for executing. Interpretation and application of these Acts are constrained by a Supreme Court order (1996), which bans green felling without a proper working plan. The National Forest (Conservation) Act (1980) and amendments (1988) along with State notification led to the establishment of JFMCs (1998) in the State followed by setting up of Sikkim Eco Development Committees as per subsequent notifications. For operation and sustainable management of natural resources from the perspective of ecotourism, the following rules and guidelines got special attention (FEWMD, 2002): Sikkim Ecology Fund Environment Cess Rules 2007; State Biological Diversity Rules 2006; State Environment Agency Guidelines 2006; Guidelines for Lake Conservation in Partnership with Gram Panchayat 2006; Sikkim Ecology Fund and Environment Cess Act 2005; and Sikkim Wildlife (Regulation of Trekking) Rules 2005.

Discussion

Preliminary study points to the fact that majority of tourists (more than 90%) are ignorant about the concept of ecotourism and its sustainability aspects. The share is more in case of domestic tourists (more than 93%) than the foreign tourists' (60%). Ecotourism is known to be practiced in protected areas (PAs), especially in biosphere reserves, wildlife sanctuaries as well as in national parks; but in Sikkim, ecotourism is practiced in trekking routes, mountaineering, village home stays over and above of wildlife sanctuaries. Thus, the concept of ecotourism is broadened in Sikkim and the visitors get an opportunity to visit this pristine environment in a hospitable atmosphere. But using the broader concept of ecotourism often lead to the question: whether ecotourism is practiced in Sikkim *et al.* Studies (FEWMD, 2009) reveal that confusion reigns among stakeholders about the concept of ecotourism and too often the term is used to suit their own objectives. There have been mistakes made in the name of ecotourism such as inappropriate construction in this pristine environment; which can lead to catastrophe in this fragile ecosystem.

Bhattacharjee and Kumari's study (2004) reported that ecotourism in the Yuksam-Dzongri trail corridor and surrounding areas has been facing immense pressure on its natural resources because of increase in the number of visitors in the Khanchendzonga National Park (KNP). The study further reveals that forest remain undisturbed on the steeper slopes and degradation increased near the settlement and tourist camp sites where interference was more pronounced. It added that firewood and fodder resources are easily accessible from the forests. Rai *et al.* (1998) aptly remarked that littering of the trekking corridor, fuel-wood extraction,

Table 18.3: Acts and Rules related to Forest Management and Biodiversity Conservation in Sikkim

Category	*Acts*	*Rules*
A. Biodiversity	(i) Biological Diversity Act 2002 and Amendment 2003	Biological Diversity Rules 2004
	(ii) Environment (Protection) Act 1986	
B. Forest Conservation	(iii) Forest (Conservation) Act 1980 and Amendment 1988.	Forest (Conservation) Rules 2003 Forest (Conservation) Rules 1981 and Amendment 1992.
	(iv) Indian Forest Act 1927	
	(v) Draft State/Union Territory Minor Forest Produce (Ownership of Forest Dependent Community) Act 2005	
	(vi) Sikkim Forests, Water Courses, Road Reserve (Protection and Preservation) Act 1988 and Amendment 2000	
	(vii) Compensatory Afforestation Strategy for the Proposed Project Act 1988	
	(viii) Forest Right Act 2006	
C. Wildlife	(xi) Wildlife Protection Amendment Act 2002 (x) Indian Wildlife (Protection) Act 1972 and Amendment 1993	National Board for Wildlife Rules 2003 The Declaration of Wildlife Stock Rules 2003 The Wildlife (Specified Plant Stock Declaration) Central Rules 1995 The Wildlife (Specified Plant Condition for Possession by License) Rules 1995 Recognition of Zoo Rules 1992 The Wildlife (Protection) Rules 1995
D. Forest Management and Biodiversity Conservation	(xi) Sikkim Ecology Fund and Environment Cess Act 2005	Sikkim Ecology Fund and Environment Cess Rules 2007 Sikkim State Biodiversity Rules 2006 State Environment Agency Guidelines 2006 Guidelines for Lake Conservation in partnership with Gram Panchayat 2006 Sikkim Wildlife (Regulation of Trekking) Rules 2005

Source: Department of Environment, Forests and Wildlife, Government of

trail site erosion as a result of large number of trekkers', pack animal movement and unregulated grazing by animals are the issues need to be addressed urgently. Chakraborty's (2009) study concluded that the construction boom in Sikkim and pattern of construction in Gangtok and other urban centres have raised serious question of transforming the State into eco-friendly destination and greenest place in India.

Rai *et al.* (1998) revealed that ecotourism can ensure greater benefits trickling down to local communities. Sikkim Biodiversity and Ecotourism Project (SBEP) has been working with this objective involving local communities, enterprises and the government for tourism development in the major trekking destinations of the State. Bhattacharjee and Kumari's study highlighted the positive aspect of community based ecotourism (CBE) in Yuksam village as there is less negative impact on resources, vegetation, forest, etc., due to localized ecotourism initiative. However, contrasting results are observed in Pelling in which due to less involvement of locales in CBE lead to severe pressure on resources on the one hand and scarcity of income and employment opportunities for the residents on the other. Maharana's study (2000) divulges that nearly 69 per cent of the total household income comes from tourism related activities, which increased the income and consumption pattern of the community. The study further reported that the local stakeholders have increased their share to conserve biodiversity through organizing themselves in Khanchendzonga Conservation Committee (KCC), and managing site enhancement activities.

However, the existing network of protected areas suffers from their small physical size, inadequate landscape level distribution and insufficient development and management of physical infrastructure. They are all small in size despite their boundaries have been repeatedly expanded (FEWMD, 2009). There are also small sized State park, butterfly park, birds park, etc., visible in most of the places of the State. Management of these types of programme requires large human resource inputs as well as financial resources. Similarly, most of the PAs are surrounded by different categories of land-use including forests. As the land-use changes over time due to overextraction of resources and land hunger, smaller PAs suffer more than the larger ones in terms of faunal collapse because spatial heterogeneity is non-existent. Meeting the habitat requirement of large ungulates and predators is important for biodiversity conservation in the parks and reserves. If a flagship species is suppressed because the small area cannot accommodate their habitat resources, including food and cover, this would not result in biodiversity conservation (FEWMD: 2009).

Joshi and Dhyani (2009) argued that increasing trend of tourists' inflow in Sikkim would create numerous jobs and income opportunity in the State, implications of the large turnout on the resources, cultural environment and ecotourism would be significant. With the declining livestock population, production of foodgrains and switch towards cash crops results in replenishing these products from outside would result in leakage and increase in the cost of popular tourist pockets. Our study reveal that during peak season tourism sector in Sikkim depend on import of goods as well as employ workers from outside the State, thus reducing the benefits accrued to the Sikkim's economy. The leakage has its effect on all spheres on tourism activities, namely, transport, tour operators, travel agents to name a few. Package tours by outside tour operators had its evil effects on the Sikkim's economy as it deprived off valuable economic resources for the locals on the one hand and also failed to develop local resource base; especially in human resource sector.

In the field of tourist transport, the State is following a restricted policy of movement of tourist vehicles from one place to another inside Sikkim; aimed at trickling down economic benefits to local vehicle operators. Tourists are also not allowed to drive hired cars within the State is also a welcome step in the right direction. However, this rule is, most often, relaxed for outside tour operators create confusion in the mind of locals. Recent introduction of officially recognized twelve luxury cars, which can be used by tour operators throughout the State, can bring a welcome change in tourist-transport facility in the State.

The present system of waste management practices and environmental clean-up call for constant review and upgradation. Municipal solid waste in Sikkim consists of garbage, refuge and other discarded solid materials from industrial, commercial and agricultural operations as well as from community activity. Sikkim generates 0.45 kg per capita of solid waste per day. The total quantity of solid waste generated is about 42 tonnes per day, majority of which collected from urban areas (GoI, 2008). The arrangement of waste disposal in Sikkim involves collection of wastes by Urban Development and Housing Board (UD & HD) through bins placed at different locations and street sweeping. After collection, the wastes are transported through trucks to the disposable sites on a daily basis and are dumped in open dumps. Some close dumps have been constructed recently. Dumping sites are located near rivers. UD & HD has initiated a project on the treatment of municipal wastes with modern plants in Gangtok. However, this system excludes wastes deposits in rural centres as well as in popular trekking routes which needs immediate and regular attention.

Lack of dispersal of ecotourism spots in a few select tourist destinations in Sikkim has created pressure on natural resources as well as human habitat. As for example, west district has become a nerve centre of ecotourism activities and, barring few select sites, commercial considerations get preference over sustainability issues. The popular trekking routes and wildlife sanctuaries are becoming congested and causing everlasting damage to environment of host destination. This would necessitate to develop and adapt tourism product based on Sikkim's exceptional nature and culture that do not damage the environment and provide for opportunities for the locales to generate income from different market segments.

Conclusion

The foregoing discussion points to fact that the spread of ecotourism destinations in Sikkim are confined a few select tourism pockets resulting congestion and has a serious implication on its sustainability. Promotion of satellite areas could be one of the possible options. But, again development of such areas involves huge amount of costs and feasibility related issues. Moreover, in spite of having outstanding plans and policies, the stakeholders found wanting in its proper execution. Though, this is not an exception to the Sikkim alone.

Ecotourism in its purest form embraces positive environmental ethic, fostering preferred tourist behaviour. It does not denigrate the resource or erosion of resource integrity. The environment must experience a net benefit from the activity including social, economic, political or scientific benefits. It promotes firsthand experience with the natural environment and not a thrill seeking or physical achievement which are consistent with adventure tourism (Butler, 1992). From this point of view, tourism practiced in Sikkim cannot be termed as ecotourism, rather a branch of nature based tourism having a concern for sustainability. However, each of the tourism destinations has its own specificities which make it imperative for them to employ the term suit their desirable ends. The promotion of Sikkim as the 'Ultimate Ecotourism Destination' is a part of building brand image to the world in general and India in particular without disregarding its sustainability concerns. Stakeholders including policy-makers, who are directly associated with tourism, must understand this basic needs and take appropriate measures for the well-being of future generations.

It can be recalled that high tourism intensity destinations in the State is experiencing tourism congestion which invariably lead to environmental degradation. Silori's study (2004) observed that growth of tourism should not be entertained cost of environment; rather closure of tourism activity in those destinations can be an option which the policy-makers can ponder over. However, in such cases, there should be an arrangement for alternative employment opportunities for local inhabitants.

According to Leong (2008), many countries have made unwise investment in tourism that is often imposed on local communities, especially rural and minority communities, at a level and speed that causes great social disruption. Darjeeling and Simla, two popular hill stations in the North Eastern and North Western India, since British colonial rule, have been victim of resource use conflict and depletion of natural resources due to expanding hotel and tourism industry (Luhomi, 2006). Dodd (2010) remarked that many destinations did not address the issue of sustainability until negative pressures were felt. In the face of such impending challenges, ecotourism industry in Sikkim is heading for a testing time in the future ahead.

References

Annual Reoprt 2010-11, Ministry of Tourism, Government of India, p. 6.

Asian Development Bank (ADB)(2008): *South Asia Subregional Economic Cooperation (SASEC) Tourism Development Project*, Final Report, Vol. I, Tourism Resource Consultant, Newzealand in association with Metcon Consultant PTE Ltd., Nepal, 2008. p. 54.

ADB (2010): Inception Report: Regional Technical Assistance for Improving Connectivity and Destination Management of Cultural and Natural Resources in the South Asian Sub-region, Sikkim, A South Asian Tourism Infrastructure Development Project, p. 34.

Bhattacharjee, Prodyut and Kumari Smriti (2004): *Application of Criteria and Indicator for Sustainable Ecotourism: Scenario Under Globalisation,* the paper submitted for the IASCP Bi-Annual Conference on 'The Commons in an Age of Global Transition: Challenges, Risks and Opportunities', at Oaxaca, Mexico from 9-14 August, 2004.

Boora, S.S. (2005): 'Ecotourism and Environmental Sustainability in India', *Bulletin of the National Institute of Ecology* 15, pp. 249-258.

Butler, J.R. (1992): *Ecotourism: Its Changing Face and Evolving Philosophy*. The paper presented to the IV World Congress on National Parks and Protected Areas, Caracus, Venezuela.

Ceballos-Lascurain, H. (1996): *Tourism, Ecotourism and Protected Areas: The State of Nature Based Tourism around the World and Guidelines for its Development*, Gland, Switzerland: The World Conservation Union (IUCN), North Bennington, Vermount: The Ecotourism Society.

Chakraborty, Anjan (2009): "Tourism in Sikkim: Quest for a Self Reliant Economy," *NEHU Journal*, Vol. III, No 1, p. 89.

Corbett-Binsar-Nalnital (CBN)(2002): Corbett-Binsar-Nainital Initiative 2002.www.corbettbn.com

Dodd, Rachel (2010): "Moving Towards or Away from Sustainability?", *Asia Pacific Journal of Tourism Research*, Vol. 15, No. 3. pp. 251-266.

FEWMD (1998): Notification No. 202/F, Gangtok, Government of Sikkim.

FEWMD (2002): Sikkim Ecotourism Notification 2002 No. 1/WL/F/76/204, Gangtok, Government of Sikkim.

FEWMD (2009): '*Preparatory Study on Integrated Project for Sustainable Development of Forest Resources in Sikkim*', Final Report (Draft), Department of Forest, Environment and Wildlife Management (FEWMD), Government of Sikkim, November 2009.

FEWMD (2011): Sikkim Ecotourism Policy 2011, Government of Sikkim.

Government of India (GoI) (2008): *Sikkim Development Report*, Planning Commission, pp. 151-54.

Islam, M.Z. and Rahmani, A.R. (2004): *Important Bird Areas in India: Priority Sites for Conservation*. Mumbai: Bombay Natural History Society.

Joshi, R. & Dhyani, P.P. (2009): 'Environment Sustainability and Tourism Implication of Trend Synergies of Tourism in Sikkim Himalaya', *Current Science*, Vol. 97, No.1.

Leong, A.M.W. (2008): 'International Tourism and World Peace', *Journal of Macau University of Science and Technology*, Vol. 2, No. 2, pp. 38-44.

Luhomi, R. (2006): *Simla Stresses Out*, Chandigarh, India: *The Tribune*.

Maharana, Iyata (2000): *Economic Benefits and Conservation Linkages from Tourism Development in the Sikkim Himalaya*, PhD Thesis submitted to the North Bengal University.

Ministry of Information and Broadcasting (MoIB) (2004): India 2004—A Reference Annual Publication Division, MoIB, GoI, New Delhi.

Rai, S.C.; Sharma, E.; Lepcha, R. and Sundriyal, R.C. (1998): 'Tourism Development in Sikkim'. In Suresh Chand Rai, Rakesh Chandra

Sundriyal and Elalabya Sharma (eds): *Sikkim Perspective Planning and Development,* Sikkkim Science Society and Bishen Singh and Mahendra Pal Singh, Dehradun, pp. 697-711.

Sharma, E.; Jain, N.; Rai, S.C. and Lepcha, R. (2000): 'Ecotourism in Sikkim: Contribution Towards Conservation of Biodiversity Resources'. In D. Marothia : *Institutionalizing Common Pool of Resources*, Concept Publishing Co. (P) Ltd., New Delhi, p. 533.

Silori, Chandra Sekhar (2004): 'Socio-economic and Ecological Consequences of the ban on Nanda Devi Biosphere Reserve, Western Himalaya'. *Biodiversity Conservation*, Vol. 13.

Tambe, Sandeep, Bhutia; K.S. and Arrawatia, M.L. (2007): 'Mainstreaming Ecotourism in Sikkim's Economy', *Sikkim's Today*, April-June, pp. 1-3.

19

Prioritization of Extension Activities for Development Work by the Non-Governmental Organizations (NGOs) in Nagaland, India

Dr. N.K. Patra, M.N. Odyuo, Dr. Sagar Mondal and *Dr. A.K. Makar*

Introduction

The present day context of liberalization of economy, privatization of public sector, globalization of trade and the revolution in information technology gave rise to the concept of 'Global Village'. Research sector has continuously been swelled enormously with the sack of technology and the applicability of the invention or reinvention in development and farming sector has also been proved, but most of them are not adopted and popularized. Accordingly, vehement changes have also taken place in development sector and their extension approaches for transfer of technology. Extension is a science of developing capability of the people for sustainable improvement in their quality of life (Ray, 2008) and for that various activities and approaches are present. The approach of altruism, providing inputs with subsidized or free of cost and prescribing technology practices to the beneficiaries have been suppressed by the skill upgradation, capacity building and empowerment of the beneficiaries with effective participation of beneficiaries in development work. Development is a continuous, pluralistic and widely participatory process and basically it means, advancement of an area, revealing, unfolding or opening up something which is latent and a change that is desirable. It is referred to as a continuous and rigorous process of progress, mobilizing the people towards self-reliance, assuring and/or ensuring equitable distribution or benefit of opportunity, resource and social justice among all sections of the society. It may be defined as, the process of creating and maintaining a situation in which all citizens of the country can lead a desirable and satisfying life. When, development is a continuous process then activities for development, that is extension work or activities are obviously simultaneous.

Government sector is unable to reach quantitatively to all the resource poor and backward people for upliftment of their existing condition. As a result they are also pressurized to change their development approach to reach the destination. Possible ways are only a few like—privatizations of development activities, private-public partnership, and GO-NGO (Government-Non-Governmental Organization) collaboration and so on.

In development sector, Non-Governmental Organizations (the organizations which are outside the direct control of government agencies or autonomous bodies and are engaged in providing financial and non-financial services to the community are called Non-Governmental Organization or NGO) are playing major role since time immemorial. For the purpose of development of beneficiaries, NGOs adopted various extension activities. The present investigation aimed at identifying meaningful extension activities and to find out the relative importance of these activities with the following objectives:

(i) The present study aimed at identifying important extension activities adopted by Non-Governmental Organizations in Nagaland to carry out developmental activities; and

(ii) To establish the hierarchy of extension activities as perceived by NGO's employees in Nagaland to carry out developmental activities.

Materials and Methods

Nagaland State was inaugurated as the sixteenth State of India on 1st December, 1963. It is bounded by Assam in the West, Myanmar on the East, Arunachal Pradesh and part of Assam on the North and Manipur in the South. The State approximately lies between 25°6′ and 27°4′ latitude; North of Equator and between the Longitudinal lines of 93°20′ and 95°15′E. Geographical area is 16,527 sq km and total population is 1,988,636 (as per 2001 Census). Density of population is around 120 per sq km. Average annual rainfall ranges from 2,000-3,000 mm and temperature ranges from 4°C to 31°C. The topography of the State is undulating, full of hill range which breaks into wide chaos of spurs and ridges. The altitudes vary between 194 to 3,840 metres above the mean sea level. The State has a beautiful landscape and it consists of 11 administrative districts, viz., Kohima, Dimapur, Kipheri, Longleng, Mokokchung, Mon, Peren, Phek, Tuensang, Wokha and Zunheboto. Out of the total 11 districts, 6 districts have been selected purposively for the present study, namely, Dimapur, Kohima, Mokokchung, Peren, Tuensang and Wokha.

In this study 85 NGOs were identified by obtaining list from reliable sources. Out of the total identified NGOs, 45 NGOs were finally selected. From every selected NGO, one respondent from the higher level of employees and minimum one respondent from the lower level of employees were considered for this study. Higher level of employees of NGOs include the top level of functionaries, like Director, Secretary, Topmost functionaries of sub-office of the large NGOs. A lower level employee of NGOs include those which are not designed in higher level of position and directly involved in grass root level implementation work. Accordingly, 45 higher level of employees and 75 lower level of employees were interviewed as respondents (total 120) which were selected as the final respondents.

The Method of Paired Comparisons

Paired comparison is a psychological scaling method and makes possible the quantitative investigation of all kinds of values and subjective experience (Edwards, 1969). In this method, the stimuli (items, statements or variables) are presented in pairs in all possible combinations and the respondents are asked to select one stimulus over the other from each pair, which is judged as more favourable. Because the stimuli are presented in pairs and one stimulus is compared over the other, this is known as *the Method of Paired Comparisons*. This method of psychological scaling also provides an estimate of the distances between each of the stimulus, in comparison to the stimulus with least preference, whose scale value is (arbitrarily) brought down to the level of 'zero'. If there are '*n*' stimuli, the numbers of pairs which may be obtained are $n(n-1)/2$. For example, if there are 4 stimuli, the number of pairs will be $4(4-1)/2=6$. The stimuli or items for judgment should be distinct from each other and easily understandable. To eliminate response bias, both the stimuli in each pair and the pairs themselves, are randomly arranged. The stimuli are then presented to the respondents, who are asked to select one stimulus over the other from each pair, which they consider as more favourable. The stimuli selected are appropriately marked.

The F-Matrix

Table 19.1 shall consist of *frequencies* corresponding to the number of times that each stimulus is judged more favourable than the other. The cell entries correspond to the frequency with which the column stimulus is judged more favourable than the row stimulus.

Table 19.1: F-Matrix of Extension Activities

	Demonstration (A)	*Training (B)*	*Campaigning (C)*	*Free Input Supply (D)*	*Input Supply on Payment (E)*
Demonstration (A)	—	61	43	33	16
Training (B)	59*	—	25	17	10
Campaigning (C)	77	95	—	28	21
Free Input Supply (D)	87	103	92	—	28
Input Supply on Payment (E)	104	110	99	92	—

* To be understood as 59 respondents preferred demonstration to training and so on (i.e. the column stimulus was judged more favourable than the row stimulus).

The P-Matrix

The P-Matrix gives the *proportion* of times the column stimulus is judged more favourable than the row stimulus. This is obtained by dividing each

Table 19.2: P-Matrix of Extension Activities

	Demonstration (A)	*Training (B)*	*Campaigning (C)*	*Free Input Supply (D)*	*Input Supply on Payment (E)*
Demonstration (A)	0.500	0.508	0.358	0.275	0.133
Training (B)	0.491	0.500	0.208	0.141	0.083
Campaigning (C)	0.641	0.791	0.500	0.233	0.175
Free Input Supply (D)	0.725	0.858	0.766	0.500	0.233
Input Supply on Payment (E)	0.866	0.916	0.825	0.766	0.500
Sum	3.223	3.573	2.657	1.915	1.124

of the cell entries in the F-Matrix by *N*, *i.e.*, total number of respondents. The cell entries in the diagonal line which are blank in the F-Matrix are assumed to be *N/2*. This again is divided by *N*, to get the proportion of 0.500 in each cell of diagonal line in the P-Matrix. (Table 19.2)

The Rearranged P-Matrix

The rearranged P-Matrix is then made with the stimulus having the smallest column sum at the left and that with the highest at the right. (Table 19.3)

Table 19.3: Rearranged P-Matrix of Extension Activities

	Input Supply on Payment (E)	*Free Input Supply (D)*	*Campaign-ing (C)*	*Demons-tration (A)*	*Train-ing (B)*
Input Supply on Payment (E)	0.500	0.766	0.825	0.866	0.916
Free Input Supply (D)	0.233	0.500	0.766	0.725	0.858
Campaigning (C)	0.175	0.233	0.500	0.641	0.791
Demonstration (A)	0.133	0.275	0.358	0.500	0.508
Training (B)	0.083	0.141	0.208	0.491	0.500
Sum	1.124	1.915	2.657	3.223	3.573

The Z-Matrix

The Z-Matrix gives the *normal deviates* corresponding to the proportions in the table of P-Matrix. The Z-Matrix corresponding to the rearranged P-matrix is obtained by converting the p_{ij} entries to z_{ij} entries with the help of the table of Normal Deviates (Edwards, 1969). The column sum (Sums z) for each stimulus is obtained by adding the respective cell entries, taking the sign into considerations. The means (Mean *z*) are obtained by dividing the sums with the number of stimuli in each column. The absolute scale value of the stimulus with the largest negative deviation is added to all the column-means to make the scale value for this stimulus zero and all others with positive sign. The hierarchies of extension activities are presented in Table 19.4.

Considering the various extension activities from various reliable sources, proper discussion with NGOs' employees and taking into consideration of findings of pilot study, researcher included important extension activities for research purpose to identify the hierarchy of extension activities by NGOs. Five widely accepted and important

Table 19.4: Z-Matrix of Extension Activities

	Input Supply on Payment (E)	*Free Input Supply (D)*	*Campaigning (C)*	*Demonstration (A)*	*Training (B)*
Input Supply on Payment (E)	0.000	0.726	0.935	1.108	1.379
Free Input Supply (D)	–0.729	0.000	0.726	0.598	1.071
Campaigning (C)	–0.935	–0.729	0.000	0.361	0.810
Demonstration (A)	–1.112	–0.598	–0.364	0.000	0.020
Training (B)	–1.385	–1.076	–0.813	–0.023	0.000
Sum Z	–4.161	–1.671	0.484	2.044	3.280
Mean Z	–0.832	–0.334	0.096	0.408	0.656
Add largest negative deviation	+0.832	+0.832	+0.832	+0.832	+0.832
Rank (scale value) R	0.000 5th	0.498 4th	0.928 3rd	1.240 2nd	1.488 1st

extension activities were considered for this study which are presented below:

A. Demonstration,
B. Training,
C. Campaigning,
D. Free input supply, and
E. Input supply on payment

These five stimuli were arranged in 10 possible pairs which were provided to the respondents and were asked to select one extension activity over the other from each pair separately, and during the selection they were asked to consider one developmental work from their experience where all the five extension activities are applicable separately (like hybrid vegetable cultivation, improved banana cultivation), which they considered to be more preferable and appropriate from their point of view. Later, the Method of Paired Comparisons (Edwards, 1969) was applied to derive a rank scale value of them. Intention was concentrated in this study to find out the relative importance and degree of differences among the considerations within the sets of five extension activities.

In paired comparisons, the method of complete data was used as there was no P_{ij} value equal to or greater than 0.99 or equal to or less than 0.01. For analysis of data, F-Matrix which consist of frequencies corresponding to the number of items that each column stimulus was judged more favourable than the row stimulus, followed by P-Matrix, rearranged P-Matrix and Z-Matrix were computed.

Result and Discussion

Developmental works were continuing with various extension activities by NGOs for all-round development of their territory of working area. Management and proper selection of extension activities at grass root level is important, and effectiveness of development approach and endeavour is relatively inclined on extension activities and prioritization of the extension activities. Five extension activities, viz., Demonstration (Demonstration is a practical exhibition or explanation of something, designed to teach or inform), Training (According to Khemmani, training is a planned communication process which results in changes of attitudes, skills and/or knowledge in accordance with specified objectives relating to desired patterns of behaviour), Campaigning (According to Reddy, it is an intensive teaching activity undertaken at an opportune time for a brief period; focusing attention in a concerted manner on a particular problem, with a view to stimulate the widest possible interest in a community, Block or other geographical area), Free Input supply and Input supply on payment were considered for the present study and method of Paired Comparisons was followed to establish the hierarchy of extension activities.

Extension activities are the bases to achieve the developmental work up to the desirable level. Various types of extension activities are available in development sector but all are not compatible/applicable to all types of developmental work; if compatible/applicable, it is difficult to handle large number of extension activities in a single developmental work. Adoption of more numbers of extension activities in a single developmental work is only possible with sufficient and experienced man-power which increase the implementation cost. NGOs may have various developmental activities for all-round development of their working area. Accordingly, proper and limited selection of extension activities for specific programme is important to achieve proper development.

Table 19.4 shows that five extension activities namely training, demonstration, campaigning, free input supply and input supply on payment are ranked accordingly with their scale value and scale value ranges from 0-1.488 where training is the highly preferred extension activity and input supply on payment is the least preferred extension activity.

Table 19.4 shows that out of 5 extension activities "Training" has the highest scale value (1.488) and considered as the first and most important extension activity which perceived by NGOs' employees of Nagaland, India and which is most widely accepted tools or extension activity throughout the world for implementation of all types of developmental work. For any developmental work, the first and foremost requirement is financial arrangement, and second important requirement is sufficient manpower for developmental work. In reality, all over the country as well as in Nagaland NGOs are running with insufficiency of fund except few reputed and high profile NGOs. Financial status is directly related to staff strength and again staff strength is directly related to selection of extension activity. In other side, efficacy of the extension activity towards the implementation of the work is another technical consideration for selection of extension activity. When any organization is continuing in such a way, i.e., lack of manpower and insufficient financial arrangement, then that organization tries to adopt such type of extension activity where requirement of manpower and involvement of fund is limited. In this juncture training is a unique extension activity where financial and manpower involvement is limited and effectiveness is up to the mark, because within low budget and less manpower it covers wide number of beneficiaries. These may be the reasons for selection of training as the first preferred extension activity and scale value difference in between first and second preference is 0.248 (1.4,88–1.240) which indicates the high preference with high scale value difference.

"Demonstration" has the second highest scale value (1.240) and has been considered as second important extension activity as perceived by the employees of NGOs. It is one of the most effective extension activity for adoption of innovation, but it necessitates to invest more manpower, much time of extension worker, and more financial involvement compared to training which could not match with the average NGOs' staff and financial profile. As a result, demonstration is a second preferred extension activity and compared to third preference scale value difference is 0.312 (1.240–0.928) which indicates that it is also highly preferred extension activity compared to campaigning, free input supply and input supply on payment.

The study shows that "Campaigning" has been placed in third position with scale value of 0.928. It is very much effective extension activity for the purpose of awareness of large number of population of a specific area about a particular innovation or addressing a certain problem within a short time span, but involvement of manpower and financial requirement are relatively more compared to training. Target group get preliminary ideas about the matter which in maximum cases are not sufficient to adopt within their enterprise or system and these are the reasons for weak and low preference of the campaigning as extension activity.

"Free input supply" has been placed in fourth position with scale value of 0.498, as perceived by the employees of NGOs. During interview, respondents have expressed that supply of input either subsidized or free of cost to the target group is not desirable. Development is a continuous process where without self-realization, aspiration and desire from beneficiaries for development and upliftment, it is difficult to develop them. If input is available, either free or as subsidized cost, then immediate profit attract them but in reality they are not prepared to adopt in their system, again it is 'helpful to demobilize' and 'grow a habit of expectation' of free inputs from development functionaries and these may be the reasons for low preference of the free input supply on payment.

"Input supply on payment" has the lowest scale value and considered as least important extension activity as perceived by the employees of NGOs with scale value is arbitrarily zero. Respondents also opined that in one way it is good for providing and supplying quality and authentic inputs to the beneficiaries but difficulties present from their organization. For this purpose huge financial involvement and additional manpower is needed which average NGOs are unable to incur due to lack of manpower and insufficiency of fund. As a result, it is relatively less viable extension activity and may be the reasons for least preferred extension activity among the selected five extension activities. In this respect NGOs are continuing collaborative work with local traders for supply of inputs as per requirements of the beneficiaries.

Conclusion

Five commonly used extension activities at NGO level in Nagaland are training, demonstration, campaigning, free input supply and input supply on payment.

Training is the highly preferred extension activity followed by demonstration, campaigning, free input supply and input supply on payment.

Capacity building and skill upgradation of beneficiaries is in top-most priority

Free of cost and subsidized input supply to the beneficiaries is not desirable for developmental work.

Maximum NGOs are continuing with insufficient staff strength and fund.

References

Edwards, A.L. (1969). *Techniques of Attitude Scale Construction.* Vakils, Feffer and Simons Private Ltd., Mumbai.

Government of Nagaland (2006). *Nagaland* Department of Tourism, Government of Nagaland, Kohima, Nagaland, India.

Government of Nagaland (2006). *Statistical Hand Book of Nagaland 2006* Directorate of Economics and Statistics, Government of Nagaland, Kohima, Nagaland, India.

Khemmani, M. and Jonathan Cook. (1985). 'Appropriate media for amateur trainers', Manila, Philippines, UNDP Asia and Pacific Programme for Development Training and Communication. Training Tips No. 6.

Ray, G.L. (2008). *Extension Communication and Management*, Kalyani Publisher, Ludhiana, India.

Reddy, A.A (1978). *Extension Education*, Sree Lakshmi Press, Bapatla (A.P.), India.

20

An Analytical Study of Developing Gender Equality through Watershed Development Programme in India

(*With special reference to Chhattisgarh*)

Dr. Rupali Satsangi and *Dr. Ayan Hazra*

Introduction

The importance of increasing women's participation in watershed development has been recognised, and efforts are being made in this direction. However, there is still need to sensitise policy-makers and staff of project implementing agencies to the core issues in ensuring benefits to women from watershed-development projects.

A major component of watershed development is to improve agriculture and increase land productivity. Agricultural development programmes have always targeted men rather than women, since women are rarely viewed as 'farmers'. Therefore, in watershed development too, it is male farmers who first come forward to participate in the programme. Women, however, often perform more task and spend more hours than men in agricultural production. This becomes all the more important since more than women are shifting to non-farm livelihoods, leaving agricultural tasks to women. However, in the absence of the men, women are not able to take any decisions related to the land, since the land titles do not belong to them. It is (male) landowner who is nominated to the decision-making body for watershed development projects, although the woman may be actually farming the land. Agarwal (1994)[1] argues that allowing women to hold land titles would motivate them to increase output and adopt better farming practices, besides increasing their access to credit, inputs and technology. Access to arable land is mainly through inheritance, which varies by region and religion. Although laws today give more rights to women, significant inequalities remain, more so because of the disinheritance that takes place in practice. Some of the important reasons leading to disinheritance are male reluctance to endow daughters with land, women's forgoing of their shares in parental property in favour of their brothers, and obstruction by government officials in the implementation of laws in favour of women.

Women's needs and priorities are similarly overlooked in relation to common-pool resources. These resources provide women with livelihoods options that are not always visible. Restricting access to them increases drudgery in fuel and fodder collection, and reduces the livelihood options available to women. Assessing the interface between livelihoods and the resource base can help keep in focus issues related to the economic survival of women resource-users through the planning and implementation stages of the project.

NWDPRA—A Holistic Approach: Watersheds as hydrologic units provide appropriate system for conceptualizing and implementing development investment (Barbier, 1988).[2] This comprises combinations of arable and non-arable land, drainage and is utilized by permanent and transient populations with varying skills and commitment to long-term resource husbandry. The range of issues relevant to watershed management is enormous and included environmental issues, crop and livestock production, a whole range of social and cultural concerns, infrastructure planning and entire questions of governance and control (Hegde, 1988).[3]

The watershed projects taken up by *Adarsha Gaon Yojana* (ideal village scheme), Indo-German watershed development projects operated by NGOs in collaboration with the Government of Maharashtra and NGOs on participatory approach have performed better. The factors that enable participatory projects to perform better are clearly explained in terms of the characteristics of semi-arid areas that distinguished from irrigated lands. In less favourable rainfed areas, the success of technical inventory often depend on location-specific physical and socio-economic conditions and requires collective action by watershed area people and farmers pursue complex strategies for producing food and earning their livelihoods (Bortrall and John, 1991).[4]

Watershed Development Projects are designed to harmonize the use of water, soil, forest and pasture resources in a way that conserves these resources while raising agricultural productivity, both by conserving moisture in the ground and increasing irrigation through tank and aquifer based water harvesting (Khepar *et al.*, 2001).[5] The few quantitative studies available tend to be based on small number of heavily supervised projects, with no information about long-term benefits. At the same time, the vast majority of projects were never evaluated, and there were good reasons to suspect that most of them had little impact (Guy, 2002).[6]

Early watershed projects introduced technologies for conservation and production without any input from farmers, all on the basis of trials in experiment started far from the villages and denied of socio-economic constraints. The lack of sustained maintenance or adoption under these circumstances is not stressing, given the difficult conditions prevailing in many rainfed areas. This background helps explain why people's participation is the key feature of the best watershed projects (Kaushal, 1994).[7] Mishra and Hussain (2001)[8] conducted impact evaluation on Peddagedda watershed of Srikakulam district in Andhra Pradesh concluded that more participatory approach would have resulted in better results.

Review of Literature

Watershed – A Unit of Improving Livelihood

Watersheds as hydrologic units provide appropriate system for conceptualizing and implementing development investment. This comprises combinations of arable and non-arable land, drainage and is utilized by permanent and transient populations with varying skills and commitment to long-term resource husband.y Barbier (1988)[9] and Bortrall and John (1991).[10]

Watershed Development Projects are designed to harmonize the use of water, soil, forest and pasture resources in a way that conserves these resources while raising agricultural productivity, both by conserving moisture in the ground and increasing irrigation through tank and aquifer based water harvesting (Khepar *et al.*, 2001).[11] The number of quantitative studies available tends to be based on number of heavily supervised projects, with huge information about long-term benefits to the beneficiaries accrued from the project. People's participation is the key feature of the best watershed projects (Kaushal, 1994).[12] Impact evaluation on Peddagedda watershed of Srikakulam district in Andhra Pradesh revealed socio-economic upliftment of farmers through participatory approach (Mishra and Hussain, 2001).[13] Palta *et al.* (1995)[14] studied the Kamar tribe of Gariyaband Block of Raipur district and she observed that tangible wealth in the form of land was found in 34.3 per cent families while the remaining 65.7 per cent were landless.

Socio-economic Characteristics

Tribal dependent on forests and forestland, not only for its natural vegetation but also as a source of livelihood and, the ties with the forest go back to times immemorial. Further, they have enjoyed freedom to use the forests, in whatever manner they like; to such an extent that they have developed a conviction that they belong to the forests and forest belongs to them (Kottakayam, 1983).[15] Gowda and Jayaramiah (1990)[16] found in Chitravathi watershed Karnataka that socio-economic status, land productivity and annual income of the small and marginal farmers have increased to considerable extent as a result of Watershed Development Programme. Babu (1991)[17] observed that the existing land-use patterns are even able to fulfil the basic needs of the rural people. All the socio-economic indicators analyzed show that agro-forestry is an ideal method for the small and marginal farmers. It helped to get that better output for their labour and also increased in the long run. Seth (1991)[18] mentioned that the participatory approach with elements of self-reliance and equity has demonstrated its capacity improve lives and production systems of resources for poor farmers rainfed area of developing countries where watershed management holds that key for economic development and restoration of ecological balance.

Mahnot *et al.* (1992)[19] concluded that the Integrated Watershed Management approach include rainwater harvesting structure and soil water conservation measures adopted in the foothill of Aravalli Region holds the key to development of the area.

Socio-personal Characteristics

Saxena *et al.* (1990)[20] revealed that education status of a farmer and adoption were found to be positively and significantly correlated. Dhyani (1994)[21] found the results indicating that farmers within watershed received 50 per cent higher income from agriculture. Further, the agricultural income is more equitably distributed than family income and distribution of income is more equitable within watershed than outside watershed farm group. Manjula (1994)[22] found that more than half of farm-women had favourable attitude towards education and decision-making. Watershed development programmes has been successful in changing and educating a sizeable portion of farm-women. Patel *et al.* (1995)[23] in Mehsana and Banaskantha district of Gujarat found that great majority of marginal, small, big and pooled sampled farmers had medium level of Techno-economic change.

Need of the Study

Increasing women's participation in watershed projects is critical to the long-term sustainability of development efforts. There is a need to sensitize policy-makers and staff of project implementing agencies to the core issues affecting women's participation in decision-making processes and the distribution of benefits between men and women. There is a need to progress from an attitude where women are treated as a 'disadvantaged group', to a point where they are treated as integral members of the community. Unless women are involved in the decision-making process, watershed development projects will remain welfare oriented as far as women are concerned.

The watershed programmes have a direct impact on their living conditions and economy. A meagre research is done particularly in the field of watershed on the socio-economic status. The NWDPRA has completed its first phase of development in the Gariyaband and Mainpur Blocks of Raipur district. A need of crucial scientific assessment of the programme in the tribal area, such assessment will be useful for extending the programme, put corrective measures regarding shortcomings and enable management and extension workers to devise methods and improve the planning and implementation procedure. The impact of programme on gender equality among tribal women is important from the point of view of the efficacy and suitability of the programme.

Objectives

The main objective of the study is to examine the present socio-economic status of the tribal of Raipur District, benefited by the NWDPRA. The specific objectives of this study are as follows:

1. To assess the benchmark socio-economic profile of the tribal women prior to implementation of the programme.
2. To identify the issues and concerns of tribal women.

3. To assess the traditional knowledge in watershed management.
4. To study the gender concerns and women empowerment in watershed programme.

Hypothesis of the Study

The basic hypothesis of the study was that the watershed programme improved the socio-economic conditions of the respondents that led to their empowerment in due course of time. It was expected that various issues, concerns, particularly the gender concerns, role of respondents, participatory activities, rural technologies and tribal women's contribution to sustainability of resources will be delineated and addressed adequately in watershed programme, that will ultimately led to self-reliance, economic independence, increased participation in decision-making and local self-governance of respondents. The following are the important points of hypothesis to be tested in the present study:

1. There is improvement in overall socio-economic conditions.
2. Various issues (such as socio-institutional) and concerns (particularly gender inequality) have been addressed adequately in watershed programme.

Outcome of Testing Hypothesis

1. There is no doubt that there are drastic changes in the socio-economic profile of the respondents. Present study quantified these aspects through various parameters. The level of improvement was not impressive but satisfactory in view of lack of staff and underemphasizing the sociological aspects in this programme.
2. The study was able to identify the crucial issues (socio-institutional and others) and concerns (particularly gender related) of respondents that created hurdles in the way of empowerment. The watershed programme lacks in addressing these issues adequately due to absence of evaluation and monitoring mechanism.

Research Methodology

(i) Methodology of the Present Study

The present study based on primary as well as secondary data. Primary data was collected by thorough interview schedule, direct dialogue, interactions and discussions with respondents, watershed officials, government, Gram Panchayat functionaries, social workers, NGOs and other secondary sources, were processed and analysed through various statistical tools like averages and percentage.

The study was conducted in Raipur district in two Blocks—(based on secondary data of Gram Panchayat BDO) Mainpur (82° 14′ 03″ E longitude and 20° 14′ 36″ N latitude) and Gariyaband (82° 03′ 37″ E longitude and 20° 37′ 58″ N latitude). The 2 Blocks were selected as it inhibit major population of Scheduled Tribe (ST) with adequate area (5148 ha) under watershed programme. Out of the 8 watersheds of district under NWDPRA, 4 were randomly selected watersheds viz. Chhaimasi Nala, Sati Nala, Pairi Nala and Urmal Nala were for the study.

Sample Design

A sample of 300 tribal women from 4 watersheds was taken considering different levels of adoption of watershed programmes. Samples from each village were selected randomly from different income levels, sub-tribes and occupation (micro-enterprises).

Table 20.1: General Information and Respondents of the Study Area

Name of Watershed	*Name of Village*	*Distance from Block (km)*	*Total population*	*No. of Respondents*
Chhaimasi Nala (Gariyaband Block)	Nagabuda	5	2159	65
	Pandaripani	4	594	18
	Total		**2753**	**83**
Sati Nala (Gariyaband Block)	Joba	18	567	20
	Amadi	20	522	18
	Total		**1089**	**38**
Urmal Nala (Mainpur Block)	Urmal	68	2105	64
	Chanabhata	65	470	15
	Total		**2575**	**79**
Pairi Nala (Mainpur Block)	Jadapadar	30	1289	39
	Mainpur Kala	1	2021	61
	Total		**3310**	**100**
Grand Total			**9727**	**300**

Source: Government of Chhattisgarh, Census, 2011.

(ii) Independent and Dependent Variables

In order to make an assessment regarding the level of improvement leading to empowerment, achieved through watershed development programme, various independent and dependent variables in respect of respondents were chosen for the study.

Independent Variables

Sl. No.	*Socio-personal*	*Socio-economic*	*Technological*
1.	Age	Landholding	Improved packages
2.	Education	Share in Annual income	Cottage industries
3.	Score of personal abilities	Share in Annual expenditure	Use of irrigation
4.	Change in women's status	Credit facility	Use of Animal dung
5.	Type and size of family	Occupation pattern	*Dona pattal* making
6.	House type	Participation in farm activities	Farm machinery
7.	Decision making and gender concerns	Engagement Schedule	Stitching and embroidery
8.	Health consciousness	Employment opportunities	Vegetable production
9.	Reduction in dropout	Marketing facility	Fish rearing
10.	Living conditions	Self Help Groups	Training opportunities
11.	Social customs	Small savings groups	Micro enterprises
12.	Availability of water	Participation in institution capacity building	Processing and value addition
13.	Problems at workplace	Contribution to sustainability of natural resources.	—
14.	Reduction in poverty	Impact of other programmes.	—
15.	Score of adoption of ITK	Role evaluation in watersheds	—

Dependent Variables

1. Level of adoption of watershed management technology.
2. Level of improvement in socio-economic conditions.
3. Intensity of social constraints affecting women empowerment.
4. Share of participation in watershed activities.
5. Share of work participation and association in institution capacity building.
6. Level of improvement in role of tribal women.
7. Level of improvement in training opportunities availed by tribal women.
8. Level of improvement in micro enterprises (entrepreneurship development).
9. Level of contribution towards sustainability of natural resources.
10. Satisfaction level of beneficiaries in respect to their socio-economic profile.
11. Investigator level of satisfaction.

Need for Gender Equity in Watershed Management

The use of a gender-sensitive approach to watershed management ensures that both women's and men's unique needs, priorities, and knowledge are incorporated into management plans and policies. Specifically, a gender equity approach can:

- Increase men's and women's participation in decision-making processes related to watershed management;
- Promote more equitable access to, control over, and distribution of natural resources among social groups;
- Ensure that watershed management interventions do not adversely affect one social group more than another;
- Consideration of gender in water management allows for the identification of women's and men's different roles in the use, supply, administration, and conservation of water resources.

Work Participation Rate

The Work Participation Rate (WPR) of the ST in the State is 53.4 per cent which is lower than national average (49.1%). There has been a marginal decennial decline of 0.7 per cent in the WPR. Male (56.7%) as well as female WPR (50.2%) among the tribes are higher than the corresponding figures (53.2% and 44.8%) at the national level. Among the total workers, 67.4 per cent are main workers and this proportion is marginally lower than the national average (68.9%). Among the major tribes, Gonds have WPR (54.2%) more than the State average whereas Oraon, Halba and Bhatra have recorded WPR below the State average (GoI, 2004).[24]

Category of Workers

The total workers can be categorized in two ways, viz., (1) According to the length of period of engagement, i.e., Main workers who are engaged in the work for sufficiently long period on regular basis, and (2) Marginal workers who are engaged for short period on temporary basis. Each of these categories can further be classified based on the nature of work, viz., cultivators, agricultural labours, household industries and other miscellaneous works. More than half (56.6%) of the total tribal workers are "Cultivators". This figure is higher than that of the country (44.7%). "Agricultural Labours" constitute (32.7%) which is comparable with the national average of 36.9 per cent. "Cultivators" and "Agricultural Labour" together constitute 89.3 per cent of the total tribal workers. "Other workers" account for 9.5 per cent only. This proportion is also considerably lower if compared to the national average of 16.3 per cent. Workers engaged in Household industry (HHI) account for a meagre 1.2 per cent that is lower than that of all tribes at the national level (2.1%). The percentage of labours employed as main workers is higher among men (65.2%) than among women (34.8%) as shown in Table 20.2.

Among the major tribes, *Kawar, Oraon* and *Halba* have more than 60 per cent workers that are "Cultivators" followed by *Gond* (59.6%). *Bhatra* have the highest proportion of "Agricultural Labour" followed by *Bhunjia* (55%). The workers engaged in household industries are highest in *Kamar* (40.2%). It is lowest in *Bhunjia* (0.3%), followed by *Halba* (0.4%) and *Gond* (0.6%).

Table 20.2: Category-wise Distribution of Workers in Chhattisgarh

Economic category	*All STs*	*Gond*	*Halba*	*Bhunjia*	*Kamar*
A. 1. Cultivators	56.6	59.6	62.1	40.7	14.2
2. Agricultural Labours	32.7	30.5	23.7	55.0	38.1
3. Household industries Workers	1.2	0.6	0.4	0.3	40.2
4. Other Workers	9.5	9.3	13.7	3.9	7.5
B. 1. Main Workers	67.4	68.3	78.2	69.2	68.8
2. Marginal Workers	32.6	31.7	21.8	30.8	31.2

Source: Office of the Registrar General, India (GoI, 2004).

Women Workers

Women contribute considerably to household income through farm and non-farm activities as well as through waged labours. Women's work as family labour is underestimated (FAO, 2004).[25] The rural female participation rate is 27.2 per cent, nearly thrice as much as the urban female participation rate of 9.7 per cent in the country. More or less equal proportion of tribal women forms main workers and marginal workers, however, it varies from tribe to tribe. *Halba,* the leading tribe in agriculture has main workers, more than twice that of marginal workers. In case of Kamar—one of the primitive tribe, the main workers are one and half times that of marginal workers.

Table 20.3: Category-wise Distribution of Women Workers in Chhattisgarh

Economic category	*All STs*	*Gond*	*Halba*	*Bhunjia*	*Kamar*
A. 1. Cultivators	50.7	53.7	62.5	30.9	10.2
2. Agricultural Labour	42.1	39.6	30.0	66.5	39.7
3. Household Industries Workers	1.2	0.6	0.3	0.2	44.1
4. Other Workers	6.0	6.1	7.2	2.5	5.9
B. 1. Main Workers	49.6	51.9	69.9	53.4	60.3
2. Marginal Workers	50.4	48.1	30.1	46.6	39.7

Source: Worked out based on the Census Data 2001: Office of the Registrar General, India (GoI, 2004).[24]

Women's Share in Tribal Workforce

The share of women in total workers is less than half (47.3%); about one-third (34.8%) in main workers and just three-fourth (73%) in marginal workers. Agricultural labours are predominantly women (60.8%) in tribes of Chhattisgarh, however, it varies from one tribe to another—*Gond* and *Halba* tribe has more than 60 per cent whereas *Bhunjia* and *Kamar* tribe has less than 60 per cent share of women. Tribal women are also involved in rural crafts and entrepreneurship for their livelihood. Their share in household industries workers is less than half (48.3%)—highest in *Kamar* (55.7%). Tribal women of Chhattisgarh have adequate share as cultivators (42.3%).

Approaches to Effective Involvement of Women in Watershed

Need to Acknowledge Women as Farmer

An important objective of watershed development is to improve land productivity. It is, therefore, farmers who first come forward to participate

Table 20.4: Category-wise Share of Women Workers in Chhattisgarh

Economic category	*All STs*	*Gond*	*Halba*	*Bhunjia*	*Kamar*
A-1. Total Workers	47.3	47.8	48.7	46.9	50.8
2. Main Workers	34.8	36.4	43.5	36.2	44.5
3. Marginal Workers	73.0	72.5	67.3	71.1	64.7
B-1. Cultivators	42.3	43.1	49.0	35.6	36.6
2. Agricultural Labourer	60.8	62.2	61.6	56.7	52.9
3. Household Industries Workers	48.3	47.2	37.0	23.5	55.7
4. Other Workers	30.0	31.2	25.6	29.6	40.0

Source: Worked out based on the Census Data 2001: Office of the Registrar General, India (GoI, 2004).

in project activities. It is the same farmers who are nominated to the local decision making bodies—including the watershed committee—set-up for the project. Women are nominated to these committees under a kind of 'reservation policy', implying that they are not members of the farming community in their own right. However, women are and always have been farmers. They are the primary food producers, contribute more hours of work and perform more tasks than men in agricultural production. They not only cultivate land belonging to their families and work as agricultural labourers, they also independently lease plots for cultivation. Women farmers have independent views about farming practices and can contribute significantly to the improvement of agriculture:

- Women reported that the shift to cash cropping resulting from increased water availability in rehabilitated watersheds had been disastrous for their families. Increased investment financed through credit, has resulted in a highly vulnerable economic condition. Given a choice, women would opt for enhanced stability and the cultivation of foodgrains.
- Men in Raipur district (Chhattisgarh) said that they preferred to marry brides who were able to share their knowledge of agricultural practices.

Need to Identify Women's Livelihoods in the Watershed Community

An effective way of ensuring that the interests of women as resource users, especially in decision-making, livelihood strategies upon which they are based. This should focus on access and control issues related to private and common resources (land, water, fuel, fodder) and on those resources which provide livelihood options to women—such as rope making, basket weaving and leaf plate making.

Watershed development requires decisions on the appropriate management of common pool resources, upon which poor and marginal groups in the community often depend for their economic survival. Common pool resources play a key role in fulfilling fodder and fuel needs, the collection of which is primarily the responsibility of women. These livelihood options are not easily visible because:

- the percentage of the population involved is small;
- income from these sources is regarded as secondary in terms of family income, even though it may be the primary source of income for the woman.

An assessment of livelihood strategies is, therefore, an important way of keeping issues related to the economic survival of women in focus.

Need to Create Male Support

While physical works were being planned, it emphasised the need to involve women in all levels of activity. This led to a debate in the community on the role and competence of women. The debate and continuous discussion fostered an atmosphere of support among the whole community. Male support was generated because of their increasing understanding of the women's work burden. Secondly, *dalit* men began to see that processes of oppression were similar in the public and private domains. For example, caste norms excluded *dalit* men from participating equals in mainstream village politics. They understood that their deprived economic situation contributed to their status, and realised that the politics of exclusion was not fair. Men came to agree that women had an equal right to participate in development processes. This enabled them to take the following decisions: all committees and associations would be paid

Table 20.5: Details of Watershed Committees

Committees	*Men*	*Women*	*Total*
Watershed central committee	5	5	10
Village-level committee	3	3	6
Watershed volunteers	4	5	9
Monitoring committee	4	4	8

equal wages; special efforts would be made to ensure work availability to vulnerable groups such as single woman; women and men would participate equally in all watershed activities.

Watershed committees were formed as shown in Table 20.5. The village-level committees have worked exceedingly well. In particular, women in the monitoring committees laid down and enforced strict quality norms.

Need to Participation of Women in Decision-Making

Along with the PIA, it is the village watershed committee that is responsible for planning and decision-making in watershed development projects. Most women are unaware of the role they can play in watershed development projects. PIA efforts to involve women are often limited to 'awareness camps', or explanations of the concept of watershed development in women's meetings.

One of the main objectives of these camps and meetings is to 'enforce' the ban on free grazing and open access to common pool resources. Results from the survey indicated that the number of villages in which women have had to resort to stealing fuel wood from others has doubled over the last ten years; in 23 per cent of the villages, women said they stole from restricted areas. More significantly, women in 53 per cent of the villages said they had to travel farther in search of fuel wood and fodder due to restrictions on village commons and forest lands. Common pool resources often remain inaccessible to women, even when resources have regenerated as a result of watershed development efforts. It is essential, therefore, that women have a say in decisions regarding watershed resources.

The mandatory requirement of 'at least one woman' or an 'adequate number of women' on committees encourages tokenism and does not demonstrate a committed effort to involve women in decision-making. For effective participation, it is recommended that at least one-third, preferably one-half, of the committee should consist of women (Pangare 1996).[24] Furthermore, female committee members need to be given specific responsibilities and made signatories to the bank account for the project, in order to emphasise the importance of their role.

As a first step towards strengthening the involvement of women in decision-making, the objectives of the PIA and the plans for intervention in the watershed should be made available to women in the community from the beginning of the project. Watershed plans are usually presented by the PIA through the *Gram Sabha* and it is, therefore, essential that full participation of women in these meetings is attained. This can be achieved by specifying that the unit of participation is the individual adult and not the household.

Need to Develop Women's Leadership

Local women's leadership was encouraged in a number of ways. Women and men participated in all training and exposure visits in equal numbers. This was a norm for the programme. If women were not ready to travel, the exposure visits were postponed. Exposure visits and training helped to give women confidence based on knowledge.

To support the development of women's leadership, separate meetings with women were conducted regularly by the woman coordinator of the watershed. These meetings discussed women's perception of their own skills and abilities, and women were encouraged to learn new skills, articulate their needs and try out new ideas. Women were also provided with detailed information about the watershed activities. As a result, women were able to exert their influence with growing confidence. Separate organisations of women created a forum to discuss problems and solutions freely. After coming to collective decisions in separate meetings, female members in different watershed committees were able to push their agenda forward, such as demanding and receiving equal wages. They could also forcefully demand changes in earlier discriminatory practices or decisions (such as payment only to male members of families). In several instances, work groups were reorganised to ensure employment of women.

Need of Voluntary Organisation in Developing Women's Leadership

The intervening agency has a significant role to play in moulding the views of men in the community. It saw the watershed programme as an opportunity to create gender justice. This understanding guided its activities. Initially, the men in the area were reluctant to pay women minimum wages and to accept equal wages along with them, because they thought that women work less than men. An analysis of the number of hours worked by men and women and the range of tasks carried out by women convinced the men that all should take an equal wage. The government commitment was essential in bringing about change.

Women were viewed as less skilled and able than men in many construction activities—a view often internalised by women. These attitudes were changed by discussing the skills needed for each kind of activity. In some cases, it became clear that men did not have the necessary skills either. A review of training needs of men and women created an atmosphere for learning, which helped women to cross gender barriers. The identification of women with leadership potential and their training led to women placing demands for gender justice. Women refused to accept unequal wages or to hand over their wages to male relatives, and made significant contributions to discussions and decisions—so a change of attitude was inevitable.

The separate organisation of women in the community and their struggles for government resources also changed the view of women as subordinate. The women's groups in the area were active in confronting local elites. They faced harassment, and dealt with issues as group. This helped them demand and receive the status of equal partners. The current experience also shows that women are able to assert themselves more in smaller groups and in their own village. In large groups, they are still hesitant to speak out. However, they have made a significant beginning to change their own situation and the attitudes of their community.

Need to Create Thrift and Credit Groups for Women

Women have been motivated to form thrift and credit groups. Within 18 months, 126 women had started a savings programme and in that period had saved ₹ 46,515. The thrift groups in the district are, however, facing problems from the local administration. They are being asked to save only under the Development of Women and Children in Rural Areas programme (DWACRA, a government sponsored thrift and credit programme to take up income-generation activities), and are being forced to stop other savings.

This is the main reason why not all women in the watershed have yet joined existing groups. The government-sponsored DWACRA programme does not meet subsistence needs, and does not make funds available at the discretion groups and their needs. This local policy (in other district of Chhattisgarh women are free to save in their own *sangams*) is hampering the growth of savings and self-help development in the watershed area. In spite of this, women are determined to manage their own money. The creation of collective assets, in the form of thrift groups, gave women confidence that they could become self-reliant. Instead of going to moneylenders, they could borrow from each other in times of distress, and could start new income-generation programmes from their own funds.

Access to collective funds has enhanced the status of women in the community.

Need to give Importance of Sensitising PIA Staff

Men dominate the decision-making hierarchies in most PIAs—especially in government PIAs—and it is essential that staffs are trained to understand issues related to women's roles and needs. Female staffs are generally recruited only when a conscious decision is taken to work with women in a project. In discussions with PIAs, one NGO staff member questioned the assumption that only female staff can work effectively with village women: "although it is true that it is easier for women staff to interact with women in the community, there is also a positive aspect to male staff speaking on behalf of women; men are often more responsive to male staff advocating greater participation by women". There is still, however, an urgent need to increase the number of female staff in PIAs. Female staff also needs to be trained in facilitating women's participation and in the technical aspects of watershed development.

Need of Technical Training for Women

Knowledge and skills determine an individual's position in the hierarchy set up to implement project activities. Unfortunately, training programmes in watershed development target men rather than women. Some PIAs hold meetings with women, or use existing women's groups as forums for explaining the objectives of a watershed development programme. Women are typically isolated from the scientific and technical aspects of watershed development. The most common training programmes for women are related to the development of nurseries for tree planting programmes; they are rarely offered training in surveying methods or the construction of conservation structures. Even in nursery training, women are used as labour and rarely contribute to the selection of species to be raised in the nursery. Due to the lack of technical training, women rarely hold supervisory positions on land development sites and only contribute to the labour component. They are also unable to participate in decisions related to the selection of sites and identification of appropriate conservation structures.

One of the common reasons given for not offering technical training to women is their lack of education. However, even illiterate women can be trained to measure the amount of work completed on construction sites. Women from two watershed villages have learned to measure trenches with the help of markings made on measuring tapes, ensuring that they receive the correct wages and that they are not being made to work more than required. Training modules need to be specifically designed for women. The purpose of offering technical training to women should be to create an opportunity for them to move up in the decision-making hierarchy. Educated women from the community can also be identified for specific training.

Need to Improve Water, Health and Hygiene

While watershed development can lead to an increase in groundwater levels and ensure water is available in the village for longer periods, obtaining water for household needs still consumes on average, one and a half to three hours of a woman's day and water sources (especially open wells) are often unhygienic. Attention should be given to this aspect, by providing women with information on the causes of drinking water contamination, its consequences for health and simple ways of purification. Water sources (open wells, hand pumps, springs) that are susceptible to contamination should be protected by building masonry aprons or structures. Wherever possible, a piped drinking water scheme within the village should be established by government schemes, other projects or community contributions. Formation of village level committees or habitation-wise user group committees can be established (preferably of women) to ensure that water sources are well maintained and protected.

Women bear the burden of the ill health of their family. The health and nutrition of women and female children are usually the last priority. Through the provision of information, nutritional status can be improved. Hence efforts along the lines of 'action oriented-learning' sessions concerning health, hygiene, sanitation, family planning and nutrition are important. Interventions such as raising kitchen gardens or homestead poultry and latrine building can help address some of these needs. Establishment of soak pits to drain waste water, as well as improve the hygiene of surroundings, can reduce skin and diarrhoeal infections. The use of improved energy conserving *chulhas* (earthen stoves) and biogas units can reduce time and energy spent on fuel collection (on an average, eight hours a week), as well as reduce smoke levels in the kitchen (the cause of many respiratory illnesses) where women and small children usually sit.

Need for Women Awareness in Education

Women lay great store in education for their children and the acquisition of information, knowledge and skills for themselves. Middle and secondary schools and higher education centres are often located far from the village, limiting attendance particularly of female children. Cultural norms and poverty necessitate that female children attend to the household chores and look after younger siblings. Sources of income provided by the project and related developments can help reverse the situation. As watershed projects work with the community, the opportunity to promote education, especially for female children, should not be missed. For tribals living in remote areas, problems are particularly acute. Apathy and a lack of hope in obtaining productive employment results from poverty and their isolation from society in general. In mixed villages—where tribals and other cultural groups live together—working side by side on watershed work, attending WC meetings and *Gram Sabhas* and SHGs and *Mahila Mandal* (MMs, women's organisation) breaks down barriers and encourages tribals to take advantage of development and send their children to school. However, in homogeneous tribal villages, special attention and efforts have to be made to promote education. The increasing integration of urban and rural areas, market development and the widespread use of mass media (radio and television) is leading to the breakdown of traditional thought patterns. Women even in remote areas, are increasingly aware that they are being bypassed by progress and are, therefore, unable to enjoy the benefits of modern development; as such, they are becoming more vocal about their rights. Fortunately women are beginning to be supported in their quest by men, who are gradually realising that their home situation is a reflection and consequence of the level of knowledge, information and skills women possess. If women are active and capably manage the home, the status of men is also increased, particularly in the larger society with which they socialise or conduct commerce. A man's status in rural society is increasingly measured by the image his wife presents socially. While previously women themselves would not think of spending a night away from the family, men increasingly allow women to participate in training of two to three days outside their villages. The experience shows that the demand for 'literacy', comes later, usually two to three years after the beginning of the project. Women's initial priority is for information, knowledge and skills related to their daily responsibilities.

Need of Cooperative Societies for Women Upliftment

To ensure long-term benefits to women, it was felt women should take up self-employment schemes. To begin with, 23 single women have been constituted into a *Balameshwari Cooperative Society*. The society will be further strengthened by including landless and very poor women. The society is planning a number of activities, including establishing brick kiln and small shops, trading in locally available tamarind, and leasing land for farming and sheep breeding. The success of the society depends on the supportive climate provided by local government.

Need to Accessing Existing Government Programmes for Women

The watershed activities galvanised the poor in the community to come together and collectively access government funds. The women's groups were able to access and acquire ownership rights over wasteland for ten women, including four single women. With the help of the groups accessed, the benefits are shown in Table 20.6.

Table 20.6: Showing Government Resources Mobilization

Benefits	Number
Ration card	10
Old-age pension	2
Widow's pensions	4
Flood relief	1
Land allocation for 10 landless women, including 4 single women	20.25 acres, worth Rs 410,000
House sites	15

Identify the Strategic Needs of Women

While developing livelihoods to meet basic needs is a long-term effort, it helped to organise women to meet their strategic needs. 'Startegic needs' are defined as enabling conditions which assist women in seeking gender justice, i.e., better living conditions and genuine choice to manage their lives (the ability and possibility of attending meetings and taking decisions is an example of meeting strategic needs).

The struggle to meet both basic and strategic needs has been strengthened through the watershed development intervention. A process of change towards establishing equal rights has been initiated. Two organisations have been formed: the Vyavasaya (agriculture) Dhan Union, and Stree Shakti. Through these organisations (the former a mixed group, and latter only for women), women's needs and demands are projected to the community and government. Men with a reputation for fair dealings were identified to support women's self-assertion. Cases of atrocities against women are taken up by the women's organisations, and justice ensured for vulnerable women. Cases handled by Stree Shakti include marital dispute, rape and cheating. The organisation of women to enforce their own rights have given them confidence to deal with different government departments, including the police. A process of change towards establishing equal rights has been initiated.

Need of Women's Rights over Common Property Resources

The watershed has a common resource of 70 acre of revenue land. This land has been neglected for many years, leading to its degradation. All the tree cover was lost through illegal tree felling, forest burning, intensive grazing and excessive fuel wood gathering. As part of the watershed implementation the community improve the common property resource. The organisation took the following initiatives:

- Discussions were held with the community on natural resource protection and management.
- 50 women formed two user groups to protect the entire 70 acres of the revenue land.
- The women's organisation took the initiative to acquire usufruct rights for the women users' group. The allocation to a user group of the usufruct rights to government revenue land is the first of its kind in the area. It could prove to be a model to other community organisations.
- The legal sanction of usufruct rights enhanced the interest and motivation of the user-group members to protect the resource.
- Essential interventions, such as soil and water conservation on severely degraded patches, seed broadcasting, planting, etc., are being carried out to speed the regeneration of the area.
- The user group developed a separate accounting system for managing the resource. Grass was plentiful after the first year of protection. This was sold locally, and the savings after deduction of wages for women watchers were deposited in the bank.
- After one year, the vegetation has improved tremendously due to good protection of the entire area. This was made possible by the commitment of the well-organised women's user group.

While the women have improved resources on the wasteland, one issue remains. The Mandal Revenue Officer has issued tree titles for the whole area with a reservation clause 'that this *patta* (title) shall be liable to be cancelled by the government either at the end of any Fasli year, or at any other time after three months notice'. In either case, no compensation can be claimed by the *pattadars* (title holders).

The women are concerned that their rights can be taken away without compensation. They feel vulnerable that after years of effort, they may not receive any benefits. It is necessary to ensure that rights remain with the user and management groups as long as they do not breach their contract.

Conclusion

In many Indian cultural traditions, women have been given a lower economic and social status than that of men. Many of the attempts currently being made to break these moulds regard women potentially as passive beneficiaries of special concessions. In reality, women are strong contributors to the economic and social well-being of rural areas and should be regarded as such. This implies that they should be given equal representation with men on the various committees dealing with watershed development, and equal wages in construction and other work. But they should also be given the technical and social support (such as childcare) necessary to allow them to play a role in watershed development. In addition, if women's interests are to be adequately represented, it will be necessary for government and project officers to be sensitised to women's roles and needs, and to ways of meeting those needs. Ways will have to be found of increasing the proportion of women officers on watershed committees and elected bodies and, especially in the case of watershed development teams, of making it easier for them to undertake field duties. Monitoring systems must be established to assess how women's interests are being defended.

Notes

1. A. Agrawal (1997), "Dying Wisdom : Rise, Fall and Potential of India's Traditional Water Harvesting System", CSE, New Delhi, p. 25.
2. Edward Barbier (1988), "The Economies of Farm Level Adoption of Soil Conservation Measures in the Uplands of Java", World Bank Environment Department, Working Paper, pp. 11-18.

3. B.R. Hegde (1988), "Concepts and Components of Watershed Development Workshop on Watershed Management for Rainfed Farming System in Hill States", *MANAGE*, Hyderabad, pp. 34-38.
4. A.F. Bortall and K.C. John (1991), "Adapting Farming Systems Research to the Needs of Collective Decision-Making", *Eastern India Farming System Research Extension Newsletter*, Vol. 5, No.3, pp. 13-16.
5. S.D. Khepar, S.K. Sondhi, J.K. Chawla and Mandeep Singh (2001), *Jour. of Soil and Water Conser*, Vol. 45, No. 1 and 2, pp. 41-49.
6. H. Guy (2002), "Principles and Practices of Integrated Watershed Management in India", (ed.) Omega Scientific Publisher, New Delhi, 2002.
7. R.C. Kaushal (1994),"Evaluation Study on Economic Viability of Watershed Management Project in the Degraded Aravali Foothills of Haryana", Ind. *J. Agril. Economy*. Vol. 49, No. 4, pp. 210-222.
8. P.K. Mishra, M.H. Hussain (2001), "Impact Evaluation on Peddagedda Watershed of Srikakulam District in Andhra Pradesh", Report– CRIDA, Hyderabad, pp. 18-20.
9. Edward Barbier (1988), "The Economies of Farm Level Adoption of Soil Conservation Measures in the Uplands of Java", World Bank Environment Department, Working Paper, pp. 11-18.
10. J. Bonnal (2004) "The Sociological Approach in Watershed Management : From Participation to Decentralization", In Chapter 9, Proc. African Regional Workshop on Watershed Management, Part 4 : Social Aspects of Watershed Management, pp. 117-122.
11. S.D. Khepar, S.K. Sondhi, J.K. Chawla and Mandeep Singh (2001), *Jour. of Soil and Water Conser*, Vol. 45, Nos. 1 & 2, pp. 41-49.
12. R.C. Kaushal (1994),"Evaluation Study on Economic Viability of Watershed Management Project in the Degraded Aravali Foothills of Haryana", *Ind. J. Agril. Economy*. Vol. 49, No. 4, pp. 210-222.
13. P.K. Mishra, M.H. Hussain (2001), "Impact Evaluation on Peddagedda Watershed of Srikakulam District in Andhra Pradesh", Report– CRIDA, Hyderabad, pp.18-20.
14. A. Palta, N. Sharma and M. Vishwakarma (1995), "Socio-Economic Profile of the Kamar's—A Primitive Tribe of M.P.", Bulletin - Tribal Research Institute, Bhopal, M.P. Vol. XXIII, No. 2, pp. 57-62.
15. J.J. Kottakayam (1983), "Social Structure and Change among the Tribals", D.K. Publishing House, New Delhi, p. 53.
16. M.J.C. Gowda and K.N. Jayaramiah (1990), "Impact of Watershed Development Programme on Socio-Economic Status, Land Productivity and Income of Small and Marginal Farmers", *Ind. J. Extn. Edu*. Vol. 26, No. 3 and 4, pp. 44-77.
17. T.H. Babu (1991), "Socio-Economic Appraisal of Agro Forestry

Technology in the Rainfed Areas of Maheshwaram Watershed Project", Int. Conf. on Extn. for Minimising Risk in Rainfed Agric., New Delhi, pp. 6-9.

18. S.L. Seth (1991), "Institutional Adjustments for Participatory Approaches on Watershed Based Sustainable Farming System Development in Rainfed Areas", Int. Conf. On Extn. for Minimising Risk in Rainfed Agric, New Delhi, pp. 6-9.
19. S.C. Mahnot, P.K. Singh and Y. Sharma (1992), "Socio-Economic Evaluation of Watershed Management Project – A Case Study", J.R.D., Hyderabad. Vol. 11, No. 2, pp. 219-227.
20. K.K. Saxena, N.C. Jain and S.C. Pandaya (1990), "Transfer of Rainfed Technology and its Adoption by the Farmers in Malwa Region", *Ind. J. Extn. Edn.*, Vol. 26, No. 3 and 4, pp. 70-73.
21. B.L. Dhyani, Ram Babu, M.L. Agrawal and Nirmal Kumar (1994), "Impact of Watershed Management on Farm Income", *Ind. J. Soil Conser.*, Vol. 22, No. 3, pp. 71-77.
22. N. Manjula (1994), Attitude of Farm Women towards Watershed Management Programme", *Mah. J. Extn. Edn.*, Vol. 13, p. 227.
23. B.S. Patel and R.S. Patel (1995), "Impact of Lab to Land Programme on Adoption Behaviour of Beneficiary and Non-Beneficiary Farmers in Gujarat", *Raj. J. Extn. Edu.*, Vol. 3, No. 1, pp. 2-25.
24. GOI (2002), "Watershed at Work—Success Stories of Watershed Programmes". (Eds.) M.M. Josh, S.K. Dalal and C.K. Haridas, Ministry of Agriculture, (GoI, New Delhi), p. 264.
25. FAO (2004), "Women's Role in Dynamic Forest-based Small Scale Enterprises: Case Studies on Uppage and Lacquerware from India", Food and Agriculture Organization of the United Nations, Bangkok, pp.10-28.

21

Capacity Building of Communities under Watershed Development Programme

Dr. Madhu Thawani and *Dr. Priti Garg*

Capacity is the essential lubricant of development; more important even than finance. The UN Development Programme has defined "capacity" as "the ability of individuals, institutions and societies to perform functions, solve problems, and set and achieve objectives in a sustainable manner".[1]

To give fluidity, flexibility and functionality to a programme/organization to adapt to changing needs of the population that is served capacity building is essential.

'Capacity Building' has been defined by UNDP (1991) as:

1. The creation of an enabling environment with appropriate policy and legal frameworks.
2. Institutional development, including community participation (of women in particular).
3. Human resources development and strengthening of managerial systems.

According to it, capacity building is a long-term, continuing process, in which all stakeholders participate (ministries, local authorities, non-governmental organizations, professional associations, academics and others).[2]

Ann Philbin, defines capacity building as the "process of developing and strengthening the skills, instincts, abilities, processes and resources that organizations and communities need to survive, adapt, and thrive in the fast-changing world."[3]

The **WCO** defines capacity building as "activities which strengthen the knowledge, abilities, skills and behaviour of individuals and improve institutional structures and processes such that the organization can efficiently meet its mission and goals in a sustainable way".[4]

Therefore, Capacity Building should include the following:

- Human resource development, the process of equipping individuals with the understanding, skills and access to information, knowledge and training that enables them to perform effectively and strengthens the capacity of people to achieve sustainable livelihood.
- Organizational development, the elaboration of management structures, processes and procedures, not only within organizations but also the management of relationships between the different organizations and sectors (public, private and community) and emphasis on technological change and innovation.
- Institutional and legal framework development, making legal and regulatory changes to enable organizations, institutions and agencies at all levels and in all sectors to enhance their capacities.[5]
- "Economic Capacity Building" which increases the capacity of any developed or developing society to improve trade, employment, economic development and quality of life.[6]

Thus, Capacity-development like sustainable development according to The UN Commission on Sustainable Development (1996, p. 2), encompasses a wide range of aspects, including the human, technological, organizational, financial, scientific, cultural and institutional.[7]

This chapter focuses on Community Capacity Building with special reference to community capacity building under the Watershed Development Programme in Songadh Taluka, Tapi District in State of Gujarat.

Community Capacity Building

Community capacity building is to empower communities engaged in development programmes, so that their capacity is sustained after the programme ends. Developing community capacity enables members of a community to draw on the skills and resources they need to take control and improve their lives.

Community capacity building leads to:

1. Stakeholder participation;
2. Increases problem assessment capacities;
3. Develops local leadership;
4. Builds and empower organizational structures;
5. Improves resource mobilization;
6. Strengthens links to other organizations and people;
7. Enhances stakeholder ability to "ask why";
8. Increases stakeholder control over programme management;
9. Creates an equitable relationship with outside agents; and
10. Encourages strategic planning, implementation and evaluation of programmes.

Areas in which capacity building is done:

- Skills;
- Information;
- Resources—natural, financial and intellectual;
- Knowledge;
- Technology; and
- Linkages.

Tools that can be used for capacity building:

- Intensive trainings;
- Forming Groups;
- Focus group workshops, seminars, discussions; and
- Exposure and exchange visits to successful projects.[8]

Community Capacity Building under Watershed Development Programme in Songadh Taluka

Watershed is a geo-hydrological unit draining at a common point by a system of streams. It is a unit comprising various interdependent resource systems in nature, e.g., vegetation growing in the watershed, surface/subsurface water, arable, non-arable lands, soil, trees, agriculture, livestock, and people accessing its resources. All these form an integral part of watershed.[9]

Depletion of the natural resource base requires the efficient management of these natural resources. For this watershed is considered as one of the ideal unit. For the development of this Watershed Unit, Government of India has formulated Watershed Development Guideline 2001 and Hariyali 2003 under which Watershed Development Programme is being implemented. Under this programme number of activities are taken up like soil and water conservation, agriculture development, forest development, animal husbandry development, community capacity building, etc.

Objectives of the Study

1. To study the tools adopted for Community Capacity Building under Watershed Development Programme.
2. To study the areas in which Community Capacity building was done under Watershed Development Programme.

Research Methodology

A qualitative and quantitative approach was adopted for the study. For this available government records, knowledgeable people-government officials, members of NGOs, elected members, certain beneficiaries were initially contacted to understand various dimensions of the study. In-depth interview of above mentioned categories of knowledgeable people were conducted to probe various aspects related to the topic. After identifying the various dimensions and attributes survey method was adopted for research.

Scope of the Study

The focus of the research study is Songadh Taluka, of Tapi District. Tapi District comprises of 5 Talukas (Valod, Vyara, Songadh, Uchhal and Nizar Talukas). Out of these 5 Talukas Watershed Programme is implemented in 4 Talukas. In Songadh Taluka there are 177 villages out of which 29 villages are covered under Watershed Development Programme.

For the purpose of the study we selected all 29 villages of Songadh Taluka where Watershed Development Programme has been implemented. For collecting primary data 10 functionaries, who were working at different levels were contacted and interviewed. At the village level 122 beneficiaries (Self-help groups and user groups) were contacted to study the Community Capacity Building task undertaken under Watershed Development Programme in Songadh Taluka. Convenience sampling method was adopted for contacting self-help groups and user group members.

Both secondary and primary data sources were tapped to collect the data. A checklist was developed. Based on this checklist in-depth interview was conducted for the functionaries. An undisguised structured questionnaire was developed for the beneficiaries. Many of the questions were of multiple choices though there were certain open ended questions also to elicit their opinion. Contact method used was personal.

Measures Taken Up and Areas Covered under Watershed Development Programme in Songadh Taluka for Community Capacity Building

Individual and Community Skill Development

- Training; and
- Organization of camps.

Institutional Capacity Building

- Entry point activity;
- Participatory rural appraisal;
- Formation of watershed committee;
- Formation of watershed association;
- Formation of self-help groups; and
- Formation of user groups.

Financial Capacity Building

- Watershed project account;
- Watershed development fund; and
- Loan facility through self-help groups and bank linkages.

Individual and Community Skill Development

Skill development activities help one to learn about new skills and technology. Skill development and information about new technology leads to economic and social development. For example learning about hybrid seeds, use of bio-fertilizers, new methods of irrigation, way of conserving soil and water conservation helps in increasing agriculture productivity. From the officials of Watershed Development Programme and also through primary data it was found that for skill development of individual and community Training, Exposure Visits and Camps were organized.

1. Training and Exposure Visit

Out of a total of 122 respondents, 77 (63%), went for training and exposure visits and learnt about making warmi compost, sowing mango *kalam*, candle making, agarbati making, soap making, pickle making, hand pump repairing, making beds, making *ubajpadia*, etc., and also learnt about high yield variety of seeds (crop demonstration plot, horticulture demonstration plot and agro-horticulture demonstration plot).

Apart from this, the respondents also learnt about hybrid variety of grass (*stylo hamta* and *dhaman*) which is more nutritive and its productivity is also very high. Besides this it was also found from the respondents that they acquired knowledge about drip, sprinkle and lift irrigation and different ways to conserve soil and water resources.

After receiving training, out of a total of 122 respondents 77 (63%) respondents engaged in alternative economic activities, 20 (16%) respondents took up nursery, 29 (24%) respondents warmi compost, 27 (22%) kitchen garden and 1 (1%) horticulture. Due to taking up of alternative economic activity out of a total of 122 respondents 57 (47%) respondents' income increased under the Programme

61 (50%) of the respondents started using hybrid seeds like dangar GR-5, GR-7, for juvar G-38, G-40 and for tuvar G-T1. Due to the use of hybrid seeds agriculture productivity of 56 (46%) respondents increased.

67 (55%) respondents started using bio-fertilizer after learning the making of warmi compost and knowing its usefulness.

Due to training and economic capacity building out of a total of 122 respondents 65 per cent respondents' confidence has increased, 42 per cent of the respondents living, dressing and eating pattern has changed and health of self and family has improved. Besides this 56 per cent, 49 per cent and 29 per cent of the respondents have understood the importance of cleanliness, education and team-work respectively. Apart from this 44 per cent respondents have become independent as they on their own are involved in economic activity, 40 per cent are participating in household decisions as they have become self-independent and their status in family and community has changed.

2. Cattle Camps

Cattle camps were organized in Songadh Taluka under the Watershed Development Programme with the support of Sumul Dairy in Bardoli. Under cattle camp vaccination and deworming facility was provided to the beneficiaries of the programme. 14,739 cattle were treated.

Out of a total of 122 respondents, 71 (58%), attended cattle camps and got their cattle vaccinated.

The organization of cattle camps helped improve the health of cattle of 40 (33%) respondents, 31 (25%) respondents learnt how to rear cattle and milk production of 23 (19%) respondents increased.

The secondary data provided also showed an increase in milch animals. Before the programme there were 3,355 milch animals but after the programme milch animals increased to 4,451—an increase by 32 per cent. Milk production also increased from 8,82,674 litres to 12,34,300 litres. Thus, milk production went up by 58 per cent. The same is the case for milk sale.

According to the primary data also out of 122 respondents 55 (45%) respondents were having livestock and 67 (55%) respondents were not having livestock. After the programme 98 (80%) respondents possess livestock and 24 (20%) do not possess livestock. Thus, there is a rise of 35 per cent of respondents who are possessing livestock after the programme. This has brought an alternative economic activity to the respondents. Loan facility available under the programme also helped the respondents purchase the livestocks.

Institutional Building at the Village Level

Institutional building at the village level helps the community to manage the resources themselves which develops local leadership and encourages stakeholder participation and control over the activities taken up. This leads to strategic planning, implementation and evaluation of the programmes. This makes them feel that they are working for themselves which leads to efficient utilization of the resources on sustainable basis.

For Institutional building at the village level under Watershed Development Programme in Songadh Taluka Watershed Associations,

Watershed Committee, Self Help Groups and User Groups were created. Besides this Entry Point Activity and Participatory Rural Appraisal Activity was carried out to create a We Feeling among the community. This is discussed below.

Entry Point Activity

Entry Point activities are undertaken to bring people together and make them aware of the programme and involve them in some common activity that is useful to the community such as constructing an approach road, or building a community hall.

Participatory Rural Appraisal Activity

The Participatory Rural Appraisal is one of the techniques used for gathering information on community resources and needs for use in literacy and community development programmes.[10] The techniques include the use of transect walks, maps, calendars, matrices, and diagrams using locally available materials.[11]

In Songadh Taluka under the Watershed Development Programme Participatory Rural Appraisal Activity was carried out. It helped the administrators and villagers to know more clearly about the need of people and problems faced by them. This led to effective planning based on the needs and problems faced by the community. In Songadh Taluka out of a total of 122 respondents, 81 (66%) were present in Participatory Rural Appraisal Activity.

Watershed Committee (WC)

Watershed Association nominates about 10-11 WC members from amongst the User Groups (4-5), Self-Help Groups (3-4), Gram Panchayat (2-3) and a member from the Watershed Development Team. While making nominations, WA ensures that the Committee has at least one-third women representatives and adequate representatives from the Scheduled Castes/Scheduled Tribes.

In Songadh Taluka for each Village a WC has been constituted consisting of 11 members from user group, self-help group, Gram Panchayat and WDT.

Watershed Committee prepares the detailed Action Plan/Treatment Plan for integrated development of the watershed area. It maintains

Watershed Project Account and Watershed Development Fund. The Chairman, Secretary and one member of the WDT operate the WP account. It constitutes Self Help Groups (SHG) and User Groups (UG) with the help of Watershed Development Team Members. Besides this it gives not more than rupees 10,000 to each self-help group for economic activity from the revolving fund which it sets up. The maximum amount in this revolving fund can be rupees 1 lakh only. WC also determines the user charges for the usage of common facilities after getting the nod from the Gram Sabha.[12]

Under the supervision of Watershed Association, the Watershed Committee undertakes the routine activities of WDP. For the smooth implementation of the project it also coordinates with different agencies involved in implementation of the project.[13]

Watershed Association

All villagers who in one way or the other are associated with the Watershed Area are members of the WA. Where the Watershed Area is same as the Village Panchayat area the Gram Sabha is deemed to be Watershed Association for that area.[14]

A minimum of 2 meetings of WA are held in a year. The following issues are generally dealt with/taken up in these meetings:

1. Elect its president.
2. Developing and/or improvising the Watershed Development programme.
3. Keep track of the progress made in the programme.
4. Give nod to the account statements.
5. Constitute self-help groups and user groups.
6. Settle any dispute arising between the groups and members of the group.
7. Give its approval to the different ways of collecting donations and contributions from the people and members.
8. Decide upon the procedure for the maintenance and operation of the assets created under the project.
9. Nominate members for WC from amongst the members of UGs/SHGs by rotation.
10. Take necessary disciplinary action for removing members from WC.[15]

Self-help Groups

SHGs are constituted from amongst poor, small and marginal farmer households, landless/assetless poor agricultural labourers, women, shepherds and SC/ST persons.[16] These Groups are homogeneous groups having common identity and interest who are dependent on the watershed area for their livelihood.[17] These groups are mainly formed for undertaking economic activities, for encouraging savings and women empowerment. 175 Self-Help Groups have been formed in all the villages covered under the Watershed Project of Songadh Taluka.

The total number of people who are members of SHGs is 3,000—134 male members and 2,866 female members. Out of 3,000 members' 1,956 members have taken loan facility under the Watershed Project. Total savings raised by the Self Help Groups is ₹ 17,56,080 out of which ₹ 14,09,000 is used for internal lending (₹ 6,32,860 is given for agriculture, ₹ 2,90,680 for health, ₹ 1,45,980 for education and ₹ 3,39,480 for social purpose).

Besides this the Self Help Groups which get graded are eligible for revolving fund and bank lending facility under the Watershed Development Programme.

Out of 175 Self Help Groups, 98 Self Help Groups have been graded and are linked to SGSY/NABARD. Out of 98 Self Help Groups which have been graded 62 Self Help Groups have got revolving fund facility and ₹ 2,23,03,600 was made available to these Self Help Groups through bank for animal husbandry and agriculture.

Apart from this out of 175 Self Help Groups, 64 Self Help Groups are doing economic activity of which 9 SHGs have carried out warmi compost activity, 35 nursery, 5 *agarbati* making, 4 *nadia* trading, 2 provision store, 2 cloth trading activity, 2 *pappad* making, and other 5 are involved in some trading activity. These 64 Self Groups have earned an Income of ₹ 5,66,000 through these economic activities in five years.

User Groups

User Groups (UGs) are constituted in all the villages covered under the Watershed Project. 158 User Groups have been formed in all the villages of Songadh Taluka. These Groups are homogeneous groups of persons who are deriving direct or indirect benefits from a particular watershed work or activity.[18] Operation and Maintenance of the assets is the responsibility of user group.[19] Different User Groups are formed on the basis of the benefits received by them directly or indirectly. The types of groups formed generally are: soil conservation group, water conservation group, agriculture group, fodder group, afforestation group, animal husbandry group, horticulture group and agriculture group.

Financial Capacity Building

Capacity of community cannot be developed only through skill development and institutional building but also requires enough financial resources for undertaking various developmental activities. Therefore, under the Watershed Programme in Songadh Taluka Watershed Project Account and Watershed Development fund was created which is managed by Chairman and Secretary of Watershed Committee. Loan facility is also available to the members of Self Help Groups from the savings raised by them. Apart from this the Self Help Groups which have completed Gradation get revolving fund and are linked to bank. This has increased the resource mobilization capacity of the beneficiaries which in turn increases the economic capacity of the beneficiaries leading to sustainable development.

Watershed Project Account

In Songadh Taluka the WC of each village has opened a Watershed Project Account in which the development fund sanctioned by the Government is transferred. Chairman of WC, one WDT member and Secretary of Watershed Project operate this account jointly.[20] The Watershed Secretary maintains the necessary records of income and expenditure from this account.

Transfer of Funds in the Watershed Committee Account and its operation by Chairman and Secretary of Watershed Committee shows that the community has been given financial powers also along with the other responsibilities of the implementation of Watershed Programme. This empowers the community to use the resources effectively to their benefit.

Watershed Development Fund (WDF)

For a village to be selected for WDP, it is necessary that it contributes to the WDF depending upon the type of land (individual or community land) on which activity is to be carried.[21] The Watershed Development Fund account has been created in Songadh Taluka. The contribution to WDF is at least 10 to 15 per cent for individual land and 5 per cent to 10 per cent for community land. All contributions are deposited in the Watershed Development Fund which is maintained separately. Fixed deposit of five years is created out of the Watershed Development Funds. It is operated after the project is completed. This account is managed by the Chairman, WC and Secretary jointly. For the upkeep of the common assets after the project is completed funds from the WDF account are used.

Total amount of Watershed Development Fund in Songadh Taluka for all 29 villages covered under the project is 14.85 lakhs.

Out of a total of 122 respondents, 77 (63%) respondents have participated by contributing cash and 71 (58%) have contributed their labour. This shows that beneficiaries have given their contribution in the development of their own resources which will lead to sustainable development of the programme.

Loan Facility

Under the watershed programme loan facility is available to the members of the Self Help Groups through Self Help Groups internal lending and Banks.

Out of a total of 122 respondents 75 (61%) of beneficiaries of the programme have taken loan from Self Help Groups. Most of the beneficiaries of the programme have taken loan for purchasing cattle which has led to taking up an alternative occupation—animal husbandry. Besides this the beneficiaries easily get loans from the Self Help Groups for agriculture, health, education and social purpose as and when required.

Summing Up

Under Watershed Development Programme various measures were adopted in different areas for Community Capacity Building like Institutional Building at Village Level, Financial Capacity Building and Community Skill Development. Under Institutional Building Watershed Committee, Watershed Association, Self Help Groups and User Groups were created in which some of the beneficiaries of the programme were members. Participatory Rural Appraisal Exercise and Entry Point Activities were also undertaken. This has led to people's participation and they themselves identifying their needs and having control over the activities. Local level leadership was also developed as the Chairman of

WC and some of the members were from amongst the villagers. The beneficiaries were motivated to choose on their own the work that could be taken up for development of the project area depending upon their needs and also organize themselves into self-help groups and user groups. This also helped them to administer the Watershed Project Account and Watershed Development Fund. Besides this, it is the Gram Sabha which sanctions the Watershed Plan after identifying the needs and problems of the people. This has led to effective planning, implementation and evaluation of the programme on sustainable basis. Apart from this, under Watershed Development Programme skills of the people were upgraded through Training and Exposure Visits and organizing Cattle Camps. They were also taught about new technological developments in agriculture, and different methods for soil and water conservation. All this helped the respondents indulge in alternative economic activity. Thus, under Watershed Programme efforts are being made by Government for Community Capacity Building like Resource Development—Natural, Financial Development, Human Resource Development; Institutional Development, Technological Development and Economic Capacity Building.

However, there is still need to strengthen links with other institutions, and diversify training programmes. Forward and backward linkages also need to be provided along with skill development. Further for equity and social cohesion, it is necessary that the whole village benefit under the programme and not part of the village only which is covered under Watershed Development Programme.

References

1. http:///uk.oneworld.net/guides/capacitybuilding.
2. www.gdrc.org/uem/capacity-define.html.
3. en.wikipedia.org/wiki/Capacity building.
4. *Ibid.*
5. *Op.cit.*, www.gdrc.org/uem/capacity-define.html.
6. *Op.cit.*, en.wikipedia.org/wiki/Capacity building.
7. Sue McGinty Community Capacity Building (2002), available at www.aare.edu.au/02pap/mcg02476.htm.
8. www.sgpindia.org/.../CAPACITY%20BUILDING%20OF%20 COMMUNITIES.doc
9. Tideman, E.M., *Watershed Management Guidelines for Indian Conditions*, New Delhi, Omega Scientific Publishers, 2003.

10. www.sil.org/.../literacy/.../glossaryofliteracyterms/WhatIsThe ParticipatoryRuralApp.htm -
11. http://www.sil.org/lingualinks/literacy/referencematerials/ GlossaryOfLiteracyTerms/. WhatIsTheParticipatoryRuralApp. htm...www.sayen.org/Volume-II.pdf.
12. www.nird.org.in/brgf/doc/HARAYALI_Guidelines.pdf
13. *Ibid.*
14. *Ibid.*
15. *Ibid.*
16. Government of India, Common Guidelines for Watershed Development Projects, 2008. nraa.gov.in/guideline.pdf
17. Ministry of Rural Development, Department of Land Resources, *Guidelines for Hariyali*, Government of India, New Delhi, 2003. www.dolr.nic.in/ HariyaliGuidelines.htm.
18. *Ibid.*
19. *Ibid*
20. Ministry of Rural Development, *Guidelines for Watershed Development*, Department of Land Resources, Government of India, New Delhi, 2001. dolr.nic.in/GuideWD.htm.
21. *Ibid.*

22

Water Resource Management

Challenges for the Future

Dr. Rajeev R. Shrivastava

Introduction

"The third world war, if ever it is fought, will be over water"

Water is an essential component of earth's natural environment. Natural ecosystem supports it to perform important functions for planetary health including sequestering carbon and recycling carbon dioxide into oxygen. Each year about 502,800 km^3 of water evaporates over the ocean and sea, 90 per cent of which (458,000 km^3) returns directly to the ocean through precipitation, while the remainder (44,800 km^3 falls over the land (Gleick, 1993). The total volume of water on the earth is 1.4 billion km^3, of which only 2.5 per cent is the volume of fresh water (Gleick, 1993). The total amount of water on the earth has remained same for million of years due to earth's atmosphere.

Water is transported in different forms within hydrological cycle or water cycle. Water constitutes 71 per cent of the Earth's surface. Ocean constitutes about 97.2 per cent of the total waterbodies of the earth surface. Glaciers, snow, permafrost 2.175 per cent and Groundwater 0.06 per cent. Lakes, swamps and rivers contribute only 0.025 per cent of the waterbodies.

Water Scenario in India

There is a general feeling that our country with mighty rivers like the Ganga, the Brahmaputra, the Krishna, the Godavari and the Narmada, etc., have abundant water resources. But from the last decade it was realized that this impression is not correct. It is, therefore, necessary to review the availability of water from quantitative and qualitative point of view.

Global Water Scenario

Over 1 billion people without safe water and 2 billion people are without sanitation facilities. There is pervasive underpricing and mismanagement of services. About 10 per cent of the world's food is grown with water from aquifers, which are being depleted faster than the rate of recharge. What does it mean for the ordinary people in the developing world?

In many parts of the world, access to water distinguishes poor from non-poor. In developing countries about six children die in every thirty minutes because of drinking of contaminated water, inadequate sanitation and the diseases associated with them. In 1990, 3 million deaths worldwide were attributed to diarrhoea but there were over 4 billion episodes, or more than a thousand times as many. Children under five are the most vulnerable, accounting for 55 per cent of all episodes but for 85 per cent of the deaths from diarrhoeal diseases. Mortality is high but morbidity is still higher.

Some comments about water in different parts of the world:

A farmer in Kenya:

> "Water is life and because we have no water, life is miserable."

A young man in Russia:

> "How can we sow anything without water? What will my cow drink? Water is our life"

An old woman in Ethiopia :

> "We live hour to hour wondering whether it will rain!"
> (How life will be without these important things.)

These are true even today in most parts of the world.

Challenges in Front of India

We have to address the 'informal' water sector. We also have to improve the productivity of 'green water'. Groundwater management is in very poor shape. There is a high transaction cost for monitoring water use and collecting water charges. Vast numbers of small-scale stakeholders and from private or community storage without any significant mediation from public agencies or organized service providers. Because the bulk of water provision takes place in the informal sector, it is difficult to pass enforceable water legislation. Dense population at both valleys and catchment areas; high population at both upstream and downstream of dams creates heavy demand for water everywhere.

Existing Scenario

Underground water recharge by way of water harvesting is not feasible because of Hilly terrain in major parts of the country. The risks of landsides and damage of water and water storage system are very high. In India, 66 per cent of the land is under reserve forest, accesses in such area are restricted. There is inadequate community participation throughout the country. There is no private sector participation and lack of funding in almost all parts of the country. There are dwindling water resources due to overexploitation or environmental degradation. Most of the sources are susceptible to natural calamity. There is catchment area protection works implementation in isolations.

Focus should be on 'quantity' of water rather than 'quality' of water.'

Water in the Twentyfirst Century

Major Issues which are Challenges for India may be summarized as:

- Groundwater depletion;
- Water quality deterioration;
- Low water use efficiency;
- Expensive new water sources;
- Resources degradation;
- Water and health;
- Massive subsidies and distorted incentives; and
- Development of water resources in all parts of the country.

Strategies to Overcome these Problems

- Rainwater harvesting;
- Comprehensive water policy reform and demand management;
- Secure water rights;
- User management of irrigation systems;
- Reformed price incentives;
- Use appropriate technologies;
- Protecting environment;
- Tradable water rights; and
- International co-operation.

Rainwater Harvesting

Water harvesting is a method of collection and storage of rainwater that can be used to meet out the household, agricultural and navigational requirements. As early as 4,000 years ago people of Negev Desert in Israel stored rainwater for household and agricultural use. In Independent India, the first successful example in large-scale water conservation is PANI PANCHAYAT of Maharashtra. Tapping the primary source of fresh water (rain) is called rainwater harvesting. In urban areas it can also help to divert flooding rainwater for useful purposes, increase soil moisture to maintain urban greenery. Rainwater harvesting may be done by two different methods:

1. **On the surface**: By collecting and accumulating rainwater from the sky on the surface catchments.
2. **Into the groundwater**: Collecting the rainwater and diverting it to groundwater aquifers for use in the distant future

Traditional Rainwater Harvesting Methods in Different Parts of India

Maharashtra	*Ramtek*
Karnataka	Kere
NW Maharashtra	Phad
Tamilnadu	Eri
Kerala (South)	Ooranies
North Malabar	Surangams
Andhra Pradesh	Cheruvus
Himachal Pradesh	Kuls
Nagaland	Zabo
Meghalaya	Bamboo pipe
Run of Cutch	Virda
Rajasthan	Tankas
Uttrakhand	Khal and Chaal

Source: S.N. Chary: *Environmental Studies.*

Rainwater Harvesting Methods in Cities

1. Collect and conserve rainwater for immediate use.
2. Collect and divert rainwater into the ground for increasing the quality and quantity of groundwater.
3. Channelize the rainwater to avoid flooding during heavy rainfall.

Towards these objectives all the buildings should harvest rainwater on the rooftops, channelize it into sumps constructed underground or into specially created seepage areas so that the rainwater percolates undergrounds. This water may be used for various purposes after cleaning and other hygiene related precautions.

Factors Governing Rainwater Harvesting

- Frequency, duration and intensity of rainfall;
- Nature of catchments; and
- Run-off characteristics.

Even if 5 per cent of rainfall we harvest properly, that would produce a substantial quantum of water to the tune of 900 million litres.

Benefits of Rainwater Harvesting

- It saves water for the future;
- Improves soil moisture;
- Increases groundwater level;
- Improves the quality of water;
- Allow drought-proofing;
- Prevents flooding of storm water drains;
- Saves energy required to lift water;
- Reduces flooding of roads;
- Reduces soil erosion;
- An ideal solution of water problem in areas having inadequate water resources;
- To improve the ground-water quality in aquifers;
- To raise the water in wells and bore wells that is drying up;
- Surface water is inadequate to meet our demand and we have to depend on groundwater;

- Due to rapid urbanization, infiltration of rainwater into the sub-soil has decreased drastically and recharging of groundwater has diminished;
- Overexploitation of groundwater resources has resulted in decline in water level in most part of the country;
- To enhance availability of groundwater of specific place and time;
- To arrest seawater ingress;
- To reduce power consumption;
- To improve the vegetation cover; and
- To avoid flooding of storm water drains.

While rainwater harvesting is very useful practice, it is only a part of the total solutions for achieving sufficiency in water. The more permanent and comprehensive solutions lies in practicing **watershed management.**

Watershed and Watershed Management

A watershed is also called catchment or basin which is a land and water area that contributes run-off to a common point. In fact all lands on the earth are a part of one watershed or another. The comprehensive development of a basin to make productive use of all its natural resources with a focus on the social and environmental aspects is termed as watershed management

Water Resources Management through Watershed Technology

Hydrological watershed could be defined as an area from which the run-off is drained through a particular point in the drainage system. Watershed management as found in the International Glossary of Hydrology is "planned use of drainage basin in accordance with the predetermined objectives" or "optimization of the quantity and quality and timing of run-off through planned use of drainage basin". The concept of developing an area on the watershed basis started playing an important role since 1920s. Watershed Management (WSM) has emerged as a new paradigm for planning development and management of land, water and biomass resources with a focus on social and institutional aspects apart from biophysical aspects. Watershed programmes are being implemented under array of national schemes/programmes (IWDP, DPAP, RVP, and Flood Prone River, NWDPRA, etc.). Most of the millions of people living in our country depend on agriculture and natural resource management for their livelihoods. The development planners are eager to implement productive, environmentally sustainable land and water management.

Aims of Watershed Management

- To control damaging run-off,
- To control erosion and sediment yield,
- To moderate flood,
- To enhance groundwater storage,
- To use land resources optimally,
- To protect, conserve, and improve lands, and
- To develop and manage water resources.

Watershed Characteristics

Shape

It may be rectangular, square, oval, fan, etc.

Shape Index (SI)

$$SI = L/W = L/A$$

where,

L = Length of watershed along the main stream,
W = Average width of watershed, and
A = Area of watershed.

Slope

Average Slope

$$S = [(M \times N)/A] \times 100$$

where,
M = Total length of contours within the watershed,
N = Contour interval, and
A = Watershed area

Drainage

It depends upon

- Drainage density,

- Drainage pattern, and
- Stream order.

Climate

It is related to

- Precipitation,
- Humidity,
- Temperature,
- Wind velocity and direction, and
- Sunshine hours, etc.

Water Conservation is connected with the following issues

1. Use or misuse/overuse is due to current lifestyle and social conditioning; and
2. It means self-restraint over its use by a section of the society in the larger interest of the entire community.

We have to save every drop of water for our present as well as future requirements. While consuming water we should think about others and save it for our future generations. We should adopt following measures for our better future.

Suggested Measures for Long-Term Solutions

1. Rainwater harvesting and water conservation:
   (a) Urban Areas
   (i) Roof top collections,
   (ii) Run-off collection and recharge, and
   (iii) Recycling of household water.
   (b) Rural Areas
   (i) Gully plugging,
   (ii) Bench terracing,
   (iii) Contour building and trenching,
   (iv) Rock-filled dams,
   (v) Check dams,
   (vi) Percolation tanks, and
   (vii) Sub-surface dams.

2. Changes in cropping pattern/less water intensive crops (like beans, pulses, peas, lentil, *etc.*).
3. Recycling of groundwater.
4. Inter-basin transfer of water.
5. Strict groundwater legislation.
6. Increase mass awareness using formal and non-formal methods.

References

Books

Asthana, M. and Asthana, D.K. (2007), *A Text Book of Environmental Studies*. S. Chand & Company Ltd., New Delhi.

Bansil, P.C. (2004) : *Water Management in India,* Concept Publishing Company (P) Ltd., New Delhi.

Chary, S.N. (2008), *Environmental Studies*. Macmillan, New Delhi.

Chaturvedi, M.C. and Rogers, P. (1985), *Water Resources System, Planning: Some Case Studies for India*, Indian Academy of Sciences, Bangalore.

Nagarjun, R. (2006), *Water Conservation, Use and Management for Semiarid Regions*, Capital Publishing Company, New Delhi.

Narwani G.S. (ed.) (2005), *Community Water Management*; Rawat Publications, Jaipur.

Palanisami, K.; Kumar, D.S.; Chandrasekharan, B. (Eds.) (2002), *Watershed Management: Issues and Policies for 21st Century*, Associated Publishing Company, New Delhi.

Prasad Kamata (ed.) (2003) : *Water Resources and Sustainable Development: Challenges of 21st Century*, Sipra Publishers, Delhi.

Ray Dutta, B. and Athparia R.P. (ed.) (2005) : *Water and Water Resource Management,* Omsons Publications New Delhi.

Singh, H.R. and Kumar, N. (2004), *Ecology and Environmental Sciences*, Vishal Publishing Co., Jallandhar.

Index